STEERING
THE
ELEPHANT

How Washington Works

STEERING THE ELEPHANT

How Washington Works

Edited by
Robert Rector and Michael Sanera

with a Foreword by Aaron Wildavsky

UNIVERSE BOOKS
New York

Published in the United States of America in 1987
by Universe Books
381 Park Avenue South, New York, NY 10016

© 1987 by Robert Rector and Michael Sanera

87 88 89 90 91 / 10 9 8 7 6 5 4 3 2 1

Printed in the United States of America

Library of Congress Cataloging-in-Publication Data

Steering the elephant.

   1. Administrative agencies—United States—
Management.   2. Bureaucracy—United States.
3. United States—Politics and government—
1945–   I. Rector, Robert. II. Sanera, Michael.
JK421.S73   1986   353   86-40225
ISBN 0-87663-499-4

We must make our choice between Economy and Liberty, or profusion and servitude. . . . If we can prevent the government from wasting the labors of the people under the Pretense of caring for them, they will be happy.

Thomas Jefferson

Contents

Acknowledgments

The editors would like to acknowledge the assistance of Gordon Jones, Suzanne Kugath, Don Hall, and Darlene Roberts. Special thanks must go to Laurie Rothenberg and Jill Friedman, who though remarking certain similarities between this endeavor and the labors of the Danaides, persisted in their invaluable support.

Foreword
The Human Side of Government

AARON WILDAVSKY

This book is a goldmine; whether one finds in it nuggets or effluvia, the real thing or fool's gold, depends on one's expectations. If readers approach *Steering the Elephant* as an effort to provide an impartial account of how Republican appointees tried to impose their preferences on administrative agencies, they will be disappointed. The book is avowedly ideological: Liberals and social conservatives need not apply. Competitive individualism, laissez-faire capitalism, with but few exceptions, is the norm. The hopes and disappointments of its advocates provide the moral and emotional center point.

The substance of *Steering* is best expressed in the deliberate irony of the title; the elephant stands both as an analogy for government—ponderous, overweight, crushing—and as a symbol of the Republican Party, divided as usual. Understandably, given the differences within the Republican Party, we are never quite sure whether the problem addressed is controlling a balky government or a recalcitrant party. Indeed, it would be fair to say that the appointees discussed in this volume had more difficulty in persuading the Republican administration to steer in the direction they thought had been agreed upon than in getting the bureaucracy to follow a clear command.

Readers who come to *Steering the Elephant* for what it does have to offer will be amply rewarded. It is fascinating. When the remains of our times are exhumed by interplanetary archeologists, they will find *Steering* to be indispensable source material about how people sharing certain values and desiring to legitimate certain social practices viewed their world, tried to act on it, and were in turn reacted upon.

One of the main focuses is on controlling a presumably hostile bureaucracy. The ambience is one of moving into uncharted islands amid hostile natives. Yet the actors (insiders now like to refer to them as "players") differ markedly in their approach to the natives. Some, expecting hostility, generate it in return, thereby reconfirming their initial hypothesis. Although dark murmurings of bureaucratic sabotage are heard, significant evidence of such behavior is seldom presented. On the contrary, there are numerous examples of bureaucratic cooperation, if not exactly of enthusiasm at having their agencies chopped and their missions thwarted. Other actors express regret at discovering, perhaps too late, that they could have made friends with many of the natives. Still others, like Jeane Kirkpatrick at the United Nations, attempt to intervene in the personnel process to assure themselves of staff who are competent and willing to support the new dispensation. They then attempt to improve the conditions of their bureaucrats so as to enable them to serve effectively. No sense in obtaining better staff if they cannot afford to live near enough to where they work. Gradually, after the identification of the "the bureaucracy" with all their troubles wears off, these bright-eyed and bushy-tailed reformers, albeit they usually want to do less rather than more, begin to realize that the disagreement on policies they once thought they were supposed to be carrying out against bureaucratic opposition has causes much closer to home.

They are all for the President, if only they are allowed to carry out what they are sure would be his wishes if he were in their place. Yet they never quite seem to get the authoritative presidential pronouncement, followed by active White House implementation, that would enable them to realize his (as well as their) aspirations. The hoped-for call from on high is just around the corner—they are in fact right about his and their policy congruence—yet it seldom comes into sight. Why is that?

By common consent, Ronald Reagan is a splendid communicator of political ideas. By my own lights, with increasing but by no means unanimous agreement, he is also a superb political strategist.[1] All the more reason, then, to depend on and welcome his help. Why does it come (read these accounts) so seldom and so late?

A leading characteristic of President Reagan's political style is that he chooses only a few high-priority items in which to invest himself. This self-imposed limitation has served him and the nation well. The sense of frittered effort and disappointed hopes that enveloped the Carter Administration in its own malaise has been avoided. Major objectives have been achieved. The "down-side" of this accomplishment for the President's appointees, however, is that they are left on their own. It is up to them to bring him the necessary support for what are undoubtedly his own policy preferences so he can afford to back them. That they have to bring support to him, not he to them, it would be fair to say, did not comport with most initial expectations. When the rules of the game are based on an anti-leadership culture, in which authority does not inhere in position but must be earned anew policy-by-policy, each relying on somewhat different coalitions, the players are limited by the overall capacity of the system.

There's the rub. The president's appointees are limited by the political system's capacity to support authority.

Now enhancing the authority of American institutions is an objective one might think conservatives would share. But these actors are not social but economic conservatives. They are individualists. They believe in competition, not in collectivism. The Republican Party, however, so well exemplified in the person of Ronald Reagan, is a coalition of hierarchical collectivism (viz., defense and abortion) and competitive individualism. The hierarchical, socially conservative wing has to be concerned about shoring up authority to legitimate intervention in social life. Even the individualistic, economically conservative wing requires presidential authority to undo governmental intervention it does not like. Why, then, do they often beat down on the bureaucracy, which is (and must be in a modern society) a major repository of authority?

One might think that a two-track approach to bureaucracy would commend itself: on the one hand, a concerted effort to abolish agencies and programs; on the other, respect for the officials who administer the programs that the representatives of the people in their wisdom have decided to retain.

The conflict—condemnation of the activity versus respect for its administrators—comes out nicely in the discussion of the Small Business Administration. Its head was apparently a splendid administrator. Evidently that is not enough to satisify those who believe that government should not subsidize industry and certainly not provide selective subsidies. Does that view, which I share, justify the actions of some players in denigrating the civil servants who continue to obey the law or the director who has greatly improved its operations? I don't think so. Conservatives, who in other areas call for defense of American institutions, cannot inculcate respect for authority by denigrating its most visible manifestations. Similarly, they would not justify any administrator's attempt to thwart presidential policy once the decision to shut down an agency had been made.

Among the many interesting uses to which *Steering* could be put would be to solicit comments from civil servants. Do they see themselves accurately portrayed here? What do they see as their proper role—doing as they are told, suggesting better alternatives for accomplishing the same purposes, rallying opposition to proposed changes (after all, members of Congress are part of government too)? What do bureaucrats think of their power? Not much, I expect. And their situation may well get worse. If liberal Democrats occupy the executive office, they will heap more tasks on the bureaucracy while challenging its authority as inegalitarian. The further the ideological differences between Democratic and Republican elites, moreover, the more difficult it will be for bureaucrats to discover what they are supposed to do or to whom they are supposed to be accountable. None of this matters, of course, except for those who care about respect for American institutions. Perhaps the actors who write about their hard times here would reply that they will love government more when it becomes small enough for them to embrace.

How much, the reader may wonder, in an effort to assess the applicability of advice on *Steering the Elephant*, would liberal activists entering a future government have to learn from these accounts? A great deal, I think. The advice given is often surprisingly neutral, almost antiseptic. Clarity of purpose, knowing what you want, is essential, though it is difficult to imagine how anyone not already gifted with this invaluable trait will be able to acquire it. Modifying what is desirable with what is feasible, not allowing the best to become the enemy of the better, makes sense. The trouble is that the advice is contradictory. If you don't try, you won't know how far you (or your ideas) might have gone. True. Gramm-Rudman-Hollings and tax reform testify to that. But if you go to the well once too often, or fail too blatantly, your future chances may be much diminished. Also true.

The importance of personal energy, a resource presumably available across the ideological spectrum, is once again reaffirmed. Keeping pushing, maintaining contacts, making yourself and your ideas available to others, pays off.

It is difficult to accomplish anything if you are worried about failure. It is difficult not to be worried, however, when you suddenly get fired or are savaged at hearings. The rule of American life—what you were before doesn't matter as it would in a class system—has now been rewritten to say that you can be held to blame from birth on. In such a heated context, political appointees are wise to cultivate friends and to seek allies against adversity. People who take the reigning ideologies too seriously, as if adherence to them constituted a protective shield, should know better. For them, as for the bureaucrats they are concerned about, government has become a dangerous place.

William Niskanen's heartfelt advice to political appointees is spot on: If they can't support the President who appointed them, they should have the good grace to resign before they bring down with them the institutions on which the proper functioning of government depends. I would add that loyalty can only imperfectly go two ways. It has to be given but it cannot always, perhaps often, be expected to be given back. Keeping your bags packed, while remembering there is life outside of Washington, as Niskanen suggests, is the best advice in the book.

"The Firing of Ed Curran" contains the moral. Upon discovering that the Secretary of Education had not assumed his position to preside over the liquidation of that empire, contrary to the President's pronouncements, Curran tried to tell the chief executive what everyone in Washington knew. In the process, he discovered something only insiders know, namely, how to address a letter with a special code bringing it to the President's personal attention. Curran couldn't have known that when the President was away a senior staffer would send that communication to the Secretary who promptly fired his subordinate. Long afterward, upon learning about what happened, the President is reported to have said that maybe the firing was a mistake. The attentive reader will observe, however, that the staffer occupies a still more prominent position while Curran does not.[2]

In the first chapter, M. Stanton Evans, whom I join in celebrating the usefulness of this volume, proposes a different theory of why conservative appointees have a hard time: The permanent government rejects them. This is why affirmative action is enforced, not because it is the law but because bureaucrats insist. I submit that the difficulty in getting the President to sign an executive order abolishing or modifying it—wasn't Reagan elected?—suggests otherwise. The reason it is necessary for appointees to follow Evans's excellent advice to get involved with the war of information is not that faceless bureaucrats and consultants prevent popular rule but rather that under the separation of powers and a disinclination to accept authority, elections cannot control most outcomes. The campaigners do not usually specify positions clearly enough. We cannot know which of their positions voters support. And the balance of power is in flux. Hence the need both for support and for clarification of alternatives is continuous. Appointees get a license to try, not a guarantee that they will catch anything except trouble.

In these necessarily brief introductory remarks, I have not been able to do justice to the many excellent contributions toward *Steering the Elephant.* The final chapter by Rector and Sanera, for example, will serve political scientists well in attempting to figure out, using well-chosen tests, how far President Reagan has succeeded in moving the domestic government. Nuggets abound throughout. The book should help students and appointees understand the loneliness of the political administrator, the difficulties of change, the varied perspectives on what success means and how it is to be achieved, found even among people who are in general agreement on public policy.

There is also a human element in these stories that sets *Steering* apart from the usual literature on the Washington community, the joyful "How I Came and Conquered" school, the proud "How I Lost but Didn't Sell Out" genre, and the dispiriting "You Can't Beat City Hall on the Potomac" wail. The editors are to be congratulated on producing a mosaic of hope emerging out of disappointment whose personal stories stay with you long after more desiccated accounts have faded from view.

Notes

1. See my "President Reagan as a Political Strategist," in *Elections In America* ed. Kay Lehman Schlozman (London and New York: Unwin Hyman, forthcoming)

2. After being fired at the Department of Education, Ed Curran served as Deputy Director of the Peace Corps, and was nominated as head of the National Endowment for the Humanities (NEH). The position at NEH would have been considerably higher than Curran's former position at the Department of Education, but his confirmation was blocked in the Senate. This latter fact points to a second lesson: Aggressive action based on one's convictions is not a sure road to personal advancement in Washington.

Introduction

ROBERT RECTOR and MICHAEL SANERA

This is a book about American politics, and specifically about the internal politics of the executive branch. It is also a book about change in public policy; how change is facilitated or frustrated, and how the very nature of the process of policy change is evolving. It is an account told by Reagan appointees about what has happened in the first six years of the Reagan Administration, providing guidelines for effective future governance.

There are currently 2.8 million civilian personnel in the executive branch of the federal government. Much of what goes on within this mammoth bureaucracy is of considerable social significance but remains largely a mystery. Executive branch politics is the unheralded component of government; largely undocumented and unexamined, its importance rivals the more publicized activities of the legislative arena. At the heart of the executive branch are 3,000 presidential appointees, about 500 of whom are in positions requiring Senate confirmation. These appointees are the President's eyes and hands—they are the instrument of presidential control. It is through them that the President, who is one man, attempts to govern an establishment of millions.

Steering the Elephant examines the political process, the role of the executive branch in that process, and the role of the political appointee within the executive branch. The book was conceived with two audiences in mind: the first, political appointees and other political figures—current and future—interested in learning techniques for becoming more effective within the policy process; the second, students of Washington politics and government—anyone truly interested in how Washington works. The materials contained in this volume are geared to both audiences. Although some of the essays involve specific advice on political management in the executive branch, they also provide a glimpse of how the government works at the ground level, and as such may be more illuminating to a general audience than much theoretical material written from a loftier and more abstract perspective.

The book is divided into five sections. The first section outlines the principal themes of the volume: the nature of the political system, the nature of the process of political change, and the role of the presidential appointee in those contexts. In the first chapter, M. Stanton Evans provides a new model of our political system. In Chapters 2 and 3, Bruce Fein and Morton Blackwell provide a conceptual framework for understanding the process of political change. In Chapter 4, Fred Smith addresses the process of change on a tactical level and from the perspective of a Washington insider. In Chapter 5, William Niskanen, a former Member of the Council of Economic Advisors under President Reagan, discusses the role of presidential appointees in the federal government. Chapter 6 examines, from a conservative policy perspective, specific pitfalls into which presidential appointees may stumble.

The second section of the book presents techniques of policy change in three arenas: litigation, legislation, and public relations. Joseph Morris, in Chapter 7, discusses the interrelationship of legislation, regulation, and litigation, providing a penetrating analysis of change in the nature of the political system itself. In Chapters 8 and 9, Clifford Barnhart and Jade West discuss relations between the executive and legislative branches of government with particular emphasis on shortcomings in the legislative strategies of the Reagan White House. In Chapter 10, Patrick Korten discusses media relations from the perspective of a Reagan appointee. Chapter 11 describes some of the hidden potential within the federal government for altering public perceptions and promoting policy change.

The third section addresses personnel and management issues within the executive branch. In Chapter 13, Donald Devine, former Director of the Office of Personnel Management, compares various theories of public administration and their impact on the President's ability to govern within the executive branch; he also provides rules for the conduct of political appointees, and a prescription of an ideal form of cabinet government. Based on her experiences at the United Nations, Ambassador Jeane Kirkpatrick offers in Chapter 14 an excellent set of management principles to guide the work of political appointees within the federal government. In the next chapter, Becky Norton Dunlop describes the crucial role of the Office of Presidential Personnel for the success of the presidency, and the reforms which the Reagan Administration has instituted in political personnel selection; she also suggests a model personnel system for use in future administrations. Chapters 16 and 17 examine what it means to "manage" in government, how management in the public and private sectors differs, and why private-sector management techniques, when imported into the public sector, often yield unforeseen and undesirable results.

The fourth section presents nine case studies drawn from the Reagan presidency. The case studies involve a variety of problems typical of those which have confronted Reagan appointees, and reveal a mixture of success and failure. The case histories were deliberately based on issues within mid-sized agencies and offices rather than on major headline-grabbing policies. The reasons for this were twofold. First, there is very little comprehensive information available to the public about operations at the middle levels of government. Second, much of what the government really does is accomplished at this nuts-and-bolts level by thousands of energetic individuals scattered across government departments and agencies. By understanding how the political process operates on this scale we may gain an improved understanding of the broader mosaic of government and policy at the macro level.

The final section of the book provides an overview of the Reagan Administration and policy change. It assesses the impact of the Reagan presidency in broad terms and describes the long-run nature of the policy change process.

The authors in this volume are either Reagan appointees or have worked closely with the Reagan Administration. All write about the problems of government from a conservative perspective. The accounts are "raw" in the sense that they are written by those actively—and emotionally—involved in the policy process. The immediacy is instructive and even those readers who do not share a conservative perspective should learn a great deal about our federal government from this volume. Indeed, much of the material in this volume may seem surprising even to those who feel they are well acquainted with Washington politics. The real world of Washington has an Alice in Wonderland quality that clashes with conventional images. We have sought to capture part of that peculiar world; if the material presented surprises and challenges the reader, we will have accomplished at least part of our task.

A final purpose of this volume, alluded to briefly above, was to uncover principles which lead to effectiveness among presidential appointees—and at a higher level, guidelines which would lead to an effective presidency. The essays and case studies presented here offer a unique picture of how Washington works; the advice contained in them is a necessary first step to understanding Washington for those who would seek to govern here, both now and in the future.

STEERING
THE
ELEPHANT
How Washington Works

1 Steering the Elephant

M. STANTON EVANS

Editors' Note: In this introductory chapter, adapted from a presentation at a Heritage Foundation Seminar, M. Stanton Evans, a thirty-year veteran observer of the Washington scene, provides a new model of the way our political system works. His model, in part, explains why policy change in Washington is so difficult to achieve. As such it offers a suitable backdrop to the rest of the material in this volume. The author concludes with a number of timely suggestions for political appointees in a conservative administration.

Our discussion begins with a paradox: Conservatism is on the rise in the United States, yet many conservatives in government are experiencing a period of discontent. Ronald Reagan, for years regarded as a hopeless outcast on the right-wing of the political system, was elected president in 1980 and triumphantly re-elected in 1984. Public opinion polls show a rising level of conservative affirmation in the country, and everyone seems to acknowledge we are in an era of an ascendant new conservative majority. Yet the policy product emerging from the federal system, six years into the Reagan Administration, is often very different from what conservatives expected. The central question we need to ask ourselves is why—given the rising tide of conservatism—it is so difficult to get conservative results out of the federal government.

I am convinced the answer to this question is that most of us have been working in terms of a mistaken model of the political system. The conventional model, which we learned in civics class or from our readings in the media, is that this is a system of representative government, based on popular sovereignty. According to this model, every two, four, or six years, the American people listen to candidates holding forth on issues and then go to the polls. They decide between candidates on the basis of their policy stands, and vote accordingly. The candidates then become officeholders. They go to Washington where they proceed to put into effect the platforms upon which they were elected. By this indirect process, the people rule. The model presupposes that the people are the ultimate sovereigns in the system and that the engine that makes the system run is the election.

Most of our political energies as conservatives over the past generation have been devoted to working within this model. We first approached the problem by recognizing that liberal policies were wrong and ineffective, and that they violated the principles that conservatives cherish—a free economy, personal freedom, a strong national defense. Conservatives then proceeded with an educational effort to get the word out, to show the American people what was happening under liberal rule. We tried to get people to cross over to the conservative side from the welfare state majority that sustained the New Deal and ruled this country up through the era of Lyndon Johnson. Once conservatives got that educational job done, they moved into the field of political action and developed political action committees and lobbies that worked to get the appropriate people elected to office and then to push for legislation that reflected the issues upon which they were elected.

Conservative efforts in this respect have not been one hundred percent effective, but to a large degree we have succeeded. We got the educational job done. We have also got a good part of the electoral job done. It still needs working on—you can't ever quit—but conservatives have done a lot of what they set out to do. And yet if we look at what actually goes on here in Washington, at the actual policies still in place, there is little comfort for those of us who have been working within this model—assuming that education and elections were the keys to changing policy.

The reason for this disappointment, I submit, is that the model conservatives have been operating under is basically incorrect. The system as it functions today is very little like the civics-book image of popular sovereignty and representative government. There is a very different kind of government here in Washington, D.C., which has a very tenuous connection, if any, to the will of the people. In many respects, indeed, it goes directly counter to the will of the people.

What is actually in place here is a permanent, self-enclosed system that operates on its own terms, toward its own ends, according to its own laws. This system of permanent government defers only reluctantly to manifestations of public sentiment expressed in elections. From its perspective, elections are an inconvenience, a distraction that must be dealt with before the people who really run things can get back to the business of governing.

The apparatus of this permanent, unelected government is extensive, embracing a number of components. The first of these is the federal bureaucracy, which has nearly 3 million civilian employees. When a new president is elected he may replace only about one-tenth of one percent of these employees. The rest of the 3 million will remain in place as if the election had never happened, and these individuals will generally act as vigorous caretakers of their departments' traditional policies and interests. Not only are the officials appointed by the president vastly outnumbered by the unelected bureaucrats, but the bureaucrats control the technical information concerning the government's policies and operations, thereby defining the issues and the options for their nominal superiors. So the appointees will have an uphill struggle even finding out what is going on in the bureaucracy they are supposed to supervise— let alone bringing about any changes.

Perhaps the worst agency in this respect is the State Department. The bureaucrats who run the Department clearly believe they inhabit a world unto themselves. I am informed that they have a nickname for political appointees: "the Christmas help." Their feeling is that government policy should be set by "professionals" and they react with annoyance to elections and other incidental factors that intrude on their "professional" operations.

A second component of our permanent government—in some ways even more important than the bureaucracy—is the federal courts, which have become the unelected legislature of the country. If we look at many of the critical issues that have caused so much turmoil in the United States from the 60's up through the 70's and even today—issues such as abortion, prayer in the schools, busing and quotas, pornography—all have been ignited by the courts. They have not come up through the legislative process. It would be almost impossible to get the U.S. Congress or state legislatures to vote into law what has been enacted by the courts.

For example, there is no statute law whatsoever to justify racial balance busing or quotas. Quite the contrary. The Civil Rights Act of 1964 repudiates the notion of racial balance busing and quotas in very explicit language. That repudiation has been reiterated over and over by Congress in many resolutions. Nonetheless, we have *had* racial balance busing and quotas in this country for twenty years because the courts and bureaucrats wanted them. If you take a look at all of the so-called law on this subject, it consists of bureaucratic regulations and decisions by courts. There is no statute law whatsoever. The same is true of all these other issues. The courts, as we well know, are insulated from public opinion. The judges are not elected and once they're there it's almost impossible to get them out.

Almost as important as the civil service bureaucracy and the courts in determining the agenda in this city are the nearly permanent staff on Capitol Hill. When conservatives get elected, they come to Washington and immediately hire a staff. Almost invariably they start by saying, "I need someone with Hill experience." You can't have a congressional office, it seems, unless you've got people with "Hill experience." So you tend to get sort of a floating group of "experienced" people who stay in place, almost irrespective of who gets elected. Although they have less formal protection than the civil service, there tends to be the same kind of stability and permanence as there is in the executive branch. So you get a large group of people who make a living off the Congress and who play a large role in seeing that the same policies remain in place year after year.

In addition to these three main elements of the permanent "unelected government," there are other components as well. These are not officially part of the government, but nonetheless they play a very important role in the system that controls things here in Washington. They constitute an "invisible" layer immediately surrounding the components of the formal, permanent government. In this category are organizations representing recipients of government largess, subsidies, or favors through the regulatory process: the unions, business organizations, retirees, etc.

In addition, there are the so-called Beltway bandits: vendors to the government; people who do studies for the government agencies; all the big law firms that specialize in regulatory practice; the influence peddlers; the public relations firms. These are people who essentially live off the government system and play a considerable role in running the system. Then there are the ideological pressure groups; these groups are less concerned with economic gain than the economic lobbying groups but they have a policy agenda they want to have enacted, generally through bigger and more intrusive government.

All of these economic and ideological lobbies are very attentive to the legislative and regulatory process, much more so than is the average American. There's really no comparison. The lobbies are here full time. They know exactly what is going on. They know exactly what levers to pull. They know exactly what the regulatory process is, they know how to get to the regulators, they know how to get to the Congress. They know how to command public attention when needed. And they're tracking everything all the time that could conceivably affect their interests.

The average American, the average consumer, the average taxpayer— who have to pay the bills for ever bigger government, or are injured by it—don't have the time, resources, or inclination to sit camped out in Washington, D.C., but even if they did, they wouldn't know what to do. They just do not have the same kind of expertise. Average Americans do not know how all of these agencies function and they really have very little input into or influence on what happens in the regulatory process or the legislative process, in most cases.

On top of all these components, there is a final, extremely influential element of the permanent governing system, and that is the media. In the conventional image, the media are supposed to be adversarial to the government. They are allegedly ferocious watchdogs of the public interest ensuring that government doesn't do something bad. That is by and large another part of the mistaken model. It is true that the media, in certain cases, act in an adversarial way toward government—but only in certain cases, i.e., those which happen to correspond to the ideological predispositions of the media. The media are selective watchdogs; not really watchdogs at all but rather active proponents of a particular outlook and a particular set of policies within the system.

If we take a look at the crusades of *The Washington Post*, the networks, or any other major media outlet, we find that almost invariably the people or the things they select to expose and to crusade against are conservative. Look, for example, at the media's treatment of the $640 toilet seats and the $7,000 coffee pots at the Pentagon. This type of waste is vigorously and incessantly exposed by the watchdogs. However, almost nothing is ever printed in *The Washington Post* or run on TV newscasts about the tremendous waste throughout every domestic agency of government. You could run rampant through an agency like the Department of Housing and Urban Development (HUD) exposing waste, fraud, and nonsense. But there is never anything about it in the press because that type of exposé does not fit the ideological agenda of most of the people in the media.

The people who work in the various components of this permanent government are here for decades. In comparison to them, an elected president and his handful of appointees are merely visitors to the nation's capital: "Christmas help." If one comes to Washington equipped with the old model of elected representative government and a view of government organizations as machinery which will automatically change in response to an elected leadership, one is not going to be very effective.

We need, therefore, a new and different model of the way our government works. I think the best model is a biological one. The permanent government resembles and reacts like an organism. Its various components mesh together to form a living entity. This entity has its own life force, its own laws of growth, its own vital interests. It has its own aspirations and beliefs—all quite distinct from the rest of society.

The election of Ronald Reagan was a threat to the vitality of this organism. From the standpoint of the permanent government, Reagan and the political appointees he brought with him to Washington are like bacteria invading the system. The system has mobilized all of its antibodies, its white blood cells, to fight off the infection which is Reaganism.

The system will try to reject, seal off, and ultimately eradicate any appointee who actually begins to threaten its well-being. If you look at the first six years of the Reagan Administration, you find that the people who have come under bitter attack, in the media and on the Hill, are almost without exception those people who were seeking most energetically to bring about change and thereby constituted the greatest threat to the system: Dick Allen; Don Devine; Ed Meese and Brad

Reynolds; Ernest Lefever (who was never confirmed); or Larry Uzzell and Eileen Gardner who lasted three days at the Department of Education. The list goes on and on. In other cases where the appointee was behaving in a way that the system approved—doing nothing or actively promoting the status quo—there has been a policy of benign neglect, few attacks, little by way of critical exposure. So the first lesson that a new appointee should bear in mind is that, rather than being a pliant machine to be controlled, the permanent government is an active entity that will resist and even seek to destroy anyone who threatens its interests.

Not only will the system reject individuals who threaten it; the permanent government will also promote its own priorities and issues, irrespective of public opinion. Events at the start of Reagan's second term illustrate this clearly. In 1984, Reagan overwhelmingly defeated Walter Mondale and the liberal policy views that Mondale represented. According to the traditional model of representative government, debate during the next year in Washington should have focused on the sentiments and concerns expressed by the public in the 1984 election and on the principles upon which the President was reelected. What actually happened at the beginning of Reagan's second term was altogether different—and highly symptomatic of the way the Washington system really works.

Consider the issue of South Africa, which has dominated recent political discussion. A naive observer of our political system in 1985 would have concluded that the American people were preoccupied with South Africa. But, in fact, South Africa was of such little concern to the American people that it was scarcely even mentioned during the entire 1984 campaign. South Africa, whatever the rights and wrongs of the situation there, was just not important to the American people, and the opinion that did exist at the time supported the president's policy: it opposed disinvestment.

In the immediate aftermath of the election, however, Randall Robinson, president of TransAfrica, and a handful of left-wing supporters began demonstrating and getting themselves politely arrested outside the South African Embassy. The media leaped on the issue; Congress then picked it up and amplified it; the disinvestment issue was echoed back and forth within the various chambers of the Washington system until it seemed that South Africa was all you could hear about.

Thus a topic that had received zero attention in the election was plucked from thin air and magically transformed into an urgent national issue. As a result, at the beginning of President Reagan's second term, an Administration that received 59 percent of the vote only a few months earlier found itself losing the policy initiative. It found itself abandoning its stated policy, reacting defensively to an issue generated by a mere handful of political operatives reinforced by the rest of the Washington system. The process simply turns the traditional idea of representative government on its head.

• • •

Once we have recognized the problem of permanent government in Washington, we need some guidelines on how to deal with it. I would suggest three major criteria for effective participation in the Reagan government. The first is that political appointees should ask themselves the question: *Why am I here?* If the answer is that the appointee wanted and needed a job, or felt that he or she deserved an appointment for services rendered, or maybe wanted to administer the government in a more efficient manner, then a certain kind of conduct will follow from that response.

If, on the other hand, the answer is that the appointee is here because *he believes in all the things that Ronald Reagan said in 1980 and 1984*, and had been saying for 20 years before that, and wanted to do something to put these ideas into effect, then a totally different kind of conduct and mindset toward the government will be indicated.

During President Reagan's first term, it was evident that some of his appointees gave one answer to the question, some the other. These answers may be understood, changing the image a bit, by thinking about a man riding on the back of an elephant. One man sees his purpose as just making sure that he does not fall off the elephant. He works very skillfully at keeping his balance on the back of the elephant as it stampedes through the jungle, crashing through the underbrush, splashing through muddy riverbeds. It is demanding work staying on the back of this large and unpredictable beast; if the man falls off, he is going to get all muddy or maybe even run over. So as the elephant stampedes along, the rider congratulates himself on what a swell job he is doing, hanging on up there on the elephant's back. The only problem with this approach is that he winds up going where the elephant wants to go and not where *he* wants to go—if he ever had any ideas about where he wanted to go in the first place.

A great many figures in the current Administration have approached their jobs in exactly that fashion. They focused their efforts on keeping their balance on top of the elephant, reacting to problems, making sure the Administration looked good in the short term. They avoided risks, controversy, and potential defeats, and tried to keep clear of criticism as much as possible. During the first four years under President Reagan, this approach was dubbed "pragmatism." Unfortunately, while the pragmatic approach may leave the appointee and presidency unmuddied up on top of the elephant, it leaves everything else that is important—direction of policy—in the control of the elephant.

The second approach—trying not only to stay on the back of the elephant but also actively trying to control its direction—is far more difficult. But it is also far more rewarding. The small group of political appointees in the Reagan Administration who have actively tried or who are actively trying to *steer the elephant* deserve enormous credit. They will certainly receive enormous criticism and condemnation from those who don't want to see the system changed.

My second recommendation to appointees is to remember the purposes of our representative system, and to avoid the trap of viewing the issues in technical, managerial terms. Technical expertise and managerial competence are important, of course, but the crucial questions in our system are neither technical nor managerial, but *political*. The ends of policy should be dictated by the voters in the polling place and carried forward by their elected representatives and by the political appointees of the president.

Appointees will discover, if they have not already, that countless people in the agency or department will be perpetually ready to tell them why some political initiative of the president cannot be accomplished, all for technical-managerial reasons. Political appointees must resist absorption into this obscurantist thicket. Policy considerations should be paramount, not made subordinate to technical considerations.

My final recommendation stems directly from my experience as a journalist. Political appointees should recognize that the battle over public policy is largely a war of information. Many political appointees do not seem to realize this. I have said that the conventional model of representative government is not working, that the government is not responsive to the popular will—but this is not inevitable. The main reason that the non-elected system can ignore the public will is that the average American does not have the foggiest notion of what is going on in Washington. Not a clue. This has to be corrected—with information.

Because they see the media as hostile and adversarial, many political appointees seem to believe it is their job simply to sit on information. I have seen this happen time after time. The real job must be to get information out. I am not talking about leaking data or about false information and propaganda. I am talking about basic information, facts and figures about what is going on in Washington.

For example, a few years ago Ed Meese made some remarks about hunger in America and about federal nutrition programs. He was immediately blitzed by an outraged press corps: "How can Meese be so callous—people are starving—the programs have all been cut back," etc. Everything the media said was nonsense; the programs had not been cut. But trying to write about this to show that Meese had been correct was a very frustrating experience. The Administration was very slow in making the relevant information available.

Time after time, the Reagan Administration does not provide the relevant data even when those data support its policies. For years I tried to get information out of the Arms Control and Disarmament Agency about Soviet violations of the SALT accords. The facts on that topic justify the Administration position across-the-board on a whole range of defense and foreign policy issues; they are very damaging to liberal beliefs. But I could not get the information. Finally, Senator Symms and others forced the Administration to let the information out.

In 1984 and 1985, Teddy Kennedy, Gerry Studds, and other statesmen of that caliber were running around defaming the Contras, the freedom fighters in Nicaragua, saying they were all butchers and Somocistas and so forth. For eight months, I tried to get information from the State Department about the Contras. The information was there; the Department just would not release it. Finally, the State Department coughed up a little pamphlet on the Contras, just ten days before the vote on Contra aid. It showed that everything the liberals were saying was untrue, but it was far too late to have an impact on public opinion and on Congress. Clearly, in this case, there were bureaucrats down in the bowels of the State Department who were opposed to Contra aid, and who managed under one pretext or another to bottle up the facts until it was too late.

Political appointees need to realize they are in an information battle. The only way a conservative president is ever going to be able to get assistance for the Contras, get the Strategic Defense Initiative, or bring the budget under control is if he has the support of the people. To the extent that he has the support of the people, he can prevail against Congress, or even come up with a better Congress the next time around. But he cannot have the support of the people unless the people know what is happening.

It is not enough just to get the President on TV every three months to talk about some major issue. Providing information has to be an ongoing process that is treated as a major responsibility by all the appointees in the Administration. The effort has to go beyond simple press releases and photo opportunities; in each agency there should be appointees who have a detailed knowledge of the facts and statistics of particular programs and policies and who are charged with a continuing effort to ensure that information is available to the appropriate analysts, journalists, and writers. These information experts could be either in a public relations office or in a program office, but, in either case, they must have a mastery over a large amount of detail and must work to put that information into the hands of those who can pass it on to the public.

Effectiveness in the information war is only one aspect of success in the process of policy management. But in company with all the arts of policy management it must be based on a recognition that winning elections is not enough. After an election is won, a whole new struggle begins; a struggle to control the federal bureaucracy; to overcome the other elements of the nonelected governing system; to produce the conservative policies that will safeguard America's freedoms in the years to come. The essays in this volume offer a great many other "do's and dont's" about controlling the governmental process. These insights, gained during the first six years of the Reagan Administration, should prove extremely useful to those who want to master the difficult task of *steering the elephant.*

2 Politics: The Art of Public Education

BRUCE E. FEIN

Editors' Note: Politics is a set of linkages between government and the rest of society. Generally, political appointees will focus on the minutiae of bureaucratic management and short-term political compromise at the expense of the underlying dimensions of change which may require a more gradual pace. In this chapter, the former General Counsel of the Federal Communications Commission offers advice for politicians who would like to shape history rather than be shaped by it.

A majority of politicians, public officeholders, and commentators perceive politics as the art of fund raising, legislative compromise, constituent service, and image building. The dominant focus and concern are on the processes of election or reelection, special-interest groups, campaign contributions and expenditures, lobbying, or scandal.

Reacting to and shaping the day-to-day media headlines absorbs the attention and energies of the typical elected or appointed official. The agendas of daily staff meetings are largely set by stories carried in the morning newspapers or the previous evening broadcast news. Events or votes are ordinarily evaluated only with regard to their potential impact at the next election day. Efforts to inject political philosophy or overarching moral or ethical principles into a politician's deliberations are generally dismissed as irrelevant or counterproductive to his success. This attitude yields elected and appointed officeholders who read shockingly few books, whether of philosophy, economics, history, law, or war. The world of scholarship or ideas is generally alien to their existence. They are staunchly wedded to the belief that influence over the nation's public policies is the preserve of those who win elections; thus they fervently insist that if a politician desires to be a pivotal public-policy architect, virtually nothing must be done that might threaten perpetuation in office.

This conventional wisdom, however, is myopic and erroneous. As John Maynard Keynes observed, "[t]he ideas of economists and political philosophers, both when they are right and when they are wrong, are more powerful than is commonly understood." Persons in authority frequently champion policies based on the ideas of "some academic scribbler of a few years back. I am sure that the power of vested interests is vastly exaggerated compared with the gradual encroachment of ideas." Keynes's understanding of the political power of ideas has been recognized by only a few who occupy the corridors of American political history.

John Adams understood that the nation's independence was won during the years preceding 1775 when protests against writs of assistance and the Stamp Act spread the idea that taxation without representation was politically illegitimate. "The Revolution," Adams explained, "was indeed effected in the period from 1761 to 1775. I mean a complete revolution in the minds of the people. A . . .change of the opinions and affections of the people and a full confidence in the practicability of a union of the colonies." Similarly, Adams noted that "[t]he precepts, reasonings and example of the United States of America" had ignited a democratic spirit in Europe that threatened every despotism, monarchy, or aristocracy.

President Franklin Roosevelt realized that the processes of government are essentially educational processes. And President Kennedy frequently sent messages and innovative bills to Congress not with the expectation of immediate enactment, but with the goal of educating and accustoming Congress to unfamiliar ideas that would blossom into public policy in the nation's future. Politicians who perceive politics as the art of public education have a claim, like President Lincoln, to belong to the ages.

The decisive forces in the politics of a nation are ideological. The victor in the battle of ideas, not the battle for political office, is the authentic overseer of public policy. Virtually all major policy questions addressed by an officeholder are decided with reference to untested or untestable assumptions of what is good or evil, ethical or immoral, virtuous or deplorable, or other evaluative criteria. For example, whether a legislator votes in favor of welfare expenditures for persons both physically and mentally unimpaired will turn on his ideas concerning free will, individual responsibility, and the duty of government to relieve poverty no matter what its cause. The ideas of legislators toward these questions generally mirror those of the community at large. To control the ascendancy of ideas within the electorate on the morality or wisdom of welfare spending is thus to control the vote of the legislator.

Identical observations are applicable to legislative votes regarding color-blindness in employment, progressive as opposed to flat tax rates, military aid to the so-called Contra forces fighting in Nicaragua, and every other item on the political policy agenda. Each vote will be informed by the prevailing ideological view of whether the results sought—an end to racial preferences, lesser tax burdens on the most economically productive, the nation's intervention in the political evolution of a foreign state—are good or evil, beneficent or unfair, enlightened or counterproductive. In sum, political questions are the mere tip of an ideological iceberg. Shaping public opinion is far more important than pork barrel blandishments or campaign contributions in determining what laws are enacted and what policies are embraced by officeholders.

Experience confirms that the failures of political parties to achieve professed public policy goals can be ascribed to high-level officials, whether elected or appointed, who are blind to the importance of ideas. These officials expend their energies and time, myopically focused on tactical daily "firefighting" to mollify contentious voices. Philosophical principles that underwrite a policy position are readily compromised; the public is thus not challenged to think about whether sets of policy assumptions are wrong or misguided. This latter deficiency explains many of the major failures of presidents and other public officials.

Astute politicians will not desist from pursuing legislation or insisting on policies simply because they have poor prospects of immediate political acceptance. The prescient officeholder will use the occasions for championing specific proposals, currently disfavored by the majority, to expound on their philosophical justifications and to educate the public as to their ethical, moral, or practical wisdom. This educational process may consume years or even a decade before public opinion is decisively changed; but once accomplished, the officeholder who set this ideological change in motion will find that his cherished policy goals will find permanent expression in the nation's laws or practices. On the other hand, an office holder who manages to sneak through minor legislative or regulatory changes by tactical skill—but who fails to overturn the conventional public wisdom—will often see his gains washed away in a few years. Policy change which is not accompanied by a change in the intellectual foundations of policy will not endure.

Attorney General Edwin Meese's insistence that the Supreme Court interpret the Constitution solely with reference to the intent of its authors exemplifies the power of the long-headed officeholder. Although assailed by many within the legal and political communities, Meese's proposed interpretive doctrine of original intent has evoked constructive debate that is curtailing public and judicial acceptance of policymaking by the Supreme Court which is camouflaged as constitutional interpretation; Meese has unleashed an idea that will do more to restrain judicial activism than any legislative proposal in the nation's history, including President Franklin Roosevelt's court-packing plan.

In sum, successful politics is, by and large, the art of public education. It is clear that public education by political actors takes place not only through utterances, speeches, and press releases, but also through concrete policy proposals on the legislative, regulatory, and judicial fronts. A newly proposed policy initiative, in and of itself, will alter the context of debate surrounding an issue. Each initiative thus has an impact on two levels: first, in the realm of ideas; second, in the more immediate realm of statute, regulation, or judicial decision. However, the more articulate the political actor is in explaining his initiative, the broader the intellectual impact.

A New Idea Agenda

President Ronald Reagan assumed office in 1981 under a banner of ideas that challenged the broad range of conventional public policy wisdom. In the economic realm, Reagan disavowed so-called Keynesian or demand-oriented formulas to buttress growth through government spending; instead, he trumpeted "supply-side" economic policies aimed at stimulating private investment by reducing taxes and increasing the rewards of hard work and entrepreneurship. Reagan further stressed the need to curb government regulation of business to spur productivity and innovation, and to eliminate costs that fueled inflation.

Concerning social policy and civil rights, the initial Reagan agenda was equally ambitious. Reagan was a tribune for: color-blind laws; opposition to court-ordered busing to integrate public schools; voluntary prayer in schools; tuition tax credits for parents with children attending nonpublic schools; and restrictions on abortions. With regard to the allocation of government power, Reagan expostulated against judicial policymaking through creative "interpretations" of the Constitution, favoring instead a restoration of many sovereign prerogatives to the states in furtherance of the principles of federalism.

What is initially arresting about the idea agenda of Reagan is how many attack the actions and policies of his immediate Republican predecessors: Presidents Richard Nixon and Gerald Ford. Sounding and acting like President Franklin Roosevelt, Nixon declared himself a Keynesian in 1971, fastened wage and price controls on the economy, and approved extravagant social security spending increases. President Nixon further signed legislation augmenting the powers of government regulatory bureaucracies, or even creating new bureaucracies. Deplored, at least philosophically, by President Reagan, these bureaucracies included the Environmental Protection Agency, the Consumer Product Safety Commission, the Commodity Futures Trading Commission, the Occupational Safety and Health Administration, and the Equal Employment Opportunity Commission.

The Nixon Administration also sanctioned the idea of racial quotas, goals, and timetables in employment through the so-called Philadelphia Plan, involving government construction contractors and unions, and through remedial decrees in civil-rights litigation that showered employment preferences on minorities or women untouched by illegal discrimination. Nixon's Department of Justice and Department of Health, Education, and Welfare embraced forced busing to desegregate public schools. The Voting Rights Act of 1970 signed by Nixon and the 1975 Voting Rights Act initialed by Gerald Ford emasculated state prerogatives over election laws and sought to guarantee a quota of electoral victories by minority candidates. Reagan's color-blind and anti-busing civil rights goals seek to undo the handiwork largely of Nixon and Ford.

Reagan's abortion and federal tuition tax credit policies are substantially responses to Supreme Court decisions authored by appointees of President Nixon: Justice Harry Blackmun (decreeing in *Roe v. Wade* [1973] that a constitutional right of privacy forecloses government restrictions on abortions, except when the fetus is viable outside the womb), and Chief Justice Warren Burger (proclaiming in *Lemon v. Kurtzman* [1971] that government aid to nonpublic schools violates the First Amendment unless: its purpose is secular; its primary effect neither advances nor inhibits religion; and its administration does not entail excessive government entanglement with religion). The judicial activism of the Supreme Court animadverted by Reagan has been sustained by Nixon (Burger, Blackmun, and Powell) and Ford (Stevens) appointees, and orchestrated by an Eisenhower (Brennan) appointee.

As this brief survey illustrates, the domestic policies of Presidents Nixon and Ford were profoundly nonideological. Neither President was either philosophically reflective or tutelary in his domestic policy actions or messages; neither challenged conventional public policy wisdom. It is thus unsurprising that the presidencies of Nixon and Ford marched to the domestic policy drummer of President Franklin Roosevelt and his successors, and bequeathed legislation and policy precedents applauded by contemporary liberal Democrats.

President Reagan has succeeded in vindicating his professed domestic idea agenda to the extent that he has expounded a coherent philosophy and instructed and exhorted the public both through speeches and action. Where Reagan has vacillated or relied upon unedifying or glib slogans, his policy goals at best have been an "incomplete success" (a phrase coined by President Jimmy Carter to characterize the ill-starred Iranian rescue mission).

Supply-side Economics

Since 1981, President Reagan has expounded and vigorously supported supply-side economics as the basis for crafting budget and tax policy. Briefly stated, supply-side theory asserts that economic growth, employment, and productivity are predominantly stimulated by expanding private investment incentives and by augmenting the rewards of labor and entrepreneurship in order to increase aggregate productivity and output and to reduce inflation. Applying this theory, President Reagan has repeatedly sought to decrease federal civilian government spending and to increase real corporate and personal income by reducing federal income taxes. Furthermore, President Reagan has frequently spoken directly to the people in explaining his economic policy premises and insisting that material rewards ought, as a matter of right, to crown those who work diligently and proficiently.

President Reagan has generally deplored the idea that government should subsidize idleness or economic hardships confronted because of misguided investments or personal indiscipline (with minor exceptions made for farmers and Continental Illinois Bank); this has not prevented Reagan from supporting a safety net for the genuinely needy whose plight cannot be ascribed to individual sloth. However, in contradiction to his basic policy, Reagan has staunchly refused to curb social security spending, and has accepted social security tax increases.

Despite occasional departures from supply-side theories, the Reagan Administration has succeeded in convincing policymakers at all levels of government, and the public, that economic policies should be informed by the idea that the private sector, through incentives that increase output and personal income, should be the pivot of growth, employment, and prosperity. The Reagan economic philosophy has dethroned the New Deal wisdom that government policy should focus on increasing the demand for outputs through government spending, by programs like the Works Progress Administration (WPA), Public Works Administration (PWA), and Agriculture Adjustment Administration (AAA). The vast majority of both Democrats and Republicans accede to Reagan's new conventional wisdom, and budget debates in Congress focus not on whether new spending programs should be initiated, but on whether program expenditures should be curtailed or eliminated. In addition, there is bipartisan consensus that tax rates should be reduced to permit the working population to retain a greater proportion of their income. The only disagreement is over the magnitude of tax reduction.

President Reagan's success in altering conventional wisdom regarding government economic policies will be an enduring legacy of his Presidency; its influence will dominate public-policy economic dialogue for at least a generation. The long-term consequences of this victory in the war of ideas will far outweigh, in importance, the immediate economic success that Reagan policies have produced.

Economic Deregulation

President Reagan has been modestly successful in circumscribing government economic regulation of business and in explaining to the nation the reasons for his deregulation policies. Reagan has eliminated oil price and allocation controls, presided over the elimination of the Civil Aeronautics Board, and urged legislation to further deregulate financial institutions, natural gas, and surface transportation. Reagan has proposed a relaxation of anti-merger laws, and successfully fought against tighter government regulation of tender offers.

On the other hand, Reagan has signed legislation that relaxes competition in the maritime industry. Moreover, Reagan's Department of Justice has erected, in conjunction with Federal District Judge Harold Greene, a virtual regulatory matrix that confounds large portions of the nation's telecommunications industry. For instance, the modified final judgment made by Judge Green prohibits local telephone companies from offering long distance services, manufacturing telephone equipment, or entering into non-telephone services without his approval.

Upon assuming office, Reagan confronted a relatively impotent philosophy favoring economic regulation. A chorus of voices favoring deregulation had begun under Gerald Ford, and proceeded forward during the Administration of President Carter. That chorus picked up, in some areas, such unlikely converts as Ted Kennedy and Ralph Nader. Accordingly, the Reagan Administration could avoid extensive public education efforts in its quest to lift economic regulatory activities of government from the necks of businessmen. But the failure to master the art of public education regarding deregulation also yielded costs. Lacking a groundswell of public support, President Reagan, as noted, has failed to obtain congressional assent to deregulate important sectors of the economy such as telecommunications, natural gas, and banking. The Reagan Administration has crystallized in the public mind, nevertheless, a conventional wisdom that makes the likelihood of any new federal government economic regulatory agency virtually nil during the forthcoming decades, irrespective of which political party is successful at the polls.

Color-blind Laws

President Reagan has equivocated on his professed commitment to color-blind laws that prohibit awards based on racial preferences to persons untouched by illegal discrimination. President Reagan signed the Voting Rights Act of 1982, which established virtual racial quotas in the election of public officials. Moreover, he has so far refused to alter a federal Executive Order that demands racial goals and timetables for employers with federal government contracts. The Reagan Administration failed to make its voice heard in the *Guardians v. Civil Service Commission* case in the Supreme Court that upheld the power of agencies to make practices with discriminatory effects illegal even when untainted by any discriminatory purpose.

On the other hand, the Department of Justice under Reagan has filed lawsuits and briefs that denounce racial quotas or preferences of any sort except when employed to aid individuals proven to have personally suffered from past discrimination. The Department's greatest success was in the *Stotts Firefighters* case, which outlawed decrees issued by judges in the arena of employment that preferred nonvictims of discrimination on the basis of race. In addition, the Equal Employment Opportunity Commission has recently ceased seeking racial goals and timetables in any lawsuits that it initiates.

President Reagan has devoted little time to expounding on the evils of racial preferences in order to alter public opinion. In the absence of any strong effort to educate the American people on the unacceptability of racial preferences in any form, President Reagan has been uninfluential in moving the country toward his professed goal of color blindness. Even though public support for the liberal status quo is at best shallow, the Reagan Administration has failed to mount consistent policies which assault the weakened conventional wisdom.

Court-ordered Busing

The Reagan Administration has repeatedly denounced court-ordered busing as a desegregation remedy when used to implement race-conscious pupil assignments. Both President Reagan in speeches, and the Civil Rights Division of the Justice Department in litigation, have opposed mandatory busing as both ineffectual and contributory to racial divisiveness unhealthy to educational endeavors. As a partial consequence, mandatory busing has been discarded in favor of neighborhood school assignments in a large number of desegration cases. A recent Court of Appeals ruling upholding the decision of Norfolk, Virginia to abandon a desegregation plan involving extensive busing, further demonstrates the discredited state of that remedy in contemporary desegregation jurisprudence. Court-ordered busing has only a handful of supporters today.

Voluntary Prayer in Schools

President Reagan has vigorously supported a constitutional amendment that would permit voluntary prayer in public schools and in other public fora. Reagan's Department of Justice has also urged the constitutionality of voluntary prayer in litigation, and has supported the enactment of a federal statute generally forbidding public schools to discriminate against religious endeavors in offering their premises for extracurricular use.

President Reagan, however, has been relatively silent on the reasons why religion in public life is an indispensible component of American democracy. He has failed to remind the American people that prayer was routine in the first Continental Congress, and that John Adams urged that American independence be commemorated by a solemn act of devotion to the God Almighty under whose providential care it had come about. In addition, it was recognized by Adams and his compatriots that inculcation of religious values is essential to the civic virtues that underwrite a healthy democracy. Because he has failed to elaborate on the reasons for enhancing religion in American life, and failed to demonstrate the nexus between religious values and a healthy functioning of democracy, President Reagan has been generally ineffectual in changing public-policy approaches to religious issues.

Abortion

President Reagan has repeatedly voiced support for statutory restrictions on abortions. The Reagan Department of Justice has urged that the landmark decision in *Roe v. Wade*, which established a constitutional right to abortion, be overturned. But President Reagan has done little to expand on the reasons for opposition to abortion, relying mainly on unedifying *ipse dixit*. He has failed to stimulate thoughtful public debate over the human attributes of a fetus, and the ethical imperatives that militate in favor of protecting human life, whether prospective or otherwise. As a consequence, public opinion remains favorable toward the right of women and young mothers to obtain abortions. Even if the Supreme Court overrules *Roe v. Wade* and returns the power to regulate abortions to states and municipalities, those government authorities would probably enact pro-abortion policies.

Curbing Judicial Activism

President Reagan and the Reagan Department of Justice have over the years 1981-85 articulately and convincingly assailed judicial arrogation of policymaking powers, powers entrusted by the Constitution to other branches of government or to the states. By the end of 1985 Reagan had appointed 252 federal judges, the vast majority of whom accept that much in current constitutional jurisprudence is misconceived. Many of his appointees, such as Robert Bork, Antonin Scalia, Ralph Winter, and Richard Posner, have written opinions that curb judicial activism and policymaking.

Reagan's Department of Justice has consistently opposed judicial policymaking. The Department has urged the overruling of *Roe v. Wade* and various decisions suggesting the constitutionality of racial preferences to nonvictims of discrimination. Moreover, the Department has successfully limited rules for excluding evidence obtained improperly and has called for eliminating the so-called *Miranda* rule that restricts police interrogation of suspects held in custody. The Department has elaborated both in writing and orally the reasons why judicial activism sullies the separation of powers theory of the Constitution, and endangers the right of the people to self-government.

As a result of these endeavors, public opinion has turned against activist judicial decisions. Judges are less inclined than at the beginning of the Reagan Administration to usurp policymaking powers of non-judicial organs of government. One of President Reagan's most profound legacies will be a federal judiciary which accepts a more circumscribed role in fashioning public policy.

Federalism

President Reagan has achieved little in the way of restoring sovereign prerogatives to the states. Indeed, the Department of Justice under Reagan has presided over litigation that has destroyed virtually any constitutional protection of states from the overriding will of Congress. (See *FERC v. Mississippi; EEOC v. Wyoming; Garcia v. San Antonio Met. Transit Authority.*) Furthermore, Congress, during the Reagan Administration, has enacted laws peeking into every aspect of American life that was traditionally of local or state concern: juvenile delinquency, runaway youngsters, spouse battering, alimony and child support, speed limits, the drinking age, education in the local school classroom, and the trial of repeat offenders charged with local crimes. Federal grants-in-aid to states have been substantially reduced, but that reduction has not augmented state power to make policy.

The major defect of President Reagan's federalism agenda has been the absence of any public explanation of why it is desirable in our democracy. Reagan has not taught that to diffuse power is to safeguard freedom, and that to encourage policy experimentation at the state level fosters enlightened legislation nationwide. Reagan has not stressed that state legislatures, unlike Congress, enjoy the salutary restraints imposed by the mobility of businesses. Because states must compete for business, they have a powerful incentive to enact reasonable tax and regulatory laws, to upgrade educational institutions, and to craft otherwise enlightened public policy. Failure to act responsibly yields economic stagnation, outmigration, and ultimately political pressure for state policy reform. Unlike the federal government, state government is self-correcting over the long run.

Without teaching its political value to the electorate, Reagan's invocation of federalism seems an arid slogan to the majority of Americans both in and out of official office. Reagan thus has been unable to suppress a fifty-year tendency of Congress to override state or local prerogatives on any matter that seems politically fetching to a Congressman or Senator.

Conclusion

Justice Louis Brandeis observed that government is the potent and omnipresent teacher; for good or ill, it teaches by example. The actions of political officeholders are most potent insofar as they convey underlying ideas to the public. If the reasons for political action are solely to attain office or to be reelected without regard to principles, ethics, or morals, then that message will be readily deduced by the electorate. The influence on public policy of a politician without philosophical commitment will be narrowly circumscribed; he will simply echo prevailing conventional wisdom. Speaker of the House of Representatives Tip O'Neill and former Senators Warren Magnusen and Jennings Randolph can be saluted for their long tenure in political office; but history will not vouchsafe the trio even a footnote in explaining the decisive forces behind public-policy change.

The genuine power to shape the nation's evolving public policies belongs to those who teach and mold public understanding of fairness and justice through well-articulated ideas convincingly advanced. To compromise principles or public morals is a political formula for long-term impotence in the governing of America. Those who wish to be architects of the nation's destiny will devote themselves to the tutelary opportunities of public life, even if the results are short-term legislative or electoral failure.

3 Building a Conservative Governing Majority

MORTON C. BLACKWELL

Editors' Note: The attention of Washington officials is often restricted to events "within the Beltway" or may extend, at best, to temporary fluctuations in public opinion in the rest of society. This chapter deals with strategies for promoting fundamental change in the American polity, without which a real change in the course of government will be infeasible. Morton Blackwell served as Special Assistant to the President for Public Liaison under President Reagan.

Sometimes you can win by accident. Sometimes you can win because the other side makes too many mistakes. Usually, though, winning any contest requires you to understand the nature of the fight. Definitions, rules, and dynamics all must be studied.

To discuss this topic we must first be clear on what we mean by "winning." For philosophically committed people, politics is primarily a contest over public policy. The measure is not what people, but what ideas win.

The public policy agenda of the 1980 election coalition, the American conservative agenda, can be covered by four headings: limited government; free enterprise; strong national defense; and traditional moral values. Everything described as politically conservative in contemporary U.S. politics fits under one or more of these categories.

In U.S. politics the words *liberal* and *conservative* have changed their meanings over time. Long ago, "liberal" meant limited government, low taxes, decentralized policy decision-making, and private generosity. Now "liberal" means big government, high taxes, centralized government, and vast public welfare spending. The lost attributes of liberalism are now characteristics of popularly defined conservatism.

The 1980 elections may have been the first flowering of a new conservative normal governing majority in U.S. politics, and may not. Certainly, changes in the framework of the debate in American politics were important to the conservative election victories of recent years.

The recent liberal vs. conservative elections were fought on two sets of themes. "Liberal vs. conservative" came out in political discourse as:

- economic stagnation vs. economic growth

- high unemployment vs. job opportunities
- high interest rates vs. lower interest rates
- high taxes vs. lower taxes
- oppressive big government vs. limited government
- policies of weakness vs. policies of strength
- hostility to voluntary prayer vs. support for voluntary prayer
- liberal welfare state vs. conservative opportunity society
- pessimism and defeatism vs. optimism and progress
- quotas for special interest groups vs. equal opportunity for all
- endorsement of moral decay vs. traditional family moral values
- politics as usual vs. politics of principle
- abuse of government funds vs. unquestioned personal integrity
- the past that won't work vs. the future that will work

Deliberate changes in the framework and terms of the debate are one aspect of conservatives' better understanding of political tactics and organizational technology. Conservatives have learned more about the real nature of politics, important practical lessons, since the days of the Barry Goldwater defeat in 1964.

Most people who start political activities motivated by their political philosophy believe, as those of us who worked to nominate Barry Goldwater believed, that being right in the sense of being correct is sufficient. We believed that if our candidates were the better candidates, if the policies they supported were better for the country than those of the opposition, if our candidates were more honest than the opposition, that somehow victory would fall into our deserving hands like ripe fruit off a tree. I call this the "Sir Galahad" theory: "I will win because my heart is pure."

Unfortunately, the real world of politics does not work this way. Different conservatives learned the real nature of politics at different rates of speed and, even today, to differing extents.

The fundamental difference between the days of defeat with Barry Goldwater and the days of victory with Ronald Reagan is this: U.S. conservatives have learned that victory in a political contest is largely determined by the number and the effectiveness of the activists on the two sides. The side that best understands and over time uses effective political tactics and organizational technology will win. And the other side will lose, no matter how right, in the sense of being correct, it may be.

This is not to say conservatives now believe that our philosophy is any less important. We have discovered that we owe it to our philosophy to study how to win. Study is a preparation for action. Not only study about issues, but also study about how to win through the system: political technology.

The 1980 winning conservative coalition was composed of a number of major elements. Most obvious was the Republican Party.[1] Next was the majority of the business oriented political community. And finally there was the growing category of conservative organizations, many of them explicitly conservative movement organizations. All three elements have enjoyed remarkable growth in the past decade, but charting that growth is not my purpose here. Rather, I intend to explore the prospects for a new conservative governing coalition. Before discussing the dynamics of building a governing coalition, it is necessary to demolish the misconception that parties govern in the United States. The nature of our political parties and their role in politics is badly misunderstood.

The Nature of Political Parties

Most people in the United States are brought up to believe that a political party has membership, that it has a unitary organizational structure, that it is an organization, that it has an enforceable decision making process, and that it has some effective disciplinary procedure for people who do not adhere to the beliefs of the party.

One good friend of mine, a nationally known New Right political leader, told me a few years ago, "I am mad at the Republican Party." My response was, "You've just made an irrational statement. It makes no more sense to say you are mad at a U.S. political party than it would to say you are mad at everyone with red hair or that you are mad at everyone born in the state of West Virginia."

People make such statements because they do not understand what a political party is in the United States. In truth, a political party here has none of the attributes I just listed. For instance, it is not an organization. There is a Republican National Committee (RNC) headed currently by Frank Fahrenkopf of Nevada. The RNC raises tens of millions of dollars every year and spends that money just about any way Frank Fahrenkopf decides it should be spent.

However, there is also a National Republican Senatorial Committee, currently headed by Senator John Heinz of Pennsylvania. That committee also raises tens of millions of dollars every year and spends that money virtually any way Senator Heinz wants the money spent. Similarly, there is a National Republican Congressional Committee, headed now, as for many years, by Congressman Guy Vander Jagt of Michigan. That committee also raises tens of millions of dollars every year and spends it just about any way Congressman Vander Jagt wants it spent.

But these three committees are completely independent of each other. There is no organic way any one of these three committees can tell the others how to conduct their affairs. They exist entirely independently, under the law and in usual practice.

There is surely no unity of philosophy. Frank Fahrenkopf is generally recognized to be a conservative Reagan-Laxalt Republican; Congressman Vander Jagt is known to be moderately conservative. Senator Heinz is commonly and correctly described as a moderate-to-liberal Republican.

Moreover, in each of the fifty states there is a totally independent state Republican Party. In my home state of Virginia, the state party committee, headquartered in Richmond, budgets about $1 million every year for its own purposes. It raises and spends that money without any control by the Republican National Committee, much less by the National Republican Senatorial Committee or the National Republican Congressional Committee.

The Republican National Committee is in law the creation of the state party organizations, each one of which elects three members of the Republican National Committee. The state parties are organized primarily under state law, not federal law. Their organizational structure and their rules of procedure are determined by state law and by the members of the respective Republican state committees.

At a lower level there exist in every major city in the United States and in almost all the counties official Republican city and county organizations. Under state law, the city or county Republican committees are created by the state party committees, but in practice they too are fiercely independent.

My wife now happens to be serving for the third time as the Arlington County Virginia Republican chairman. Each year she raises about $30,000 for the Arlington County Republican Party. She and her committee spend that money any way they please. No one from state party headquarters in Richmond, much less anyone from the national Republican organizations in Washington, would dare to tell her how to conduct Republican politics in our county. So it's dead wrong to say the Republican Party is *an* organization.

Membership in a political party is very hard to define in the United States. In Virginia one does not register as a Republican or a Democrat or an Independent. One simply registers to vote. Occasionally, both the Republican Party and the Democratic Party in our state happen to hold party primaries on the same day. If you are a registered voter in Virginia, you may then vote in either the Republican nominating contest or the Democratic nominating contest, even if your name is Gus Hall and you are known to be the general secretary of the Communist Party in the United States.

If you move to Virginia and register to vote, you may show up at a primary election or a Republican mass meeting and vote in that party contest, even though every other person in the room, every other person who calls himself a Republican in the whole state of Virginia, might not want you there. You have a legal right to participate.

Across the Potomac, in the state of Maryland, things run a bit differently. The end result is much the same, though. If Gus Hall of the Communist Party moved to Maryland, he could choose to register in the Republican Party. He could not be denied the right to vote in the Maryland Republican primary elections, even though every other registered Republican in the state of Maryland would prefer, and urge, and even demand, that he not vote in that Republican primary.

The law varies greatly from state to state. Each is unique. A most extreme case is the state of Washington where there is a totally open nominating primary. In Washington State, if you are a registered voter, you vote on primary day on a huge, broadsheet ballot. You are privileged there, if you choose, to vote simultaneously in the Republican primary for governor, the Democratic primary for United States senator, the Republican primary for Congress, the Socialist Party primary for mayor if there is one, and so on. So, I ask you, how can one ever define a member of the Republican Party in the state of Washington?

In other countries, parties can and do discipline their members and throw out undesirables. But there is no expulsion procedure from membership in the Republican or Democratic parties. And unlike the practice in virtually every other country, no one in the United States may be required by his party to pay membership dues.

There is also no decision-making apparatus within the Republican Party that is binding on all the party. Yes, there is a national convention every four years that nominates candidates for president and vice president and adopts a platform. That platform is adopted after much debate and many struggles, but it is not binding on anyone. There is some presumed moral obligation for candidates for president and vice president to adhere to what is promised in the party platform. But no candidate does all of those things "his" platform pledged.

Candidates for the United States Senate or the United States Congress feel little, if any, obligation to adhere to the principles outlined in the party national platforms. Even less do candidates for governor, state legislature, sheriff, or mayor feel in any way bound by commitments made in their national party platforms.

Everything that I have said about the Republican Party has its close parallel in the Democratic Party. Our two major parties are without definable membership. They don't have expulsion procedures. They are not single organizations. They don't have unitary structures. They don't have enforceable decision-making processes.

I think it can safely be argued that this is precisely the sort of outcome intended by the founding fathers of the United States. They wanted to avoid the formation of unitary parties. If one reads *The Federalist Papers* and correspondence among those who adopted the United States Constitution, one will find that all have, to one degree or another, an abhorrence of political parties or, as they sometimes referred to them, factions. Thomas Jefferson said, in 1787, "If I could not go to Heaven but with a party, I would not choose to go there."

The founding fathers set up a separation of governmental powers with a national executive in tension against the legislative branch. The two chambers of the Congress are in political tension with one another. The federal government is in political tension against the states. *It's not widely understood, but U.S. political party institutions have developed parallel structures and tensions.*

The national committee of each party is almost totally responsive to the party's national ticket. The Republican presidential nominee designates someone to head the Republican National Committee, and the members of the National Committee dutifully vote for his choice. And when a Republican is in the White House, the tenure of the Republican National Committee chairman is, in practice, at the pleasure of the head of the executive branch.

But the president has absolutely no influence on who becomes chairman of the National Republican Congressional Committee or the National Republican Senatorial Committee. If a presidential nominee or a president should endeavor to influence the selection of chairmen of the senatorial and congressional campaign committees of his party, there would be immense outrage. Frankly, it would be counterproductive.

I've mentioned all these things that a U.S. political party is not. I think now it is useful to define *what an American political party is.* In my judgment, a political party is this and nothing more: a legal label used by a wide variety of individuals to advance either their principles or their interests or both. A party has meaning only as people who say they are members of the party use the party label or party apparatus to further some political aim.

Our founding fathers did not like what they saw of factional politics in Great Britain, where if you were a Tory it was your accepted responsibility to destroy any Whig, no matter how honest, no matter how upright he might be. Similarly, if you were a Whig it was your duty to destroy politically any Tory no matter how brilliant or patriotic.

The founding fathers of the United States saw unitary parties as enemies of the national interest, truth, justice, and other desirable attributes in a public policy environment. The system they designed has produced a result that today, I think, would be fairly much to their liking.

Voluntary party loyalty is a strong factor, but for a declining number of Americans. For most politicians, it is useful. For most voters, it's nothing more than a casual habit. Our parties as organizations are fictions. Party unity cannot be enforced and therefore is dependent on voluntary cooperation. By their nature, our parties are not suited to govern. They do not govern. Their importance is real, but vastly overrated.

To the extent it can be said that our country is governed, decisions are made by an enduring coalition of segments of the population which form a governing majority. The formation, growth, and decline of these coalitions is the real drama of governing America. A party is at most the vehicle through which this drama unfolds.

Building a New Governing Majority

We now return to the question of whether or not the 1980 winning coalition is a new, normal governing majority in politics. It has been a long time since a new, normal governing majority has been assembled in the United States. The last time was 1932, when Franklin Roosevelt performed the feat. Between 1932 and 1980 there were 48 years of a normal governing majority operating under the label of the Democratic Party. During that period, Roosevelt's coalition controlled either the Congress or the White House or both for all but two years. Only in the first two years of the Eisenhower Administration did the Republican Party control both the White House and the Congress.

For conservatives there are many lessons to be learned from Franklin Roosevelt's success. I think he has proved to be thus far the most successful president of the 20th century. His new, normal governing majority lasted far beyond his lifetime.

President Eisenhower, on the other hand, quickly lost his early strength in the Congress. He remained personally popular, but he struggled with hostile, Democratic majorities for his last six years in the White House. And his vice-president lost the ensuing attempt to succeed him.

Roosevelt's success stemmed from a number of factors.

- FDR built and retained his winning coalition by keeping the issue initiative by launching and fighting hard for a steady stream of policy proposals even though he knew many of them would lose in the Congress. He knew that many items which passed the Congress would be declared unconstitutional by the Supreme Court. But he kept the nation speaking about his proposed solutions for the great problems facing the United States. He reduced what was left of the Republican Party simply to reacting and complainng about what he was proposing. Thus the Republican Party lost its credibility as an alternative vehicle for governing.

- Roosevelt kept his coalition together by giving each element of it frequent, solid reasons to stay aboard. No ally was taken for granted.

- To the extent that he could, Roosevelt ran each ensuing election on the central themes of his 1932 success. Specifically, he attempted to pit the always more numerous "have nots" in society against the "haves." And even today, the "liberal" political coalition lineally descended from FDR tries to convince people that conservatives are on the side of only those people who are rich while the "liberals" are working for everyone who is not rich. As long as that argument was persuasive, the liberal coalition remained the normal governing majority.

- Roosevelt used legislation, his administrative powers, and the prestige of his office to build the political power of the key elements of his coalition, particularly organized labor. Changes made to our labor law during the 1930's gave long-lasting advantages to the growth of monopoly union power. And today the political power of unions is such that, in most areas of the United States, Democratic candidates are wasting their time and money if the unions are against them.

- Roosevelt cheerfully used confrontation with his opponents in order to motivate his coalition. Once Roosevelt announced a draconian regulation of prices that could be charged by businesses across the country. Sewell Avery, president of Montgomery Ward, one of the largest corporations in the country, announced that he would keep Montgomery Ward prices as low as he could and that he would ignore Roosevelt's price-fixing regulations. Roosevelt could simply have filed a legal action against Sewell Avery and Montgomery Ward, but he didn't. Instead, he sent federal officers into Sewell Avery's office. They picked Avery up from behind his desk and dragged him off. Of course, Roosevelt thoughtfully informed the news media, so there were many dramatic pictures of the president of a major corporation being hauled away.

- Roosevelt almost cheerfully accepted the most intense unpopularity with a smaller number of Americans in order to achieve unique popularity with the majority of Americans. I think it is fair to say that Roosevelt was both the most popular and the least popular President in our century. That is to say, a greater number of Americans revered Roosevelt more than any other president of our century, and a greater number loathed and despised him.

We should not forget that FDR built a stable, winning coalition while the Great Depression raged all during the 1930's. At least for Roosevelt, economic prosperity, or his lack of success in creating it, proved largely irrelevant to his political success.

Nor did Roosevelt's coalition lack mutually antagonistic elements. It contained most of the Jewish population, most of the devoutly Catholic urban ethnics, and most of the Southern Protestants who regarded the Roman Catholic Church as the Whore of Babylon. It was home to liberal intellectuals who abhorred racial segregation but also to Ku Kluxers and to labor unions with "white only" membership restrictions. These and other polar elements submerged their differences sufficiently to govern together in coalition for two generations.

The election of Ronald Reagan and so many other conservatives in 1980 put this country at a crossroads. The materials are at hand for a new, stable governing coalition. My belief is that by shouldering the whole burden of the issues on which he ran and won, and by taking unmistakable actions to confront his opponents on these issues, President Reagan could revive the winning coalition for future elections. Given also the growing competence in organizational technology of the major elements of his coalition, Reagan's victory could mark the start of a new lasting governing majority.

But if conservatives, the Reagan Administration, and Republicans in the Congress fail to take decided actions based on the wide range of issues set forth in the 1980 elections, I think this opportunity to build a new, normal governing majority will be lost. Already, instead of moving forward, we have seen the 1980 election gains in the House and Senate begin to erode. Republicans might then have to depend in future national elections on the Democrats' nominating brazen McGovernites, a course I think they are highly unlikely to take.

The Role of Social Issues

In order to understand the current dynamics of coalition building we must focus our attention on the role of noneconomic or "social" issues. Social issues have unusual potency within our political system, a potency not shared by many other issues. At root, most of these issues get their strength from *moral outrage*. Moral outrage is a tremendous motivating force within the political process. Here are some sample sentiments:

> "They will take my gun only by prying it from my cold, dead fingers. God made man, but Winchester made men equal."

> "Abortion is the murder of tiny babies."

> "Union goons beat up innocent workers and force people to pay them tribute for the simple right to work."

> "I won't send my kids to drug-filled schools which denigrate

God and can't even teach the three R's."

"Rampant pornography is stamping out all vestiges of
morality in our country."

"The commies want to destroy America, and we have to be
strong or we'll have to choose between being slaves or corpses."

In these and other such high-intensity issues, most of the liberal
Democratic leadership is firmly locked in to the wrong political position.
Millions of traditional Democrats will vote conservative and Republican
when organized around these issues.

President Reagan states each of these high-intensity positions much
more graciously than was just done above. I tried to word them at their
strongest. But I believe the President is clearly on the right side in each
case, not only the philosophically right side but the politically right side.
As Roosevelt's brilliant manager James A. Farley once put it, "Sound
doctrine is sound politics."

Unfortunately, all six of those issues and their kin are now pale shadows
of their intensity in 1980. Beneficiaries of the 1980 winning coalition have
indulged in unilateral moral disarmament. In rhetoric and, more important, in action, many in the Reagan Administration and in the congressional leadership of the Republican Party behave as if these issues were
skunks at our garden party.

But moral outrage, in my judgment the most powerful motivator in
politics, is alive and well in America today. Unfortunately, official GOP
leadership has granted almost a monopoly to the opposition in the use
of moral outrage.

Liberals and most of the major national news media are systematically
and successfully directing moral outrage at conservatives. Here are some
sample sentiments from their point of view:

"They are spending more money on bombs and rockets while
people are losing their homes and starving."

"The rich are getting richer and the poor are getting poorer. It
isn't fair."

"They are raping the environment for private greed."

"They want to make your home ground zero in an insane
nuclear exchange with the Soviets."

"They are deliberately destroying your jobs in order to
increase the profits of the privileged few."

Yes, the liberal Democratic leadership understands the political use of
moral outrage.

If the public sees the national political contest as primarily between
"those who will give help to the have-nots who badly need it" and "those

whose policies enable capital formation so that productive businesses can make profits so that employers can offer jobs so that all who want to work can work"—perhaps a steady minority of 45 percent will vote Republican or conservative.

But a conservative and Republican majority forms if, as in 1980, the public sees the national contest as primarily between those on the one hand, the conservatives, who have a difficult-to-grasp but clearly well-meaning economic policy, and those on the other hand, the liberals, who say they want to help the poor but really want to "take children away from home and neighborhood by forced busing in Soviet tanks into the clutches of counter-culture teachers who would fill their heads with pornography, abortion, and gun control, and prevent them from praying."

After the 1980 elections, leaders of every major conservative group feared that their contributors would reduce their giving. The reverse proved true. Virtually every conservative group continued to grow rapidly in income and in members in the years after the 1980 elections. It became reasonable to expect a much better than usual midterm election in 1982. Unfortunately, greater resources did not translate into greater conservative group activism in the 1982 elections. The coalition was not reactivated.

In fact, most of these groups spent far less on grassroots activism in 1982 than in 1980. Figures for long distance telephone bills, travel budgets to targeted races, and numbers of voter letters mailed told the story. Much of the 1980 Reagan coalition was largely dormant in the 1982 elections. And also in the 1984 congressional races, even though the President was again on the ballot. In 1982 and 1984 we found that conservative activists did have someplace else to go—home. The defeats of many Republican candidates at every level were in large measure due to this decline in activism.

Many conservative organization leaders placed the entire blame for the 1982 defeats on failures of the Reagan Administration to make good on the 1980 Reagan promises. And many inside the Reagan Administration said that the election results of 1982 proved that the conservative movement was overrated. In my view, there's plenty of blame to go around. One trend is unmistakable and undeniable: The Reagan Administration, the liberal Democratic leadership in the Congress, and quite often the Republican congressional leadership chose deliberately to concentrate on economic battles.

It took more than five years after the 1980 election to get votes in both houses of Congress on a major piece of legislation affecting gun ownership. We've had very few votes on "right to life." There were more record votes in 1979 and 1980 on right to life in the Congress than in the next six years. We had one vote in one house on the President's school-prayer amendment. We had virtually no votes in the Congress on pornography. We had virtually no votes on the death penalty. We had one vote in one house in six years on tuition tax credits. We had virtually no votes on forced school busing; what votes we had were on judicial jurisdiction limitation. We've had very few up-or-down votes on defense preparedness. It took more than five years in this Administration to get one floor vote in the Senate on eliminating the Hobbs Act exemption from prosecution of union violence; still no votes in the House. We had virtually no votes on the political use of compulsory union dues. We had only one short fight in both houses on the balanced-budget tax-limitation amendment, a vote which was held on short notice and too soon before the 1982 elections to have much impact. Thus most of the conservative issues on which millions of people have been identified and activated were virtually absent from the headlines and from the TV news programs.

For ten years prior to the 1980 elections, the *Congressional Record* had been for conservatives a gold mine of debate and record votes on most of these issues. But not in the years since. So how could groups organized around these issues fire up their grassroots supporters to hold liberal Democrats accountable in the elections for their liberalism? They couldn't.

In the protracted fight against president Carter's Panama Canal treaties, conservative groups identified and activated hundreds of thousand of people, all the while fully expecting to get many liberal senators' votes, or their seats. But by the choice of the leaders of both political parties, there have been very few protracted battles useful in this way to conservative activism in the years since 1980. That's not the way to build and sustain a governing majority.

For six years, the liberal Democratic Party leadership has done all it can to evoke moral outrage against the Republican Party and the Reagan Administration. The halls of Congress and the national news media have rung with liberal Democrats' emotional attacks on the Republican Party's "rampant military spending, insane nuclear weapons, deliberate policies of unemployment, favoritism to the rich, unfairness to the poor, raping of the environment, callous insensitivity to women, racist attitudes toward blacks, and reckless imperialism against reformers in Central America."

All of these charges against conservatives are bum raps. But they work politically, each with a different mix of voters. The conservative response to this attack, particularly from political appointees in the departments and agencies of the federal government and in elected leadership positions in the Congress, has been pathetic. Inordinately defensive party leadership has used its media access to drone: "It ain't so, it ain't so."

In short, conservatives have conceded the rhetorical initiative. Liberal

Democrats choose most of the debate topics in the Congress, and Republican leadership obligingly stays away from other issues. This is the formula for the Republican Party to remain the normal minority party, achieving office only when the opposition blunders badly.

How different from the years leading to the Reagan winning coalition victory in 1980. In the latter 1970's and 1980 liberal Democrats were kept on the defensive. Bound with hoops of steel to groups with McGovernite agendas, liberal politicians were forced to take the left-wing side on issues of great importance to millions of traditionally conservative Democratic voters.

Ongoing battles and frequent votes in both houses of Congress kept public attention where the liberal Democrats are most vulnerable. Rather than raising the issues they are now voicing against Republicans during the Reagan Administration, the liberal Democrats were dealing again and again with charges of gun grabbing, government-funded abortions, parental rights, compulsory unionism, voluntary school prayer, tuition tax credits, forced school busing, crushing tax burdens, and giving away our canal in Panama. There were multiple battles on most of these issues in each house each year. Each of these issues was a net benefit to the Republican Party. And each of these issues drove wedges between major elements of the old Franklin Roosevelt Democratic coalition.

But why this GOP failure to understand the requisites of coalition building? Has the Republican Party been afflicted with terminal niceness? Do we so enjoy the heady business of governing that we forget how we got here? Did we learn any lessons as we built strength before the 1980 elections?

The Source of the Problem

After considerable thought, I concluded that the general run of the Republican leadership, particularly in the Congress, is now unable, or unwilling to lead. The activism, which in 1980 at least temporarily changed the balance of power in favor of the GOP label as the embodiment of conservatism, was not created by the then existing party hierarchy. That activism was created by Ronald Reagan and a galaxy of coalition-building conservative leaders largely in the GOP structure but not in the party's top leadership.

Terminal niceness is not the problem today, nor was it in the past. In fact, GOP officials stand ready for action to harass and embarrass liberal Democrats with only one major reservation: No Republican may be offended. Unfortunately, a leadership that strives above all to offend neither Senator Jesse Helms nor Senator Lowell Weicker is unsuited to lead a majority party.

Lowest-common-denominator politics is not Tip O'Neill's way. As long as Speaker O'Neill believes an action will do damage to his opposition and produce net benefit to his own party, he moves. He does not worry much about the sensibilities of conservative Democrats in the House. If they get out of line, he handles them the way he handled former Democratic Congressman Phil Gramm. Most of Gramm's conservative Democratic "boll weevil" former colleagues know that they cannot make the same successful transition between parties that he did.

The Washington Post, always generous with advice for Republicans, ran an editorial on August 30, 1983 entitled "Giving up the Senate." After noting the current weakness of the GOP in many states, the *Post* lavished praise on the Republican Senate. "They have put on the back burner many issues that belong there. Their leaders have often been brilliant and their backbenchers have been suitably quiet. They have certainly been more unified than Senate Democrats in recent Congresses. Should they lose control, it will be less from the merits than from bad luck."

Baloney. Unity of a sort is usually attainable if one operates on the lowest-common-denominator basis. But it's not a winning strategy. Leaders of vital elements of stable governing coalitions don't get or expect to get their way in everything. But their enthusiasm wanes quickly if the coalition appears to lose interest in its constituencies' highest priorities. The high-intensity issues now languishing on the back burner in the Congress were those forcefully raised by conservative backbenchers in the years before the 1980 election, the very issues of benefit to the GOP and most destructive to the liberal Democrats' coalition. No wonder the *Post* was pleased.

In 1983, I had an unexpected debate before the National Association of Homebuilders with then Democratic National Chairman Charles Manatt. In our discussion, I reviewed the high-intensity, liberal vs. conservative issues largely or entirely avoided in the Congress since 1980. Manatt replied that he hoped that these issues would remain buried. He's no dummy.

Major GOP leaders, including many in elected or appointed office, have lost, if they ever had, the entrepreneurial spirit for solid political growth and sustained success. The strength of the President's winning coalition is drained by consensus decision-making, bureaucratic fear of controversy, and paralysis that masquerades as pragmatism.

Successful political leadership necessarily has its confrontational aspect. Skill at confrontation is not incompatible with a "nice guy" public image, as in "I paid for this microphone" and "There you go again."

Defensive political tactics have their uses. But wise leaders seek out battles in areas where their opponents are most vulnerable. If you do not go on the offensive, you never win ground. In a series of battles on the defensive, you hold the line in some cases and lose ground in others. Long term, you lose. Conservatives who behave this way are the only ones *The Washington Post* loves to praise as statesmen.

The pervasively defensive mentality of too many current Republican leaders can be measured by reviewing newspaper headlines and noting radio and TV news broadcasts. By ratios from 3:1 to 10:1, news items these days describe GOP leaders as "defending" rather than carrying the fight to the opposition by criticizing the liberal Democratic leadership.

Remember, despite his huge majorities in both houses, President Franklin Roosevelt constantly directed much of his thunder at Republicans rather than responding defensively to their criticisms. The nation's news media in the 1930's rang with FDR's attacks at Republicans as "malefactors of great wealth" and "economic royalists."

The grassroots organizations that poured activists into the 1980 campaigns of President Reagan and so many other winning conservative candidates still exist. Almost all these groups are better funded now, and they have larger memberships. They grew in finances and mailing lists because their leaders became proficient in print media advertising, direct mail, television and radio appeals, telephone solicitation, and other forms of fund-raising and recruitment. In time, they learned the dynamics of coalition-building.

These organizations continued to grow, not because their issues were being widely debated in the halls of Congress or on the national news media. They grew because their leaders became effective organizational entrepreneurs. What these sources of support lacked in 1982 and the congressional races of 1984 were sufficient reasons to throw themselves and their adherents fully into the campaigns. Until that situation changes, they will continue to lack those reasons in future elections.

For three years I was President Reagan's liaison to all the conservative organizations in the United States. Virtually every effective conservative group's leaders privately would express to me their disappointment, ranging from dismay to disgust, with the lack of Republican leadership. I heard this repeated almost every day I was in the White House. Sometimes I felt as if I were the receptionist at a home for battered wives.

Conclusion

If conservative and Republican candidates are to run in future elections with the 1980 coalition revived and enthusiastic, the issues of 1980 will have to be reclaimed, and with vigor. The process is relatively simple, but it will not be easy, given the current GOP predilections.

Simply put, each high-intensity liberal vs. conservative issue must be brought repeatedly to the floor of both houses. For maximum effect, legislative battles on each issue must be guaranteed two or more months before House or Senate consideration. Few of the conservative grassroots groups have instantly ready armies of D.C.-based lobbyists. For communication with their many supporters, they depend largely on direct mail, television and radio, rallies, word of mouth, and other channels that require a fairly long lead time.

Given the invigorating battles they need and the time to activate their troops, the groups that helped build the 1980 winning coalition can and will do so again in future elections. These groups are capable of organizing voter registration drives that overshadow the highly successful efforts of Jesse Jackson. And they've proved they can generate more grassroots activity than can organized labor.

White House meetings with organization leaders are not enough. Repeated presidential remarks on these issues are no longer sufficient without actions. Without action these issues will have little impact in future elections no matter how cordial are the personal relations of the president with the leaders of supportive groups.

There are formidable obstacles to the implementation of the plan I advocate:

- the heterogeneous staffing of the administration
- the deadening effect of the GOP's consensus decision making
- the difficulty of teaching a whole generation of old leaders new behavior
- the failure to understand how it is often possible to lose legislatively but win politically
- the notion that social issues are like mechanical rabbits which can keep those interested in them running futilely around the track forever
- the expectation that leaders and organizers of supportive massed-based groups will be willing to keep pretending that token efforts on their issues are real efforts
- the current preference for making a small retreat rather than risking a small defeat
- the false notion that somehow, always "next year", we can "pick one or two issues" and get the whole 1980 coalition activated again

Perhaps consolidation of a new governing coalition will have to wait until the next solidly conservative president is elected. But because President Reagan is already committed and on the public record on the politically right side of all the necessary issues, there are ways around, over, and through these obstacles now.

To put the Administration squarely and convincingly behind a winning coalition-building strategy on the legislative issues most damaging to liberal Democrats, the President could:

- issue to all relevant Administration appointees unmistakable, specific orders to push forward with vigor on all these legislative fronts
- demote or fire a few who then drag their feet. (During my three years in the Reagan White House I cannot recall a single instance where anyone was disciplined, much less fired for dragging his feet on the President's issue agenda.)
- identify and fire a few of the "leakers" who sneak over to the media to snipe at the President's views
- meet privately with GOP congressional leaders to urge them to end "lowest common denominator" party legislative decision-making
- meet privately with "back-bench" legislators who are personally strongly committed to the President's position on each useful issue. (The President could encourage them to stop being "suitably quiet" and to force battles and record votes when the party leadership fails, as it is wont to do.)

For protracted legislative struggles leading to frequent record votes on these politically potent, coalition-building issues, the time to start was 1981. But at minimum, the time to start is now.

Note

1. *Editor's Note:* The author addresses the relationship between the Republican Party and conservative ideas. He notes that the current Republican Party is scarcely a pristine embodiment of conservative principles. Moreover, the links between sets of ideas and political parties shift over time. Historically, the Democratic Party has been the standard bearer for ideas that are now regarded as indispensable conservative principles, specifically free trade and a strong interventionist foreign policy. The parameters of what is considered "conservative" are not constant. President Truman's campaign against the threat of communism, internal and external, would be considered almost radical by contemporary standards. President Kennedy's economic, trade, military, and foreign policies could be judged to be highly conservative in comparison to the policies of the Reagan Administration. While the Republican Party is currently the focal point for the advance of conservative political principles, this need not invariably be the case.

In addition, the author notes that importance of political parties as organizations is greatly overrated. What does matter in the political system is a coalition of overriding ideas tied to a social majority. The art of governing consists of processes for implicitly linking groups with diverse interests or viewpoints; or of binding together a mobilizing core of political ideas with a broad-based foundation of popular support.

4 Learning the Washington Game: Political Strategy and Tactics

FRED SMITH

Editors' Note: Dubbed the "leprechaun of free enterprise" by The Washington Times, Fred Smith, President of the Competitive Enterprise Institute, is among the foremost of a new breed of political organizers and activists in Washington. With uncanny insight, this article covers a wide range of issues relating to political strategy; it should be required reading for anyone holding office in the federal government.

Those entering the federal government who seek to redirect the system to place greater emphasis on the role of the individual and the marketplace have much to learn. Specifically, we would do well to observe the strategies and tactics that the modern liberals have used so successfully to dominate the Washington scene. Conservatives, after all, seek a world that provides opportunities for all citizens; conservatives wish to maintain and enhance the quality of the environment and strive to ensure that society considers the risks inherent in technological and economic change. Why have our approaches received so little attention in the implementation of policy options?

Clearly, we have not done well. In the sixth year of an administration led by an extremely popular and articulate president who embodies the conservative philosophy of government, we have yet to achieve any lasting shift in the fundamental political landscape. Government spending has increased at unprecedented rates. Outlandish federal programs such as Amtrak, the Economic Development Administration, the Small Business Adminstration, and the Export-Import Bank have been momentarily trimmed around the edges, but they vigorously resist half-hearted efforts to terminate them. Privatization initiatives such as the sale of Conrail, disposal of federal property, and turning federal Power Marketing Administrations over to the private sector have stalled well short of implementation. Deregulation has been de-emphasized, with gains limited largely to agencies most independent of the White House (such as the ICC and FCC). Proposals for enterprise zones, tuition tax credits, and education vouchers have been featured in speeches but neglected in congressional lobbying plans. In general, the Reagan Revolution hasn't failed—it really hasn't been tried.

True, there has been a shift in the language used in the policy debate. The expressed belief that government expansion is an effective way of resolving most social concerns has disappeared, and Democrats as well as Republicans discuss issues in more market-oriented terms. However, this rhetorical shift has yet to become a policy reality. And although we should not underestimate the value of this shift in the language of policy discourse—hypocrisy, after all, is the tribute paid by Vice to Virtue—it is not enough.

It is important that we examine why it is that change has been so difficult to achieve. That explanation must in particular account for why our successes in the field of ideas have not been followed by success in the field of policy change. The changes in the world of ideas have been profound. A decade or so ago, all ideas were liberal. The concept of a conservative think tank seemed an absurdity. The future was clear. America would become a planned economy run on sound scientific principles for the egalitarian good of all. Indeed, President Johnson suggested that his generation was probably the last in which conservatives would even exist.

The intellectual transformation has been overwhelming. Few liberal thinkers challenge the dominance of today's market-oriented theorists. Privatization, deregulation, tax reform, free trade—all are policies without significant intellectual opposition. Individualists today have at their disposal a massive intellectual arsenal of well-considered policy ammunition to fight in virtually every field of government.

Why then has success in the implementation of these ideas been so slow and so disappointing? Answering that question and suggesting steps that will improve future performance is the intent of this paper.

Ideas Aren't Enough   To understand public policy, one is well advised to consider an earlier and better explored area of conflict—military tactics and strategy. In war, the victory does not always go to those having the largest armies or the most sophisticated equipment. At the beginning of the Second World War, both the French and the British had tanks superior to those used by the Panzer Divisions. However, the Germans knew how to employ their weapons, while the Allied Forces did not. This lesson applies to political conflict as well. Superior ideas alone will not carry the day; we must become sophisticated in the use of intellectual ammunition in policy debate.

There are difficulties in regrouping our intellectual forces to fight the implementation battle. The skills required in the political arena are different and not always easily learned by those more comfortable in the analytic arena. The strengths of the intellectual often lie in developing technical arguments for or against specific policies—cost-benefit analysis, for example. In the political arena, these efforts are important, but alone they seldom determine the outcome. In a pluralistic society, there are always many battlefields, and it is essential that separate and appropriate tactics be used on each.

Liberals have long realized that the internal analytic battles within a government agency, while important, are not the only and indeed often not the decisive field in which issues will be resolved. Liberals often fight with skill and courage major internal bureaucratic battles to expand government regulatory authorities and budgets—but they have also understood that it is important to mobilize allies elsewhere (in and out of government) and that they must ensure that their side of the story is effectively presented in the press.

Too often, conservatives have failed at this test. Consider the setbacks suffered in the areas of environmental, tax, and budget policies. Superfund has been blindly expanded without any ability to achieve its toxic-waste cleanup goals, most of the 1981 tax cut has been nibbled to death by a subsequent series of "revenue enhancement" measures, and a long list of proposed domestic spending program terminations failed to get off David Stockman's notepad.

The remainder of this paper elaborates on these ideas. Section I discusses some of the misconceptions that conservatives often bring into the political arena and how these limit their effectiveness. Section II reviews a number of tactical lessons that are often overlooked by newcomers to the Washington scene. Section III provides an integrated strategy for policy change.

I. Selling Ourselves Short: Conservative Preconceptions and Political Realities

Conservatives in general remain ambivalent about politics. Too often, they view political activities in the same way that the Victorians regarded sex—a messy necessity that should not be openly discussed and certainly should not be enjoyed. This genteel view of politics handicaps its practitioners in the tug of war over government policy. If you don't like politics, you probably aren't going to be very good at it.

Mainline Republicans often bring into government a modified version of this basic problem. They act as if they are intruding upon the policy preserve of liberals. If they are cautious, polite, and well mannered in "managing" the liberal agenda, they seem to believe, the liberals might let them play with the trappings of government power for a little while longer. Or liberals might allow them to help make policy a bit more reasonable and efficient. This attitude of conservative restraint—allowing the liberals to ratchet up the role of government while conservatives come in and make the resulting expansion a little more manageable and bearable, to set the scene for the next liberal expansionary initiative— should be firmly rejected by anyone seeking to restore the American dream. From these attitudes toward government emerge many mistakes. The following section lists some of these.

The Tendency to Pre-Compromise   One of the most common and serious mistakes made by the newcomer to the Washington scene is to pre-compromise. A young analyst asked to review a specific issue swiftly realizes that current policy is absurd and prepares a recommended shift. At that point, however, he begins to think of the political context in which he operates. He thinks of how *The Washington Post*, the liberal activists, and the congressional review committees might react to such a strong reversal of policy and thus elects to water down—however slightly—his original paper. His boss receives only this "final draft" of the original paper and, in turn, often goes through the same reasoning. An even more bland product is passed up the intellectual food chain. Eventually, the diluted recommendation reaches the desk of an official able to do something, but he notes its close relationship to the current situation and decides that a fight for such small stakes would be irrational.

The nature of this problem is obvious. Every mid-level political appointee entertains delusions of grandeur as a master strategist. The desire to incorporate political factors and tactics into an early analysis is almost irresistible. Yet it is fatal to bold thinking. What is possible in the political world is rarely known in advance. Weak positions (e.g. the Clean Air Act) turn out to be impregnable, while long-respected political redoubts (the Clark Amendment barring aid to UNITA forces in Angola) may be taken without a fight. For the analyst to substitute his political judgment for that of the political boss is to forgo the one benefit his involvement in the policy process might produce—objectively reasoned policy alternatives. Politics is the art of the possible, but it is unlikely that any new hand in Washington is expert enough about that process to justify sabotaging the case for radical change at the outset.

Too often, conservatives within government refuse even to ask that rational alternatives to existing policy be considered. In 1981, the Department of Transportation (DOT) effectively dismantled a large portion of the existing structure for federal air traffic control in firing PATCO members who attempted an illegal strike. DOT chose to limp along with a crippled, undermanned system without considering the unique opportunity suddenly available for bold reform—privatization of a regionally dispersed air traffic control system. Support for such a step could even be mobilized among the fired union members, since private operators of air traffic control centers would be free to "rehire" them. DOT instinctively brushes aside such a "radical" proposal because "there is no political support for such a move." But support is something one must work to gain. It does not appear spontaneously without clear analysis of new opportunities as they unfold. Supply-side agents of political change must first invest capital before they can reap long-term gains.

The short-sighted tendency to pre-compromise policy should be fought at all times. The initial policy analyst should perform objective analysis and present the policy alternative that best serves the public interest. That is what he is paid to do. He needn't worry; the ideas will have plenty of opportunity to be compromised at all levels even if the analyst continues to fight for "unreasonable" changes. (It also doesn't hurt to insulate one's proposals with personal conviction at the start to help withstand the gradual erosion and watering down effects of the policy process.)

The Tendency to Dawdle—The "When the Right Time Comes, I'll Take a Stand" Bias Like all fallacies, this viewpoint has an element of truth. One cannot fight every battle, every day. An unprepared stance can undermine one's ability to gain an audience. Nonetheless, the valid risks of occasional instances of excessive aggressiveness should not blind one to the far more common Washington trait of excessive caution. Risk taking is virtually unknown within the Washington community, especially among conservatives. Political capital is husbanded carefully—to the point where one scarcely sees any of it being expended. Consider the gentle handling of an area crying out for bold reform—the nation's welfare system. Years after the intellectual groundwork was laid for a bold assault on its record of tragic failure, the Reagan Administration only recently could summon enough "daring" to delegate consideration of reform to a second-level White House committee, under the vaguest of charters.

In practice, this dictum could be best thought of as the political equivalent of the "Not now dear, I have a headache" rule of marriage. In politics, one often hears the statement, "This year is an election year (or soon to become an election year) and thus is not a propitious time to rock the boat." Since some special circumstances can be ascribed to just about every year, time passes while action languishes. The perfect "moment" to start the reform ball rolling rarely announces itself, and can easily pass quietly, never to return. Nothing is ventured, and nothing is gained. Another "conservative" year goes by with nothing accomplished.

The Engineering Trap—Excessive Pre-Planning A related professional bias that can limit the effectiveness of conservatives is that of excessive preparation. One seeks to foresee every contingency, to avoid every future obstacle. Obviously, planning is essential, but again, the nature of the political process renders any fine-tuning effort foolish. As Clausewitz noted long ago, "No battle plan survives first encounter with the enemy." The objective instead must be to design a robust plan, to have prepared the ground, and to be ready to adjust to events during a long campaign—not to seek the neat micro-management of change possible only in the controlled environments of science or engineering. One must be ready to make midcourse changes "on the fly" in response to the dynamics of policy debate. The original game plan for the Reagan tax cut in 1981, for instance, never anticipated the sudden appearance of congressional proposals to reduce the top rate from 70 to 50 percent and to index future tax rates against the effects of inflation.

Avoiding Capture and the Pressure to "Go Native"　　One of the more serious problems encountered in any conflict is the possibility that key officials will change sides in the heat of battle. Benedict Arnold, after all, was an American hero at the Battle of Saratoga, but lived to fight another day—on the other side. Too often, "conservative" appointees have weak ideological roots and lack a firm intellectual grasp of how the objectives of their agency might better be achieved via nongovernmental or less burdensome approaches. Such individuals are easily captured by the dedicated career officials who readily adapt conservative rhetoric in service of existing agency programs, while explaining that *substantive* change "can't be done."

In all too many cases, we see old programs dressed up in new conservative lingo. The World Bank has absorbed all of its leaders with no change in policy, save to make the agency even more statist in its approach to economic development. The Department of Education, the Small Business Administration, the Department of Transportation, and numerous other agencies have changed little if at all during the Reagan era, because their newly appointed heads soon developed chronic cases of "clientitis." They adopted the perspective of interest-group constituencies defending the status quo, becoming effective spokesmen for the policies of the past.

The urge to "get along" with the career bureaucracy must be kept within narrow limits. A political appointee swimming in the waters of a liberal-infested agency may need to develop a relatively formal attitude. He should remember that everything said and done is "on the record," and should distinguish between careerist guidance on process as opposed to policy. He should rely on a loyal circle of political allies to handle sensitive matters.

The "Poor Li'l Ole Me in a Hostile Environment" Problem　　The newcomer to Washington may soon experience a feeling of powerlessness. Decisive orders cannot readily be given in a world controlled by civil service rules, watched closely by liberal media, and protected by vigilant congressional committee overseers. Soon, a feeling of helplessness can occur and give rise to apathy and disinvolvement. Conservatives in both the Environmental Protection Agency and the Department of the Interior fell victim to this "bunker mentality" during the final stages of assault against their embattled leaders, Anne Burford and Jim Watt.

Such attitudes, however, stem from a misunderstanding of the nature of power in a fragmented, politicized world. The power of an agency official is primarily the power to mobilize opinion, to advance ideas, to provide forceful direction to the bureaucracy, and to arrange the setting of an issue so it becomes more or less likely to advance—in other words, to take risks. Here again, there should be no underestimation of the strength of a risk-taker in caution-prone Washington. Whistle blowers provide an interesting illustration of that reality.

In a world of wimps, those having the conviction to take decisive positions fill the power vacuum. That risk-taking propensity should not be flaunted recklessly, but it is real and can be flexed to gain influence in many areas. Remember that one need not be a superman; most political struggles are lost by the the opponent finally making a decisive mistake. But political appointees should not simply try to keep the ball passively in play and refrain from forcing the issue. Taking the offensive and applying pressure on the opposition is what creates the other side's mistakes.

The Superman Illusion The obverse mistake of viewing oneself as powerless is the attitude that "I give the orders and what I say goes." In this respect, the famous anecdote about President Lincoln being asked to intercede in the career prospects for a Union soldier is instructive. Lincoln asked the inquiring lady if she had spoken with Seward and Stanton (two of the most prominent members of his Cabinet) and she noted that she had, but to no avail. At that point, Lincoln threw up his hands and said, "Well, what can I do? I'm only the President."

No one in Washington can achieve much in isolation from other allies. Efforts to bulldoze a tunnel of change à la David Stockman are likely to prove counterproductive. In this town, one has to build a coalition of forces, develop understanding of other viewpoints, shape convincing moral arguments, and be prepared for the long struggle. Kamikaze efforts to succeed "my way" or not at all may occasionally lead to lucrative book contracts, but they are more likely to drag the conservative cause down in flames.

Power in Washington is an elusive attribute. It is built on perceptions only partly grounded in reality. It always reflects one's ability to draw upon the resources of others; politics is team sport and it is important to realize that fact.

"Chameleon Victories"   To many, winning on any terms is the goal. For them, the continuing victories of liberals on many fronts require that we adopt their approach. Thus, if polls indicate that Americans accept the welfare state, favor EPA, believe in protectionism, and generally approve of affirmative action—well, then, vox populi, vox Dei—let's get on with adapting ourselves to the shortest route for gaining power. But if conservative "victories" require that we become liberals, how valuable and how lasting will those victories be? The challenge to conservatives is not to gain a chair at the control panel by promising not to turn many of the dials. Rather, we have to explain our approach to government in a way that gains and reinforces political acceptance. Instead of playing the transitory game of poll-ish popularity, we must find ways to restore respect for individual rights; and to better insulate those rights from the threats posed by momentary passions—regardless of who wields the tools of demagoguery.

Failure to do this leaves us helplessly on the defensive. The inability to articulate an acceptable alternative vision in such areas as environmental policy, civil rights, and trade protectionism has placed many conservatives in the situation of choosing between the role of liberal soundalikes and that of flinthearted naysayers.

Liberals have been extremely effective, and we can learn much from their operational tactics and strategy. But we should not confuse means with ends. We may respect our opponent's abilities and the broad goals we share in common. But liberal policy approaches are flawed and retard rather than advance the causes they so nobly espouse. To attack the liberals' discredited policies requires a rejection of the current framing of issues, and a determined resistance to popular misconceptions. In their place, we must invent a new language of politics to ensure that our ideas gain respect and that our policies become politically feasible.

The "Waiting for Godot" Tactic   One often hears, in this town, statements to the effect that we want to move on an issue but we aren't getting any leadership. That statement says much about the top-down command-and-control mentality that so dominates this city. To await leadership from top-level politicians is foolish and unlikely to result in any swift results. Leadership is exercised by leading, and one can take direction from below as well as above.

Too often, Reagan appointees are willing and eager to go on the offensive, but they await passively the leadership that never arrives. The battle ends and they have never seen combat. Leaders are valuable, and an agency led by a politically capable individual espousing conservative goals is invaluable, but one cannot depend upon leaders in all cases. If they do not exist, then the individual must be prepared to assume that role directly. The story of "contracting out" at the National Oceanic and Atmospheric Administration presented in Chapter 24 of this book is an excellent example of leadership from below. Another example, at a higher level, was Secretary of Transportation Drew Lewis's promotion of a gasoline tax increase in 1982. Although this policy was not desirable from a conservative perspective, Secretary Lewis serves as a model of effectiveness. Seizing the initiative and with carefully orchestrated outside support, Lewis successfully realigned the Administration's policy and won a strong legislative victory.

II. Neglected Tactical Lessons

There are many important tactical lessons to be learned about orchestrating political change. Some of the more salient of these are listed below.

Prepare the Ground Too often, ideas are dropped into a hostile environment with no effort to explain their rationale or how they will actually advance the objectives of the program. An example was the way the idea of weather-satellite privatization reached public attention. The Department of Commerce (the National Oceanic and Atmospheric Administration) was investigating the feasibility of requiring the major networks and industrial users of weather data to pay their way, but the story was leaked in *The Washington Post* as the Reagan Administration plan of making the public pay for good weather, and the idea swiftly died. Had this story been presented accurately as the elimination of corporate welfare, the chances for change might well have been improved. Certainly, the *Post* would not have characterized the move as it did.

Timing Considerations It is important that conservatives think carefully about the timing of their activities. An analytic support document should be circulated soon enough to have impact, but not so soon as to allow time for opposition sources to mount a counterattack. The legislative session is a two-year cycle, and conservatives should seek to match their activities with the ebb and flow of these political tides.

One of the most critical requirements is that you *let your friends know of your timing*. Far too many conservative ideas have been destroyed by failure to notify in advance those who would provide support and assistance. Conservatives are often the last to know, and that is foolish. The view that ethics requires that only the enemy know one's battle plans is hard to rationalize. One need not give away any memos or detailed discussions of the internal deliberations of White House working groups to ensure that sympathetic people on the outside know something is going on. Hints and clues should be adequate—but an informal network that ensures that one's friends are not surprised is essential to a strategic campaign.

Conservatives should also realize that policy warfare consists not only of one decisive battle but rather of multi-year campaigns with many fronts and many possible gains and losses. One of the greatest mistakes made by the German army in Russia was its failure to prepare for a multi-year campaign. Similarly, conservatives tend to think of issues in terms of an occasional burst of energy rather than a sustained effort. This summer-soldier approach is unlikely to win many battles.

There is a ritual to legislative change. First, an idea is proposed in the annual Presidential Address to Congress. Even to gain that mention will require several months of advance effort. Once the President has suggested the idea, legislation must be prepared, hearings scheduled, witness lists compiled, and so forth. Typically, the first hearings reveal problems, and the proposal must be remanded to the appropriate agency for rework. All this takes considerable time and is unlikely to be completed in any one session of Congress.

Beyond this there are longer campaigns. Significant policy initiatives may require a decade of research, discussion, and public education before the time becomes ripe for actual change; the President's 1981 tax cut had a legislative history that could be traced back a half-decade or more. Since there is likely to be a correlation between the significance of change and the length of time needed to prepare for it, policy development should not be ignored simply because the prospects for change are not immediate. Liberals have mastered this long-term process; many conservatives seem to barely know it exists.

Exploit Breakthroughs   In warfare, much has recently been made of the tactics of mobility and focused force in contrast with the view of battle fronts as monolithic entities that should be attacked uniformly at all places and all times. Actual success occurs when one achieves a breakthrough and is able to exploit that breakthrough. The NASA disaster, for example, offers a unique opportunity to consider the value of private space alternatives; the Imelda Marcos shoe collection brings into question the whole debate over the efficacy of foreign aid; the PATCO strike provided a brief window of opportunity to consider the privatization of air traffic control. Be alert for opportunities—or be prepared to create that opportunity. In any event, when something fortuitous happens, don't be hesitant about discontinuing operations on fronts offering major resistance and redeploying that time and energy to the breakthrough.

Trial Efforts In war, again, one often finds that eventual success has been preceded by demonstration efforts that were sometimes disastrous. The Normandy invasion, for example, was preceded by the Dieppe raid, which was a catastrophe. Nonetheless, that raid led to much being learned and made possible the eventual successful landing two years later. In public policy, we may well wish to push vigorously for demonstration programs, for experiments in areas where knowledge is uncertain and doubts are great. The information gained from these experiments can often be of great value in redesigning a program and gaining greater acceptance.

Role of Allies In warfare, few belligerents seek to go alone. Efforts to identify and gain allies are a critical part of the overall struggle, and so it should be in a political arena. Allies do much to attract support from groups who might normally oppose conservative initiatives; moreover, allies can fight in ways and methods that may be impossible for an appointed official. Allied commands are never easy, but they can yield high payoffs. Recall that in the Second World War, the Allies sought out and equipped several divisions of the Free French troops. That was done not because there were no more American or British soldiers, or because equipment was so plentiful that there was no cost to this diversion. It was certainly not because De Gaulle was the easiest person to work with. No, the effort to liberate France was seen as having greater credibility if the French were involved. Moreover, there were certain situations—what to do if the Germans decided to use Notre Dame as a defensive point, for example—that would be best handled by French forces.

It is often useful in developing an alliance to reach beyond an immediate circle of natural allies and appeal to a wider cast of groups. When a large number of organizations come together to focus on one particular issue, there is no requirement that these organizations generally agree on anything, except on the specific issue. The umbrella group puts aside all other disagreements.

Many conservatives handicap themselves with the knee-jerk attitude that any overtures to liberal groups simply strengthen the latter's credibility. We need to be more confident of our abilities to convert past adversaries on one issue at a time whenever the opportunity arises. The payoff from imaginative coalition building is richly rewarding. First, we can gain valuable allies who know what they are doing on the tactical level, add specialized skills to the battle, and may provide protective coloration ("How bad can a conservative policy be if liberal groups are backing it for different reasons?"). Second, it helps generate a bandwagon aura of widespread support. Third, we keep liberals busy working on our agenda, diverting energy and resources from their own projects.

One recent effort—the Clinch River Breeder Reactor campaign—demonstrates the potential power of pulling in unnatural allies to form a broad coalition. The breeder reactor project was launched in the early 1970's; government subsidies were used to commercialize nuclear energy development processes. The case for government aid was premised on the notion that uranium was suddenly becoming scarce. Initial opposition to the breeder came from anti-nuclear groups. When they couldn't stop the project on their own, they went shopping for allies at the National Taxpayers' Union and the conservative Council for a Competitive Economy.

Conservatives said we opposed the breeder reactor, but on different terms. Our position—that every energy source should pay its own way without special advantages from government—was based on economic grounds. This argument was more persuasive and made it possible to draw in conservative support. Our coalition reframed the issue to appeal to liberals, church groups, "good-government" types, and, most significantly, social conservatives. When the last crucial vote in the Senate came, several of the Senate's social conservative leaders came out in opposition to the breeder on the grounds that they opposed corporate welfare at the expense of social welfare; this populist approach was the final straw in defeating the Breeder Reactor Project. A similar left-right coalition came very close to blocking funding to the International Monetary Fund in 1983. In both cases, the lesson learned is that variety within a coalition provides influence on a broader segment of the public and Congress.

III. An Integrated Strategy for Change

This section rests upon the preceding tactical lesson, namely, that politics is a team sport in which allies are indispensable. An integrated strategy for issue management calls for coordinating the activity of players in the executive branch, the legislative branch, and nongovernmental groups. (In some cases, if regulatory as opposed to legislative change is desired, coordination between the executive branch and outside groups will be sufficient.) The following discussion provides recommendations for individuals operating in each of these fora.

Any strategy for policy change must progress through four stages or task areas. The task areas are generally sequential, although some tasks may be performed concurrently. The four stages of an integrated strategy thus are:

1. *Analysis* (Intelligence & Planning): In this stage a policy initiative is developed. A comprehensive data base, to justify the policy and to serve as a foundation to later tasks, is assembled.
2. *Educational Outreach* (Propaganda, Psychological Warfare): Educational outreach means delivering the appropriate message to people who will influence the final decision-makers. Precise targeting requires matching the media delivery vehicle to the target audience. In other words, this stage of the campaign is political advertising where the "issue" is the candidate.
3. *Coalition Development* (Diplomacy): In this task, an initial circle of natural allies for the issue is formed, then techniques are fashioned for appealing to a wider cast of groups. The issue should be reformulated in several ways to market it to a variety of interests. Once a coalition is formed, one nongovernmental organization should serve as a clearinghouse for communication and coordination within the group.
4. *Advocacy* (Command & Control, Leadership, Field Generalship): In this final stage, all resources are brought directly to bear on the ultimate decision-makers. If the arena is legislative, congressional advocates are identified and supported; uncertain votes are located and Congressmen are personally lobbied by relevant coalition members. If the issue is a regulatory one, popular pressure is directed at executive branch decision-makers.

Conceptualizing a campaign for policy change within this framework will mean that many of the pitfalls previously discussed (such as the superman illusion or failing to prepare the ground) will be avoided. However, accomplishment in each task area is no simple matter; there are many lessons to be learned.

Focusing Analysis   Analysis encompasses the gathering of all the intelligence information needed to construct a foundation beneath the public campaign. One canvasses the existing field of policy experts and think-tank scholars in search of supportive material. It may be necessary to stimulate new research to fill gaps in the issue base. (Political appointees who can free research funds within their own agencies should play a key role here.) Public opinion polls are useful early barometers of how much freedom of action one has in mobilizing support.

However, in developing a relevant information base, one must place emphasis on its political value. As noted, the strength of conservatism often lies in its intellectual achievements; the conceptual and empirical data to support departures from liberal orthodoxy are usually well established. But the conservative intellectual case often fails to detail the *politically relevant argument.*

The market for policy change is not the economics profession or even intellectuals per se, but rather those who have traditionally backed the program and would be willing to reconsider if convinced by new evidence. That group is likely to be interested in the distributional consequences of policy change. For example, a critique of mass transit will gain from information on the income status of those benefitting from the present system. Such information can be damning; in the Washington, D.C. area, those benefiting from the heavily subsidized Metro system have a much higher annual income than the average American taxpayer or even the local D.C. taxpayer. Such facts allow one to combine the general argument against federal subsidies with the specific moral argument that we are robbing the poor to help the rich. In arguing against trade protectionism, the general argument for free trade should be coupled with information identifying the specific industries and localities that will be injured, how consumer prices on specific products would be affected, etc.

The most useful information thus will be based on the politics of that issue: what motivates the various interest groups involved in the policy and what factors are likely to persuade them to support our position. Politically relevant information, not abstract studies on "efficiency" or "cost effectiveness," should be the goal of this area of policy inquiry.

A related category of valuable research will take off from the public choice perspective which examines the hypocrisy of existing policy. Do the poor benefit or is the measure an elaborate way of propping up union salary structures? Is the bill for mine safety or does it eliminate the smaller non-union mine? Is the Clean Air Act protecting the environment or Ohio industrialists? Analysis examining these types of questions can often undermine the moral standing of the defenders of the status quo.

A final valuable element of the research task is that of examining the "government failure" aspects of the question. For too long, public policy has been little more than a wired game. In case after case, the private-sector performance was not all we might have hoped for and thus the need for a new government program was considered as proven. George Stigler, the Nobel Prize economist, noted that this would be like having a singing contest with two contestants in which one listened to the first singer, found her less than perfect, and thus awarded the prize to the second. Stigler suggests that we listen closely to the bureaucratic singer as well and decide what represents the best of the available options—not that we simply decide that the market has failed to realize some utopian ideal.

Improving Education Outreach   This task is the critical one of ensuring that the facts of the case reach those most likely to have influence
on the decision process. Being right has little value if no one is aware of
that fact. Conservatives need to make more and deeper contacts with
those in the media world. The biases of the newspeople are obvious, but
they are also professionals and like good stories. Their favorite framing
of the issue is White Hats vs. Black Hats; if conservatives intervene, we
confuse that framing and also make it possible to gain greater representation for our values and our data.

In large part, today, information is disseminated and ideas gain
respectability via the media. Thus, it is critical that conservatives begin
to meet the press, provide them newsworthy materials, inform them of
the value of the steps being advocated by the Administration, grant them
early warning of breaking events, and so on. A trust relationship must be
established with those with whom one wishes to work and that may
well require a considerable investment in time and energy. But it is
worthwhile.

Conservatives sometimes have an obsessive desire for secrecy—
believing that nothing can be told until everything is ready. That obses-
sion is understandable—in a hostile world, prepare for surprises—but as
a goal it is unattainable. Everything one does or says in Washington may
well appear the following day on the front page of *The Washington Post*.
The solution is to be careful and to consider not only your statements and
goals, but also how these will appear to those hostile to individual freedom. One may prefer that plans remain confidential, but one should have
no illusion that this can be guaranteed.

One should be aware that the relevant audience will differ from issue
to issue and be prepared to target one's educational campaign to that
audience most likely to advance the policy position. For example, if one
were to take on the marketing order issue (regulations which raise the
price of certain foods by restricting supply), the logical audience that
might support change would be the liberal and consumer forces in most
American metropolitan regions. The group most likely to oppose the
effort would be the grower and agricultural co-ops in the relevant growing
regions. The best strategy, then, would be to focus articles emphasizing
costs-to-consumer in major American cities and to avoid anything that
might further activate the opponents in their bastions.

In other cases—antitrust reform, for example—much of the debate will
occur in the trade press and an article in that forum will have a far greater
effect than will one aimed at a mass audience. In still other cases, such
as issues involving air traffic control, one might wish to target editorials

and news stories to the regional papers of those chairing the relevant congressional committees (Senator Kassebaum of Kansas and Congressman Mineta of California, for example). In brief, think not only of gaining media attention but of what that media attention is intended to achieve.

There are also a number of specific monitoring tasks that are essential to this task area. One needs to establish the prevailing tone of the media treatment of the issue, among the leading writers on the topic, and monitor how this changes as the issue evolves. How are the opponents' arguments playing in the press? Are your counter-arguments and positive analyses having any impact? Recall, too, that the media are a multi-faced outlet. The editorial page battle may be going well but is that success matched by treatment of the issue in the news system?

Coalition Building   Bell Telephone recently mounted a major advertising campaign with the theme, "Reach out, reach out and touch someone." That should be a basic goal of all who are seeking to effect policy change. As noted earlier, allies are essential in any effort to change policies. Allies can achieve results and play a role different from one's own. The first step in this task area is to create a road map or guide to the players—who are the groups that care about this issue, what are their current positions, what concerns do they express, what materials and experts do they rely on to guide their policies, and so forth. In other words, one must first know the terrain on which the battle will be fought.

Having developed an understanding of that terrain, one must then decide which groups are supportive, which opposed, and which might be persuaded to support the policy initiative. For each group, you should then prepare separate marketing plans: One plan to assist your allies in becoming more effective. Another plan to seek to nullify the fighting strengths of your opponents. And a final plan seeking to elicit support from the neutrals.

Appointees in a conservative administration have valuable resources that can be mobilized in this effort. For example, conservative appointees should always consider holding hearings to examine the pros and cons of their initiatives. The value of this is obvious: Any effort to disturb the status quo will automatically stimulate opposition and hearings will do little to further increase that opposition; in contrast, the constituency that will benefit from change is likely to be quiescent and uninformed. A formal hearing provides an opportunity to mobilize that group in an impressive setting—the Old Executive Office Building, a ceremonial room at an agency, with formal invitations. All this can be heady stuff, even to the average Washington operators, and it is likely to encourage them to become far more active on the issue.

Careful orchestration of coalition-building can also be invaluable in creating the view that one's policies are snowballing. One might well wish to plan a well-tempered effort in which success within the Administration fired expectations outside and vice versa. An element of *smoke-and-mirrors* is often at the basis of any successful policy campaign. One first seeks to create the illusion of movement within the Administration and to use that illusion of action to stimulate a similar outside response. Handled well, this can lead to illusion becoming reality. This approach was a valuable element of the overall campaign that led to transportation deregulation.

Improving Advocacy   All campaigns culminate in battle, and victory requires that one succeed in "getting there furstest with the mostest." Forces not present on the field of battle will decide no issue, nor will unfired ammunition nor untried tactics. Advocacy efforts seek to marshall the cumulative support generated on the outside and refocus its full force on the final salient decision-makers. Grassroots pressure is combined with personal lobbying of congressional members (or top administration officials). If the earlier stages of the issue management campaign have proceeded well, one will have media and interest-group support and a developed data base indicating the rationality and grounds for change.

Testimony is provided to congressional hearings and supplemented with additional written statements. A constant flow of fact sheets on the issue to Congressmen is followed up with personal calls and visits. Voting head-counts are updated to isolate wavering and undecided targets of opportunity. Direct mail and action calls before the final stages of the campaign activate coalition members to magnify the force behind the effort.

In addition, an issue management campaign must enlist leaders as well as troops. Political champions having the stature and skills required to pilot an initiative through the minefields of the legislative or regulatory process must be identified and encouraged to assure an active leadership role.

In the political world, true champions do not exist. However, all politicians seek to find areas where they can shine. The issue manager should develop a situation in which the politician gains from his role in championing an issue. That means close attention to the press to ensure that the efforts are treated favorably, that home press focuses in on his activities, and that he receives letters and calls reinforcing his actions. Leaders in the political world require reassurance, and that reassurance should be continuously forthcoming.

Conclusion

The battle for individual and economic rights will be a long one. Those favoring a statist solution to all public problems have long been in control, both in the United States and abroad. The current intellectual shifts create the opportunity to rethink statist policies and to gain new appreciation for conservative positions. But we must not count on the assurances of Mammy Yokum of Li'l Abner that good will win over evil "'cause it's nicer." More will be required. We will have to be smarter, self-critical, and goal-oriented. The fight is clearly worthwhile, but we had best be prepared for a long, long campaign and expect to be bloodied many times before the conflict is over.

5 Lessons for Political Appointees

WILLIAM NISKANEN, JR.

Editors' Note: This chapter is based on a speech delivered by Dr. Niskanen, a former member of the President's Council of Economic Advisors, to new political appointees entering the Reagan Administration. He provides an excellent set of summary guidelines for conduct in office. We can only hope his lessons will be followed by all appointees both in the current administration and in future conservative administrations.

I would like to offer political appointees a half-dozen lessons about operating as an effective manager in the Reagan Administration. *The first and maybe most important lesson a political appointee should remember is who appointed you.* Remember who was elected President in 1980 and 1984. Most political managers in government, unfortunately, very quickly drift into a sense that the people to whom they really ought to be responsive are the constituency groups and the congressional committees to which the agency reports. It is too easy to become comfortable with one's own staff and agency objectives.

But remember who appointed you in the first place. While your foremost political loyalties must be to the Constitution, very close to that remember that you were appointed by a President with an explicit agenda. In the area of economics it is probably the most explicit agenda of any president in history. The general themes of that agenda are really very clear. Make government smaller. President Reagan attributes many of our economic problems to the size and extensiveness of government. Rely more on markets. Rely more on state and local governments. These ideas were set forth in very substantial detail in the original program spelled out by the President.

If you're ever in doubt about the policy of the Reagan Administration in a given area, the best test is probably to ask yourself: If the program or the regulation did not exist, would you expect President Reagan to create it? If the answer is no, then your long-term objective must be to eliminate the program or regulation.

Don't get captured by the status quo and don't get caught by the incrementalist thinking of this town. A lot of what goes on in Washington consists of programs, regulations, statutes, and so forth that the Reagan

Administration clearly would not initiate if they did not already exist. So ask yourself, *Would Ronald Reagan wish to create this program if it did not exist?* The answer to that question can be the best guide to Reagan policy in areas where the policy is not explicit.

The second lesson is loyalty up. Remember loyalty up is, first of all, loyalty to the Constitution and, very close to that, a loyalty to the President who appointed you. Any political coalition that is large enough to elect a president, is going to have an agenda that is broader than those issues you may be particularly concerned about. It may even include elements that you do not support. But if you cannot support the policy of the Administration in your particular area of responsibility, you're in the wrong job. If you feel you cannot support the President's policy and still get along with your immediate superiors, you're probably in the wrong job. Because the system cannot work encumbered by guerrilla warfare from the bottom. It's got to work through a tiered system of responsibility upward toward the President.

The third lesson, right behind loyalty up, is loyalty down. Expect loyalty from your own subordinates in the same way that the White House expects loyalty from you and be loyal to them as well. Be willing to share credit for success when the activities of your agency are praised. Share credit with your staff. Be prepared to accept blame for innocent mistakes by your staff, at least in any public role. The White House, unfortunately, has all too often failed to recognize that loyalty down is an essential condition of loyalty up. There have been, from my perspective, too many occasions in which a wholly loyal, able, middle manager or political administrator has been dumped on in one way or another by the White House. This occurs, in many cases, even after they were asked to go out on a limb on a particular issue. But that's a lesson that we should all learn, and I hope that at some stage the White House learns it as well.

A fourth lesson I think is quite important: Set a few, not very many, key objectives for your own tenure in the job. Decide what it is that you want to accomplish in the job. I hope that most political appointees in the Reagan Administration are not just looking for a job in Washington and don't regard a political appointment as a way of paying the grocery bills and the mortgage. President Reagan was elected to bring about change in the government, and he has selected people with the expectation that they will contribute to that change. Don't let the staff set your agenda. Now, in my own experience in three government jobs, I found that most of my term was, almost by necessity, spent trying to head off new mischief. A lot of the new mischief originated within the Administration, within one's own agency sometimes. Fighting off new mischief can be a full-time job. Beyond that, you have to work especially hard to preserve time, attention, and resources to attempt to correct even a small part of the old mischief that existed before you got there.

Unless you set your own agenda, your own objectives in the agency, you will find yourself overwhelmed by your daily calendar, by the paper flow, and by other people's agenda. Set some items of your own agenda, things that you want to accomplish. You should set aside maybe half a day per week, not necessarily at the same time each week, but set aside some of your own time and say, "I'm going to preserve that time." Keep it free from meetings. Keep it free from the daily paper flow. Keep it free from other people's agendas, and work on trying to accomplish your own agenda.

Conventional politics, by its nature, is incremental. It asks what should we do relative to where we are now? That is often, however, a very poor guide to clear thinking. In many cases, what we ought to do is go back and start from first principles and address what, if anything, government ought to be doing in a given area. And in particular what, if anything, the federal government ought to be doing? Don't assume that the status quo has any special normative qualities. Address the problem from a zero-base perspective even if you recognize that the political process and the internal governmental review process, by and large, work on a strictly incremental perspective.

The fifth lesson concerns how political appointees conduct themselves in office. Here let me suggest three standards for conduct. The first I call the *Teddy Kennedy standard.* By that I mean, when you're designing a program or designing regulations or designing implementation plans—design them as if the next Kennedy Administration were going to administer it. Don't act as if your own friends and Reagan people are going to be in office forever. Don't act as if even intelligent people are going to be in office forever. Design the program in a way that will at least avoid extraordinary mischief if administered by your worst political enemies.

The second standard I call the *Caesar's wife standard.* Because the President has such an explicit agenda for change in Washington, it threatens a lot of people. It threatens the establishment thinkers in the press and in the academy. It threatens the bureaucracy and it threatens interest groups. It threatens congressional staffs and congressmen. In short, all the iron triangles.* Because of that, political appointees in the

---

Editors' note: The term "iron triangle" will be used throughout this book to refer to the symbiotic relationship among congressional committees, interest groups, and government agencies. When these three groups agree on a particular policy it is very difficult for any president to oppose that power. For example, see Chapter 22 which describes the power relationship created by the Small Business Administration, the small business interest groups, and the Senate Committee on Small Business.

Administration will be in the spotlight in terms of their own personal behavior. Unfortunately, there have been occasions in which even some of the most able managers, by careless remarks or by careless relationships with lobbyists or whatever, have undermined their own potential. In part because those same people were pressing the system, they became targeted and vulnerable to criticisms about personal behavior. You should expect to be judged by a standard that is far superior to that by which other people are judged—because if you're effective in your job you will threaten the system. The effective political appointee must be careful. It isn't that one has to live the life of a saint; it just means caution, prudence, and setting that higher standard for yourself and expecting it of other colleagues at your level.

Another standard I call the frustration standard. If you're not frustrated in your job, you have the wrong job. If you're not frustrated in your job, the Reagan Administration has appointed the wrong person. Reagan came to Washington after twenty years in the political outback and is regarded as an outsider. He came to this town to change it, and frustration is inherent in trying to bring about change.

Washington moves like a mountain of jelly; you touch it or you carve away in one spot and it seems to just ooze back. It's an inherently frustrating task to try to carve away some of this mountain. But, I'm telling you, if you don't feel frustrated in what you're trying to do in your own job, you've got your objectives misplaced. If you have resolved your frustration, you are very likely a part of the problem rather than a part of the solution. Frustration is inherent in the job of a political appointee if you're doing the job well, because it means that you are setting goals for yourself and for your agency that are higher than what is necessary just to get along.

The final lesson is to maintain the perspective of an outsider. Act as you would want somebody else to act in your own position; act as if you were among the people affected by those actions outside of the government, as if you were the taxpayers, the people who are subject to the regulation, the people who are subject to the program benefits. Act as you would want somebody else to act in your own position but on the assumption that you are outside the process rather than a part of the process. This has a solid ethical basis either from a religious perspective or from John Rawls' perspective of making judgments from behind a veil of ignorance. That is, design rules, laws, tax structures, and benefit programs, as if you don't know whether you are going to be a taxpayer or a recipient, whether you are going to be an administrator or somebody being regulated. Maintain an outsider's perspective. Don't get caught up in the "within-the-Beltway" set of mutual expectations about going along and accommodating the system.

One last aspect of being an outsider that is important to remember is that *you should keep your bags packed.* Don't act as if you're going to be here forever. The only way to maintain an outside perspective is to recognize that there is a world outside of the Beltway. There is even a world outside the government that pays all the taxes and bears all the burdens. Don't act as if you're going to spend the rest of your life in your government job. Don't act as if the only possible basis for promotion and greater reward is through the channels of government. Because once you set your expectations on that limited basis you will be adopting very different standards for your own behavior than if you regard yourself as being a Jeffersonian free man who is asked to serve the President for a short period of time in the interest of the general citizenry.

Keep your bags packed; maintain your outside perspective; there is life after Washington. Most of us have experienced it beforehand and some of us have experienced it afterward. I think remembering that simple fact is essential to maintaining one's sanity in a political job as well as maintaining one's commitment to the kinds of changes that we all wished to bring about when we first came to Washington as political appointees.

6 Agenda Deflection

ROBERT RECTOR and MICHAEL SANERA

Editors' Note: This chapter discusses central problems that have emerged in policy-making during the Reagan Administration. An understanding of these concepts is essential to the success or failure of political appointees in conservative administrations, present and future. These concepts form an analytic background to many of the case studies presented in Part IV of this book.

This chapter is about how conservative administrations fail—or, at least, about some of the central causes of failure. It is about how the policy agenda or policy goals of an administration are deflected or dissipated; how conservative policy initiatives become stillborn within the executive branch, or how a conservative administration may even collaborate in replacing its own agenda with that of the bureaucracy or the opposition. The processes described have been drawn from a study of the first six years of the Reagan Administration, but they represent perennial problems that will plague any administration—present or future—with conservative objectives.

Development and implementation of an agenda must be the foremost task of a presidential administration. In turn, it is the single most important aspect of a political appointee's job. Often, the simple development of an agenda or set of policy goals is the most crucial responsibility facing an administration because an alternative agenda—if forcefully presented along with its underlying conservative analysis—may sharply alter the context of national debate, irrespective of any short-term success or failure to implement that agenda legislatively. Failure to develop and adhere to a strong policy agenda means that there will not even be an effort to implement real policy change.

In a business organization, the primary goal must be to make a profit. The measure of success or failure is the "bottom line" that provides a guide to day-to-day management decisions. In political management, there is no bottom line; it must be replaced by another measurement tool. The policy agenda serves this purpose. A policy agenda allows a political manager to evelute his success or failure, and provides a target toward which he will direct his energies and channel the resources of his organization. The goal of a business, the bottom line, is given by the nature of the organization. A political agenda, on the other hand, must be developed. It is the function of a political appointee to take the overarching philosophy of the president and apply it to his agency or program in order to articulate a specific agenda.

Generally, there will be confusion, deliberate or nondeliberate, concerning the development of an agenda. Imagine, for a moment, a private business that was confused about its primary purpose. Some members of management believed that the intent was to make profits; some argued that the firm existed to benefit workers; others believed that it was an aid to community groups; and still others viewed the organization as a social club. Obviously, this business would not be very effective. Yet such confusion over primary purposes is the norm in government, not the exception.

Modes of Agenda Deflection

With the concept of "agenda deflection," we are concerned with the underlying mechanisms by which the philosophy and principles with which Ronald Reagan has been associated, both as a candidate over the years and as president, may become derailed within his own administration. Many of these underlying institutional processes and management styles linked to agenda deflection are not unique to the Reagan Administration or even to conservative administrations. However, to a moderate or liberal presidency (that is, a presidency committed to maintaining or expanding the role of the federal government in America), these factors may appear only as an inconvenience, or in some cases may even be seen as laudatory. For a conservative administration, these factors represent attitudes and management problems that must be overcome if desired policy outcomes are to be achieved.

Examination of the Reagan Administration reveals four modes by which the political agenda has been deflected within the President's own departments and agencies. These four modes of agenda deflection correspond to four management styles or four different types of political appointee:

- green eyeshade Republicans
- interest-group representatives
- liberal Republicans
- captured appointees

These modes are not mutually exclusive; a single appointee can embody more than one category.

Green Eyeshade Republicans

Both political parties, but especially the Republican Party, have a penchant for believing that the problem with government is that it is not run like a business. Therefore, the solution is to appoint businessmen to come to Washington and apply the latest business management principles to government. Such appointees have been termed "green eyeshade Republicans" because they set as their objective improving the economy and efficiency of government operations. They fail to recognize that a true conservative agenda must aim at changing the role of government in society, at changing or eliminating liberal programs, not making them run more efficiently. Thomas Gale Moore of the Hoover Institution has taken note of this fact when he states: "Traditionally, the Republicans have played the role of reforming *how* the government works, while Democrats have played the role of changing *what* the government does."[1] (Emphasis in original.) Unfortunately, green eyeshade Republicans will spend large amounts of time and resources making liberal programs run well. Such appointees will neglect opportunities for making more fundamental change or, when such change is thrust on them, will often resist it.

Liberals are quite comfortable with this type of "conservative." Such individuals may even play a necessary role in sustaining the welfare state or "transfer society." As Irving Kristol has noted,

> It has long been a cliché of liberal discourse that what this country needs is a truly intelligent and sophisticated conservatism to replace the rather primitive, philistine, and often racist conservatism that our history is only too familiar with. This new and desirable conservatism should have . . . a nebulous but definitely genteel political dimension, since it is likely that we shall always, at intervals, need a brief interregnum of conservative government whose function it is to consolidate and ratify liberal reforms. The ideal conservative President, from this liberal point of view, would be a Dwight Eisenhower who read Lionel Trilling instead of paperback Westerns, who listened to chamber music instead of playing golf—but who would be, in all other respects, as inert as the real President Eisenhower in fact was.
>
> What we absolutely do *not* need or want, from this liberal perspective, is a conservatism with strong ideas of its own about economic policy, social policy, or foreign policy—especially if these ideas can pass academic muster and survive intellectual debate. Such a conservatism might actually affect public policy, even become a shaping force in American politics, and this is simply impermissible. The very possibility

of such a conservatism is a specter that haunts the liberal imagination and can propel it into frenzies of exorcism.[2] (Emphasis in original.)

Making marginal changes in liberal programs or making those programs more efficient is not an effective means of reducing the size of government. Another drawback is that it allows liberals to frame the context of the debate. Liberals will always be willing to admit that in their rush to erect programs to meet an array of unmet human needs, in their vital concern over those needs, they may have let efficiency slip a notch or two. As Irving Kristol noted, liberals will graciously allow an occasional role to bespectacled Republicans to tidy up the many good works the liberals have bestowed on the American public. Debating whether sound liberal programs can be run with marginally greater efficiency concedes the rhetorical and electoral advantage permanently to the liberal camp. The challenge for conservatives must be to develop alternatives or, more important, to demonstrate why no government role is often best.

A final drawback of green eyeshade management is that it often directly frustrates efforts to bring about actual change. Real policy change requires a commitment of resources: Appropriate policy analysts must be hired; outside consultants must be located; policies must be developed and research conducted; research findings and policy proposals must be broadly publicized. Unfortunately, these are precisely the sorts of things that are likely to fall under the scalpel of a zealous green eyeshade manager concerned with marginal cost savings.

Throughout the Reagan Administration it is common to find appointees who are unable to prepare for and promote policy change because they are literally swamped with the tasks of managing Great Society programs. This is a question of misplaced priorities. Efficiency in government is a worthwhile goal, but it cannot be the primary goal of a conservative presidency or of the appointees within it. Efficient management should not distract resources—attention, time, and staff—from the more basic process of governmental change.

The story of James Sanders, Administrator of the Small Business Administration discussed in Chapter 22, is an excellent example of a green eyeshade manager in operation. As a manager of existing operations instilling efficiency into a lackluster agency, Sanders was quite effective. However, when it came to dealing with the more fundamental aspects of his job, Sanders was at a complete loss. He was incapable of examining critically the underlying economic rationale of his agency. He was incapable of analyzing his agency in terms of an overarching free-market economic policy, and most important he seemed oblivious to the long-run political implications of the growing dependence on government of vast segments of the population through a variety of income transfer programs. (Other aspects of this case will be discussed in a following section.)

Interest-Group Representatives

Many appointees at the assistant secretary level are in charge of large organizations with technical missions: vocational education, fish and wildlife, energy research, farm commodity programs. Such appointees may need technical qualifications and experience in the issue area. The result is that the political appointees often have educational and experience backgrounds that are similar to the career bureaucrats in the office and to the interest groups served. Thus they may have more in common with these forces and their interests than with the president and his policy agenda. Often they see their job as supporting the interest groups served by the agency. The life of such a political appointee will be relatively easy because he fits in the "iron triangle" of the agency. The interest group is happy because services are expanded; the bureaucracy is happy because its role is reinforced and expanded; and the members of the congressional committee are pleased because the benefits continue to flow to their districts. The only possible flak originates in the White House because the President's agenda is not being served. But White House officials are very busy on a wide range of issues; open controversy will prove exhausting and will bring charges of "management difficulties," so it is likely that the matter will simply be ignored.

It is desirable to select appointees with a professional knowledge of the issues they will be managing. However, there is a thin dividing line between selecting someone with knowledge of the field and getting an interest-group representative. It is often impossible for the White House to know in advance what role the appointee will assume. This dilemma is least important in foreign policy and most important with respect to programs where entire professions or industries have become dependent on government support or intervention.

One way of bypassing the interest representative dilemma is to search out academic experts who have written critically about the policy in question and who have no direct economic interest in it; such individuals may, however, be opposed in the confirmation process by the relevant interest groups. Overall, a political appointee with a conservative policy orientation but no knowledge of the field is more desirable than an "expert" with an ambiguous or uncertain policy perspective. Secretary of Education Terrel Bell in the first Reagan Administration is a clear example of an interest-group representative effectively at work. (See Chapter 26.)

Liberal Republicans

President Reagan is a president with a clear commitment to a conservative philosophy. The Republican Party, on the other hand, represents a broad ideological spectrum. It includes individuals who routinely vote as far to the left as Ted Kennedy. Even though President Reagan is conservative and represents the conservative wing of the Party, the Lowell Weickers still have influence on the Party and some of their supporters are appointed to executive branch positions. Popular impressions diverge greatly from reality in this regard. Contrary to popular conceptions, political staffing of the executive branch is not systematic and one can find in any presidency appointees of a very wide range of ideological hues. According to press accounts, the Reagan Administration contained within its ranks for a considerable period one high-level appointee in a position related to national security, who repeatedly proclaimed himself to be a McGovern Democrat.[3] This individual represented an extreme case, but was not completely atypical.

Such appointees may not be very effective in promoting a liberal agenda, but by virtue of their positions, they will be very effective in incommoding other appointees with conservative agendas. At times, the liberal appointee will be in direct conflict with conservative appointees. (See Howard Dana at the Legal Services Corporation, in Chapter 20.) At other times, even if the liberal appointee does not directly attack conservative policies, he can frustrate the efforts of those around him by quietly refusing to cooperate; Chapter 24 of this book, on the National Oceanic and Atmospheric Administration (NOAA), depicts a liberal appointee operating in this fashion. Delaying tactics can be an extremely effective political weapon. The turnover among political appointees is rapid, and tenure is short; incremental delays of a few months each calling for further study or reexamination of a policy may mean that the initiative is stalled until the sponsoring appointee leaves office; a new appointee arrives with a different approach or priorities, and the cycle begins afresh. In the aggregate, the result is stagnation.

A related problem, of perhaps equal consequence, pertains to moderate Republicans. The Republican Party has traveled a considerable ideological distance from the early 1970s to the second term of Ronald Reagan. For example, President Nixon regarded himself as a "new conservative," "a conservative with liberal ideas." As such, he supported the welfare state; did not regard the federal government as too large; did not regard taxes as too high; did not feel the level of taxation had any impact on economic growth; and viewed economic policy as a matter of tinkering with deficits and the money supply to moderate business cycles.[4] Such viewpoints have little support today within the Republican Party or among the American people; however, they still exist within the Party hierarchy. Appointees entering the executive branch with views such as these are likely to be ineffectual in producing real policy change even if they wished to; however, they may again be very effective in stalling initiatives within the executive branch, even if inadvertently.

Captured Appointees

Capture is the process by which political appointees are converted from being agents of the President's political agenda to being agents of the bureaucracy's agenda. This process is also referred to as "the bridge over the River Kwai syndrome." Capture of political appointees is a widespread phenomenon. It occurs in both liberal and conservative administrations and has been commented on in Washington for years.

At its heart, capture is a socialization process. In this process, the norms, values, and perspectives of the agency are imparted to the political appointee. The appointee absorbs the "bureaucratic ideology" of the institution: an implicit vision of the beneficial role of the organization and its necessary part in the functioning of a good society. This is a natural process by which new members are assimilated into any group or organization, such as a business firm, club, or church. However, in government the process, though natural, is highly disruptive.

The socialization process gains effectiveness due to the inherent informational bias of the appointee's position. The appointee will be absorbed almost totally by the problems and concerns of the agency and its programs. He will have most of his daily contact with agency staff and will spend most of his time reading materials prepared for him by the bureaucracy. Most of these materials will subtly lobby for the agency viewpoint if only by neglecting alternatives. Invariably agency staff will adopt an initial flattering attitude toward the appointee, and their viewpoints will be couched in such a way as to make them appear fully consistent with the administration's broader philosophy.

This does not necessarily imply a conspiratorial attitude on the part of the career staff. Rather, they may simply be offering views that they authentically believe; it is difficult to work for years on a program or policy without coming to believe in its value. They may be unaware of alternatives. The effectiveness of the process will be compounded by the fact that top-level career staff will be bright, energetic, and knowledgeable.

Gradually the appointee comes to understand the agency's mission, its importance, and the practical limits on change; he sees also that there is often an incomplete understanding of the agency in the outside world.

"Capture" is a compelling, unconscious process; although it occurs with great frequency, *one will never meet a political appointee who will allow that he has been captured by the institution he is supposed to be managing.*

The entire socialization process is often reinforced by the fact that the appointee has been thrust into an alien environment in Washington and may be dealing with unfamiliar problems. Hugh Heclo of The Brookings Institution describes the process of isolation and conversion:

> Weaknesses among political executives lead inevitably to White House complaints about their "going native" in the bureaucracy. The image is apt. To a large extent the particular agencies and bureaus are the native villages of executive politics. Even the most presidentially minded political executive will discover that his own agency provides the one relatively secure reference point amid all the other uncertainties of Washington. In their own agencies, appointees usually have at least some knowledge of each other and a common identity with particular programs. Outside the agency it is more like life in the big city among large numbers of anonymous people who have unknown lineages. Any common kinship in the political party or a shared political vocation is improbable, and in the background are always the suspicions of the President's "true" family of supporters in the White House. Political appointees in the larger Washington environment may deal frequently with each other, but these are likely to be the kind of ad hoc, instrumental relations of the city, where people interact without truly knowing each other. . . . Among political executives themselves there is little need to worry about joint action to enforce community norms, because there is no community.[5]

An excellent example of the capture process is the story of James Sanders, Administrator of the Small Business Administration (SBA) presented in Chapter 22. As noted previously, Sanders began his career as a green eyeshade manager but soon found himself surrounded by the adulation of the agency staff and the interest groups dependent on the SBA. Sanders was touted as SBA's "best administrator"; his reforms were lavishly praised and his leadership was eventually credited by supporters of the SBA with having "saved the agency." These sentiments were reciprocated; Sanders developed a profound emotional loyalty to the generally disreputable agency, a loyalty which brought him into open conflict with the White House when it decreed that the SBA would be shut down.

The SBA case represents the extreme. Capture is usually more subtle. Its more common and important effects are largely invisible: initiatives that never surface because they conflict with institutional interests, or footdragging and vacillation on those initiatives that do emerge.

Preventive Measures

Many of these problems can be solved through an increased awareness of their relevance early in the appointment process. Others can be mitigated by an improved understanding among political appointees of their proper role in government and the pressures and influences that will be brought to bear on them. Of the four modes of agenda deflection, capture is particularly prevalent. As noted, capture will occur in any presidency. For a liberal president, however, capture is not always a problem. It is not particularly distressing if, for example, during the Carter Presidency the secretary of HUD was captured by her institution and took on the role of an impassioned White Knight crusading for an expansion of agency programs; this may even help the liberal agenda in the long run. For conservatives, on the other hand, capture is a disaster. In many instances, it has meant that the "Reagan Revolution" was aborted before it commenced. It means that a conservative electoral mandate will not be translated into executive branch policy; in effect, it short-circuits democracy.

Capture, or "going native," occurs in varying degrees. It can happen even to the best of political appointees. Although it is very common, however, capture is also more correctable than other modes of agenda deflection. With this in mind, we offer the following *anti-capture* techniques to current and prospective appointees. (Some of these techniques may also have a bearing on appointees who have tendency to fall into the interest-group representative or green eyeshade manager roles.)

1. When the political appointee catches himself thinking "It's true that government is too big and wasteful, and spending should be sharply cut, but my agency/program is really different, it accomplishes worthwhile goals"—he should be aware that the capture process has begun to take hold. Because it is very difficult to spend money without satisfying someone or achieving some results, virtually any government program can appear to produce "positive" benefits. In many cases, the only way to fail to accomplish some good would be to hide the money under a mattress. Those working within an agency will directly perceive these apparent "accomplishments"—projects completed, funds dispersed— while the question of relating these "benefits" to societal costs will remain theoretical and remote; if government should be cut, it should always be some other program (one that is really wasteful). Political appointees should be wary of this type of bias in their thinking and decision-making.

2. In order to maintain a proper orientation toward his program or

agency, a political appointee should begin by asking himself the question introduced in the previous chapter: If this program did not exist, would the President seek to create it? If the answer is no, the political appointee should devote his efforts toward the ultimate goal of eliminating his agency or program, thereby making a personal contribution toward the gradual reduction of government.

3. The political appointee should break the traditional Washington "budget game." The traditional budget game consists of subordinate bureaus within a department lobbying the department head for more funds (or at least for a mitigation of proposed cutbacks), and of the departments lobbying the Office of Management and Budget in a similar manner. To a surprising degree, this ritual pattern has persisted within the Reagan Administration. Its continuation is to a degree a result of appointees seeking to assure that budget "restraint" is proportional and that their programs get a "fair share" of available funds. Such activities are highly detrimental to a conservative agenda and should be avoided at all costs.

4. Political appointees are often inundated by the flow of paper arriving in their in-boxes. They find themselves spending their time reacting to things initiated elsewhere. In these circumstances, appointees will end up merely "managing" their agency, and very little positive policy change will be achieved. To avoid this fate and break out of the reactive mode, it is important that the political appointee control the allocation of his time—a certain portion of each day should be set aside during which the appointee will be free to work on projects he has initiated as opposed to those that the bureaucracy, the press, and interest groups have initiated. President Nixon had an ideal method of formalizing this technique. In order to maintain blocks of time free for his own agenda, Nixon would periodically schedule times to leave the Oval Office and cross the street to the Old Executive Office Building, where he had a separate, spartan office. Once he was secluded in this simple hideaway, his staff knew not to disturb him except in true emergencies. Nixon was thus able to preserve time to concentrate on his own plans and on the issues that were of greatest concern to him.[6]

5. Finally, within Washington, the political appointee will have most of his daily contact with individuals within his own agency. He will be relatively isolated even from other political appointees within the Administration. This is part of the process by which the appointee learns to absorb agency goals and perspectives. To break down this pattern, the appointee must make a special effort to remain in daily contact with conservative groups and individuals outside the agency.

These techniques will not guarantee that a political appointee will be successful in advancing a conservative policy agenda. But they will increase the prospects of success by ensuring that some of the most obvious pitfalls are avoided.

Notes

1. Thomas Gale Moore, "Reagan's Regulatory Record," in *To Promote Prosperity: U.S. Domestic Policy in the Mid-1980s*, ed. John H. Moore (Stanford, Calif.: Hoover Institution Press, 1984), p. 244.

2. Irving Kristol, *Reflections of a Neoconservative: Looking Back, Looking Ahead* (New York: Basic Books, 1983), pp. 73–74.

3. Tom Diaz, "U.S. Officials Tried to Fire Worker for His Conservatism, Counsel Says," *The Washington Times*, January 4, 1985, p. 24.

4. Herbert Stein, *Presidential Economics: The Making of Economic Policy From Roosevelt to Reagan and Beyond* (New York: Simon & Schuster, 1984), pp. 133–209.

5. Hugh Heclo, *A Government of Strangers* (Washington, D.C.: The Brookings Institution, 1977), pp. 111–112.

6. David Asman and Adam Meyerson, eds., *The Wall Street Journal on Management: The Best of the Manager's Journal* (Homewood, Ill.: Dow Jones-Irwin, 1985), p. 42.

7 Clausewitz Updated: Litigation as the Continuation of Policy Making by Other Means

JOSEPH A. MORRIS

Editors' Note: This chapter focuses on the role of litigation in our political system. In pursuit of his primary target, the Chief of Staff and the Counsel to the Director of the U.S. Information Agency, redefines many features of the contemporary political landscape with unique insight.

"War," observed Karl von Clausewitz, the seminal 19th-century Prussian military thinker, "is the continuation of foreign policy by other means." That statement contains a great deal of meaning, not all of it obvious. For one thing, it reminds us that people do not usually make war as an end in itself; wars serve political goals. Clausewitz's dictum also warns foreign policymakers that war is necessarily one tool that they—and their adversaries—may take up in the execution of policy; the policymaker who discounts war and the threat of war as viable options in carrying out national policy does so at his own grave peril. Put another way, a foreign policymaker may truly not want war, but he cannot—indeed, he dare not—fail to think about war. War is a tool of policy; he who will understand war must seek out the political interests that it is meant to serve; he who will understand policy must look for the dimensions of policy that may make war into someone's viable option.

Litigation is also the continuation of policy by other means. In the domain of foreign policy, litigation between and among states is at the other end of the spectrum of governmental action from acts of violence. International adjudication and arbitration are perceived, generally quite correctly, as healthy substitutes for combat. The fact of the matter is, of course, that governments that are willing to sue each other (and are able to agree upon some process of suit and some forum in which to try suits) are probably sufficiently friendly that violence was never actually a likely course for either of them. There are, to be sure, exceptions to this generalization; the claim prosecuted by Nicaragua against the United States in the International Court of Justice is an example. In that case, a lawsuit is undertaken essentially as an exercise in public diplomacy that is intended to abet and, to some extent, to mask Nicaragua's prosecution of war against its neighbors. But as a rule, international litigation is far from an extreme measure in the conduct of foreign policy.

In the realm of a democracy's domestic policy, however, litigation is virtually the most extreme of measures. Perhaps, under a parliamentary constitution, forcing a legislative vote of confidence—with the attendant danger to the sitting government that the outcome may arrest its powers, dissolve the legislature, and compel a general election—is a more extreme matter. But under a constitution such as that of the United States, which carefully and relatively rigorously separates legislative, executive, and judicial powers, litigation is probably the most remarkable weapon that can be wielded against or in defense of a policy choice.

Simply put, litigation in the context of policy-making is the process of referring to the judiciary a question that has arisen in the political branches of government and has hitherto been treated as a political matter—that is, as something fit for disposition by the discretionary action of Congress or the president and the executive branch. Judicial review of legislative and executive action is one of the remarkable and generally distinguishing features of America's political landscape. Our courts have a power, long since popularly accepted, to review congressional enactments for consistency with the Constitution and acts of Congress. Judicial review may be invoked not just by Congress or the president, but often by private citizens and their businesses and organizations, as well as by the several states. It is possible, for example, for an individual to bring suit against the president of the United States— indeed, against the United States government in its entirety. Americans not only sue their sovereigns, they view such suits as almost commonplace. These facts, when first encountered, often boggle the minds of foreign observers.

Just because a suit is brought against the government (or one or more of its officials or agencies) by someone attacking a policy (or the statute, rule, order, or conduct embodying it) does not mean in and of itself that the courts have power to decide the case. They may lack jurisdiction over the subject matter, for example, or the plaintiffs involved may lack standing to sue, or the question presented may not be "ripe" for decision. Scores of reasons may keep a court from taking up a case involving governmental policy, and even though a case ultimately is taken up, that fact alone does not mean that, in deciding the case, the court will decide the ultimate public policy question that is involved. Indeed, just because a court is wrestling with an issue does not necessarily mean that Congress and the executive branch have been utterly shorn of their abilities to deal with the problem, too. But it is an interesting fact of American political life that, once an issue is put in litigation, "time out" tends to be called on other policy-making fields of play and the disputants tend to marshal their resources for legal battle. Even after the courts have spoken in a case, and even where the judicial outcome in fact imposes no restraint upon further legislative or executive action, legislators and executive branch officials tend to display exhaustion, to declare that "the courts have spoken," and to retire from the issue, whether or not they have prevailed on the merits.

Two attributes of litigation thus serve to make it an extreme measure when taken in the context of a policy dispute. First, it either removes the dispute entirely from the ordinary political policy-making processes (e.g., elections, legislation, and executive decision-making), or it at least intrudes a putatively nonpolitical participant—the judiciary—onto the field. A corollary of this first attribute is that it necessarily involves a highly specialized profession in the policy process: lawyers, who bring with them their peculiar habits of mind, methods of combat, and language, often displacing from the field any number of individual policy-makers who see themselves as attached to, if not proprietors of, the policy questions at issue. The second attribute is litigation's aura of finality. Even when a judicial decision does not, in truth, dispose of a question, forever binding the hands of legislators and executives, there will invariably be some participants in the policy debate who, for one reason or another (ranging from substantive satisfaction with the judicial outcome, to fear of the consequences of appearing to dwell on the losing side of a dispute, to sheer boredom), will urge that, the courts having spoken, the matter be dropped.

Just as foreign policymakers need to keep themselves ever mindful of the integral role of force and war in international affairs, so domestic policymakers must learn the laws of litigation and their bearing on contemporary politics. If there is one profound distinction between war and litigation, in their respective realms of relation to policy change, it is this: Whereas war, even when successful, almost always entails horror, litigation, even when it fails, almost always entails opportunity. Policymakers justifiably have an abhorrence of war and prudently resort to it with great reluctance. But litigation is not necessarily something to be avoided at all costs. Whether by conscious congressional preference or by simple default, it has become, in fact, an essential part of the federal policy-making process.

As war must be kept in the mind of makers of foreign policy, so litigation must be kept in the mind of the domestic policymaker, both as a threat to be deflected and as an arrow to be fired. The wise policymaker will study litigation and learn to use it to advance his policy interests. With this in mind, here are propounded, as addenda to Clausewitz, "Ten Laws on Litigation and Policy Change."

Law No. 1: *Litigation is the continuation of policy-making by other means*. Litigation has become an intended consequence of the operation of our domestic policy-making system. This will be discerned in any candid examination of the heart of the American governmental process, the making of laws. In truth, over the course of at least the last half-century, the primary hidden agenda of the legislative process has been to permit Congress as an institution to avoid ultimate responsibility for the making of difficult or controversial decisions.[1]

Consider, for example, the actual case of a proposal for the federal government to dam a river. In one set of legislative enactments, Congress authorized that a dam be built and appropriated funds for the work. Manifold reasons justified this decision: The dam would arrest soil erosion, enhance flood controls and drainage systems, produce hydroelectric power, facilitate field irrigation, furnish recreational opportunities, and create numerous jobs along the way. Many advantages would flow from such congressional action, and individual congressmen and their committees made sure that the relevant publics were made aware of its asserted benefits.

On the other hand, Congress also enacted legislation to protect the natural environment. These measures prohibited the construction of any public work if it would endanger the life of a species. The public benefits behind that statute were also manifold: It would conserve nature, retain nature's beauty, preserve for future generations interesting, beautiful, and productive species that had important roles to play in the ecosystem, and inculcate general respect for the natural environment. Again, Congress took pains to make sure that the voters appreciated the wisdom of this legislation.

Alas, the idyl was disturbed by reports from environmental scientists that construction of the dam would destroy the only known habitat of a rare and endangered species of fish. Assuming that factual assertion to be true, then the two measures so proudly advanced by Congress would come directly at loggerheads. One set of statutes would command that the dam be built, while the other would declare the dam prohibited. Thus spoke Congress.

When Congress speaks on both sides of a question, as in the illustration just tendered, who is to resolve the contradiction? The answer, at least in the first instance, is very often the president and the executive branch. Action—execution—is of the essence of the president's function. The Constitution commands him to "take Care that the Laws be faithfully executed." The executive branch thus rarely has the luxury to defer a matter for lengthy study; action is normally the order of the day, a point on which Congress is itself particularly insistent, as, for example, in the prohibitions it has purported to place upon the president's power to *refuse* to spend appropriated money. In the illustration before us, the question before the executive branch is quite simple: Shall or shall not the dam be built?

To execute the laws, the president and his assistants must know what the laws are and what they mean. They must therefore undertake to reconcile conflicting laws when they are encountered. Sometimes conflicts occur within, as well as between, laws; more often, statutes are simply vague or ambiguous, unclear as to meaning or susceptible of more than one reasonable interpretation. The task therefore falls upon federal executives to make working decisions as to what the relevant law—that is, the controlling choices of Congress—may be. When such executive branch decisions prove controversial, some review at a higher level of the executive is often possible; ultimately, of course, review may be had in the courts, with several layers of judicial review typically available.

A consequence of this process is that difficult public-policy choices, though nominally the province of Congress, are in fact made in the executive and judicial branches. What is remarkable is that the public rarely seems to notice that Congress has actually abandoned the field of decision-making to others. Congress has done *something*; it has *appeared* to act. That a congressional enactment is vague or in conflict with another law often seems a subtlety lost in the press of public business. Thus, the opprobrium for a policy choice that is unpopular with a particular constituency is visited not upon Congress, which has taken pains to convince the constituency of its sympathy and sincerity, but upon the executives or judges who, in essaying to divine and apply the intent of Congress, are perceived as working their own wills, interposing their own (presumably perverse) policy choices. Each competing constituency will argue, of course, that the congressional enactment under debate was intended by Congress to benefit its interests; bureaucratic or judicial interpretations merely stray from the path that Congress had desired. The net effect is to insulate Congress, as an institution, from accountability for unpopular decisions, while preserving for Congress credit for choices that prove popular.

It will be noted that an institutional interest of Congress is served by this system's dependence upon formalized contests as to the meanings of congressional enactments; that is, litigation is a highly convenient vehicle in which to transfer a thorny public-policy problem from the halls of Congress to the chambers of the executive and the judiciary.

There is a second congressional device that achieves similar results. First, Congress identifies a problem: pollution, carnage on the highways, children who cannot read. Second, Congress holds hearings on the problem where many speeches are given deploring it. Third, a government agency is established, with funds and personnel, to deal with the problem. Fourth, Congress gives the agency the name of the problem:

hence, the Environmental Protection Agency, the National Highway Transportation Safety Administration, or the Department of Education. Fifth, Congress gives the agency a very vague mandate to correct the problem; the mandate may itself be internally inconsistent, as in a direction to curb pollution without impairing production, closing factories, or costing jobs.

Then Congress gives the agency the power to make rules. Rules, of course, are laws; they are made through regulatory procedures, but, if validly promulgated, they undeniably have the force and effect of law. By this means, Congress delegates to the executive branch its constitutional authority to legislate. Moreover, Congress frequently caps such an exercise by conferring upon the agency—already empowered to make rules and to enforce them—the authority to adjudicate cases that arise under its regulations, including a power to interpret its own rules as well as the act of Congress that gives rise to the whole establishment. The agency thereupon hires administrative law judges, sets up hearing structures, and develops a caseload. Finally, of course, Congress will typically provide for the courts to review the agency's decisions.

By this second device, Congress has identified and deplored a public problem and has created the appearance of doing something about it. In fact, though, it has been left to someone else to decide how the problem is to be resolved. Whether it is the proscription of an industrial process or the prescription of an airbag, the decision will be made by an executive agency or a court and not by Congress. When a constituency is pleased with the decision, Congress will expect and accept credit; when another constituency is displeased by the same decision, Congress will blame the agency or the court.

For present purposes, the salient fact is not the desire of Congress to open itself to praise while simultaneously insulating itself from criticism; rather, it is the central and necessary role that litigation plays in achieving such a state of affairs. Litigation is not an accident of policy-making; it is an intended consequence of it, and will remain a central feature of the policy-making landscape unless and until Congress as an institution wishes to resume being openly accountable for policy decisions.

There is litigation over rule-making, litigation over the failure to make rules, litigation over the substance of rules, litigation over the application and interpretation of rules. An administrative law judge may well make more law and policy for his agency than does his agency's head, because law is often made case by case, interstitial decision by interstitial decision. The whole policy matrix is at times controlled at least as much by lawyers through litigation as it is by administrators who move the levers of policy in accordance with their own timetables and agendas. Law No. 1 therefore teaches the policymaker to recognize that federal public policy is, to an extraordinary degree, made, vindicated, and overturned through litigation. Litigation therefore must not be seen as alien to the business of policy-making, at least in the federal context, but as an inherent part of it.

By way of completing the historical record, it should be noted that, in the case of the disputed dam, the executive branch ultimately resolved the contradiction between acts of Congress in favor of proceeding with construction. Litigation followed, eventually making its way to the Supreme Court. For once the Court was unable to finesse the statutory contradiction by devising some miraculously reconciling reading of the competing enactments. The policy choice was virtually binary, a stark election between building or not. The Court therefore applied some reasonable rules of statutory construction and concluded that Congress had intended to stop the dam; the Court's logic was no more questionable than if it had decided that matter in exactly the opposite way. Interestingly, the Court's decision made it quite apparent, for once, to interested constituents that Congress was the real decision-maker, and *vox populi* was soon heard clearly on Capitol Hill. Congress finally addressed the policy problem in an unambiguous way, directing unequivocally that the dam proceed. The case was unusual precisely in its being an exception to the general rule; the ultimate decisional power of Congress was not masked and it was Congress that, in the end, visibly made the final, dispositive policy choice. (The biological story seems to have a generally happy ending, too. It turns out that the endangered piscine species not only thrives in the shadow of the dam but has been found to have other natural habitats as well.)

Law No. 2: *Litigation defense can be policy-making offense.* A responsible federal executive will be sued and sued often. One's natural instinct, when made a defendant in a federal lawsuit, is to think that one has done something wrong. On the contrary, when the conscientious federal executive is sued, chances are that he has done something right. Interest groups that oppose a policy will sue to interdict or reverse it. It is a free country and the courts are open to them; having lost a policy battle in one forum, interest groups will often roll the dice in court to see if an administration's policy objectives can be frustrated there. It is entirely legitimate—indeed, it is of the essence of one's duties—for the federal executive to defend his policies in court. The forum should be used to defend agency action, including policies, rules, and operational judgments. Litigation should be viewed as an opportunity to explain and to defend the administration's policy choices. The loss of a single lawsuit does not necessarily spell defeat for an entire policy; but victory in a lawsuit can often strengthen a policy and encourage the trend of policy-making from which it emerges.

Law No. 3: *In the federal sector, transaction cost analysis is largely irrelevant to litigation decisions.* In the private sector, when two businessmen sue each other, the lawsuit is about market share, profits, or who is responsible for a loss that has occurred in a particular transaction. The disputants are people engaged in commercial relationships who doubtless wish to maximize and continue their trading relations. They are not engaged in litigation on behalf of numerous third parties and generations yet unborn. Rather, they are typically disputing relatively microscopic aspects of normal commercial transactions that have encountered unanticipated adversities. Under such circumstances, if the controversy is purely about money—and most commercial litigation is—then it makes no sense to throw good money after bad. The parties will typically engage in enough pre-trial skirmishing—lawyers call it "discovery" and "motion practice"—to sort out the facts and the probabilities of liability and loss, and then settle out of court. Why flirt with the risk of complete loss when attorneys' fees and the other costs of litigation will consume the greater part of one's potential winnings? That is why more than 95 percent of all commercial lawsuits in the private sector are settled before trial. The parties make a modest investment in litigation as a tool of fact-finding and persuasion needed to negotiate a reasonable, mutually acceptable result. The lawsuit serves, in a sense, as a laboratory of market forces in which to approximate how a transaction would have turned out had the parties not breached their relations. Since commercial litigants value real business more than abstract models, their goal is to settle disputes reasonably, resume relations if possible, and go on to the next mutually profitable transaction. It is not a fight to the death.

In the federal sector, as well, settlements may often make sense. This is particularly so when the lawsuit results from a commercial transaction of a commonplace kind. But settlements of policy-based lawsuits make sense on the basis of a calculus that is entirely different from that which applies to commercial litigation. The federal government is not normally concerned with making profit; it is more typically interested in the effectuation of a policy or, as is more likely to result in litigation, a policy change. The interests of third parties (including future generations of the taxed, the regulated, and the benefited) will typically be involved, and the federal executive will be expected to conceive of his "bottom line" as the public interest broadly understood.

Now, it is true that the government's legal expenses can be outrageous, particularly in light of relatively recent statutes that have often made the government pay not only its own costs but also the expenses and attorney's fees of those who sue it. Nonetheless, the transaction costs of litigation over federal policy will typically pale in comparison to the downstream economic, political, social, and cultural costs and benefits associated with the policy questions at issue in the litigation. What is more, not only is the actual dollar value of a policy dispute often much greater than that present in the typical private commercial case, but the intangible values at issue are beyond cognizable dollar measurement. Accordingly, investment in litigation for policy change often makes a great deal more sense than an investment of comparable magnitude would make in the context of a lawsuit over a private business dispute.

Law No. 4: *The key to success at policy change is the effective fusion of policy vision and legal strategy.* A government agency's career counsel tend to be risk averse. They tend to advise against disturbances of routine and to inflate the signficance of adverse precedents. Their instincts are to preserve the status quo and they are therefore likely to be unsympathetic, at least initially, to policy change. Far from being a sinister phenomenon, this characteristic of career government counsel is common to most lawyers, who are generally conservative in the sense that they are trained to encourage prudence and that they serve a legal system that is designed, quite correctly, to act as a brake upon radical change.[2]

The prudent government executive, committed to policy change, will do well to listen carefully to his career counsel, but the entire legal picture will not be understood unless it is also evaluated by a lawyer who shares the commitment to policy change. Sometimes conflict should be avoided, but at other times the interests of justice require the government either to provoke it or to commence it directly. There are times when the proper role for government is that of peacemaker and conciliator, but there are other times when responsible officials must willingly enter the crucible of litigation in order to vindicate a policy judgment—whether the judgment is that of Congress, the president, or their own agency. Litigation should not be courted without cause, but policies and operations should not be mangled merely to avoid lawsuits. Consequently, there is a crucial role in American government for politically appointed counsel. It is at the juncture of law and policy, where the calculus of risk and reward must be sorted out and where the policymaker must hear candid advice from one who is faithful both to the administration's policy mandate and to the system of justice.

These observations apply no less to the Department of Justice than to the federal agencies whom the Department will ordinarily represent in the courts. But it must be stressed that the Department of Justice cannot be expected to have any clearer understanding of the policy goals of its client agencies than the agencies impart to it. It is therefore essential that an agency's general counsel cultivate good personal working relations with the assistant attorneys general and United States attorneys around the country whose divisions and offices will be handling his agency's affairs. These channels of communication should be used assiduously to convey articulable senses of the agency's policy objectives and its operational needs.

Law No. 5: *Losing a lawsuit is not necessarily losing the policy war.* Bad cases can make good policy, by informing public sentiment and thereby setting the stage for policy change in Congress, in the executive branch, at the polls, and even at higher levels of the judiciary. There are many attentive publics to be informed: the general public, media elites, the bar and other professions, Congress, the higher courts, the academic community, and others. Loss of a case can give rise to an opportunity to appeal. It can serve as a stimulus to continued litigation, in both the same court and other courts, at both the same level and above. It can also create opportunities to explain a policy and a controversy to the public. It can highlight the absurd consequences of the rule or policy that the administration proposes to change. Indeed, it can stimulate correction through rule-making or by legislation. It may even affect the opinions that people take with them to the polls.

Law No. 6: *Persistence pays rewards.* A single loss in a single forum does not by any means necessarily end the policy war or even the litigation strategy. Victory may still be possible in another case, in another forum, on another day. The Supreme Court exists, after all, in important part precisely to resolve conflicts among decisions of lower courts.

The Supreme Court itself has been known to overrule its own precedents. A hallmark of the litigation approach of President Reagan's administration has been its laudable willingness to encourage courts to reexamine precedents and, where they are found to be bad law, to overrule them. Neither the president nor the Congress nor the courts should be ashamed to correct themselves when they have made wrong decisions.

Such logic certainly applies, too, to the lower courts and the adminstrative tribunals. An example of success born of persistence may be seen in a recent case won by the Office of Personnel Management (OPM). OPM, the goverment's central personnel and labor-relations agency, for years disputed the contention of federal-sector labor unions that the Civil Service Reform Act of 1978 required government agencies to pay the travel and *per diem* expenses of union representatives negotiating agreements around the country between federal agency units and the unions representing their work forces. OPM held the view that it is for the provision of such services that unions exist and union members pay dues; it is unfair to make the taxpayers pay for bargaining both for themselves and against themselves. Time after time the issue was taken to the Federal Labor Relations Authority, and time after time OPM lost. OPM took the matter to the courts of appeals and lost again. Finally, OPM persuaded the Supreme Court to take up one such case to examine the issue. The Supreme Court held for OPM, thereby overturning the precedents established in numerous cases below and vindicating OPM's policy for future application.

Law No. 7: *The quality of justice rises in inverse proportion to proximity to Washington.* It may surprise those whose knowledge of the judiciary is derived exclusively from the pages of *The Washington Post*, but the United States District Court for the District of Columbia and the United States Court of Appeals for the District of Columbia Circuit are not the only courts, besides the Supreme Court, that exist. There are, in fact, twelve other circuits and scores of districts. Just as approximately 90 percent of the personnel of the executive branch will be found outside the Washington area, so the overwhelming majority of courts, lawyers, and lawsuits will be found outside the Washington Beltway.

This has practical significance. Very often an agency with far-flung operations has the opportunity to sue (or be sued) somewhere outside of Washington. In all candor, public sentiment and the opinions of benches, bars, and juries across the nation are often more sympathetic to the goals of conservative policy change than are their counterparts within the Beltway. Just as journalism "inside the Beltway" should not be thought to define the temperament and opinions of the nation as a whole, so it should not be assumed that the bench and bar of Washington necessarily represent the sentiment of the nation's legal community. The atmosphere of the nation's capital is sufficiently rarefied that many who dwell there for extended periods of time may well lose touch with the day-to-day realities of life across the land.

The gravamen of Law No. 7 is not so much that the bench and bar of the other twelve circuits are vastly superior to those found in the District of Columbia as it is that they exist at all. Policy-makers must think in terms of the nation as a whole, not just of Washington. This is true no less when it comes to the evaluation of legal risks and the development of legal strategy than it is in terms of sounding public opinion or measuring the general welfare.

Law No. 8: *Sue and be sued over things that matter.* Time is the most precious resource of policymakers and their counsel. Their attention must therefore be focused on the issues, policy questions included, that really make a difference. They should not be bogged down in litigation—or, for that matter, any kind of controversy—that does not serve their adminstration's agenda for policy change. Irrelevant litigation is certainly the first domain in which to seek candidates for settlement and the avoidance of costs and risks.

Law No. 9: *Enforce the law as it exists, but criticize the law when it is unjust.* When a policymaker enters office he finds a thick fabric of statutes, regulations, and case law that governs him. As a conscientious public servant he must uphold the law, taking the actions required by the law as it exists.

But this does not mean that laws are beyond criticism. They are often vague and ambiguous, inconsistent with themselves and with other enactments, and inimical in practice to the interests that they purport to serve. All these things may be pointed out quite constructively with a view toward informing relevant opinion as a step toward change. Nothing in our system requires a public official to like the laws that he enforces, and one may conspicuously hold one's nose while still doing one's duty. There are times when the most convincing way to demonstrate the folly of a law is precisely by its rigorous enforcement. The law's consequences may then be seen by all whom it affects, and the enforcer is armed with both experience and credibility as he calls for appropriate reform.

To enforce the law as one finds it, by the way, necessarily entails a serious effort to learn what the law is. The diligent policymaker, particularly when first taking on his official responsibilities, will arrange for counsel to brief him thoroughly on the laws committed to his care. The policymaker should attend critically to such briefings, and should insist that they include comprehensive discussions not only of the statutory and regulatory materials that apply, but also of the relevant judge-made law, including consent decrees. Although generally uncodified, court opinions and decrees can significantly color the legal terrain and can furnish unexpected impediments to—or support for—policy change.

Law No. 10: *Policy advocacy through litigation should be coordinated with policy advocacy in other fora.* Litigation is one of several tools by which the policymaker seeks to achieve wholesome change. Other tools include relations with Congress, communication through the news media, dealings with interested constituency groups, discussions with the central government management agencies (such as the White House, OPM, and the Office of Management and Budget), and the like. These tools should be understood as strategic means toward the development and implementation of a policy agenda, and should be conscientiously coordinated to serve the president's policy goals. Thus, while lawsuits should not be tried in the newspapers, an agency should not be shy about explaining to Congress and the public the policy goals that may be at issue in litigation. At the same time, courts should be candidly apprised, through proper procedures, of the policy dimensions of the cases before them. This will often improve the administration of justice by focusing judicial attention upon the most relevant points of legal and policy conflict.

Conclusion

A raging passion for litigation, a quickening erosion of the constitutional separation of powers, and an ever more pronounced congressional distaste for public accountability all characterize our time, and all have contributed to the increasingly common resort to the courts for the resolution of public-policy disputes. Even domains of policy choice once unthinkably surrenderable to judicial processes have come under judicial sway, often at the very invitation of their traditional overlords. Congressmen themselves have brought suits seeking, for example, to forestall the abrogation of treaties, enjoin the president's deferral of the expenditure of appropriated funds, and inhibit furnishing aid to armed partisans resisting foreign tyrannies. In other times, such controversies among members of Congress and the executive would have been addressed by ordinary political means, including legislation, public education, and elections. Today, it appears, they are ever more likely to be addressed (at least in the attempt) by extraordinary means: litigation.

It is hardly the purpose of this essay to justify, let alone to commend, this state of affairs. Indeed, the weight of the evidence overwhelmingly shows that the dependence of our public policy-making system on litigation is lamentable, both corruptive of policy and corrosive of the law. But the reality must be faced. Litigation is, today, a significant part of the process of making and sustaining policy choices. Legislators no less than interest groups choose to make themselves plaintiffs. Venerable legal notions such as standing, ripeness, and the requirement of an actual case or controversy are either distorted beyond recognition or discarded altogether. With others having selected the weapons and chosen the field of battle, the president and his executives are called upon to defend the choices of policy—and the changes in policy—that they have made. The theme of this essay is that such disputes can be won, even on the field of litigation, if policy-makers do not cower before the attack but bear up under it, recognizing policy litigation for what it is—an extension of the policy-making process itself. Litigation is probably an unavoidable path to the vindication of most contemporary policy change.

Litigation is certainly a necessary path to the ultimate restoration of the proper distinctions between policy and law. The boundaries of policy and law, of politics and justice, of the sphere of will and the sphere of reason, have first been trespassed, then disfigured, and then erased in little increments, enactment by enactment, lawsuit by lawsuit, acquiescence by acquiescence, over time. James Madison warned that "there are more instances of the abridgment of freedom of the people by gradual and silent encroachments of those in power than by violent and sudden usurpations." A great challenge of our time is whether or not those encroachments can be redressed in the same way, step by step, case by case, until the freedom of the people and the Constitution's limitations upon government are restored. The first step in taking up the challenge is understanding squarely the part that litigation will have in the struggles to come.

Notes

1.   This theme and its larger juridical and economic implications are explored in Joseph A. Morris, "Congressional Cowardice: An Inquiry into the Causes of the Public Law Explosion" in National Legal Center for the Public Interest, *The Legal Assault on the Economy* (1986), 1.

2.   More and more the law has come to be seen by some as the decisive tool for the redistribution of rights and property. Contemporary "legal activists" seek the creation of new kinds of lawsuits and remedies to achieve radical redistributionist ends. It is helpful to remember, therefore, that our underlying common law heritage is anything but redistributionist. Its clear goal is the protection of property, including voluntary transactions involving property. Thus, the paradigm of justice at common law is the restoration of the victim of a tort or of a breach of contract to the condition (or its economic equivalent) that he would have been in but for the wrongful conduct of the tortfeasor or contract-breaker, such restoration to be paid for by (and only by) the wrongdoer. Hence, my assertion that lawyers—or at least common lawyers—represent a kind of conservative impulse.

8 Preemptive Compromise and Other Pitfalls in Legislative Strategy

CLIFFORD BARNHART

Editors' Note: This chapter examines legislative strategy during the Reagan Administration. Clifford Barnhart, a pseudonym for an individual with a great deal of Hill experience, explains the reasons behind the early 1981 legislative successes and why those successes have not been repeated. Practical suggestions are provided for the conservative political appointee who wants to learn how to "work" the Hill.

Ronald Reagan's election in 1980 was the beginning of a revolution. During the campaign he proposed to fundamentally redirect the role, expanse, and power of the federal government. His sweeping victory brought in a Republican-controlled Senate for the first time in 25 years, and a House of Representatives dominated by a conservative majority coalition. Thus, all the factors necessary to move the Reagan Revolution forward were in place when the President was inaugurated in January 1981.

A decision was made to limit the legislative program in the first months of the new Administration to economic issues: the budget and tax reduction. All of the President's electoral coalition agreed to this initial focus, assuming that their broader agenda would be dealt with after these economic issues were voted on.

There was a boldness of approach in the first months of 1981 that had not been seen in Washington since the early days of the New Deal. Many players in the White House were new to Washington, or to Ronald Reagan's inner circle, or to the legislative arena. Their newness to Washington made the early White House team much more susceptible to taking advice from allies on the Hill; a close working relationship emerged that has not since been resurrected. Those who would later consolidate authority to say "no" within the White House had not yet done so.

These factors, combined with the overwhelming mandate of the 1980 election and the aggressive proposals of the transition teams and outside forces like The Heritage Foundation, helped to force the pace of change. In a sense, because the people in the White House did not know that what they were doing was impossible, they were able to succeed. Ignorance and naiveté made them much better partners to conservatives on the Hill in the effort to implement President Reagan's proposals. Instead of trimming their sails, they moved forward resolutely.

In this first phase, the legislative program of the White House and the style of leadership was *entrepreneurial*. The political operatives were willing to stake out a clear position and to pursue what had to be done to make the economic program succeed—even at the risk of losing on a vote in the House or Senate. They were guided by what needed to be done, not merely by what could be achieved. If this meant a legislative defeat, they were willing to accept that risk. If they suffered a loss, the plan was to go over the heads of the Congress directly to the voters.

There are three major examples of this entrepreneurial leadership: the budget act (outlining spending priorities), the budget reconciliation package (implementing domestic spending cuts), and the tax reduction act. All were debated, passed, and signed into law by August 1981.

The initial budget proposal by the Administration was an about-face from the proposals that had dominated since the days of the Great Society. It ended some programs, combined others into block grants, and altered the priorities of the federal government. It was a fairly radical document. Throughout the month before the vote on the House floor, it appeared certain that the Administration was going to lose on this first major test. The reaction of the White House was not to alter its goal, but to adopt an aggressive plan to target wavering Congressmen to get them to support the President. Working with grassroots organizations, the White House made a concerted drive to go to the voters, who, in turn, would bring pressure on their elected representatives. There was no talk of compromising on the substance of the proposal in order to win. While, in retrospect, the budget act was passed easily, no one expected that to be the case at the time. The first major victory was a result of setting a tough agenda and going over the head of the Congress to achieve it.

On two more occasions, the budget reconcilation and tax reduction bills, this strategy was used successfully. A good bit of horse trading occurred on both bills, but the White House never surrendered on policy substance. When it came down to the final critical votes in the House, the Administration was willing to take the risk of losing the vote rather than give more ground. In the case of the reconciliation bill, this meant going so far as to join in public support of a challenge to the rule under which the bill was to be considered. It was virtually unprecedented for a president to risk his prestige on a technical issue of this sort, yet it was done, and what is more, it was done on a moment's notice, on the request of conservative congressional leaders. Few more successful examples of effective teamwork between the White House and the Hill exist.

General opinion was again certain that the Administration would lose. Informal head counts often showed the Administration far behind. The White House never wavered in its course. In a period of two days, on both substantive and procedural votes, the Administration and its supporters never won any of these decisions by more than four votes. But they never blinked, nor did they lose any of the critical votes—thus the Reagan Revolution was born.

The tax reduction act was much the same story. At the beginning of the week before the vote took place, House Speaker Tip O'Neill predicted, and the newspapers headlined, that the Administration would lose on the proposed tax reform. In fact, the White House strategy proved out, and once again *without a preemptive compromise* the Administration was victorious. In all three of these cases, the Administration took a risk and was willing to lose a vote if that was necessary to carry the fight forward. Still, the entrepreneurial phase of leadership came to an abrupt end after the August recess of 1981.

For the remainder of President Reagan's first term, the manner of leadership from the White House senior staff was custodial as opposed to entrepreneurial. The emphasis was on *risk aversion*. The goal was to keep the record clean and undefeated. If this meant compromising before the vote, then that was what happened. For example, the President vetoed the continuing appropriations resolution in 1981. But instead of standing firm with the threat of a second veto and insisting on the double-digit cuts originally requested, the Administration settled for a $4-billion cut. Tax increases were proposed and passed in 1982 to take the pressure off budget cuts. In 1983, the Social Security Commission built a compromise that took the issue away from the White House and the people who were proposing fundamental reforms in the pension and retirement system. Again, the strategy was to evade a difficult problem—not to change government policy.

As stated, during this second phase of the Administration, a premium was put on winning. Above all else, *the President could not be on the losing side* even if a tactical loss might have led to a strategic victory. Unfortunately, an adversary who is unwilling to take a risk is an adversary who can be manipulated.

A second change in the Administration concerned the focus of legislative strategy. During the initial phase of the Reagan Presidency, the focus had been on the slim conservative majorities in the House and the Senate. Legislation was developed and compromises were struck with the aim of keeping the membership of this group intact and in line for the passage of each bill. During the second phase of the Reagan Presidency, the focus shifted. For no apparent reason, the White House began to seek legislative support among the liberal opposition. Compromises were struck accordingly. This search for a broader base of support was in keeping with a goal of risk aversion, but it also led to a significant dilution of legislative content.

A third change was the decision not to promote seriously the social agenda of the Reagan coalition. As one high White House official reportedly said of "social issue" conservative groups: "We will give them nothing but rhetoric." This strategic choice had important indirect consequences that were not fully understood by the White House staff. As it became increasingly apparent that the social agenda would be left to languish, the multitude of right wing groups concerned with these issues never rejected President Reagan; but their willingness to mobilize and expend effort in support of the White House naturally waned.

In 1981, the active support of these groups, with their vast grassroots networks, had played an integral part in the success of the Reagan Administration on economic legislation even though economics was not their primary concern. In later years, the decline in activism of these groups significantly weakened the Reagan Administration on all fronts: economic, military, and foreign policy. Thus, the ironic decision to exclude from the White House agenda many of the key issues and forces responsible for placing Ronald Reagan in the White House limited what the President could accomplish in later years in office.

Each of these changes in legislative approach preceded the losses in the off-year elections of 1982 and therefore cannot be attributed to a weakened position on the Hill. On the contrary, the changes in legislative strategy themselves probably contributed to the 1982 election losses.

The change in senior staff at the White House in January 1985 resulted in yet another approach to Congress. This new style might best be characterized as *risk limitation*. A high regard is placed on winning, but no longer to the exclusion of virtually everything else. Also, while the current regime is highly centralized, there are more people who have involvement in legislative strategy and, paradoxically, greater independence among those participants.

Two examples will serve to identify the current style of leadership. Both incidents occurred on the Contra aid bill proposed by President Reagan. First, during the weeks leading up to the initial House vote in March 1986, a no-compromise attitude was struck by the White House. The Administration proposal was already an accommodation on what was thought to be politically possible, and it was determined that any further retreat might be untenable on policy grounds.

At first, it was difficult to convince members of the House that the usual compromise would not be forthcoming. Over a period of several weeks, the steadfast Administration position began to persuade members that in fact there would be no alternative. However, just at the critical moment, a senior White House staffer told the press that, if necessary to win, they would consider a compromise. The effort to gather votes for the strong initial Administration position was stopped cold.

The second example occurred after the House voted to defeat the President's plan and the Senate voted to approve aid to the freedom fighters. The Nicaraguan military launched an attack against the Contras into Honduras. This offered the Administration a chance to move quickly to get a second vote in the House of Representatives. It would have entailed a risk because the House had already adjourned for its Easter recess and a special session would have been necessary. Unfortunately, caution prevailed and the Congress was not called back into session. As a result, the opportunity was lost. Still, in late June 1986 the Administration was able to put together with the aid of conservative Republicans and Democrats a joint humanitarian/military aid package which narrowly passed in the House. This enactment serves as a perfect example of a risk-limitation strategy which resulted in less aid and harmful delay but which still, through diligence, yielded a success of sorts.

• • •

In retrospect, there is no doubt that the first efforts of the Reagan White House team were the most successful. They set forth the boundaries of the economic revolution and achieved a significant first step toward changing the direction of our government. The legislative strategy practiced during this initial period provides many useful lessons for the future.

Clearly, holding to initial proposals and risking a temporary loss was worth the reward. Such a policy of judicious brinkmanship provides distinct advantages. Since votes cannot be precisely forecast, significant victories may emerge on seemingly "non-winnable" legislation. Each of the economic victories of 1981 demonstrates this. Narrow vote margins and significant policy change often go hand in hand, while a tendency to steer clear of tough fights on the ground that Presidential prestige might be damaged ensures that change will be muted.

Consistent *preemptive compromise* weakens the bargaining position of the White House. "Fence-sitters," who do not wish to support an Administration policy but who would be embarrassed by a clear vote against it, learn they can wait for the usual watered-down alternative to emerge from the White House. Correspondingly, allies of the White House who would be willing to go along with the Administration, even at a personal political cost, will also stand aside if they expect a future compromise to render sacrifices pointless. Friends will not go out on a limb if they expect the limb to be needlessly sawed off. Allies inside Congress and outside, as well, are unlikely to expend effort on a battleline that they expect will quickly and arbitrarily shift or disappear in order to create a continual appearance of "winning."

Acceptance of losses must be part of a sound legislative approach. Though losing can never be the ultimate aim of any endeavor, often a tactical loss can lead to strategic victory. A clear, uncompromised vote, even if lost, allows the Administration to define the issue, focuses public attention, and places the opposition on record. That record then becomes the basis for discrediting opponents in the future. A succession of losses on an important issue raises the ante for fence-sitting Congressmen. It may be all right with the folks back home (who aren't paying close attention) to vote against the Nicaraguan freedom fighters once, but voting against them four, five, or six times may be another matter. In this way, loss may be translated into victory.

The political balance on the Hill is not permanent, and aggressive legislative strategy can be used to change that balance. Such a strategy may include repeated, deliberate tactical losses on issues where the opposition is most politically vulnerable. These votes can focus attention, raise activism, and do maximum damage to political opponents in the next election. Such a strategy is of course the exact opposite of one that steers clear of losses in order to preserve White House prestige; it is also a strategy aimed at changing the government and expanding political power—as opposed to treading water.

Another mistaken notion linked to risk aversion is that you can fight only one battle at a time. In fact, the number of issues can be widened greatly, because each victory makes you stronger. The President's persuasive ability is not a set stock of capital that can only be drawn down. Rather, it is a resource that can be built on and added to, if used correctly. To avoid risk is to avoid opportunity; without taking a chance there can be no reward.

A realistic legislative strategy must also recognize that effective political power stems not from transient polls of Presidential popularity, but from a coalition of active supporting groups. Legislative strategy must seek to build and expand the electoral coalition, not take it for granted. A related lesson for groups within the coalition is that political power means mutual support; once some groups decide to "sit out" fights on issues that are crucial to other members of the coalition, the coalition begins to unravel and everyone loses.

There are a few additional useful rules for dealing with Congress that are the same whether one is at the White House or elsewhere in the executive branch. One important rule, which is both obvious and neglected, is to remember that elected officials have interests of their own. Each has his own unique strengths and weaknesses. To be successful, one must understand the individual personalities and strengths of the Congressmen and Senators.

Such an understanding helps in targeting the right Congressman. It is essential to find a "hero" to carry an issue or idea forward. For example, Henry Hyde is the "hero" on right-to-life issues, Jack Kemp is the "hero" on supply-side economics, and Jim McClure is the "hero" on SALT II. Without finding a champion, it is difficult to get an issue carried to a conclusion. Considering the enormous number of issues on which Congressmen must work, without some personal involvement it is impossible to keep an issue at the forefront.

To enhance the chances of success, one should start on the issue when it is in subcommittee. Often this is when it is easiest to form a coalition to move an issue forward. At this point, most Congressmen will not have taken a stand; an early start thus eliminates the policy surprises that elected officials particularly dislike. There is no quicker way to fail than to come to a Congressman or Senator after he has taken a position on an issue.

Sometimes it is impossible to find a hero or even an advocate on a sub-committee or committee. Then a little wildcatting is in order. There are certain Congressmen and Senators who are more willing to offer amendments on the floor. In addition, there are groups in both the House and the Senate who are devoted allies of the Reagan program. In the Senate, the Senate Steering Committee is a helpful ally. In the House, the Republican Study Committee and the Conservative Opportunity Society are the most active advocates of the Reagan agenda. These are good places to look if one intends to bypass a committee and introduce an issue on the floor. They are also good places to look if a political appointee would like to generate legislative activity on a conservative initiative that has, for one reason or another, become stalled in the executive branch.

There are two final rules of thumb which it behooves any advocate to remember. First, make an effort to meet people before you need them. It is much more advantageous to come begging to a friend, rather than a stranger, no matter how philosophically compatible he may be. Second, every relationship is a two-way street, and one's requests will receive a much better hearing if there is a sympathetic ear on the return call.

The Reagan Revolution has changed the federal government. Although the speed and the extent of the changes may not be fast enough or go far enough for many of the Reagan faithful, the transition has been made. In addition, a new group of conservative leaders is being trained on the job. In future administrations, the lessons learned will help move the conservative revolution forward.

9 Working with the Hill

JADE WEST

Editors' Note: Football, we are often told, is a question of block-ing and tackling. Success lies in the fundamentals. In this piece Mrs. West, the Executive Director of the Senate Steering Committee, deals with "blocking and tackling" in the legislative process from which larger successes spring.

Any analysis of how to have an impact on Capitol Hill should begin with the oft-cited sentiment that no man's life, liberty or property is safe while the legislature is in session. Those most likely to agree with that state-ment are probably conservative Hill staffers with close first-hand knowledge of how Congress works—or fails to work. Conservatives both on the Hill and in government agencies may well long for the "good old days" when the Congress was a part-time institution and life, liberty, and property were safe for at least a few months a year. One might also point to a number of states which prove that governments can in fact run quite well—and often better financially—with part-time legislatures. Neverthe-less, the unavoidable fact is that the U.S. Congress is a full-time body, in session more than it is out; and one must deal with that reality to have an impact on policy in the legislative arena.

Moreover, it is arguable that Congress is not in fact making policy attuned to the conservative rhetoric of the Reagan Administration, but is merely slowing down the constant leftward drift. If that is so, it is even more necessary for conservatives to become effective on the Hill in order to implement a conservative legislative agenda.

It is critically important to remember that "The Congress" has no specific policies, platforms, or positions. "The Congress" is 535 individual members working with thousands of staff members to enact, defeat, or amend a wide range of legislative initiatives. It is not uncommon for Administration personnel to bemoan the fact that their agency cannot pursue a specific policy initiative because "The Congress" is opposed to it. To suggest that a policy should be abandoned because "The Congress" is against it is tantamount to conceding defeat before the rules of the game are clearly established.

One must first, then, be willing to play the game. Given that willingness, one must have a clearly-defined and constant policy to sell—failure on this score would be the subject of a book in and of itself. Assuming both a consistent policy and a willingness to promote it, one then must have a basic understanding of Hill operations. That means understanding legislative scheduling and timetables as well as the basic civics-class description of the process by which legislation is introduced, amended, conferenced, and enacted or defeated. It is not necessary to know the intricacies of the complex, even Byzantine, rules of the House or Senate, although it would not hurt to have a contact who is familiar with procedural nuances.

Start with the basic principles. For example, there are specific deadlines in the spring for the reporting and adoption of a First Concurrent Resolution on the Budget, after the adoption of which authorizations and appropriations are properly considered. Funds cannot be appropriated for an agency until a budget is adopted and an authorization is passed. Another example is the House of Representatives' extremely strict rule for the germaneness of amendments and the inhibitions that rule imposes on legislative initiatives. Similarly, even in the more open Senate it is not in order to legislate on an appropriations bill.

Hill staff understand better than outsiders that these rules often are comprised of "smoke and mirrors," and that such restrictions as specific timetables set forth in the Budget Act are honored more in the breach than in the practice. In reality, the primary rule in the Senate is that "you can do anything with the unanimous consent of the members."

The rules, however, do exist, at least on paper. And they provide ready-made excuses for inaction. For example, if an idea for a legislative initiative is brought to the Hill after an agency with arguable jurisdiction over the subject matter has been authorized, any Hill staffer has a perfectly good reason not to be of help: "We have already passed that authorization, and it would not be in order to offer that as an amendment to an appropriations bill. Sorry." Thus, failure to understand and operate within well-established legislative timetables, however arbitrary they may be, invites rejection of good ideas and minimizes conservative impact on policies. By understanding and operating within congressional timetables, one is much more likely to get Hill staff to cooperate, or at least to come up with a creative reason for not doing so.

On a similar note, it is often suggested that each new administration has but one year in which to propose real legislative initiatives. The relative success of the Reagan Administration in 1981 in comparison to any subsequent year confirms that hypothesis. Although an administration cannot simply stop promoting legislation once that first year is over, a general rule of thumb applies; the earlier in a Congress that an initiative is brought forward, the greater its chance for success. As with every rule, there are exceptions, especially in the Senate where non-germane amendments provide an ongoing opportunity for legislative initiatives. Nevertheless, if an agency wants to find a member of Congress who will take a policy idea and implement it, that member should be given enough time to be effective. If on the other hand one is simply looking for a bill number on a piece of paper for political purposes, timing and the likelihood of enactment become irrelevant. By and large, if ideas are to have a real impact on Congress they must be given time to percolate in congressional offices and then to turn the wheels of the legislative process.

Given that knowledge of the process is important (and that is equally true in terms of the need for Hill staff to understand how agencies function), it is even more fundamental to have a consistent policy and to know with whom to deal in order to effectively advance it. One of the most frequently heard complaints among conservatives on the Hill is that this Administration seems more intent on accommodating its enemies than in working with its friends. At present the Democrats run the House, which makes a successful guerrilla operation necessary for promotion of a conservative agenda. Unfortunately, with the liberal predominance in the Senate, despite nominal GOP control, the same need exists in that chamber. It would be logical, therefore, to assume that a successful conservative guerrilla operation also best serves this Administration.

All too often conservatives on the Hill find that our main opponent is not the liberal establishment in Congress, but people within the Reagan Administration. Agency or Administration opposition to a congressional conservative initiative is both discouraging and demoralizing. The tendency of executive branch personnel to negotiate with their opposition and ignore or even oppose their congressional friends constitutes concession of defeat on policy issues without a fight, and undermines conservative allies who are trying to move a conservative Reagan agenda on the Hill. The consequences may be that the next time the Administration needs help, those allies may not be willing to provide it.

To the extent that conservatives in the Administration influence or control policy, they should remember that negotiating with the opposition on the Hill while ignoring allies sabotages not only their allies but their policies, and thus allows the opposition to dictate terms and run the show. Default in leadership by the Administration irreparably damages the ability of conservatives on the Hill to implement conservative policy.

The result can be the same even when the executive branch merely allows policy to shift and drift, without actively compromising with the opposition. Eventually the agency concerned—or the White House—will be unable to find members of Congress and staffers willing to cooperate.

If a friendly member of Congress is willing to take an issue and push the Administration's agenda, agency conservatives should make a heroic and valiant effort to give their congressional ally full and consistent support. If conservative members of Congress are unwilling to take active roles in promoting policy initiatives for fear of being left stranded, the entire conservative movement suffers.

Because not all conservatives in the agencies, regrettably, have direct control over policy, agency staffers should maintain their access by developing good rapport with Hill allies. To be operationally effective, there are a few basic assumptions one should make about Hill people. (A Hill bias is fully admitted here; conversely many Hill staff could use a similar briefing on how to deal effectively with federal agencies.) The assumptions: (1) Hill staff are very busy; (2) they have some knowledge of the issues of interest to most agency staffers, but possibly not as much knowledge as an agency specialist; (3) conservatives on the Hill are just as interested in implementing a conservative agenda as are conservatives in other areas of government; and (4) yes, Hill staff tend to be a little arrogant.

Assume that Hill staff are very busy. Of course they are. So are agency staff. Washington is a city of very busy people. Those that really aren't all that busy pretend they are; the more senior the position, the busier the individual is likely to be (or pretend to be). And the busier an individual genuinely is, the more valuable he is likely to be as a Hill contact. These are not simply gratuitous points: assuming that the most useful contacts are also the busiest, one should be careful not to waste time in dealing with them. For example, do not call the Staff Director of a congressional committee to ask what time a hearing is scheduled to begin. Do not call a member's Administrative Assistant (AA) or Legislative Director (LD) to request a copy of yesterday's *Congressional Record.* However, if the need is for political insights as to how a committee member is likely to vote or what testimony will be most effective in upcoming hearings, call the most senior committee staff contact reachable. If the need is to determine whether a member is willing to introduce an amendment of particular importance to an agency, call that member's AA or LD. In short, an executive branch appointee should waste others' time no more than he enjoys having other people waste his.

Assume that a Hill contact knows something about the issue on which one is working, but that he does not know everything. Many agency staffers are specialists in a field; most Hill staff are generalists. An AA or an LD must have a working knowledge of a range of issues that may include foreign policy and fiscal and domestic issues and a little about "bombs and rockets." A Committee Staff Director must be familiar with every issue over which his committee has jurisdiction. A generalist simply cannot spend sufficient time to become an expert on each issue with which he deals. Understanding that liability and being a reliable source of information and assistance can make one an invaluable ally in dealing with contacts on the Hill. Do not assume that Hill allies are nitwits in need of special training (many *are* even specialists in their fields), but more points are earned by offering information and shared knowledge than by assuming that everyone knows as much as an agency specialist.

Also assume that proven reliably conservative allies on the Hill are just as committed to promoting the conservative agenda as are those in the agencies. If a Hill contact declines to take on a project, do not immediately assume he has sold out on that issue. Occasionally a conservative contact simply cannot provide a requested favor or service. This is not necessarily an abdication of philosophy any more than it is when the slow turning of bureaucracy's wheels makes impossible action which the Hill would like to see an agency take.

Assume that Hill staff are occasionally arrogant. So are agency personnel. Not taking oneself, one's position, or one's importance too seriously (as well as maintaining a slightly irreverent sense of humor about inside-the-Beltway Washington) not only helps keep one from being too arrogant; it also makes it easier to deal with those who are.

On the practical side, when preparing information for Hill staff and members of Congress, keep it short. Members of Congress are given hundreds of pages of material to read daily, covering the entire spectrum of political and legislative issues (occasionally a snide comment can be heard as to the length of the average member's attention span, but no one could read the amount of material that appears on a member's desk each day). The material that gets read is concise, to the point, and full of useful data. If there is a lot of material to be presented, summarize it in a cover sheet and attach the more lengthy documentation. Don't waste good, well-researched material by making it so long that a major commitment of time is required to use it.

In testifying before congressional committees, direct the written testimony to the proper audience—the staff who read and use the technical information agency personnel can provide. Use actual verbal testimony to make salient points aimed at the members of Congress physically present at the hearing or who might read the hearing transcript itself.

A point that should always be of concern: be absolutely certain that any information provided to a congressional staffer is accurate. The first rule of success—and survival—for Hill staff is "Protect your boss." This includes providing the member with current, up-to-date, and unerringly accurate (or at least politically defensible) information. A staffer who writes a floor statement or speech for a Congressman or Senator and has included incorrect, incomplete, inaccurate, or simply untrue information will probably not write any more speeches. The member of Congress may never learn of the source of that information, but the staffer will never forget, regardless of whether or not he remains on the Hill.

Do not make the mistake, as we all so often do, of losing overall perspective or becoming so involved in an issue that all others are ignored. The appointee should not presume that everyone else in this political city necessarily agrees that the appointee's issue is the most critical issue facing the Administration—not to mention the country, and Western civilization. As exaggerated as that may seem, there has been at least one agency congressional affairs officer who was so intense in stressing the importance of *his* issue to the conservative movement that many of his natural allies on the Hill simply refused to take or return his calls.

At risk of grossly oversimplifying, a few additional observations might be in order. In attempting to enact conservative philosophy through legislation, success can often depend on the simple element of access. And access depends often on small and seemingly unimportant details. First of all, one should identify the Hill people who work in the offices and committees important to one's agency. Specifically, avoid calling a friend who handles foreign policy to inquire about a tax bill. Callers that prove repeatedly annoying eventually will not have their calls taken or returned.

One should avoid asking Hill staff contacts to do some favor every time one calls. An occasional call from an agency appointee offering unsolicited but valuable information will be much welcomed, and will keep the door open. Hill staff learn quickly which agency staffers always call with a request for help that involves time and effort. Those calls are taken more and more reluctantly, resulting in a loss of access.

In short, the executive branch appointee should treat Hill contacts and colleagues much as the appointee himself or herself would prefer to be treated. Don't always ask for something; occasionally offer something. Consider conservative Hill associates as allies and friends and not as adversaries, antagonists, or subservients.

Conservatives share a common objective and, unfortunately, a long road ahead before we have achieved our goals. It is important to always keep foremost in mind that common objective. The successful implementation of legislative initiatives, and the making of real public policy from shared conservative philosophy—not the acquisition of personal power, prestige, or position—should be the basis for conservative action and cooperation.

10 Building Private Sector/ Public Sector Coalitions

RONALD D. UTT

Editors' Note: In 1787 James Madison wrote that interest groups "must be involved in the necessary and ordinary operations of the government." Too often in American politics, Madison's prescription has meant that narrow special interests receive special favors and advantages from government action. In this chapter, Dr. Utt, the Deputy Chief Economist at the U.S. Chamber of Commerce, provides practical advice for conservative political appointees who wish to build broad-based legislative coalitions that work for the passage of legislation which more accurately represents the public interest.

I am afraid that I am going to have to begin this chapter on a sour note, calling attention to one more failing that can be attributed to political executives and officials in both the executive and legislative branches. In doing this I should note that I myself have served as a manager in the federal bureaucracy and can easily appreciate the multitude of difficulties appointees confront each day in trying to perform their responsibilities. Indeed, many of the observations below are drawn from my own experience and failings during short careers at the Department of Housing and Urban Development (HUD) and the Office of Management and Budget (OMB).

My complaint is simply this: in fighting the many battles to implement the President's agenda, the typical political executive fails to solicit or take advantage of the resources that are available to him in what euphemistically passes for Washington's private sector—the vast array of trade associations, professional organizations, public-interest advocacy groups, and (shudder) law firms that populate this town in an alarming number. Appointees will often fail to utilize outside resources even when they are offered.

In my more than five years of work in the public policy arena from the perspective of an economist/lobbyist at the Chamber of Commerce, I have pondered this failing—frequently in frustration. I have concluded that there are probably three reasons to explain it. All are easy to understand.

- The first reason is that political appointees are simply not aware of the help that outside groups could offer in the struggle to implement policies.

- The second reason is that what little contact political appointees have had with outside groups (and I use that term broadly to describe anyone vaguely involved in lobbying) has been unfavorable and has thus encouraged conservative appointees to lump all groups into the category of potential opponents and obstacles.

- The third reason is that as an embattled minority often attacked from all sides, appointees adopt forms of emotional protection that encourage them to stay with their own kind and refrain from venturing out into hostile territory.

I am sure that there are some pseudo-sophisticated psychological explanations for this last sort of behavior, but since I am not adept at that field of inquiry, I will simply note the tendency in passing and focus my remarks on the first two.

On the first two points let me say the following: in my experience it is the rare public servant, in Congress or the executive branch, who knows how to work the Washington advocacy groups to his or her advantage in the pursuit of public policy goals. Let me also say that those few who do know how to do this, or who even bother to seek such support, have been remarkably successful in meeting their objectives. But because most political executives don't bother to seek out and take advantage of potential allies, their public policy struggles generally take the form of themselves versus the world. In these "heroic struggles," the outcome is predictable—the appointee loses, and so does the nation. As a consequence, the appointee spends the rest of his or her career administering someone else's agenda; all too often it is an agenda that the President is opposed to and is committed to change.[1]

Let's consider reason number one: the ignorance factor. There are thousands of advocacy groups in Washington. They range in size from one person working on one tiny issue on a part-time basis to massive organizations like the Chamber of Commerce with a staff of a thousand following hundreds of diverse issues. To further complicate matters, these organizations often form into temporary ad hoc coalitions to work on a single issue. The Chamber of Commerce participates in eighty-seven such coalitions at the moment, which is an increase of more than fourteen from a year ago. Bearing names such as the Hydroelectric Relicensing Strategy Coalition and the Coalition to Clarify the Foreign Corrupt Practices Act (I didn't make either of these up), these coalitions cover numerous issues and have as their purpose some change in some specific public policy. Many of these permanent groups and ad hoc coalitions offer potential resources to help executive branch appointees achieve their public policy objectives whenever there is a conformity of views.

But how does one find such groups? Obviously, there is no way that anyone can keep apprised of the existence or changing interests of the thousands of advocacy groups in Washington, but that shouldn't deter one from looking. If an appointee knows his issue as well as he should, he should also have a good idea of what sorts of businesses and advocacy groups might have an interest in it. Most large companies have an office in town. Most large trade associations like the Chamber of Commerce or the National Association of Manufacturers have a large number of staff specialists and publish staff directories that can assist in a search. Having identified potentially relevant groups, the appointee should give them a call and determine their position on the issue. They might not be able to help, but chances are pretty good that they can give the names of people and organizations that might. One thing leads to another, and before one knows it, the makings of a coalition emerge. But one cannot be shy or deterred by rejection. All this might sound simple-minded and plati-tudinous, but this is, quite simply, what people like myself do for a living. It is what every conservative appointee should be doing to enhance the prospects for policy change. It works.

Whenever I am confronted with a public policy problem or opportunity, the first thing I do is get on the phone and try to find some good allies. Invariably, I find them and, of course, advance my prospects for success well beyond what they would be if I tried to do it alone. Why do these other groups help? Or, better yet, why should they help an appointee in the executive branch? There are a number of reasons. The first is unremitting self-interest. Any change in law or policy can create both winners and losers. The losers are easy to identify: they're the first ones to call up and complain. The winners are tougher to find for reasons related to human nature that are not easily articulated but can readily be envisioned in the form of an average American sitting back and watching the news on TV of some initiative that might benefit him, and saying to himself: "Well, isn't that nice," and then switching the channel. Because the political system ignores all social impacts except those which are translated into immediate political pressure, it is important that these diffuse and silent beneficiaries of policy change become involved in the process. A deliber-ate effort must be made to inform and motivate the relevant groups and representatives.

The second reason an outside group might help is simply because of the principle involved. Although the policy proposal may not directly affect them, their business, or their constituency one way or the other, they may, as good citizens, agree with President Reagan's agenda and be willing to do something to insure its success. All they need is a little motivation and direction. Believe it or not, there are a lot of people in

Washington who are motivated by issues of principle. Strange but true.

Finally, there is motivation based on guilt or the simple process of horse trading. A political executive should not underestimate the power of his office or the respect with which appointees are held by the private sector. A request by the White House or by an officer of the executive branch is not something that is treated lightly by folks on the outside. In the end, we may not be able to help, but sometimes we will. Sometimes we will help just because we were asked and we cannot think of a good reason to say no. Related to this is horse trading, the desire on the part of many of us in the advocacy community to do a favor for someone in government who might later be able to do a favor for us. Do not underestimate this motive as an important way to garner support. A good political manager on the outside must have a pocketful of chips that he can use on the proper occasion, and will work to build his store. I know because I always have a couple of chips in my pocket and they do come in handy at the most unexpected times.

Appointees who do not actively seek outside support are forced to react to what others in the advocacy community want from them. In that case it is all give and no gain and the appointee's influence is diminished accordingly. This relates to the second reason I cited why government executives do not seem to rely as much as they should on outside support. To the extent that most appointees have had any dealings with advocacy groups, they have generally been instigated by a special interest group approaching the appointee for some favor or concession—often at the expense of the larger public interest. The process need not work in only this way, but the appointee is the only one that can reverse it.

Let me illustrate some of the points made above with case studies drawn from recent advocacy campaigns. A very successful instance of joint action between government officials and outside advocacy groups was an effort to halt the $9-billion bailout of the Rural Electrification Administration's (REA) loan fund in 1984. Backed by the National Rural Electrification Cooperative Association (NRECA), the powerful and well-financed trade group representing the co-ops receiving subsidized government loans, the House of Representatives passed, by a wide margin, a $9-billion bailout of the near-insolvent loan fund. The bill was opposed by the White House and the REA, the government agency that administers the program. Working by itself and depending only upon the unassailable logic of its arguments, the REA was unable to avoid an overwhelming loss in the House. But in the brief interval between House passage and Senate consideration, the officials at the REA began to look around town for allies. It was their good fortune to come to a meeting of the Jefferson Group, one of the many informal coalitions mentioned earlier, and make an appeal for help on grounds of fiscal responsibility and economic efficiency. Several of the groups agreed to help out, and an action-oriented coalition was formed.

The campaign that ensued was one of the most difficult legislative battles in which I have ever been involved. The NRECA boasts an annual operating budget of over $29 million. Since this was its only legislative initiative of the year, the NRECA was able to throw the full resources of its organization, including an extensive grassroots network, into the effort. Arrayed against them was a loose coalition of a few business trade associations, a couple of free-market oriented public interest groups, the leadership of the Department of Agriculture and the REA, and a few concerned Senators.

Working closely together and determined to win, this opposition group, which never numbered more than a dozen concerned individuals, was able to thwart every attempt of the NRECA to advance its costly legislation. Our coordinated effort was designed to take advantage of the unique skills that each of us possessed: Some groups specialized in press relations—where we became especially effective; others handled congressional relations—dividing up the Senate according to which organization had the best relations with a particular group of Senators; while others did the detailed analysis needed to refute the proponents' claims. When victory finally came in the form of an adjourning Senate that had refused to consider the bill, we had managed to convince the majority of the Senators that this was one of the worst pieces of legislation put before them that year. Indeed, we were so successful that the legislation was not introduced in the next Congress.

What was unique about this operation was the day-to-day working arrangement we had with REA staff members during the fight in the Senate. They kept us fully briefed on what was happening and were not shy about asking for our help when it could make a difference. Importantly, they made us feel as if we were an integral part of the process. They frequently sought our advice, and on one occasion Harold Hunter, the Administrator for the REA, even paid me a visit to thank us for our help. This type of behavior is rare indeed. As a consequence of their skillful and thoughtful efforts, all of us made the initiative a top priority. Although the NRECA was the toughest opponent we have ever confronted, we managed to beat them despite the vast resources they devoted to this single piece of legislation. And we could not have done it without the close coordination of the officials at the REA.

Another recent example of a well-coordinated public/private legislative initiative was the enactment of the Gramm-Rudman-Hollings Act and Senator Gramm's masterful performance in building up support for it. Unlike many other legislators, Phil Gramm is adept at putting together and managing a grassroots coalition to support his initiatives. Well before Gramm-Rudman had even been introduced as a bill, Phil Gramm called representatives of advocacy groups to his office for a private meeting about his intentions. Although he had a rough idea of what he wanted to do and how to do it, he nonetheless took the time to consult with each of the major advocacy groups and seek our advice and support. By the time the bill was introduced on the floor of the Senate, all of the major business advocacy and tax limitation groups were fully informed on the initiative, and had their plan of action in place. We were ready to roll. As the battle was fought, Senator Gramm and his staff were always available to meet with us and guide the strategy over changing terrain. Because of this close working relationship with the Senator's office, we were able to send up-to-the-minute lobbying information by way of the Chamber's electronic mail system to our massive grassroots organization. As a result of this and similar efforts by other groups, we managed to get the Congress to pass one of the most radical pieces of budget control legislation ever enacted.

There have been other successes as well—repealing the withholding on interest and dividends is one. The Senate's FY 1986 budget resolution is another. But these successes are overwhelmed by the many failures in trying to advance the agenda of limited government in recent years. What sticks out in these examples of success is the close working relationship that was formed between the government official or elected representative who sponsored the initiative and the outside groups who supported it. Conversely, I suspect that if we study those efforts that did not succeed, we will find that one of the important causes of failure was a neglect of potential support groups that could have made a difference.

For example, the delays in selling Conrail can be partly attributed to the failure to put together outside support beyond Norfolk-Southern Co. Once a coalition was formed, approval of the sale squeaked through the Senate. Unfortunately, the delay in putting such a group together allowed the opponents free rein to set the agenda, present alternatives, and do their "studies." This could create future problems in the House. Similarly, farm policy reforms consistently meet a dismal fate in Congress. The opponents are well organized while the proponents are not. Why no one makes the effort to organize the millions of households which are stuck paying higher food prices and higher taxes totally escapes me, particularly in this age of consumerism.

I hope I have alerted the political appointee to the services available from the Washington advocacy community. I want to emphasize that these services do not come easy and are not without their own frustrations. It will take work on the part of the political appointee, first in just getting to know outside groups and then figuring out who might be of help on emerging conservative issues. This will involve significant search costs, but the potential rewards are very real. Once potential allies are identified, there remains the job of motivating them to do something, particularly if it is not directly related to what their members pay them to do. This will take some creativity and marketing skills, but again, it will be well worth the effort. Building a network of allies requires lead time. It is important to make the initial investment in developing allies before help is actually needed.

An easy way to do this, mentioned earlier, is to contact the big organizations first and get an office staff directory listing areas of responsibility. If some of the staff seem to be involved in issues similar to yours, give them a call, introduce yourself, and seek out their interests. While they may not be able to help, they should certainly be able to direct the appointee to places where help can be found. In this way, you will soon see the beginnings of a future coalition emerge on your Rolodex.

Note

1. The law prohibits officials in the executive branch from using appropriated funds to influence members of Congress. Nothing in this chapter should be taken as encouraging officials to engage in illegal actions. However, there is nothing in the law to prevent officials from seeking out and notifying groups about particular issues; explaining issues and interests to relevant groups; and making an ongoing effort to keep groups apprised of prospects and problems in the evolution of a particular legislative initiative.

11 Media Relations for Reaganauts

PAT KORTEN

Editors' Note: Media relations are an integral part of the work of a political appointee. They are essential to a strategy based on the notion of politics as public education. In this chapter Pat Korten, Deputy Director of Public Affairs for Attorney General Ed Meese, has provided a primer in media relations for political appointees in the Reagan Administration. The author indicates that conservatives play the media relations game with a handicap and must adopt tactics accordingly. Nevertheless, a positive, as opposed to a defensive, style is urged—the author in his own work being a passionate and successful follower of his own advice.

Of all the banana peels of life, this one is among the slipperiest. Dealing with the news media is tough enough for political appointees serving in a Democratic administration. But after all they're dealing with a press corps largely sympathetic to their agenda. But for a conservative Republican—a *Reagan* Republican—tangling with a bunch of reporters who would not in their worst nightmares vote for Ronald Reagan for dogcatcher can be more than unnerving. It can be disastrous.

In some quarters, "media relations" is public relations in the conventional sense. Put out a news release. Hold a news conference. Take a reporter to lunch—or vice versa. Media relations is all of these things, of course. But there's no point in simply repeating here advice that can be found in a dozen public relations texts at the nearest library. Media relations in the Reagan Administration is different. It is trench warfare. It is three-dimensional chess. It is seven-card stud, and the next card is the appointee's ticket back to Omaha. It is political life and death, and the rules of the game are unique in a great many ways.

This chapter has been written as a primer for the conservative struggling to consolidate and expand the Reagan Revolution in the mid-1980's. The circumstances in which this struggle is taking place are far different from those of 50 years ago, or even 15 years ago.

Two things have changed: politics and journalism. Journalism has long been a rough-and-tumble business, but until the 1960's, "good copy" more often had a sensational cast than a political one. Publishers had their biases—Henry Luce wasn't especially fond of Franklin Roosevelt, and it showed—but there remained a certain respect for positions of public leadership, if not always for those who occupied those positions. Dwight Eisenhower and John Kennedy held news conferences, like presidents before them, and the conferences were civil. Though the questions could be tough, there was always an implicit respect in the proceedings. The purpose was to elicit information, to evoke a candid response. Journalist and public officeholder did not function on an equal plane: The public official made the tough decisions and bore the responsibility, while the journalist did his or her best to ensure that the public got the fullest possible account of how, why, and in what fashion those tough decisions got made, and by whom.

Today, to understate the matter, things are different. Respect for public office has all but vanished from the typical Washington news conference. It is virtually unknown on television interview programs. Journalists behave as if they were on an equal plane with the President, the Secretary of State, or the Attorney General. Rather than seeking to draw out their interview guest on a given subject, they *debate* with him, often not even bothering to attribute the argument they're presenting to some third party.

In the course of all this, journalists, especially TV journalists, have taken on the mantle of coequal partner in the establishment of public policy. If the president makes a broadcast address to the nation, a panel of journalists follows immediately with commentary on why he's wrong, misguided, unrealistic, and reprehensibly insensitive to the needs of the poor, world peace, etc.

In a grotesque parody of all this, one network (ABC) even went so far as to put a Soviet "journalist" in this catbird seat following President Reagan's nationally televised address on the defense budget in February 1986. This "journalist," Vladimir Posner, is nothing more than a skilled paid propagandist for the Moscow regime. So twisted has the role of the American journalist become that network executives now seem to find it difficult to distinguish between journalist and propagandist, either here or abroad.

In short, American journalists, especially those in Washington, now regard it as axiomatic that their role includes an affirmative responsiblity to *advocate* public policy positions they regard as wise. Advocacy journalism would be bad enough if the ranks of professional journalists were roughly divided between liberals and conservatives. But the division is anything but equal. Seventy-five percent or more have voted for the Democratic candidate for president in each of the last six presidential elections. The deck is stacked, and success in this area requires that conservatives come to terms with this fact right up front.

Interestingly, one other thing has changed a lot over the past twenty years, and that's politics. In 1964, the American liberal establishment danced on the grave of the Goldwater candidacy and looked forward to an unchallenged pursuit of the modern welfare state. The story of how American conservatism got from there to here is, in large measure, a story of the limitations of the media in their influence upon the course of political history. Learning about these *limitations* is the key to advancing the conservative agenda in the 80's.

Avoiding the Media Filter: The End Run

The media wield political influence by acting as a window through which the American people witness newsmaking events. Needless to say, the glass in the window isn't always perfectly clear. It may be smoked glass, through which one can only barely make out what really happened. The glass may be oddly shaped, and make a thin person look fat or a fat person thin. We may be dealing with stained glass, in which the scene we see bears no resemblance to the scene in the daylight beyond. All of what we see is filtered through the window designed by the glassmakers of the media. Necessarily, this filter governs public perception, and thus has a powerful influence over public policy. It is important to remember, however, that there are several means of communication that the "media filter" cannot control, because they bypass the media entirely. Ronald Reagan and the conservative movement used them all on the road to success. They are all for marathon runners, not sprinters. The "rubber chicken" circuit is exhausting and anything but a key to overnight success. But it is one of the most effective ways of talking directly to the people you want to hear your message. Direct mail designed more to educate than to raise funds can also have a big impact if done right.

On the other hand, the approach offering the most impressive results and the broadest penetration in the body politic is not to bypass the media but *to use the media in spite of themselves*. As with football's running back, there are basically two choices when it comes to getting your message to the public despite the media: You can run through them, or you can run around them. The difference is that you've got to do it without an offensive line looking out for your welfare.

In this game, the *end run* is often the most effective technique, but it requires a lot of preparation and should be attempted mainly by those who are very quick on their feet. In media relations the equivalent of an end run is the *live on-air unedited interview*. Stated simply, whenever you've got the opportunity to do this type of interview, take it. The "filter" disappears entirely for a brief period or has a hole punched in it, and the audience sees, or hears, exactly what the appointee has to say, exactly as he or she wants it said. The interview show host may be easy, or may be rough, but the appointee remains in the driver's seat. The "game" is yours to win or lose. Be sharp and well prepared, and there's no reason you can't come out on top.

Preparation is the key to success, and must involve a plan that

1. maps out in advance, and very specifically, the points you want to make no matter what questions are asked
2. includes a few catchy, quotable comments composed in advance that can be used to make your points memorable and that are a sure bet for the lead in tomorrow's newspaper account
3. prepares you for the toughest, meanest, most difficult questions imaginable in an interview setting

Let's take these one at a time. Point one is the most important, because it will make the difference between an interview conducted on hostile turf and one conducted in significant degree on *your* turf.

First, of course, you must decide upon a handful of important points you want to make. There may be a recent poll that proves conclusively that a large majority of the public favors some controversial conservative policy, but *The New York Times* managed to bury the poll results back on page 64. The appointee's job, then, is to get that bit of information out to the public at every opportunity.

Or perhaps the agency has just inaugurated a new policy of racial neutrality, and the civil rights establishment is painting it as "racism" or "a return to Jim Crow." At every turn the appointee will want to use the term "color-blind society" or something similar. This is not a minor matter of semantics—it has an enormous impact on the way people perceive a major public issue. Ask the folks in the pro-life movement. Met anyone lately who's "anti-life"?

When it comes to squeezing this stuff into an interview, many veteran politicians will state the dictum this way: "No matter what the question is, give them the answer you want to give." My advice would be to use a little finesse. Give a polite, but brief, answer to the [usually] hostile question, then quickly segue into a point you want to make, making the whole thing as seamless as possible.

Here's a real-life example from an interview with Attorney General Meese not too long ago:

Interviewer: "You've said you are the people's lawyer. Are you the people's lawyer or the President's lawyer?"
Attorney General: "I'm both. So far as I know, there's never been a contradiction between these two responsibilities, and I don't think there ever will be with this President. [So much for the loaded question, which is dispensed with in five seconds. Now, without pausing to take a breath . . .] I think the people of the United States demonstrated rather clearly in November of 1984 that the President certainly represented the mainstream of political thinking in the United States and that his

philosophy was what they wanted to have implemented in this country, and that's why it's my job to help implement that." [Central message, repeated again and again: The Reagan philosophy, conservatism, is the mainstream of American political thought. Everyone who hears that message out there in middle America will feel more comfortable in sharing that philosophy, and will more easily resist that criticism coming from the liberal left, whatever the issue.]

Point two—catchy phrase-making—is important whether one is doing a short TV interview or talking with a print reporter. The temptation in government, even among political appointees who ought to know better, is to speak "bureaucratese." It's not unusual to find oneself falling into this trap after only a few short months on the job. Avoid it at all cost.

Don't be afraid of being colloquial. Save the high-flown stuff for a master's thesis or your next government memo. The only voters who are impressed with people who talk that way live in Rhode Island and for some inexplicable reason keep re-electing Claiborne Pell to the Senate. Diligently practice saying "ain't" and "c'mon" and "heck."

The main idea is to plan in advance on using a word or short phrase to make a key point that'll fit in a headline or a ten-second film clip. For some people, this comes naturally. Follow Bob Dole around for a day to see what I mean. Is the federal program you're about to try to zero out "no longer needed," or is it "a scandalous waste of the taxpayer's hard-earned money"? Be boring if you wish, but don't plan on making any news.

Point three—rehearsal—could be the difference between success and miserable failure when faced with a tough interviewer. Here's a good technique to use whether you're the interview subject or the department official you work for will be in the hot seat:

- No more than a day in advance of the interview, sit down around a table with at least several key staff members who, among them, are knowledgeable about everything that is liable to come up in an interview. Don't try this with more than ten people in the room, though—things get too muddled.
- Tell everyone you've invited to this session to come prepared with the toughest questions he can think of regarding issues and subjects that may come up in the interview. Your public affairs people should take the lead in this—they have a good idea of how reporters are liable to attack. Get everyone to psych themselves for the role.
- Throw in some "softball" questions. It is best to give at least a little thought to the possibility that the interview might unexpectedly turn out to be easy and pleasant. This seldom happens, but be prepared nonetheless.

- Critique the answers honestly and frankly. If there's a better way of handling an especially tough question, discuss it. If a proposed answer is a disaster waiting to happen, say that, too.

This preparation technique requires that the interview subject be a secure and self-confident individual. One can get pretty rattled otherwise. But remember: The tough questions can be confronted in rehearsal, or they can be confronted without preparation in front of a camera or microphone with the whole world watching. No one in his right mind would want the latter if given a choice.

Bear in mind that preparation should be different for a three-minute interview than for a one-hour talk show appearance. In the short interview, any reply that lasts more than 20 seconds is wasted breath. For the "quickie" interview, psych yourself for a session of "bumper strip politicking." Short, catchy, and upbeat repartee will leave a solid and favorable impression in the viewer's/listener's mind. But use these same techniques without adaptation on a one-hour talk show and you'll run out of things to talk about in ten minutes.

For the most part, the preparation methods outlined above will work equally well in getting ready for news conferences and other types of news interviews that won't be broadcast live and uncut. I have given all the attention to the one-on-one live interview format because it's the most desirable format from a conservative point of view.

There are other, more expensive, and more exotic, methods of getting the message straight out to middle America, performing an end run on the journalistic filter. Buying satellite time isn't as costly as it once was, and there are a number of companies who would love to sell a half hour on one of their transponders hovering in geosynchronous orbit.

With this approach, you can target one of several kinds of audiences. One is *local* as opposed to *national* media. Local TV news departments might just jump at the chance to do their own "Washington stories" if they can pick up an agency head's news conference, for free, right off the satellite. The Agriculture Department has had a lot of success with this approach, and although its material is picked up largely by smaller stations in agricultural areas, the principle is sound. Local stations are more likely than the network to do longer features, with a more favorable tone, if offered this kind of opportunity.

A variation on this theme is to set up an interactive news conference in which the local stations actually participate, rather than just taping an event occuring in Washington. This costs about the same as a straight satellite feed, but requires that someone be in charge of receiving and screening phone calls from the local stations and putting them into the ear of the interview subject.

The other approach is to set up a satellite feed aimed at a general audience of one sort or another, rather than a group of journalists. The Chamber of Commerce "Biznet" program represents such an effort. The White House recently began setting up such feeds on an occasional basis. You can set up your own, but it's a lot of work and won't be an everyday sort of a thing in the near future.

Running the Gauntlet

So much for direct media techniques that avoid, or minimize, the journalistic "filter." Much of the time, the appointee will have to settle for working with the filter, rather than having direct access to the audience. In this situation the media will have enormous opportunity to edit, interpret, distort or simply ignore your message. In football terms this is the equivalent of running through them: "three yards and a cloud of dust." This is less efficient than the direct access methods described above; it is hard work, but in the long run it pays off. It requires a somewhat different, but equally important, set of skills.

Here are a few of the most important rules to follow when dealing with reporters in this context:

Rule One: Don't deal with reporters. The only exceptions to this rule are people who are paid to do public affairs work, and high-level agency officials who occasionally just can't avoid it.

Dealing with reporters, especially those from the big-time newspapers and networks, can be extremely risky work. Public affairs people know these folks, their prejudices, their habits, their interview techniques, their strong points, their weak points, how many kids they have, and who's competing with whom for the next promotion back in the reporter's newsroom. No one who doesn't do this for a living can possibly be completely prepared to deal with a determined reporter covering a sensitive subject.

If an item is politically sensitive, make sure that a political appointee in the public affairs shop handles it. Don't keep that person in the dark— give him whatever information he needs to have a fairly complete working knowledge of the issue. Your public affairs people are effective only to the degree that they are *credible* in the eyes of the reporters who cover the agency. If they are uninformed or misinformed because of your action or inaction, then you have torpedoed one of your most valuable assets.

If you choose to ignore Rule One, or are left with no choice but to deal with reporters, then observe the following additional rules religiously.

Rule Two: Harbor no illusions—about yourself or about the roles the two of you are playing. A conservative appointee and a reporter are not "jest folks" having a chat. The appointee's role is to advance the policies and programs of the president and of the head of the agency. The reporter's role is to find out everything he/she can about what's going on in your operation. Occasionally, these roles are not in conflict.

At other times, however, the reporter with whom you are dealing will have either a conscious or subconscious desire to do you in because he's not exactly a Reaganaut and you are. If there's not a philosophical difference, there may be a personality conflict, or the reporter may just be ornery. (I will ignore the situation where the appointee has done something ethically or legally wrong and they're after him for that. If that's what you're up to, you're on your own.)

Analyze yourself. Are you a wee bit naive? Do you lack sales resistance? Did you travel 200 miles to a resort development last summer just to get your free gift? Are you susceptible to flattery? Gentle persuasion? Are you easy pickings when a high-pressure car salesman is trying to sell you a piece of junk? If the answer to most or all of these is yes, see Rule One.

If, on the other hand, you know how to say "no" when the situation demands it; if you were a whiz on the debate circuit in school; if you are persuasive, aggressive, and can hold your own in a bowlful of barracudas; and most of all if you can control yourself in tense situations where level-headedness is difficult indeed, then proceed to Rule Three.

Rule Three: Be prepared. Everyone learned this one in the Boy Scouts (or Girl Scouts, I presume), and there's never been better all-purpose advice. Don't just pick up the phone and call a reporter. An interview is psychological warfare, and you can't just walk in unarmed.

Know what you intend to say. Think through the subject or subjects you expect to come up in the phone conversation or in-person interview. Heavy-duty interviews demand the kind of rehearsal described earlier in this chapter. But for many encounters with the Fourth Estate, it is sufficient simply to think for a few minutes before the encounter.

Rule Four: Consider carefully the ground rules of the interview. There are many ways in which conversations with the press take place in Washington. For the most part appointees will do interviews *on the record*: This means that you will be directly quoted and the remarks will be attributed to you. But now and then there is an advantage to speaking *on background*: This means you will be directly quoted but will not be mentioned by name—the remark will be attributed to a "high government official" or a "knowledgeable source." This is also known as being "off the record." You may wish to speak on *deep background*: This means there will be no direct quotation; your remarks will be paraphrased; they may or may not be attributed to a "government official." Finally, one may give guidance: In this mode no information you provide will be used directly in the story, you are merely providing direction and context to the reporter in developing the story; there will be no personal reference, quotation, or paraphrase. Note that these terms have different meanings to different reporters; the interviewee must spell out with the reporter in complete detail what exactly is meant by the term being used—before the interview begins.

This is tricky ground; these techniques are not for novices. If you are not already familiar with these terms, you should stay with the on-the-record interview. If, on the other hand, these terms have a ring of familiarity, consider the many ways they may help the cause. Off-the-record leaks, and especially deep background leaks, have an irresistible appeal to the workaday journalist. If it's juicy enough to get the political appointee into trouble if his or her name is associated with it, then it obviously must be juicy enough to make headlines tomorrow morning. There are people in this town who rarely make news any other way than through off-the-record interviews; they accept the theory that the surest way to kill a story is to put out a news release on it. There's some truth to that, but I'd recommend a reasonable balance. You've got to have at least some public visibility to be effective.

Resist the temptation, however, to play this game simply because you think it's fun, or perhaps because you have your own agenda. It is legitimate in my book only if it is being used to help advance the Reagan agenda. I don't think there's anything lower than indulging in what Fred Barnes calls the "anti-policy leak." Dave Stockman is said to have engaged in a lot of this in trying to promote a tax hike at the same time his President was dead set against one. That's lower than a snake's belly.

Barnes also describes a second type of leak, just-for-kicks conversations or loose-tongue leaks. People like to talk to reporters, especially in Washington, and especially if they see those reporters' bylines in print every day. It makes the appointee feel important (or even more important than he already feels). It makes him feel that he's *arrived* on the Washington scene. Don't even think about it. Your time here is short; you've got much more important things to do.

Rule Five: Be sincere. There are two excellent reasons for this. First, an experienced reporter can smell a phony a mile away. You're not going to kid anybody. Second, you are much more likely to be taken seriously if you're obviously sincere and *earnest* in advancing the themes and policies you are discussing.

If it's not inconsistent with your personality, go the extra step: Be *passionate*. Reporters in Washington are so accustomed to politicians who spend their whole lives posturing that it is actually refreshing to come across someone who really believes strongly in what he says. This doesn't always work, and you ought to pay attention to how it seems to be going over. If you push it too far, they may just decide you're a fanatic and you may as well hang it up.

There is one more reason that a little passion in the presentation can be an advantage: It gives you a lift. It's not always easy to get really up for an interview on something like ending support prices for spaghetti noodles. Psyching yourself up for it—getting worked up a little—can make an interesting interview out of a potentially dull one. This is especially true for a radio or TV interview, where your attitude, be it bored or excited, is there for all to see in an instant.

Rule Six: Be quotable. I covered this a little earlier, but it's worth repeating here. For some, this comes naturally. Others have to work at it. Ronald Reagan is one of those wonderful folks who fall into both categories—he's quick with the spontaneous quip, even when he's just been shot and is on the way into the operating room ("All in all, I'd rather be in Philadelphia"), and he also knows the value of a remark that's carefully composed and brought out in just the right spot in a speech. In any case, quotability is often the difference between getting a conservative "spin" on a story and not being mentioned at all.

A short, catchy phrase, or a cute colloquialism gets attention. They don't all have to be cute, of course; some weightier subjects demand a more serious tone. Use your judgment, but in all cases be quotable.

Rule Seven: Don't treat reporters like the enemy—even if they are. A lot more flies are caught with honey than with vinegar. Conservatives are especially prone to erring here; they will vent their anger at any reporter who crosses their path. That is one reason conservatives were buried so deep in the newspaper for so many years. Not that being a nice guy will get better coverage, or even any coverage at all. I am simply suggesting that an appointee avoid the inevitable negative consequences of starting out with a chip on his shoulder.

Reporters are people, too. They are doing a job, just as you are. Respect that. Respect them (even if they don't always deserve it). Be understanding of the difficulties and pressures that they face, just as you would like them to understand yours.

Rule Eight: Sex sells. You don't need to go to Madison Avenue to know that a little pizazz will lift a page five story up to page one if you play your cards right. A story that might not make the cut at all will make it if a little glitz is added.

Sometimes the difference is as simple as having the agency head get out front on an issue personally. When Bill Bennett personally goes out to a high school classroom to teach the classics, it sends the message more powerfully than a hundred news releases and a thousand glossy brochures. When Ed Meese goes out and personally stomps around in the middle of a marijuana patch during an eradication campaign, everyone knows we're talking serious commitment.

Other times, it will be the way the message is composed on a printed page. You can guarantee failure by using the same old boilerplate lead on a statistical release, or you can make each one fresh, built around a survey result that is truly interesting/extraordinary/unexpected.

Before I became the Assistant Director for Public Affairs at the Office of Personnel Management, the monthly releases on total government employment started out with something like "U.S. government employment stood at 2,720,893 in January, compared with 2,711,674 a month earlier." Very shortly, we began to herald "the seventh consecutive month of cutting the size of the federal bureaucracy." That's not exactly an ad for Jordache jeans, but you get the point.

Now Get Out There and Sell!

This is far from being a complete guide to media relations. It is really designed to be a ready reference guide—a list of do's and don'ts an appointee can use to refresh the memory the next time a reporter wants to come by and chat. It will at least keep you out of trouble, and may just inspire you to make a special effort to get the word out about some important aspect of the conservative revolution.

The conservative appointee should always give a little thought to how to get the word out on the next important initiative in the agenda. Formulating the policy and getting all the memos in the right order is only half the battle. Making sure the public knows *what* we're doing, and *why* we're doing it, is crucial. Don't be shy. At a personal level, it may be enough to know that the work one is doing is both rewarding and important to the future of the nation. But remember that cementing the gains made during the eight Reagan years will depend to an important degree on the *national consensus* that is built in support of the changes that have been made.

In some ways, helping to achieve this consensus is the most difficult task of all. Ronald Reagan himself is the foremost weapon in this battle, but each political appointee who serves him has an indispensable role to play. In politics, as in football, the team that spends more time on offense than on defense generally wins the game. A bold, aggressive public affairs effort is the key to staying on the offensive.

I mentioned earlier that many conservatives make the mistake of dealing with the news media as if they were the enemy. A closely related error is forgetting about members of the media who are not hostile. I'm forever being told by friends of mine who are conservative journalists that people in the Reagan Administration always seem to cozy up to the big-name types in the major newspapers and networks who are frankly liberal in outlook and are anything but friendly to the Administration. There *are* conservative journalists out there, and you should pay special attention to them and the conservative columnists and editorial writers who would be happy to write about something that you consider important if only you'd invite them over to talk about it.

Finally, bear in mind Vince Lombardi's famous dictum: Winning isn't everything—it's the only thing. Revolutions are won by those who spend every waking moment looking for ways to win. Smart media relations can be one of the most important elements of a victory.

12 Government Statistics, Public Education, and Politics

ROBERT RECTOR

*Editors' Note: Conservative appointees entering the govern-
ment generally act like unwelcome house guests or like Vikings
on a raiding party. There is little understanding that any serious
effort to change the role of government in society must entail the
positive and long-term use of instrumentalities of government
itself toward that end.*

The federal government has had a major involvement in the production
and distribution of social and economic statistics since the 1930's.
Almost all federal departments and agencies participate in these activities. From the outset, government statistics or "social indicators" have
had two aspects: one which is scientific/technical and another which is
informational/propagandistic.

Liberals have traditionally understood and exploited the propagandistic aspects of government statistics with far greater ingenuity than
conservatives. This asymmetry seems to arise from two sources. First, the
political predominance of liberalism in the federal government over the
last half-century has given liberals greater experience in mobilizing and
channeling government resources to promote their preferred public
policies. Second, conservative administrations often approach government from the perspective of seeking marginal cost savings often at the
expense of larger policy goals. Thus conservatives will regard statistical
programs with an accountant's mindset, oblivious to the public relations
possibilities which are hidden within such programs. This preoccupation
with marginal cost savings has seldom inhibited liberal administrations.

During the 1960's and 1970's liberals erected a whole new array of
government social indicators which were designed to serve as the public
relations vanguard for new social programs. Liberals became increasingly frank about the propagandistic intent behind these social indicators. As one leading proponent of the liberal "new public administration"
doctrine put it:

Social indicators can be seen as enhancing change in the direction of
social equity. . . . Social indicators are designed to show variation in

socioeconomic circumstances in the hopes that attempts will be made
to improve the conditions of those who are shown to be disadvantaged.
[Indicators] have only a surface neutrality or good management character. Under the surface they are devices by which [career] administrators and executives try to bring about change. It is no wonder they are
so widely favored in Public Administration circles.[1]

One example of liberals' increased use of social indicators is especially
striking. In 1963, Molly Orshansky, a mid-level career economist in
charge of a statistical program at HEW, developed a new measurement:
"the definition of poverty." According to this measure, in 1963, a family
of four would be considered "poor" if it had an income below $3,165. An
individual living alone was considered "poor" with an income less than
$1,540.[2] This definition was remarkable in many respects—it meant that
an American family could have an income 29 times greater than the
world per capita median income and still be considered "poor." An
individual in America could have a higher income than 93 percent of the
world's population and still be judged "in poverty."[3] In historical terms
the contrast was just as striking—measured in inflation-adjusted dollars,
the specified $3,165 level was almost two and a half times greater than
the average annual earnings of American workers at the turn of the
century. Over 60 percent of U.S. households in the 1920's had incomes
below the specified $3,165 level after adjustment for inflation; needless
to say, few of these households in earlier periods regarded themselves as
poor, and many saw themselves as quite prosperous.[4]

Despite its arbitrary nature, Orshansky's "measurement of poverty"
was quickly institutionalized by the government. The entire population
was measured periodically and statistics were published at least on a
semiannual basis in succeeding years. Related indicators were quickly
"spun off," including: female, ethnic, urban, elderly, and child poverty
rates. These were followed in a few years by more ambitious "near poverty
rates." In short order, an entire government industry for the measurement
of poverty sprang up and was coupled with an expanding network of
government offices and subsidized research centers devoted to publicizing the relevant numbers.

This institutionalization of "the definition of poverty" into a recurring
"official" government statistic clearly demonstrates the greater sophis-
tication of liberals in exploiting government resources to advance their
policy goals. Rather than producing a single esoteric report on poverty
in 1963 with a few concomitant press releases, the institutionalization
of the new social indicator allowed liberals to frame the terms of debate
for over two decades. Rather than a single study and a handful of press
releases, the result has been literally tens of thousands of press releases

and stories relating to "measured poverty" over the succeeding 23 years.

Even today when a conservative columnist or speech-writer sits down at his desk to write about poverty, he must grapple with Molly Orshansky and her poverty measurement system. This system will define the terms in which the speech-writer will address the "poverty problem." In a very real sense, Molly Orshansky will be leaning over the conservative speech-writer's shoulder, determining what can and cannot be said on the subject. If this is not political genius, what is?

Unfortunately, there are no conservative equivalents to Molly Orshansky and her poverty statistics. While it is easy to find hundreds of government social indicators created by liberals for liberal policy objectives, it is impossible—outside of crime statistics—to find social/economic indicators created by conservatives to further conservative policies. It is not at all difficult to think of dozens of useful conservative statistical indicators that could be established. These might include:

- "The Quarterly Cost of Protectionism Index" measuring the aggregate cost of existing quotas and tariffs to American consumers
- "The Cost of Protectionism Per Family Index" measuring the annual cost of the protection "tax" to the average family of four, with added reference to black families and the urban poor
- "The Illegitimacy/Poverty Index" measuring the percentage of poverty that is caused by illegitimate childbearing, especially among teenagers
- "The Annual State Burden Index" measuring the aggregate cost of regulation, protection, government borrowing, and taxation by federal, state, and local governments on the population, the average family, etc.
- "The Self Support Index" measuring the percentage of the population that maintains itself above the poverty level without government handouts

The last measure, if produced, would automatically declare the government's entire war against poverty to be a complete failure each and every time the statistic was released. Of course, such measures do not exist.

When confronted with the idea of developing new government social indicators on a given subject, many Reagan appointees will counter by saying, "We did a press release on that subject two months ago" or "Did you see our last study on that subject?" Such responses show a clear failure to recognize the difference in public relations impact between a single press release or study and a regularly issued government indicator. As stated, Molly Orshansky's "measurement of poverty" was effective precisely because it was not restricted to a single academic study but was converted into a routine government statistic to be issued year after year—and circulated to every college, press room, and library across the country through thousands upon thousands of government publications.

In general, repetitive government statistics will have a number of consistent advantages over single-shot studies, speeches, and press releases. Because extreme repetition is needed to bring any fact or issue before the public's attention, it is rare that any single study will have an impact on public opinion; routinely published government indicators, though less spectacular than other public relations tools, often have a greater long-term impact on public awareness through cumulative reinforcement. Although the liberal press corps may well ignore a single press release or study, they will find it more difficult to ignore a scientific government indicator published periodically over the course of a decade. Moreover, routine government statistics—because they are accessible—come to be utilized and cited through force of habit. In the field of public policy, certain types of information are passed back and forth with enormous frequency by the press and commentators. Once a government indicator has become familiar, it often becomes the most widely known and most accessible point of reference on a given subject. The indicator, in effect, becomes a respository of information on a topic in lieu of more obscure data analysis. The influence of "poverty statistics" or "unemployment statistics" derives, in large part, from this type of familiarity.

Finally, once government indicators are established, they are very difficult to abolish. Entire offices of bureaucrats and their families become dependent on the continuation of "their" indicator. Even when an opposing administration comes into power, it will have a difficult time eliminating or changing the indicator because its efforts will be met with charges that it is "politicizing" a scientific measurement and thereby seeking to conceal its own policy failures. Government indicators therefore tend to influence public debate over the long term; they are a remarkable means of maintaining a particular public relations effort irrespective of incidental changes in the presidency.

A hypothetical Reagan appointee who created a "Quarterly Cost of Protectionism to the American Consumer Index" (previously mentioned) would find himself having an impact on public policy long after he left the scene. For example, imagine that in 1996, after a slimmer Ted Kennedy wins the presidency, he decides to protect the American economy by imposing import quotas on lawnmowers, stereos, tennis rackets, and frozen pizzas. The Kennedy publicist charged with a press campaign to justify these quotas would find himself confronting not merely an unorganized handful of dissenting academics but the government's own well-established indicator—"The Quarterly Cost of Protectionism to the

American Consumer." This indicator would spell out in now familiar terms the expanded social costs imposed by the new quota policy. (Is it not possible that the press could eventually focus as much attention on "cost of protection" statistics as they now do on the far less meaningful monthly trade balance figures?) In such circumstances, our hypothetical Kennedy publicist, as he sits at his desk trying to draft a policy justification, will find himself with a long-vanished Reagan appointee leaning over his shoulder dictating what could and could not be said in the press release, defining the nature of the debate. That is the essence of political power.

Conservative appointees who seek to create new social/economic indicators will find themselves facing two obstacles. The first is technical. Foot-dragging professionals will object that there is a wide range of debate over the proper methodology of measurement on issue "X." An endless series of conferences and papers will be proposed to discover the correct methodology. It may also be argued that the data base needed for the measurement cannot realistically be created. Such objections may be partially correct; they would no doubt apply to nearly all of the statistics that the government has ever generated. For example, problems in the government's consumer price index are infamous. Similarly, government income distribution and poverty statistics are notorious for their shaky data bases and their tenuous connection to the concepts they purport to measure; this has never stopped the liberals from publishing and promoting these statistics.[5] Imperfections in poverty measurement are so severe that they led to a spate of policies to solve a special problem of the "elderly poor" that probably never existed in the first place.[6] Nevertheless, liberals are now fighting to prevent correction of even the most obvious deficiencies in poverty measures. Reagan appointees seeking to establish new social indicators should not allow themselves to be deterred by inevitable methodological quibbling.

The second objection the Reagan appointee will encounter will be cost. He may have difficulty finding funds for new statistical measures in an era of retrenchment. Such impediments reflect the Republican tradition of straining at the gnat while swallowing the camel. The cost of failing to re-direct the public policy debate will always outweigh the cost of added public relations efforts, many thousand times over. For example, the current cost of protectionism to the American consumer is estimated by some to be around $60 billion to $80 billion per annum. In comparison, a few hundred thousand dollars spent to establish and operate the hypothetical "Quarterly Cost of Protectionism to the American Consumer Index" are scarcely worth mentioning. Such funds directed toward staving off increased protectionism would save the nation billions.

During the first term of the Reagan Administration, most political appointees showed the traditional indifference to social indicators as public relations instruments. Conservative political appointees must take a lesson from the success of Molly Orshansky and begin to create their own social and economic indicators.[7] The United States is enmeshed in a fundamental public policy debate that will persist for generations. It is time to recognize that fact and take the necessary steps to influence the course of future dialogue.

Notes

1. H. George Frederickson, "Toward a New Public Administration," in *Classics of Public Administration*, eds. Jay M. Shafritz and Albert C. Hyde (Oak Park, Ill.: Moore Publishing, 1978), p. 393.

2. In her seminal 1963 article, Orshansky referred to the $3,165 family of four level as a conservative estimate and proposed an alternative measure which was actually 25% higher! The poverty rate for individuals was devised slightly after the original family figures. See Molly Orshansky, "Children of the Poor," *Social Security Bulletin*, July 1963, pp. 3–17, and "Courting the Poor: Another Look at the Poverty Profile," *Social Security Bulletin*, January 1965, pp. 3–28. The family poverty rate concept was loudly trumpeted by President Johnson's Council of Economic Advisers in 1963.

3. The international comparisons were made by comparing the 1959 poverty levels against global income data for 1958. See Simon Kuznets, *Modern Economic Growth: Rate, Structure, and Spread* (New Haven and London: Yale University Press, 1967), pp. 359–90. The comparisons were made using official currency exchange rates, which are sometimes regarded as underestimating purchasing power in the third world; if comparisons were made by purchasing power parity, the differentials between U.S. poverty levels and world median income might be reduced by 50 percent.

4. See *Historical Statistics of the United States: Colonial Times to 1970*, Vol. 1 (Washington, D.C.: U.S. Department of Commerce, Bureau of the Census, 1972), series E135 and D722.

5. See Martin Anderson, *Welfare: The Political Economy of Welfare Reform in the United States* (Palo Alto, Calif.: Hoover Institution Press, 1978).

6. The number of persons "in poverty" is exaggerated by a substantial underreporting of income; this problem is particularly marked among the elderly.

7. Nothing in this chapter should be construed as advocating the creation of false, bogus, or misleading indicators. As noted at the beginning of the article, indicators have a scientific as well as a public educational aspect. The existing indicators criticized do contribute, albeit imperfectly, to objective knowledge about society. The main point is to stress a recognition that many indicators have, in their formulation, applied policy implications.

13 Political Administration: The Right Way

DONALD J. DEVINE

Editors' Note: Donald J. Devine, former Director of the Office of Personnel Management and University of Maryland Professor, is one of the foremost practitioners of the art forms we know as politics and administration. In this essay, he indicates what is wrong with the the the ruling liberal model of public administration and shares with the conservative political appointee his principles of conservative public administration. Success for the conservative appointee in the making and implementing of conservative public policy depends on mastering the principles he describes.

The liberal myth of government administration is that management is merely a technical task, to be handed over to neutral experts. That myth is a vain attempt to escape from politics. It is as old as the Progressives' turn-of-the-century vision of a neutral civil service and it is still alive and well among us today. At its heart lies the question of who shall control government and to what ends.

The myth of neutral/technical government management was brought to America by Woodrow Wilson. In his seminal article "The Study of Administration," published in 1887, Wilson argued for a broad expansion of the role of government for a new positive government.[1] While for the founders the pivotal question of government had been to discover means to restrain state power, for Wilson the central problem was to unleash government power and to establish techniques for exercising that power effectively. As he stated, "Seeing every day new things which the state ought to do the next thing is to see clearly how to do them."[2]

In order to achieve effectiveness in government it was necessary that much of government operate apart from direct political control. A vast new apparatus of positive government was to be erected and to be manned by an elite bureaucratic corps trained in "the science of administration." Armed with unique knowledge, the professional bureaucrats would bring efficiency and rationality to state management. With most government operations under their command, the trained experts would be shielded from the merely "political," and thereby would be assisted in their service to the public. Their decisions would be "scientific," resting on objective fact and "universal law," not on values and opinions. Value judgments would be relegated to the older, prescientific sphere of politics which was nonrational and generally ignorant of the details of government programs.

Wilson justified this elitist doctrine on the basis that the vast bureaucratic apparatus of positive government would merely be engaged in "administration." Nonelected career professionals would exercise power only in executing the broad policy goals set by the elected government. However, by the the midpoint of this century, it was clearly recognized that much of what passed for "administration" by the nonelected bureaucracy was in fact independent policy-making. The attempt to escape from politics really meant and still means that the policy decision-making power that inherently exists in the management of government operations was given to a nonelected managerial corps to be exercised beyond direct popular control.

This realization, implying a state of affairs in direct conflict with democratic tenets, threw mainstream public administration theory into a disarray from which it has never recovered. On the one hand, there were calls for the nonelected bureaucracy to bring its neutral expertise and objective "institutional knowledge" directly to bear on policy-making, with some even arguing that the bureaucracy is uniquely capable of discerning the broader public interest, substituting an enhanced "professional" vision for the narrower outlook of legislators and political executives.[3]

On the other hand, at the practical level things continued largely unchanged. Career civil servants still propounded the useful myth of "neutral administration" to hold power. Few believed they really had special expertise or knowledge to actually solve problems objectively. Yet somehow it was still regarded as wrong for mere "politicians" to engage in administration and management. "Politicians" were untrained, and if permitted to influence agency management in a detailed way, they would introduce the nonrational political factors that had been so carefully excluded. They would insert "ideology" and political values into a sphere that had been reserved for "neutral" administration.

Currently, the myth of neutral administration is given legitimacy by national organizations such as the National Academy of Public Administration (NAPA), the American Society for Public Administration (ASPA), and the National Institute of Public Administration (NIPA). But they have their interests. These organizations conduct training and hold conferences for hundreds of top-level career bureaucrats every year. Attendance of career officials is generally paid for by government training funds. At these sessions the gospel of neutral administration is preached to the congregation assembled. Those who suggest that more political appointees are needed to increase the accountability of the bureaucracy to the public are castigated as heretics.

NAPA provides a particularly interesting example. NAPA's power is illustrated by the fact that it is one of only two congressionally-recognized private academies. (It seems that Congress recognizes an ally in the bureaucracy when it wants to oppose presidential power.) NAPA conducts studies and writes reports regarding the state of the federal bureaucracy and the executive branch. Recommendations in recent reports illustrate its commitment to the liberal myth of neutral administration. NAPA recommends:

- Fewer political appointees should serve in the executive branch.
- Presidents should draw more heavily on the career civil service as a valuable source of presidential appointees.
- Candidates for the presidency should not attack the federal civil service during the campaign. Instead, campaign speeches should encourage, inspire, and challenge the career civil service.[4]

This last recommendation fails to recognize that politicians are reflecting the public dissatisfaction with an unaccountable bureaucracy. NAPA's solution is not to achieve more accountability, but to place the bureaucracy outside the bounds of national political debate—another attempt of the bureaucracy to escape politics and political accountability.

Arrogantly entitled *America's Unelected Government: Appointing the President's Team*, a recent NAPA book discusses the process of appointing political executives to the Reagan Administration.[5] It seems that political executives who are appointed by the president are considered illegitimate holders of power because they are unelected, but it is legitimate for career staff to engage in public policy, even though they, unlike the political appointees, have no connection whatsoever with the electoral mandate.

The Conservative View of Politics and Administration

In 1981, all Reagan Administration political appointees were confronted with the liberal myth of neutral administration. Those appointees with strong conservative backgrounds were better able to resist the dogma because they were better schooled in the reality of politics and administration. First, the conservative view of public administration starts with a skepticism about government and politics, with the understanding that governmental power is a constant threat to human freedom. But that skepticism also assumes that politics exists and, indeed, is an intrinsic part of human nature and its liberty. Reexamine *The Federalist Papers* on this subject. Second, as *The Federalist* also teaches, conservatives are republicans, who believe electoral politics is the means by which governments are changed by the consent of the governed. Politics is one means by which people can contest government's threat to their freedom. Politics is a necessary part of government.[6]

Finally, conservatives have learned about how organizations operate through Ludwig von Mises's magisterial *Bureaucracy*[7] and Friedrich Hayek's *Road to Serfdom*.[8] Private organizations operate with freedom, while government operates by using coercion. Governments do not have the built-in efficiency device of private administration, which is regulated through the marvelous market mechanism. Conservatives learned that it is the market's "bottom line" that allows decisions to be decentralized, which forces them to be efficient. Government does not have the bottom line because it does not operate in a free market. It follows with an iron logic that if government does not have this mechanism, it has to be organized and managed differently.

In sum, conservatives learned that government was political. They knew that by its very nature government must deal with diverse individuals with different values. If these individuals refused to settle those differences freely in a market, they would express them through interest groups in politics and government. Conservatives were among the first to identify the role of interest groups in expressing narrow interests outside of free markets, and the need for political parties to forge those interests into a party platform, which could aggregate interests to create a party philosophy that had some claim to the public interest. A party nomination was recognized as a contest to determine that philosophy which would define the party through its candidates. It was this realism relative to politics that led conservatives to first change the Republican Party philosophy in 1964 through the nomination of Barry Goldwater, and later to institute that program through the nomination and election of Ronald Reagan in 1980 and 1984.

What conservatives have not always recognized is the need to continue politics in the administration of government. Too often, especially in Republican administrations before Reagan's, the politics that won the election were forgotten in managing the government. Once the election was won, too often Republicans turned over administration to the technocrats. In a most prophetic statement, John P. Sears—who had helped elect Richard Nixon and then lost out in the administration of his White House to the Haldeman-Dean amoral technocrats—told me early in 1979 that there was a good chance the same would happen under the Reagan Administration. He said, "I'll be the first one out when the [Michael] Deaver bureaucrats come in."

Ronald Reagan was not unaware of the problem of administering government. He once told a *New Republic* reporter that it was frustration with civil service regulations, when he was personnel officer at Culver City during World War II, that led him, in part, to become a conservative. He found that under the rules he could not fire an obvious incompetent. It made him realize that the presumably "neutral" rules of the civil service were actually structured to protect the bureaucrats from accountability. Early in his Administration, President Reagan articulated this same theme by expressing his frustration with the fact that some civil servants believed that they would outlast the Administration and could hamper implementation of his programs. The President did not just stop there; he also established the principle that he expected responsibility from all officials in the executive branch.

In my first public speech as Director of President Reagan's civil service, I advised an ASPA convention that we in the Reagan Administration would view administration differently. We rejected the liberal, progressive, welfare-state view that government could be handed to technocrats. Rather, the President and his appointees would set the new agenda. In the field of public administration, we would start by looking back to the beginnings of public administration, and to its founder, Max Weber. In his seminal "Politics as a Vocation," Weber first made a distinction between policymaker and administrator; he said that the politician's role is "to take a stand" on policy, while the administering civil servant's is "exactly the opposite principle, [that] of responsibility." Indeed, the very "honor of the civil servant is vested in his ability to execute conscientiously the order of superior authorities. Without this moral discipline and self-denial, in the highest sense, the whole apparatus would fall to pieces."[9]

Of course, the Reagan Administration would recognize that the line between policy and administration will always be blurred. The dictum that political executives are "on top" and career executives are "on tap" is too simplistic—but it makes an important point. A political leader—legitimized by a popular election—must be on top of the bureaucratic structure and provide the policy leadership for government administration. Without this, there is no legitimacy for the democratic regime. The skill and technical expertise of the career service must be utilized, but it must be utilized under the direct authority and personal supervision of the political leader who has the moral authority flowing from the people through an election—otherwise, "the whole apparatus would fall to pieces." In many agencies and departments, career executives have forsaken responsibility and have fallen to the temptation of political power. They have established their own political agendas and pursue them in spite of the policy directives of political administrators. In these cases, political appointees have the legal and moral obligation not only to control policy-making but to control the detailed administration of the President's policies.

Fortunately for the Reagan Administration, tools for controlling policy-making and administration in the government already existed in Jimmy Carter's legacy to the nation, the Civil Service Reform Act (CSRA) of 1978. The CSRA provided for a technically sound performance-appraisal system, which allows the conscientious political and career manager to fairly evaluate and control subordinate employee performance. Political executives serve at the pleasure of the agency head; while for career executives, the CSRA also allows the political manager to reward and motivate those civil servants who perform well with substantial bonuses, to reassign those who need different working environments to be effective team members, and to discipline those who perform poorly or who will not follow policy directives. It was left to the Reagan Administration to implement these new tools in 1981, and they were later given legal status in Merit System Protection Board and court decisions. By the end of the first Reagan Administration, all of the knowledge and mechanisms were available for proper conservative public administration.

Conservative Public Administration: Principles of Political Leadership

This conservative philosophy of public administration was implemented during Ronald Reagan's first term. It was based upon the critical insight noted by von Mises that the private sector executive can refer to different cost centers, with separate bottom lines, which allows him to delegate authority while still knowing how successfully his subordinates are operating. The bookkeeping and budgetary tools of financial administration that allow for diffuse responsibility in a market setting, however, simply do not provide the same critical information in government, as David Stockman has candidly admitted.[10] So government administration must be primarily political.

After six years of experience, it is possible more precisely to define the principles of this conservative public administration. First, directly from von Mises's insight about the private executive, it follows that a public manager *cannot decentralize* anywhere near as much as his private counterpart. He himself must have a greater across-the-board knowledge about his political and cultural environment, and be able personally to respond to political pressures. Very important, he must also know much more about the details of administration—for in government much of administration actually is policy. It is critical to know the details of administration, because if he does not, the political leader will lose control of policy, which is his first responsibility. Unless he has much more detailed knowledge of his operations than his equivalent in the private sector—who can just refer to those marvelous bottom lines—he will become a figurehead, and turn policy over to those below him who do not have the legal or moral authority to set policy for the public. By corollary, since the political administrator must delegate less, he must also follow up more.

The second principle is that the political administrator must have a *clearer vision of his agenda.* He can master the necessary details only if he has a clear knowledge of alternatives and precisely how they should be implemented. This agenda will be set in the first instance by the program announced by the president, but must be further fleshed out in every specific policy area by the appropriate representative of the president. The political executive must develop this agenda in the spirit in which the president would develop it himself, if the president had the time personally to deal with each of the myriad policies of government.

Since this political relationship demands an empathetic presidential-appointee symbiosis, the third principle requires that the appointee must be politically *loyal* to the president so that he can develop a program, in detail, that truly represents what the president would otherwise have developed. Potential loyalty can be tested through work on presidential campaigns.

The most pertinent political fact that a government administrator must face is that his program must be developed in a "fishbowl," where all is made public, often prematurely through the Washington institution called "leaks." Therefore, the fourth principle is for the political executive to ask himself, in each decision and for every item he puts on paper, "How would this look on the front page of *The Washington Post?*" Calculated propriety in every action becomes essential to very survival.

From this follows a fifth principle: The political executive must *keep his agenda close.* This is not an attempt to freeze career employees out of policy, as is often alleged by the NAPA/ASPA public administration community, but a matter of self-preservation, no matter whether it involves political or career subordinates. The sixth principle is that if a political administrator implements the changes in policy promised by the president, he must have the *courage to live with the inevitable negative reaction.* A porous government bureaucracy will advise the media of any warts. The media, in turn, will be pleased to print every one of them. The appointee's family and friends will see him splashed all over the news-papers and television screen in the most unflattering light. Since no one can do everything perfectly in an environment of limited delegation, these negative images are an integral part of public policy-making; they can be minimized but not avoided. The only way to avoid criticism is to do nothing. Indeed, this is the favorite tactic of the political manager who wants only to survive, even though he does so at the cost of violating the only reason for his existence within the government.

The executive who remains a true political administrator must, seventh, be *confident in the knowledge that he has the legal right to act: he is the boss.* American law clearly gives authority to the political appointee, and expects him to make the policy decisions, under the direction of the president and the checking authority of the Congress and the courts. It is difficult to maintain the poise needed for political leadership in the rough-and-tumble environment of Washington; but that is what is legally expected and what is proper. The civil service is expected in democratic theory and in American law to carry out the orders of the political head.

To maintain poise, the political executive needs three final principles: Eighth, it is easy to become isolated, given the lonely perch. *Building friendships* with other political appointees who are in the same situation and keeping friends outside Washington's distorted insularity sustains poise. There is life beyond the Beltway; and it is important to visit the real world to remember that there are people who are outside of the "gimme" environment of Washington's interest-group politics where people seem to believe that making a living is walking around with your hand out. Ninth, *other political appointees must be trained* to help share the burden of political leadership, while at the same time providing direction for career subordinates. Tenth, he must *laugh* often at the ridiculous situation he has gotten himself into. This is the world of political administration.

Conservative Public Administration: Establishing Cabinet Government

Creating a conservative administration starts with political executives who understand and have internalized these principles of political leadership. Essentially, the task of implementing a conservative public administration is to build the political team. The president should begin a conservative administration by personally choosing the twenty to thirty agency chief executives (not just those formally included in today's Cabinet) who will manage the major agencies of his government—based upon their understanding of and agreement with his program, their knowledge of the subject matter, and their agreement with the principles of conservative public administration. Above all, these critical leaders must possess loyalty to the president or the system will lack accountability; it simply will not work according to republican principles.

The president must take the time to personally review and interview in a detailed way those executives who will determine whether his administration is successful. Otherwise, there will be no political team responsible to him. Then the president should give general directions; and, finally, under criteria set by him, he should allow each of his agency heads to choose their political subordinates. If the heads are not capable of choosing their team, they should not be the heads of the agencies in the first place. Moreover, each agency head should allow his subordinates to do likewise, under the same logic. Of course, the operation of the system must be evaluated by the president's personnel team; but if the agencies follow the president's directions, they should be given the primary responsibility.

In determining how political appointees should be assigned below the level of major division head, James Watt, former Secretary of the Interior, devised what he called the "rule of three." Into every major subunit of the government organization, the agency head should send three political appointees. One should have the leadership skills and knowledge necessary to run the bureau. The second should have the knowledge and administrative competence to see that his superior's orders are implemented. The third need not have technical skills at all. His job is to make sure that the other two remember why they were appointed by the president.

Each of the thirty or so critical agencies of the executive branch would be staffed in this manner under a conservative public administration. The "rule of three" would push this model down through several levels of agency organization, to each major component of the bureaucracy. The president would give each initial instructions and leave his appointees to carry out his program. He would review performance at Cabinet meetings. Sound simple? Well, essentially it is. As President Reagan has said, there are simple solutions if you are clever enough to recognize them.

Well, what about the fact that there are overlapping responsibilities for programs between agencies in the government? The most obvious answer would be to eliminate these overlapping responsibilities, so each administration should make some effort to rationalize government organization under a conservative public administration. Yet, Congress would be reluctant, so a prudent president would create councils of the Cabinet consisting of the agency heads who share this overlapping responsibility, such as those created during the first Reagan Administration. In addition, for each program area—environment, civil rights, etc.—the president would choose one person as principal subordinate in that policy area. That person would chair the Cabinet Council and would receive from the president executive-like responsibility over all programs in that area, even those under the organizational purview of another agency head. By giving a clear "leading minister" role to one head and providing a forum to discuss differences, he would see to it that conflicts could at least be minimized. Any abuse of power by an agency head would be kept in check by the existence of a Cabinet government. Ultimately, all disputes would be settled before the president at the Cabinet table.

Conclusion

The essential ingredient for a right public administration is the political willingness to use this knowledge to implement a conservative agenda. This depends upon will. Andrew S. Grove, author of *High Output*

Management and president of Intel Corporation, noted that the same ingredient is critical in private sector management. At bottom, despite critical differences, the essential element in both private and public sectors is human leadership. And that requires, according to Grove, two things. First, if "we want performance in the workplace, somebody has to have the courage and competence to determine whether we are getting it or not."[11] And second, after evaluating what is necessary, "we managers need to stop rationalizing and stiffen our resolve and do what we're paid to do," and that is to "manage our organizations."[12]

Right political administration likewise requires courage and competence, resolve and willingness to act. But, politics—being the rougher game—requires tougher leaders, held together in a more loyal team. A conservative theory of public administration can define what those leaders need to know and that they must become a team—but it would create another misleading myth to promise any easy means to find or build the team. That is the real political art of governance.

What is certain is that the liberal technocratic view of public administration is becoming increasingly discredited. Public administration is an inherently political act. It is difficult to comprehend that anyone could believe otherwise. Yet, it is hard to believe that anyone could swallow liberal economics either. Even the European nations—which invented the myth of neutral governance and which were used by American liberals as models of how American administration should be organized—are now shifting to the American model of multiple levels of political appointees throughout the government bureaucracy.

Fortunately, American conservatives were taught well about government administration. They learned that government was different and had to be administered politically. The Reagan Administration has given them the opportunity to prove their theory. We still have two years to determine how well they handle the opportunity.

Notes

1.　Woodrow Wilson, "The Study of Administration," in *Classics of Public Administration*, eds. Jay M. Shafritz and Albert C. Hyde (Oak Park, Ill.: Moore Publishing Co., 1978), pp. 3–16. [Originally published, *Political Science Quarterly* II (June 1887)].

2.　Ibid., p. 5.

3.　For an example of this view and its lineage see Mark W. Huddleston, "The Carter Civil Service Reforms: Some Implications for Political Theory and Public Administration," *Political Science Quarterly* 96 (Winter 1981–82): 607–21.

4.　John W. Macy, Burce Adams, and J. Jackson Walter, *America's*

Unelected Government: Appointing the President's Team (Cambridge, Mass: Ballinger, 1983), pp. 100 and 104.

5. Ibid.

6. Alexander Hamilton, James Madison, and John Jay, *The Federalist Papers* (New York: New American Library, 1961).

7. Ludwig von Mises, *Bureaucracy* (New Rochelle, N.Y.: Arlington House, 1969) (originally published 1944).

8. Friedrich A. Hayek, *The Road to Serfdom* (Chicago: University of Chicago Press, 1980).

9. Max Weber, "Politics as a Vocation," in *Max Weber: Essays in Sociology*, eds. H. H. Gerth and C. Wright Mills (New York: Oxford University Press, 1946), p. 95.

10. William Greider, "The Education of David Stockman," *The Atlantic*, December 1981, pp. 27–54.

11. Andrew S. Grove, "Keeping Favoritism and Prejudice Out of Employee Evaluations," in *The Wall Street Journal on Management: The Best of the Manager's Journal*, eds. David Asman and Adam Meyerson (Homewood, Ill.: Dow Jones-Irwin, 1985), p. 102.

12. Ibid., p. 105.

14 Management at the U.S. Mission to the United Nations

JEANE J. KIRKPATRICK

Editors' Note: In this chapter, based on a speech delivered to Reagan appointees, Ambassador Kirkpatrick outlines a philosophy of management based on her personal experience at the United Nations. The principles set forth are excellent and have broad application across government. Although some of the prerogatives that Ambassador Kirkpatrick exercised in her management of the career bureaucracy were unique to her position in the United Nations, her ideas give salutary guidance as to the type of institutional arrangements that will best serve as a foundation to the effective conduct of foreign policy.

The most important advantage an executive can have in entering into a new and complex function like managing an aspect of foreign policy—or managing foreign policy in a particular venue—is to be able to choose key elements of a team that one can be certain shares a sense of purpose, brings the kind of expertise that will be the most useful to the job, behaves responsibly—a team in which one has confidence, and with whose members one thinks one might even enjoy working.

I was very fortunate in having an Andrew Young precede me at the United Nations. That helped in a lot of ways. One of the ways it helped was that Andrew Young had managed through the help of his loyal supporter, President Jimmy Carter, to expand the number of political appointees at the U.S. Mission to the United Nations (USUN) from what had been a minuscule number like four to a dozen or so. I took full advantage of that. I also had the reliable assistance and support of the White House and White House personnel. They were a little worried about me in the beginning because, after all, I was a Democrat. So I was rather solemnly told early on that I should remember that I was not to fill the U.S. Mission to the United Nations with Democrats. I told them I understood, and once we got that straight we had nothing but the most pleasant relations.

As I said, it is very useful and important in a managerial position to be able to bring along a few key members of the team—not because there are not people already there who are highly qualified; not perhaps because those people are going to be unloyal, but just because it is good to have a team who one has chosen. A team who one is sure will be compatible, a team who one is sure will be competent, and who one is sure shares one's purposes.

Foreign policy, like domestic policy, must be responsive to the American electorate. It is the American people whose will is expressed through elections. I do not, therefore, believe that the fundamental lines of policy should be identical from one administration to another, particularly if the change of administration also involves a change of party. When changes of parties occur, as in the election of 1980 and later reaffirmed in 1984, then it is appropriate and important that the broad lines of the nation's policies be adjusted to reflect the issues as they were presented in the campaign just past. I believe, in short, in political mandates, not only in their legitimacy, but in their necessity in a democracy. Otherwise, if government continues on a single course, regardless of the decisions of the electorate, then democracy has in an important respect failed.

Some may say, "But in an election there are so many issues that we do not know what the people think about any one issue." The fact is that it is not so difficult, particularly in elections like 1980 and 1984, to discern broad differences in orientation, priorities, and lines of policy—for example, in foreign policy as between the administrations of Jimmy Carter and Ronald Reagan, or between the campaigns of Carter and Reagan or Mondale and Reagan. The choice before the people was clear, and the mandate of the American people was clear, as well.

I frankly do not see how any agency or department can expect to have a sense of direction that reflects a popular mandate in presidential policy orientation and priorities without an executive-political team that understands that orientation and is committed to it. That is the *sine qua non* of implementing the popular mandate and the President's policies. Career civil servants can and must play an important role in the implementation of foreign policy and domestic policy, but it is the unique responsibility of the executive-political team to articulate that policy on behalf of the President and to give the kind of guidance and direction that will ensure that policy in fact reflects the presidential orientation. It is the appropriate job of the permanent bureaucracy, on the other hand, to do what has always been defined as the bureaucracy's appropriate task, namely, to implement policy that is articulated and approved by elected or appointed officials empowered by the popular elective process.

In order that the executive-political team may effectively fulfill its role of guiding policy, the formation of that team must be undertaken with care. I believe it is important to bear in mind substantive competence when selecting all persons for an executive team. I do not think that anyone should ever be chosen for political reasons alone. I used to feel very frustrated in listening to discussions about foreign policy that juxtaposed "political" appointees and "career professionals" as though they were juxtaposing amateur and professional. What is required for the successful conduct of foreign policy, obviously, is professionalism. But not necessarily the professionalism of the foreign service. What is required is a professional competence and substantive knowledge among career and political officials alike.

I do not believe in the all-purpose manager. This is something I agree with Lee Iacocca on. I was struck by a paragraph in his recent book where he stated that some people believe that a man who could successfully manage one enterprise could manage any other enterprise in the world. He argues that that is like saying that a first-class obstetrician would be great at heart surgery. He thinks this doesn't work; I feel the same way.

I do not think that a political executive without any real substantive knowledge—professional knowledge, if you will—can harness and guide a large establishment of career bureaucrats. I just do not think that's possible. The executive who is devoid of substantive competence and professional information will immediately find himself or herself totally dependent on the career bureaucracy—on subordinates, that is—for all the information and the analyses on the basis of which decisions are made. Now if you are totally dependent on somebody else for information and analysis, you are probably totally dependent on somebody else— period. This somebody else will be the person who is in fact guiding policy. So I think it is very important when putting together a team to choose people who have genuine substantive competence and professional experience in problems similar to those with which you will be dealing in your department or agency. The expertise need not be identical—in fact, it can seldom be identical—but it needs to be relevant to the problems at hand.

At USUN, we very carefully chose people for substantive competence. In ambassadors, for example, we sought diverse skills. Since in the UN it is necessary to deal with all the countries in the world and all the problems in the world, you have got to have diverse expertise. If you do not have the relevant expertise collectively in your executive team then you can do nothing to respond to a given problem but accept whatever instructions the bureaucracy bubbles up to you. There is no alternative because you cannot stop the functions of your enterprise while you develop the kind of expertise you need.

I also believe that there is no substitute for spending long hours following the multiple, difficult, and various problems of the enterprise that one is directing. I do not think that one can eliminate paperwork and hope to get at five o'clock in the afternoon four memoranda of not more than two pages each, which will describe to you all the aspects of the problem, which you need only read and then check off an option: yes or no. If that is what an appointee relies on for directing the activity which he or she is directing it will not work. Whoever is writing the memoranda and reading all the data that goes into them will be making the decisions. One really should disabuse oneself of any illusions to the contrary.

In addition, if an appointee is interested in guiding and implementing policy in accord with a general presidential orientation legitimized by an election, it is very important that the career service be sensitive to the guidance of the executive team. Thus, it helps if the new political managerial team chooses the career bureaucrats who fill key slots. We did that at USUN and I believe that it is important to do so.

This point underscores an interesting lesson about policy-making in general—sometimes one can be effective operating in the interstices of structure. There are a good many aspects of our government about which little is known; one of these is the job of U.S. Permanent Representative to the United Nations.

I learned some things about staffing USUN before I went there. I talked with many of my predecessors. I questioned. They answered, and I listened carefully. One of the things I learned is that an assignment to USUN has for a long time been considered a particularly undesirable assignment in the foreign service. This was true for a lot of reasons: It is a very short-term assignment; it is not a place where most foreign service officers plan to live out their lives after retirement; and unlike short-term assignments abroad, there was no housing allowance. Recently we have been reading about housing allowances to USUN and there has been some suggestion that they were too high. I accept responsibility for having worked hard to get those housing allowances for career officials assigned to the U.S. Mission to the United Nations, because it was very clear to me, as it had been to a lot of my predecessors who had studied the situation, that you could not attract or hold top-flight career bureaucrats for a brief job in New York unless you were prepared to give them some kind of financial subsidization. It was just not financially feasible otherwise. Their incomes are not high enough to absorb the additional cost of living in the New York area for a brief period. So we worked on the problem, and eventually we solved it.

It is an example of the team effort. We solved it with the help of an ambassador whom I had selected (with White House support, of course) who was a career Foreign Service Officer. He worked with the Foreign Service to secure support for the housing benefit, and I worked with the Congress. In the past, housing benefits for career officers in New York had been blocked either by the Foreign Service, by the State Department, or by the Congress. By double-teaming, we finally solved the problem.

Another way I worked on the problem of choosing career officers was simply to announce that henceforth I should not like any career officers to be assigned to the U.S. Mission to the United Nations whom I did not personally interview and approve. Somebody said to me after I had been doing that for a few months, "You can't do that. That is against the rules of the Foreign Service." And I said, "But the rules don't apply to the U.S.

Permanent Representative to the United Nations." The Permanent Representative is a very ambiguous post: You are part of the State Department but you are also a Cabinet member. Well, nobody was sure whether the rules did or did not apply to the U.S. Permanent Representative to the United Nations, so I happily continued interviewing and approving career officers who applied to USUN.

That helped in two ways. One, it helped make certain that the people we were getting were the very best people we could get. Second, it gave the people whom we chose a sense of being chosen—of being preferred. It was very clear that they were not simply being sloughed off to this slot, but that they had applied for it and had been considered and had been chosen. That is a nice basis on which to join a team.

Another important factor in dealing with career staff is clarity. In seeking to administer foreign policy, and I suspect domestic policy as well, it is important to be clear about what one is trying to achieve. Goals are the single most important component of policy. If you do not know where you are going, you cannot hope to get there. You cannot rely on purposes' simply bubbling up. Purposes are not just given in nature, and they do not just bubble up. They must be articulated by the executive team. If they are clearly articulated, they provide guidance for everyone engaged in the mission. If they are not clearly articulated, then you cannot blame anyone for not knowing what it is they are trying to accomplish. Clarity in articulating goals is extremely important, and that is another reason why it is important to have an executive team who are themselves clear about the purposes they are trying to achieve in the roles to which they are assigned.

At USUN we spent a lot of time discussing, explaining, what it was we were trying to accomplish. During the General Assembly, for example, we had daily staff meetings in which everyone in the Mission was welcome. The top-level professional officers were all required to attend, but everybody else was invited and virtually everybody came. We talked about what we would try to accomplish that day and that week, what our long-range purposes were, what everybody's jobs were that day. We did a lot of informal talking up and down and throughout the Mission at a lot of different levels. I think that we honestly did persuade many people that there *was* a different way to represent the United States, and that our way had a lot of advantages.

It is also very important in managing foreign policy, or any other area of policy, to clearly assign responsibilities. The biggest single organizational deficiency of U.S. foreign policy now and in the past is the diffusion of responsibility which permits a nearly complete escape from responsibility. Responsibility for a given activity is sometimes chopped into so many small pieces—cut so many ways—that finally no one is responsible.

Therefore, no one is charged with making certain the policy works and no one suffers the consequences of failure.

Evasion of responsibility manifests itself in a number of ways. I sometimes think that what "the experts" are expert in is intra-system communication, intra-system relationships and manipulations. It seems that success in intra-system communication and relations governs promotions, raises, demotions, and so on. Incentives are not tied to responsibility for success in the world outside, which is the presumed object of one's activities.

This is deadly. The goal of governing is not to have an impact on the system; it is to have an impact on the world. The goal of foreign policy is not to have an impact on the State Department; it is to have an impact on Ghana or Zimbabwe or wherever. For almost any task it is exceedingly important to say *you* are responsible. *You* do this and report back tomorrow morning and tell us about how *you* got it done. I do not care whether it is a file clerk or an ambassador; it is important to the file clerk or the ambassador to understand his responsibility and then to be held accountable.

In management of bureaucracy, it is important to respect people but not necessarily to respect the existing lines of communications and authority. From time to time, I found it interesting and productive (and sometimes rather amusing) to violate bureaucratic patterns of communication by calling someone seven levels below me to inquire about how a particular project was coming. This creates a lot of consternation (in case you are interested in creating consternation—which I was not), but it is necessary if you are interested in talking to the person who is actually doing the work on which you are going to rely for the achievement of your objective. If that individual was seven levels below and things did not seem to be going right, then that was the person I wanted to talk to. Respecting the people with whom you are working does not require respecting every convention of the organization.

Overall, at USUN we strove to create conditions to attract first-class people, and by clear communication and persuasion to convince them of the correctness of our policies and the appropriateness of their working very hard in support of them. We did this in earnest and I think with success. By the beginning of the third year at USUN we were, I believe, what can be called a happy mission. Most of the career officials were happy to be there. What makes me think so? The fact that almost all of them applied for extensions. They wanted to stay longer.

This provided added benefits, because in most bureaucratic jobs—certainly in foreign policy, certainly in the State Department—the turnover is much too rapid for genuine expertise to develop and accumulate. Expertise, after all, includes human relations with people in the area in which you are working. Too often a person is sent to a new post, and about the time he learns who is who and what is what and develops good working relations, he is moved on to another post. Then somebody new comes in and fills the job who does not know who is who and what is what and does not have good working relations. About the time he learns, then he too is moved on. This is the way that the Peter Principle applies in foreign policy to ensure failure.

I understand that this phenomenon is sometimes referred to as "personnel turbulence." In the interesting new book called *Military Incompetence*, personnel turbulence is shown to be one of the causes of incompetence in the Pentagon as well.[1] I believe it is crucial to dramatically reduce turnover. Once a team has been established, it is important to keep that team relatively stable and intact. This can only enhance the prospects for success in one's endeavors.

Success, of course, is the ultimate persuader. When we first arrived in USUN, there was a habit of U.S. failure in that institution. It was so habitual for the United States to lose that an attitude had developed in much of the permanent bureaucracy that failure was the only appropriate outcome. That was what we were supposed to do. That was what we were there for: to take the rap, to fail, and to be a kind of living example of impotence.

We, however, entered the scene intent on turning things around. We entered with the absolute conviction that it was not America's God-given role in the world to take the rap. America was not, in fact, responsible for all the ills of the world. It helped no one for us to pretend or for them to imagine that we were responsible for all the world's ills. We took off the "Kick Me" sign.

In the beginning, resistance to success was very great. The nay-sayers declared, "Terrible things will happen, you are not supposed to do it that way, you will never succeed." The intriguing thing is that we did succeed. I knew in advance it would take a long-term effort. I suppose another moral of our story is be patient and persistent. We were in our second year before we won a major issue. It was a vote on Puerto Rico, and it was the first time the United States had won a contested issue of principle against someone in the Soviet bloc since around 1973. We won that vote, and that was the first of several victories. Well, the career officers found that they liked winning too. You can develop a taste for winning. Once they found that it was possible to win and that the sky did not fall, they enjoyed it as much as we did.

I truly believe that by the end of the third year most of the career officers were getting as much satisfaction out of our successes in the UN as any of us political appointees. Some of them also paid the same prices. Career officers at times pay a heavy price for faithfully serving strong-minded political appointees. Some of our officers are now experiencing career misfortunes, principally for having served the President with unusual loyalty and skill for four years, and in the process having offended certain career colleagues back in the State Department who were not as pleased with our U.N. successes as we were.

Despite this lack of enthusiasm in some quarters, we did enjoy a good deal of success. How was this success achieved? I think that successful administration of foreign policy requires, to a very important degree, using American power to achieve American objectives: identifying the leverage that is available to you to achieve objectives, harnessing it, bringing it to bear on the achievement of your objectives. If we do not use the leverage available to the United States in the achievement of our objectives, no one thinks you are serious about them, least of all the other countries with whom you are dealing.

To be more specific, in the case of U.S. policy in the United Nations, it seems clear that the biggest single obstacle to American effectiveness in the U.N. system has been our failure to link bilateral diplomacy to multilateral diplomacy. We have focused historically on bilateral relations and treated multilateral relations as though they were at best marginally relevant to our relations with other countries.

For example, inside the United Nations, Ghana always votes against us. At least today Ghana knows that we know that it always votes against us—and while we are still giving some economic assistance to Ghana, Ghana understands that it is less certain than it used to be. The government of Ghana understands now that the American Ambassador in Ghana knows that Ghana's behavior in the U.N. is relevant to our relations. How do the Ghanaians know that? Because our Ambassador goes in and tells them—and often.

Zimbabwe understands not only that its treatment of American interests in the U.N. is relevant to our bilateral relations, but also that it may cost Zimbabwe $40 million per year to be too utterly contemptuous of American interests in the U.N. system for too long a time, particularly if Zimbabwe is also behaving badly toward our values and interests in other areas. If we do not link the instrumentalities of influence to the goals we are trying to implement, then those whom we are trying to influence do not take us seriously. It is a challenge for a manager in foreign policy to identify the various kinds of leverage available and to make use of them, as discreetly and prudently as possible—but still make use of them as part of being a serious representative of a serious nation.

These, then, are the key elements in the effective management of foreign policy. First, selection of a political-executive team that has a clear sense of and commitment to presidential policies, and that has professional knowledge sufficient to guide the bureaucracy rather than be guided by it. Second, a willingness to immerse oneself in the complex details of problems in order to be able to make reasoned and informed policy decisions. Third, selection of a talented career staff that is responsive to political leadership. Fourth, a clear articulation of purposes and a clear assignment of responsibility. Fifth, relative stability among the relevant members of the policy team. And finally, a willingness to use leverage in pursuit of goals.

These principles serve as a foundation to the effective conduct of policy. They will not, in themselves, guarantee success, though they may contribute to it. On the other hand, to ignore these principles is, I believe, to make failure almost inevitable.

Note

1. Richard A. Gabriel, *Military Incompetence* (New York: Hill and Wang, 1985).

15 The Role of the White House Office of Presidential Personnel

BECKY NORTON DUNLOP

Editors' Note: This chapter deals with the political personnel process in the executive branch, specifically with the White House Office of Presidential Personnel (OPP). It is interesting how traditional political science literature has neglected the linkage between the personnel process and policy-making in general, and the role of OPP in particular. The Office truly lies at the hub of policy-making in Washington. If all Reagan appointees had shown the same commitment to conservative policy change as the author, who served as Deputy Director of the Office of Presidential Personnel in the first Reagan Administration, many of the problems addressed in other parts of this book which confronted the Reagan Administration would never have emerged.

Personnel is policy. That assertion is the underlying premise of this paper. For if personnel is not policy, then all a president need do is hire the best head-hunter in the nation and charge him with finding the best techno-crats available to serve. The result might be a well-run government but it would also certainly be a business-as-usual government.

A candidate for president who has a clearly articulated policy perspective as to what the role of government should be and, therefore, what the role of the departments and agencies should be, must of necessity choose personnel who understand and support his policy perspective. If he does not choose like-minded personnel, he will either be forced to attempt to micro-manage the government, to hope for the best, or to accept whatever comes.

Conservatives tend to support candidates for president who articulate a clear policy perspective and plan for dramatic adjustments in govern-ment activities. Thus, these are exactly the types of candidates for whom personnel must be policy. Indeed, Ronald Reagan is this type of president.

This paper discusses several aspects of personnel: the Reagan philosophy of personnel at its inception; the role and operation of the White House Office of Presidential Personnel (OPP); suggestions for improvement; and guidelines for a future conservative president in establishing personnel policy. It does not intend to be a definitive piece on the Reagan personnel process. That is best left for a future paper that can be more complete in its evaluation.

The Reagan Philosophy of Personnel and Initial Selections

In a number of speeches, President Reagan has laid out what he is looking for in political personnel. The following are a sample of his basic themes:

> My basic rule is that I want people who don't want a job in government. I want people who are already so successful that they would regard a government job as a step down, not a step up.[1]

> I don't want empire builders. I want people who will be the first to tell me if their jobs are unnecessary.[2]

> Out there in the private sector, there's an awful lot of brains and talent in people who haven't learned all the things you can't do.[3]

> [We will have] a new structuring of the presidential Cabinet that will make Cabinet officers the managers of the national Administration—not captives of the bureaucracy or special interests in the departments they are supposed to direct.[4]

E. Pendleton James was the executive search professional selected to direct the staff effort on personnel selection. At the beginning of the first Reagan Administration, James added to Reagan's basic themes five widely announced criteria: "commitment to Reagan's objectives, integrity, competence, teamwork, and toughness."[5] A sixth criterion, "commitment to change," was later added.[6]

Pen James had served in the personnel office under President Nixon and knew, in advance, the type of operation that would serve the requirements the President had articulated. Unquestionably, the guidelines that he established are excellent and adequately provide a conservative administration with the framework for selecting the "best, brightest, and most qualified" people.[7]

As for the initial Cabinet and sub-Cabinet selection process itself, President Reagan used a Transition Advisory Committee, often referred to as the "extended kitchen cabinet." This group sifted through the names and material provided about potential candidates. (Often they were the source of the names although the staff operation supplied names as well.) They pared the candidates down to a short list that the committee would then discuss with the President. Included in the personnel decision-making process in addition to the kitchen cabinet were the Vice President, Michael Deaver, and James Baker. Although the President made the final Cabinet selections himself, all reports indicate that he followed the consensus of his advisors in almost every case.[8]

Interestingly, despite a process that seemed to be designed to select an atypical Cabinet, the results were not as expected. G. Calvin Mackenzie has noted in a paper on the Reagan personnel process that even with the guidelines and process which the Reagan team employed, the characteristics of the Reagan Cabinet were not substantially different from the traditional pattern. In fact, Mackenzie states, "In superficial appearances, at least, most of these early appointments could have been made as easily and comfortably by Richard Nixon or Gerald Ford as by Ronald Reagan."[9] William French Smith was quoted at the time as saying that he wouldn't be surprised if some of the people who supported Reagan would be unhappy with our choices.[10]

Thus, the system set in place was designed to ensure selection of top-level appointees based on a set of guidelines and principles dedicated to change. But in practice, it appeared that other factors played a greater role than was originally envisioned. First, some believe that the personnel selection process was deliberately used to heal the fissure between the two wings of the Republican Party. If this were true, it would account for the use of certain conventional networks of recruitment that were not fully consistent with the formally announced selection criteria. Second, personal relationships or recommendations from influential figures outside the White House at times facilitated the progress of a particular candidate through the personnel system at the expense of competing candidates who were favored by more objective criteria. Too often these personal recommendations were not well thought out, but nevertheless outweighed the more careful and painstaking evaluations of the staff.

A third, often overlooked, factor influencing the selection process was simply the unwillingness of some individuals to serve. In many cases, excellent candidates were offered high-level positions but for one reason or another turned them down, leaving the field open for other, less desirable, prospects. Fourth, personnel selection is not a science; there is an inherent unpredictability in the process. Often individuals who by all standards seemed to be impeccable choices turned out to be otherwise. The degree of unpredictability was enhanced by the fact that many appointees were entering a new environment in Washington, an environment in which they had never operated or been tested.

Perhaps the individuals involved in the original selection process underestimated the entrenched power of the status quo in Washington; they did not comprehend that the battle to control policy after an election would be as hard fought as the battle to win the election. Nonetheless, some of the problems in personnel selection that emerged at the onset of the Reagan Administration have persisted in subsequent years. In any respect, the Reagan experience has clearly underscored from the beginning that personnel *is* policy, though not always with the results desired.

Role of the Office of Presidential Personnel

Following the original selection of top-level officials, the task of staffing the Administration has largely fallen to the White House Office of Presidential Personnel (OPP). OPP has had as its mission the recruitment and selection of the best, brightest, and most qualified individuals committed to carrying out the President's stated agenda. What is the President's stated agenda? For starters, it was his campaign statements, commitments, and promises. Upon assuming office, the agenda is further defined by his speeches and his budget recommendations.

Anyone who is considered for a position in the Administration should have a clearly demonstrated support for this agenda. *Anyone, without regard to personal friendships or high-powered supporters, who cannot demonstrate a commitment to the President's agenda should not be recruited for his Cabinet or for head of an agency.* Recruiting people with demonstrated commitment to the President's policy goals does not guarantee that the appointee will be successful but it does insure that the effort to carry out the mandate will be made.

Nature of the System

There is an ongoing debate regarding personnel selection in an administration. One argument favors a centralized process with recruitment and clearance procedures handled exclusively by a White House office with a large enough staff to handle the 3,000-plus political positions within the executive branch. The alternative argument favors a completely decentralized process. In this system, recruitment for Cabinet and agency head positions would be handled by the White House, all other positions being filled directly by the departments and agencies; a small White House staff would be used for processing the necessary legal documents. The third option, and the one the Reagan Administration has pursued generally, is a combination of the two insuring that the President retains ultimate authority over political appointments at all levels within the executive branch, while receiving input from Cabinet secretaries and agency heads concerning subordinate appointments within their own organizations.

In the current system, Presidential Personnel recruits and selects persons for Cabinet-level and agency-head positions. OPP is also directly involved in recruiting and approving persons for all political positions at levels below the Cabinet right down to private secretaries. However, the departments and agencies are encouraged to recruit candidates at these sub-Cabinet levels as well. Both the White House staff and the departmental staffs conduct interviews and each wields substantial influence over the candidate selection process; however, all selections must ultimately meet with White House approval. Through this two-channel process, the universe of candidates being considered is enlarged, and both the President (through his personnel office) and the Cabinet secretary or agency head are assured that their qualifications can be met. Of course, this method demonstrates quite clearly the need for the White House and the Cabinet officers to have the same policy objectives, since different objectives would likely result in different requirements or qualifications.

A president such as Ronald Reagan who comes to the federal government with a clear set of principles, goals, and expectations for his Administration, which have been forcefully enunciated over a period of years, needs some centralization of the process to insure that personnel decisions government-wide reflect his priorities. On the other hand, he wants to be able to delegate authority to his Cabinet secretaries to the maximum permitting them the broadest possible flexibility on personnel matters. Thus, the hybrid personnel process meets both needs in theory.

This, indeed, seemed to be the decision made by candidate Ronald Reagan and his team of advisors. They established a centralized process early, even before the election, and handled recruitment of all Cabinet people exclusively. Then, as Cabinet members were selected, they were included in the decision-making process for the sub-Cabinet personnel in their respective departments. A clearance process was also established for the first time for the balance of the political appointees to set the standard to which all noncareer personnel would be held. All noncareer/political personnel were expected to have voted in the 1980 election and to have given some level of support to the Reagan/Bush campaign or to a candidate for another office who supported Reagan/Bush. Designated officials on the White House staff had to approve each of these noncareer appointees before they were to be hired.[11]

This hybrid system is the right system for any Administration that wants to hold to standards such as were laid out for Reagan Administration appointees. It is the right system for any conservative president who wants to make a difference. Criticisms of the Reagan presidential personnel process can be laid at the door of individual decisions but not at the door of the process. Indeed, each of us who served in the Presidential Personnel Office is willing to admit that we made mistakes on individual personnel decisions.

The System in Operation

As one reviews the record of Presidential Personnel in the Reagan White House, it must be remembered that the structure of the White House staff for the first four years had enormous impact on the selection process and the decision-making process of the personnel office. James Baker, the Chief of Staff, Michael Deaver, the Deputy Chief of Staff, and Ed Meese, the Counselor to the President, were the three people who had the final review on all personnel recommendations before they were submitted to the President. They also could give a direct order to the OPP regarding any position or person below the level requiring Senate confirmation, although that seldom occurred.

These three very powerful people were extrememly busy with all of their various responsibilities, and personnel was just one item on their agendas, an item to which they could give little time. The OPP took into consideration each of their approaches to personnel and their interests during the selection process, so that sensitivities would be dealt with before the name or position hit their desks. For one, it was policy and management experience; for another, it was politics and business; and for the third, it was more personal—positions in which he had a special interest or people he regarded as high priorities. These were not exclusive concerns but rather general perspectives that OPP tried to anticipate. The point is that OPP was trying to select people who would meet quite explicit criteria satisfying to the President, the relevant Cabinet secretary, and three very different top presidential advisors. (Also involved was the White House counsel's office, which had the responsibility for reviewing, commenting, and advising upon the broad and thorough security investigations that every Presidential Appointee with Senate confirmation (PAS) must undergo.) This was all in addition to the professional qualities which were identified as necessary for each particular position to be filled.

Of course, another factor that played a key role in the selection process was the Congress. Congress is always in the back of the personnel officer's mind, particularly when Senate confirmation is required for a particular position. Members of Congress play a key role in the president's program and need to have their concerns considered if not always accommodated. Powerful members control agendas, committee hearings, budgets, critical votes; and they require attention. Often the input is welcome: good candidates, good information, or consideration of a constituent's interest. At other times, the input is less welcome. But whatever the input, it will influence the decision and must be carefully considered.

There were other problems as well. Forum-shopping is a term often used in the political world, and it is quite applicable to the personnel process, unfortunately. Forum-shopping takes place when a person or persons look for the most favorable arena in which to present his or her point of view in hopes of winning an ally if not the battle. Candidates shopped the White House staff looking for a powerful figure to push their names through the process; Cabinet secretaries shopped the White House staff to find one who would support their candidates or force a personnel decision to be overridden; members of Congress shopped for the right time and right place to demand their "must hires" or to solicit assistance to place "just one," since, it would be argued, that none of their recommendations to the personnel office were ever hired. In these forum-shopping cases, too often personnel decisions were made too quickly or traded too quickly by officials who should have said, "Let me get the details from personnel and I will get back to you." Such a response would have surely resulted in better personnel decisions or at least in the White House getting an even deal in the trade.

Improving the System

The OPP has always been treated as a stepchild in the ranks of White House offices. This does not enable the office to do the best job possible for the president. It is not a part of the policy-making apparatus, the legislative apparatus, or the political apparatus. Thus, it tends to conduct its affairs in a vacuum. This is not a desirable situation and can lead to difficulty and sometimes disaster. We have seen a few of these incidents in the past six years.

Communication among White House staff on personnel matters is among the most important work that can be done. Such communication can speed up the process, sort out pitfalls and difficulties, clarify policy goals, identify past failures, create good will among concerned constituent groups, and, in general, create a more collegial spirit among all members of the Administration.

The Reagan Administration recognized the potential pitfall early and accorded Pen James the rank of Assistant to the President, housing him in the West Wing of the White House to visibly demonstrate the importance that President Reagan placed on the role personnel played in his Administration. This positioning also provided James with the access necessary for constant interaction with his peers on the senior White House staff. This recognition is essential for any administration that believes that personnel is policy.

Beyond this, a recommendation has been made to give the Assistant to the President for Cabinet Affairs overall responsibility for the personnel office and the policy office combined. This would insure that all candidates for high office would have their policy views evaluated by those White House staff who develop policy and have a clear understanding of the President's policy goals. The Assistant to the President for Cabinet Affairs would have charge not only of personnel selection but also of evaluating the performance of appointees in office. That is, the policy office and the Cabinet office could provide feedback on performance of political appointees in carrying out the President's policies. Such a program of systematic review during the selection process *and* during the tenure of appointees would improve the team approach of selecting senior policy-makers and regularize the evaluation of their performance. Although this recommendation may not be fully appropriate from an organizational perspective, the purpose of the suggestion remains valid and should be seriously considered in future conservative White House organizational structures.

This brings us to a weak link in the personnel process in the Administration: removal of an appointee who is not pulling his/her load or who is openly thwarting the President's programs. Mistakes are always made in the selection process because you never really know how people will perform in the federal government setting until they are tested under fire. However, once it becomes apparent that the appointee cannot carry out the mission or will not carry out the mission, that person should be counseled. He or she should then either move to a new position—if the problem is one of the wrong fit—or be asked to leave the Administration if the problem is simply refusal to accept the President's decisions on budget or policy matters.

Becoming captured by a bureaucracy as opposed to leading and managing the bureaucracy is not uncommon, and those appointees who fall prey to this malady must be dealt with by the President's senior policy advisors carefully but quickly. The result will be improved performance by all appointees within the Administration.

Today, there are several persons still serving in high-level positions who have lobbied against presidential decisions, fought and subverted the President's budget after if was submitted to Congress, and worked actively to undermine overall goals of the Reagan Administration. Some have engaged in this activity out of misdirection or misunderstanding, while the motives of others are not so easily explained. These individuals are able to remain in their positions because there is no coherent system in place for handling such people—particularly when they have friends in important Administration posts. A review system would permit action to proceed in a routine manner and would strengthen the personnel process overall.

Of course, there are a few examples where quick action was taken to remove someone from a high-level position who was deemed to be a problem. These decisions have not, however, resulted from policy or budget insubordination but rather from legal problems. There are few easy decisions, but legal problems make the decision to remove someone easier.

Another aspect of the process that should be strengthened is that of rewarding superior performance. Too often, it seems, those who take on responsibilities in various departments and carry out the agenda of the President in a timely, efficient, and successful manner are passed over by the OPP when other vacancies occur. These vacancies are often filled with qualified people from outside the government when the most prudent decision would be to move a current appointee into a new position, thereby rewarding him for a job well done. This would renew the appointee's enthusiasm with a new challenge, and take advantage of his knowledge and expertise in managing operations in the government.

In recent months, a number of people have left the Reagan Administration because there has been little evidence of this reward incentive. Still others wait patiently after two, three, or four years of excellent service to see if their efforts will be rewarded. Too often, their expectations fail to be met.

A third link that needs to be strengthened is that of preparing incoming personnel for the task which they face. Pen James talked early about the need for providing some guidance to appointees before they were thrust into the unknown bureaucracy. This idea was expanded somewhat during the early years of the Reagan Administration, but it needs to be formalized and implemented right at the start of a new conservative administration. The Heritage Foundation proposed an excellent program providing multifaceted training from "policy to process" in conjunction with appropriate Administration agencies. But the program was never approved.

Finally, Presidential Personnel has worked very hard to establish and maintain good relationships with the White House liaisons in the various departments and agencies. This is a critical link in the teamwork of the personnel operation. Efforts to bolster this role should be continued.

Results

Has the Reagan personnel operation been successful? I would have to argue that the results have been mixed. I believe that a fair evaluation reveals that a revolutionary system was set in place by the Reagan Administration, a system that should have provided for the President to select and appoint all the Cabinet and sub-Cabinet members based on specific conservative criteria that he established. The White House personnel office established and maintained standards (admittedly they have varied somewhat from director to director but they were nevertheless government-wide standards) to which all noncareer personnel were held. The top personnel officer was accorded senior staff rank and position, emphasizing the importance the President placed on the role of personnel.

Though we can all find great successes and perhaps great failures for which the personnel process must accept responsibility, examples of the success of the process have been profoundly demonstrated at the Executive Forum held in Constitution Hall for three of the last four years. (This is a huge meeting of all political appointees in the Administration.) At each of these events, the single member of the Cabinet who is most closely identified with the Reagan Revolution and its principles and goals has been accorded an obvious and overwhelming reception by the attendees, the foot soldiers of the Reagan Revolution. In 1983, this ovation was given to Jim Watt; in 1984, to Jeane Kirkpatrick; and in 1986, to Ed Meese. Clearly as these individuals demonstrate, something within the personnel process has worked right.[12]

Guidelines for the Future

So, what of the future? What should a conservative president do to insure the success of his policy? The following recommendations are a good place to start.

- Start early on the organization. Pick your first personnel advisors carefully. Remember, personnel is policy.
- Establish the guidelines and principles quickly. Reagan's are excellent: commitment to the president's objectives, integrity, competence, teamwork, toughness, and a commitment to change. But remember, without commitment to change, all else is irrelevant.
- Insure that your personnel officer is well versed in policy and that the White House policy office has key responsibility in personnel selection.
- Establish your top personnel officer as a key member of your senior advisors who is integrated into the daily management of the presidency.
- Maintain the integrity of the personnel system by involving your personnel staff in every decision and discussion on staffing the government. If this team concept is not supported by the president, the system will fail.

Notes

1. James Reston, "Reagan's Recruiting Philosophy," *The New York Times*, November 12, 1980.

2. Ibid.

3. Ibid.

4. Hedrick Smith, "Reagan Seeks to Emphasize Role of Cabinet Members as Advisers," special to *The New York Times*, November 8, 1980.

5. Dick Kirschten, "Wanted: 275 Reagan Team Players; Empire Builders Need Not Apply," *National Journal*, Vol. 12, No. 49.

6. Calvin MacKenzie, interview with E. Pendleton James, The White House, Washington, D.C., July 13, 1981, p. 2077.

7. Many people believe that Pen James also placed heavy emphasis on recruiting persons with prior government experience. To my knowledge, James did not place a heavy emphasis on this criterion.

8. Stephen Weisman, "Reagan's 'Kitchen Cabinet' Strengthening Its Influence," special to *The New York Times*, November 30, 1980.

9. MacKenzie, "Cabinet and Subcabinet Personnel Selection in Reagan's First Year: New Variation on Some Not-So-Old Themes," paper delivered at the annual meeting of the American Political Science Association, New York, September 1981.

10. "Choosing for the Chairman," *Time*, December 8, 1980.

11. The one exception to this is in certain independent agencies where White House control over staffing subordinate positions is legally limited.

12. Another aspect of success in the personnel process is invisible. It consists of bad potential appointments which are blocked. In this respect, OPP has been consistently active and effective. Much that the Reagan Administration has accomplished can be attributed to this persistent exercise of preventive medicine.

16 Differences in Public- and Private-Sector Management

ROBERT RECTOR

Editors' Note: When the White House asks an individual to manage a department, agency, or program, it is rare that anyone bothers to explain exactly what is meant by "managing" in government. Failure to clarify what it means to be a "manager" in the public sector has led otherwise able individuals to flounder in a hostile political environment. On the other hand, an understanding of the principal dimensions of political/public-sector management and how such management differs from that in the private sector is a prerequisite to success as a political appointee.

All presidents come to Washington with an ambitious agenda. They want to correct the mistakes of past administrations and make their mark on the future. To do this they need help, and they often call upon the "best and brightest" to help them. Within the ranks of the helpers are often a high proportion of skilled managers from the private sector. This is particularly true of Republican administrations because, as noted in previous chapters, Republicans are fond of the notion that the problem with government is that it is not run as efficiently as a business. Therefore, the solution to government inefficiency is to hire skilled business managers. A related notion is that administrative skills should be paramount in selecting political appointees: that it is important to have individuals with proven abilities in directing vast organizations—hence again a tendency to import such individuals from the business sector.

These concepts are reinforced by a trend in one part of the academic community to regard public- and private-sector management as essentially alike and to regard management skills as transferable between the two sectors. As one professor puts it:

> For perhaps two generations scholars and practitioners have realized that management can be viewed as a generic process, with universal implications and with application in any political setting—whether a private firm or a public agency.[1]

Another "expert" contends:

> As things stand, a fairly straightforward business management

approach is probably appropriate for a large number of government activities.²

In reality, these notions are inaccurate. Success in private-sector management does not necessarily lead to success in government. Public-sector and private-sector management are not alike because the functions and nature of organizations in the two sectors are not alike. Indeed, techniques and perspectives learned in the private sector may be highly inappropriate when transposed into government.

Four essential differences between the public and private sectors can be identified. These relate both to inherent differences in the nature of the respective organizations and to corresponding differences in the role of management within those organizations. These four basic differences are:

1. In the private sector the marketplace is the "ultimate manager"; in the public sector the political appointee, Congress, the bureaucracy, and interest groups compete over the role of ultimate manager.

2. The marketplace imposes a uniformity of goals and behavior on the members of a private-sector firm; the absence of such a disciplining factor in government allows a plurality of competitive goals to persist in a single organization.

3. As a corollary of the above, the goals of a private-sector manager are set by the very nature of his organization; on the other hand, the single most important function of a political appointee is to select among policy goals based on competing social values and philosophies—a function that simply does not exist in the job of a private-sector executive.

4. The information system used in private-sector management, based on profit-and-loss statements, does not exist in government organizations; the very nature of management is thereby different.

The conservative economic view holds that organizations are never naturally efficient or rational. Indeed, we might say that if left to their own devices, most organizations inherently tend to become inefficient and stagnant. In the private sector, the external hand of the market forces the organization to be efficient. The market's discipline imposes rationality on private-sector organizations; once that discipline is removed, the internal rationality of the organization will evaporate. The external competitive environment also demands that private-sector organizations be more manageable than public-sector organizations; marketplace firms that cannot be managed cannot survive.

In the marketplace, the public speaks directly to the firm with its dollars by purchasing or refusing to purchase goods. There is little room for evasion, equivocation, or misunderstanding in this type of highly articulate exchange. The marketplace is the ultimate manager—clear, authoritative, and firm in its decisions.

The public-sector bureaucracy is insulated from the general public; it has far fewer incentives to adjust or change. In the public sector there is no equivalent to the discriminating consumer; elections are a very pale substitute. Even the significance of an election may be diffuse, since there are many mixed issues before the voters at once. The election's impact will not be direct—as, for example, a downturn of sales and profits—but will be mitigated through many layers of competing political power, both official and unofficial. To many bureaucracies, an election—even decisive elections such as those of 1980 and 1984—is like a distant earthquake. It is sometimes annoying but seldom more than that.

In democratic theory, the political appointee represents the will of the people delegated through the elected president. Thus, the political appointee is not the equivalent of a private-sector manager—as some contend—but should be considered, by analogy, as equivalent to the external market forces sending signals to the private-sector firm. Rather than being a simple manager, the political appointee is a vital part of the chain of communication that passes information and values from the voting public through the president to the bureaucracy. Thus, while the private-sector executive has a single role—managing the response of the organization to signals communicated by the marketplace—the political appointee in the public sector plays two roles: (1) a conveyor of signals and values from the electoral process to the bureaucracy; (2) a manager of the organizational response to electoral signals. The management style of the political appointee must reflect this dual responsibility.

In attempting to fulfill the role of ultimate manager that is played by the marketplace in the private sector, the political appointee faces a very difficult task. Unfortunately, the political appointee is far less powerful than the consumer. Given our system of separation of powers, he cannot simply refuse to give more money to an agency that produces wasteful, inefficient, or even destructive services. He must compete with other forces that seek to direct the agency; change is far more difficult to achieve in a public-sector organization than in the private sector.

A second way that private- and public-sector organizations differ is that in the private sector members of the organization must share the same goals. The external forces of the market compel the individuals in the firm to subordinate their personal goals to the necessary goals of the firm—efficiency, innovation, and growth. Managers within the private-sector firm may disagree about the best way to achieve the firm's goals; labor and management may be at odds. But the competitive environment places definite limits on how far internal dissension may go without jeopardizing the firm and the livelihood of all its members.

All members of a private-sector organization are thus, to a degree, players on the same team. There may be disagreements, but if the members rock the boat too much it will capsize; the firm will be swamped by competitive market pressures and sink. It is perhaps regrettable that no one has developed such a simple means for sinking a government bureaucracy.

By contrast, political appointees and the members of their government bureaucracy do not necessarily share the same goals. There is no external disciplining force that compels career members of the organizations to subordinate their personal goals to those of the political leadership. If a government bureaucracy is paralyzed by internal dissent, it won't go bankrupt; it may even get more money.

In many bureaucracies a conservative political appointee arriving to take control is like a new general manager arriving at a Ford auto plant. He finds that his deputy directors were hired by and are employees of GM. He also finds that many workers on the assembly line are also employees of GM—and that another large group of employees believes that automobiles are metaphysically evil and shouldn't be built at all because they will destroy the environment. Then the new manager discovers that he cannot fire any of these subordinates and that he can reassign some of them only with difficulty.

Clearly if this manager is to be successful he must adopt management techniques that differ widely from those used in most private-sector firms. So too, a successful conservative appointee must often adopt management techniques that differ from those of the private sector. He must also adopt techniques that differ from those of liberal political appointees in government.

The third major difference between the public and private sectors is related to the second. By the very nature of his organization and of the marketplace, the goals of a private-sector manager are established for him: Increase profits and production; expand market share; and cut costs. The political appointee, on the other hand, does not have pre-established goals; instead, he has a range of what, at times, may be disquieting, theoretical freedom.

Choice of policy goals—the political agenda—is the foremost task of a political appointee. If the appointee is misguided in this task, all his other efforts will be wasted. The fact that the principal task of a political appointee—selecting the goals of his organization from a nearly limitless range of options—is not a responsibility of a private-sector manager belies any contention concerning the fundamental similarity of the two styles of management.

The existence of a number of polite buzz words in political discourse such as "strong America," "economic prosperity," and "fairness" does not mean that there are in fact uniform goals behind these words, equivalent to the common goals of private businesses. The Soviet Union and the United States both profess to seek "world peace," but hardly on the same terms. Political reality, both internationally and domestically, consists of competition between sharply divergent social visions. One either believes the government takes too great a share of the national economy, or one does not. One either accepts the notion that the government should substantially redistribute income, or one does not. One either accepts color-blind justice which does not discriminate on the basis of race, or one promotes an arbitrary equality of results through quotas that discriminate against certain groups.

The job of a political appointee is to chart a coherent policy course within this environment of clashing social visions. In this endeavor, his first guide must be the overarching philosophy of the president who appointed him. However, there are thousands of issues before the government today; a president cannot establish explicit policy on every issue. It is the task of the political appointee to interpret the general philosophy of the president as it pertains to his specific agency or programs.

In selecting a policy agenda, the political appointee will also be influenced by criteria from economic theory, ethics, political philosophy, and history. His decisions will be undergirded by notions of proper social order, and by his approach to complex questions concerning the delicate balance between the governmental, economic, social, cultural, and religious spheres of society. If the appointee has no explicit ideological viewpoint in these areas, his views will simply echo the conventional wisdom of the society around him; the policy change such an appointee will accomplish is likely to be inconsequential or counterproductive. Clearly, decisions made in this realm have little to do with the day-to-day practical decisions of a business executive; the knowledge required is not knowledge of business management.

Most political appointees who fail do so at this initial level of formulating a policy agenda. Often they will formulate no agenda at all, or will have an agenda thrust upon them by the bureaucracy, by interest groups, or by political opponents. Or they will "pre-compromise" their goals, making an agenda that is politically palatable but that is no more than a variation of the status quo. Such appointees will leave little mark on the government.

The fourth major difference between public- and private-sector management pertains to the information systems within the respective organizations. The private-sector executive is equipped with a "profit-and-loss" accounting system that covers his entire operation. Although this information does not make the executive omniscient, it does provide a reasonably accurate set of tools with which to make decisions. The eminent Austrian economist Ludwig von Mises, discussing the differences between market and governmental organizations, stressed the importance of the profit-and-loss statement in the day-to-day operational management of a firm.

> The elaborate methods of modern bookkeeping, accounting, and business statistics provide the enterpriser with a faithful image of all his operations. He is in a position to learn how successful or unsuccessful every one of his transactions was. *With the aid of these statements he can check the activities of all departments of his concern no matter how large it may be.* There is, to be sure, some amount of discretion in determining the distribution of overhead costs. But apart from this, the figures provide a faithful reflection of all that is going on in every branch or department. The books and the balance sheets are the conscience of business. *They are also the businessman's compass. . . . By means of this . . . the businessman can at any time survey the general whole, without needing to perplex himself with the details.*[3] (Emphasis added.)

The manager of a government organization has no information system equivalent to the profit-and-loss statement, which, while far from perfect, must reflect objective conditions and can only be "fudged" in a limited way. Government productivity measures and program evaluations, on the other hand, produce extremely "soft" information and may be deliberately misleading. Moreover, even low-quality information of this sort is often unavailable within the government.

Thus, while crucial information is provided automatically to the private-sector executive by the firm's financial accounting system, the political executive is in a constant battle to obtain meaningful information about the operations he is nominally managing. Even worse, because government information is "soft," the political appointee may become inundated by information pushing the bureaucracy's viewpoint and bias his decisions accordingly. To counteract for these deficiencies, the political appointee must develop a unique management style.

Although the businessman may delegate wide authority to subordinates and hold them accountable for the results, the political executive cannot do this because he lacks the information to check on the results: the content of the program. Consequently, political managers must delegate far less than business managers. Political managers must assume they have far less information than they appear to have; they must monitor their organization closely and become deeply involved in the administrative details of their organization. The appointee needs a large staff of political subordinates to help him in his struggle for information. (Proper management would require that the number of political personnel in the executive branch be doubled from present numbers.) The appointee should also use outside consultants and keep in close contact with external organizations to ensure that he is getting balanced information.

• • •

The differences between private- and public-sector management are great. This does not mean that businessmen should not serve as appointees in the executive branch, but rather that they should be prepared, upon entering the government, with a proper understanding of the differences in the role of management in the two spheres. It does mean that many of the factors that will contribute to success among political appointees will not be relevant to business-sector decision-making.

The nature of management in government has often been misunderstood. Given the vague and contradictory nature of much contemporary legislation, the job of the political manager in the executive branch is often to set policy by establishing those regulations that implement the law. (See Chapter 7.) Beyond this, the appointee will also shape policy through budgetary decisions and through proposals for new legislation. The role of the political manager in government is not to "make the trains run on time." It is to determine where the trains will go or if they should run at all. The importance of his decisions will often not be in his immediate impact on particular government operations but on his indirect and long-term impact on the economy, on society, and on the dimensions of human freedom.

Notes

1. Michael Murray, "Comparing Public and Private Management: An Explanatory Essay," *Public Administration Review* 35, July/August 1975, p. 364.

2. Howard E. McCurdy, "Selecting and Training Public Managers: Business Skills Versus Public Administration," *Public Administration Review* 38, November/December 1978, p. 577.

3. Ludwig von Mises, *Bureaucracy* (New Rochelle, N.Y.: Arlington House, 1969), p. 32.

17 Paradoxical Lessons From
In Search of Excellence

MICHAEL SANERA

Editors' Note: This article continues the discussion of the preceeding chapter. Similarities and differences between management in the public and private sectors are explored. Difficulties in borrowing techniques from the private sector are examined.

Introduction

It is often argued that management lessons learned from successful private-sector companies can be applied to the public sector. In 1982, when Thomas Peters and Robert Waterman published their phenomenal bestseller *In Search of Excellence (ISE)*, the book not only achieved instant success in the private sector, but also became very popular among public-sector managers.[1] It was thought by many that the lessons of *ISE* could be applied directly to government. One public-sector manager who believed this was Paul Carlin, who, when appointed Postmaster General in 1985, sent 12,000 copies of *ISE* to Postal Service managers and instructed them to implement its management recommendations. Apparently, the book's advice did not work: Carlin was fired by the Board of Governors less than a year after his appointment and replaced by Albert Casey, former American Airlines chairman.[2]

However, Paul Carlin was not alone. Many political appointees in the federal government sought to emulate the success of private firms by importing into government the management techniques described by Peters and Waterman. Carlin's effort was but the latest episode in a long tradition of attempting to graft the twig of business management onto the tree of the public sector. As in the past, this attempt failed because of a lack of understanding of the fundamental differences between the two sectors that were described in the preceeding chapter. These differences are:

- In the private sector the market guides; in the public sector the political executive guides in competition with other forces.
- In the private sector, organizations are unified by a single goal; in the public sector, organizations contain a diversity of conflicting goals.

- In the private sector, management goals are given; in the public sector, the essence of management is the selection of goals.
- The private and public sectors operate on different information systems.

Unless these basic differences are understood, any attempt to translate insights from one sector to the other will produce gibberish.

This does not mean, of course, that there is nothing that can be learned from *ISE*. Because Peters and Waterman offer insight into the nature of institutions, they have much to offer the student of government and the political executive in government. By combining an understanding of the inherent differences between the private and public sectors with insights into organizational behavior garnered from Peters and Waterman, we may be able to draw useful lessons about governmental management. However, these lessons will differ sharply from those produced by a simplistic imitation of private business. Indeed, many of the lessons will be the diametric opposite of the conventional wisdom inappropriately derived from Peters and Waterman's best seller; they will be *lessons of paradox.*

The purpose of this chapter thus is to review the management recommendations found in *ISE* and adjust them on the basis of the differences between the sectors. Six key factors that Peters and Waterman believe distinguish successful from unsuccessful companies have been selected for discussion. These six factors are:

- Organizational Culture
- Management of Values
- Use of Hands-On Management
- Bias for Action
- People-Oriented Management
- Habit-Breaking Reorganizations

Organizational Culture

Perhaps the most consistent theme propounded by Peters and Waterman is that successful companies develop and maintain strong organizational cultures.[3] These cultures represent a set of shared values that guide the day-to-day decision-making of all levels of the organization. Every McDonald's employee knows the values instilled and enforced by its founder Ray Kroc: quality, service, cleanliness, and value. Everyone at Procter & Gamble knows that product quality is number one. And everyone at IBM knows that "IBM means service." These values are instilled in all members of the firm and act as a control mechanism. Employees, being part of the culture, automatically adjust their behavior to conform to the corporate values.

The creator of an organizational culture is usually the founder. He shapes the development of the organization using symbols, rituals, and myths. Founders take on the roles of mythic proportions, as illustrated by the legends that surround them. Mythical stories abound about Thomas J. Watson of IBM, A. P. Giannini of Bank of America, and Robert Wood Johnson of Johnson & Johnson, many of which are told by employees who have never even seen these men. The rich tapestry of myths and legends produces the feeling of belonging needed by members of the corporation. Their jobs are not just activities that fill time between 8 and 5, but are an extremely meaningful part of their lives because they are part of a culture of shared values. The threat of sanction by either management or a worker's peers is extremely significant because it means ostracism from the cultural context.[4]

The most important part of this strong cultural context is the way it impacts on employee behavior. Employees within a strong organizational culture, as Peters and Waterman indicate, are at the same time both controlled and free. Managers allow considerable opportunity for personal autonomy to innovate and even fail because employees and managers share a common set of values that constrain the actions of all employees. In reality, the actual range of possible employee behaviors is limited by the culture, and wide deviations from the cultural norms do not occur.[5]

Since the corporate culture is so important to the success of these firms, they do not leave the nurturing of the culture to chance. *ISE* notes that successful firms conduct extensive training of new employees in order to "socialize" them into the culture. New employees at Disneyland must attend extensive training sessions even if their job is as mundane as taking tickets. Training emphasizes the learning of a new language. At Disneyland, employees are no longer employees but "cast members." The personnel department is called the "casting office." Cast members are not on duty but "on stage," and the customers are "Guests" with a capital "G."[6] This change in language transmits the culture and values of Disneyland to the new employees. Cast members automatically know that they are in the entertainment business, and their objective is to insure that the Guests have a good time. Thus, socialization into the corporate culture is a key component of the success of the private business enterprise.

Public-sector organizations have similar organizational cultures, but with essential differences. Public-sector cultures are not created by the corporate founder, but by the statute establishing the agency. The values of the organization originate in the heroic purpose of the statute: Eliminate poverty, clean up the air and water, make the country energy independent, etc. This noble mission is usually based on the liberal assumption of the effectiveness of positive government. When a societal problem is identified, liberal "reformers" create a government agency to address the problem. Action by the government, it is claimed, will "eliminate" the problem. This positive view of government action runs counter to the philosophy of a conservative president such as Ronald Reagan.[7] It should be obvious that a conservative political executive emphasizing the negative consequences of government action and the superiority of the market and quasi-market approaches will come into conflict with the bureaucratic culture in most agencies.

After the authorizing statute is passed, the development of the agency culture is almost entirely in the hands of those who believe in the benefits of positive government, whether they are career bureaucrats or liberal political appointees, or both. Each agency culture develops patterns of myths and legends over its history. Similarly, new employees are socialized into the organizational culture. In both sectors, socialization takes place at the bottom and top levels, but the crucial socialization that affects policy change in the public sector takes place at the top. Political executives who are supposed to control the agency are subjected to an intense indoctrination into the values of the agency culture by career executives. Although this is, in part, unavoidable due to the fact that career employees must inform new political executives of statutory constraints on policy, the process has an automatic bias toward preservation of the status quo and maintenance of bureaucratic power.

Mechanisms for this socialization are many. The initial briefings by career executives, the sixty pounds of briefing books prepared by the career staff, the obligatory tour of the field locations are all components of the process. These mechanisms are all loaded with the language of the bureaucratic culture. For example, the Small Business Administration uses a language that stresses its vital assistance to the small business community even though it provides loans to less than 0.2 percent of small businesses each year, and 20 to 40 percent of those loans will end in default (see Chapter 22). If the new political executive adopts that language, he will be effectively socialized into that culture. Peters and Waterman's image of a strong organizational culture should be recognized by every political appointee. Many presidents have recognized the power of agency cultures by reflecting that so many of their political appointees have "gone native in the bureaucracy."

The political executives who are especially susceptible to socialization are those who are without a strong political value system or those who view their role as improving the management efficiency of government. Both types of political executives are easy prey for the cultural values of the agency. On the other hand, political executives who are strongly committed to President Reagan's conservative philosophy are best able to resist the socialization process and win the cultural war between conservative and bureaucratic values.

Key differences between the public- and private-sector organization exist because cultural values in private-sector institutions are and should be constant over time. One does not expect the shared cultural values of McDonald's to change from year to year; all McDonald's employees from the top to the bottom conform to these consistent values. In the public sector, on the other hand, elections often demand a rapid change in the institutional values. The new political executive will bring "alien values" into the government organization. The government organization will respond, as noted, by trying to neutralize these foreign values and to absorb the appointee into the prevailing institutional culture. This absorption process replicates similar processes that exist in successful private-sector firms, but its consequences in the public sector are anything but benign; to the extent that absorption occurs, stagnation or even government expansion will reign in Washington.

The successful political executive will maintain a separate set of values that are in fundamental contradiction to the value culture of the organization he is managing. This may often result in a level of intra-institutional tension and conflict that has no counterpart in successful private-sector firms but that is essential to the effective operation of a democracy.

Management of Values

Peters and Waterman found that leaders of successful companies actively manage the values of their organizations. Specifically, they identify the role of the chief executive as the control over the "values of the organization."[8] They argue that the academic world supports their findings in excellent companies. They cite that often overlooked book, *Leadership and Administration* by Philip Selznick, as evidence of the qualities of the organizational leader.

> The art of the creative leader is the art of institution building, the re-working of human and technological materials to fashion an organism that embodies new and enduring values. . . . To institutionalize is to infuse with value beyond the technical requirements of the task at hand. . . . The institutional leader, then, is primarily *an expert in the promotion and protection of values.*[9] (Emphasis added.)

But what values should be promoted and protected? Peters and Waterman found that excellent companies strove to be the best. McDonald's strives to be the best at providing quality, service, cleanliness, and value.

Maytag builds the best washing machines. And Caterpillar provides the best service, as illustrated by its motto, "Forty-eight-hour parts service anywhere in the world." These values are not only exalted by excellent companies, but ruthlessly enforced. Peters and Waterman note that "All [corporate leaders] were ruthless [toward employees] when their core values of service to the customer and unstinting quality were violated."[10]

Within the context of the firm's sacred values, Ray Kroc (McDonald's), Tom Watson (IBM), and J. Willard Marriott have led the way in treating employees as adults and members of their families, but when violations of the core values occur they are "tough as nails."[11] Peters and Waterman conclude that "The excellent companies are marked by very strong cultures, so strong that you either buy into their norms or get out."[12]

Is it the job of the political executive to manage values within his organization? Yes, but with a key difference. Political executives must become skillful managers of two sets of values. The first are the values of the president. President Reagan clearly articulated conservative political values during both of his election campaigns. In this case, it is the President's conservative political values that are to be promoted and protected by the political executive, and when violations of the President's core values occur within the bureaucracy, the political executive should, as Peters and Waterman advise, be "tough as nails."

It is interesting to note that some private-sector executives use the political analogy to describe their management of values. Ed Carlson of United Airlines travels 200,000 miles every year to express his concern for the operations of the company. He remarked that it felt more like running for public office than running a large corporation.[13] This offhand analogy should be instructive for the political executive. Too many appointees believe that their job is simply to manage the operations of their agency. They leave the political values of the campaign behind and concentrate on "good management." But leading a large bureaucracy to produce conservative policy change is like running a campaign for office. The political values of the President must be first and foremost, not only in the mind, but on the tongue of every political appointee.

In addition to the President's values, a second set of values exists that will assist the political executive in his task of policy change: the theoretical bureaucratic ideal termed "responsive competency." Political executives are expected to change policy, and career executives are expected to willingly use their technical competency to aid the political executive in his role as policy-changer. When career executives willingly use their technical competency and expertise to aid in significant policy change, they are conforming to the ideal known as "responsive competency."[14] Political executives must manage the values of responsive competency by creating high expectations for career executives to live up to those values in their daily job performance. Career executives who are uncooperative in assisting the political executive with his policy changes should be reminded that the democratic system of government requires career executives to assist the political executive with the implementation of the President's policies. Better yet, the political executive should create an atmosphere where the cooperative career executives use peer pressure on the uncooperative career personnel to enforce the values of responsive competency.

Unfortunately, these role expectations are not always realistic in all agencies. The political executive must evaluate his situation by estimating the distance between his political values and the values of the organizational culture he is trying to change. If his political agenda is to abolish the SBA or privatize the Weather Service, the distance between his values and the values of the agency will probably be too great to expect a great deal of responsive competency from career executives. (See Chapter 20 on the Legal Services Corporation and Chapter 24 on NOAA case studies for examples of career officials who do not live up to the values of responsive competency.) On the other hand, if the policy objective is to decrease the Park Service appropriation by increasing user fees, then he may be able to manage the career ranks and secure their assistance by calling upon the values of responsive competency.

Use of Hands-on Management

Peters and Waterman indicate that successful companies have managers who manage company values in a "hands on" fashion.

> We are struck by the explicit attention they [excellent companies] pay to values, and by the way in which their leaders have created exciting environments, through personal attention, persistence, and direct intervention—*far down the line.*[15]

> An effective leader must be the master of two ends of the spectrum: ideas at the highest level of abstraction and actions at the *most mundane level of detail.* The value-shaping leader is concerned, on the one hand, with soaring, lofty visions that will generate excitement and enthusiasm of tens or hundreds of thousands of people. . . . On the other hand, it seems the only way to instill enthusiasm is through scores of daily events, with the value-shaping manager becoming an implementer par excellence. *In this role, the leader is a bug for detail, and directly instills values through deeds rather than words: No opportunity is too small. So it is at once attention to ideas and attention to detail.*[16] (Emphasis added.)

These leaders reinforce their values not from their plush offices via memos, but with their sleeves rolled up, standing on the shop floor and in the field office. Ray Kroc personally inspected thousands of McDonald's restaurants. J. Willard Marriott personally inspected the lobbies of his hotels. Only through highly visible, persistent actions, which are devoted to doing the little things right, are the values transmitted to the organization. Only through constant evangelistic behavior, preaching the truth of his values directly to the employees face to face, can values be instilled in the work force.

The political executive must also be a manager who practices hands-on, value-driven management, but with essential differences. J. Willard Marriott inspected the lobbies of his hotels to show his personal concern for the details of his company's operations. The conservative political executive is not in the same position. In most cases, the conservative political executive is leading an organization that, as stated earlier, is based on the assumptions of positive government. Showing concern for the existing agency operations will further a liberal program. The conservative appointee's task is to change that program.

At the highest level, the agency head must be an evangelist for the President's political values. He must translate those values into specific detailed actions and then must personally, in a hands-on way, transmit those values into action at all levels of the bureaucracy. He must personally supervise the policy-development process to insure that his values are not deflected by career staff. He must personally supervise the implementation of policy in order to prevent delays.

Personal contact with the lower ranks of the bureaucracy is essential. Often, sympathetic members of the career bureaucracy can be found in the lower ranks. The single greatest reward that can be offered to middle- and lower-level career staff members is the personal contact with the agency head. When career staff demonstrate that they are committed to the political executive's values, he should personally meet with those staff members to congratulate them on their accomplishments. This sends a message to the entire organization regarding the values of the political executive and his concern for their development and implementation.

In addition to finding and rewarding loyal career staff at the lower-levels, hands-on, value-driven management in the public sector prevents information distortion by mid-level managers. One of the greatest problems mentioned in the preceding chapter faced by the public manager is the lack of the profit-and-loss information. Without this information, learning about what is actually happening within the organization is exceedingly difficult. The opportunity for mid- and high-level managers to distort information, to produce "happiness data" is tremendous. Hands-on management within the organization that produces personal contact with professional staff is essential to prevent information distortion and learn what is actually happening within the agency.

Finally, hands-on management in the public sector allows the agency head to discover resistance to his values. Knowledge of when and where resistance occurs is essential to the management of conservative policy change. When it occurs, the political executive must be equally emphatic in words and deeds that deviation from the President's values will not be tolerated.

Bias for Action

In addition to hands-on, value-driven management, Peters and Waterman found that successful corporate leaders have a strong bias for action. Instead of spending time developing long-range plans, they act. They encourage the organization to act by creating a fluid organization of ad hoc committees, task forces, and small groups that experiment with new product ideas or production processes. Peters and Waterman report that success in the oil business is not dependent on having the best geologists or the most sophisticated equipment, but on how many wells the company digs. Dig more wells and you will find more oil.[17] The number of experiments or small groups working within a company is critical.

Thus, the manager's job is to start and stop these activities. The best project management and experimenting management is like playing poker.

> Making it work simply means treating major projects as nothing more than experiments, which is indeed what all of them are, and having the poker player's mental toughness to fold one hand and immediately start another whenever the current hand stops looking promising.[18]

Successful business leaders create fluid organizations where a great number of small groups experiment with ideas. These leaders see their task as encouraging the experiments and selecting those that contribute to the prosperity of the organization.

This practice by private-sector managers is perhaps the most potentially dangerous when blindly transferred to the public sector. The conservative political executive who starts a great number of policy task forces populated by career staff is courting disaster. The reason task forces work in the private sector is that they operate inside a very strong organizational culture and must constantly face the results of test markets. Both of these factors tightly constrain the operations of private-sector task forces. Neither of these constraints operates the same way in the public sector. The agency culture will very likely produce pressures that will work against the development and implementation of conservative policy; test markets revealing direct public choices do not exist. If uncontrolled, the bias for action in government will mean a bias for government expansion, a propensity to discover more and more societal needs the government "must" meet.

For these reasons, task forces and ad hoc groups should not be given the same freedom as in the private-sector. Policy task forces which are designed to develop or implement conservative policy should be heavily populated by political appointees, and the agency head should take a very close personal interest in the supervision of the working of these groups. That is not to say that career personnel should be excluded. Career personnel, especially those who support the President's values, should be included and should be active participants. But close supervision and political participation should be used to insure that task forces carry out the assigned mission: the development and/or implementation of conservative policy.

People-Oriented Management

Peters and Waterman discovered that in the excellent companies they studied there was a strong people orientation, but that there were two sides to that people orientation. On the one hand, these firms engage in what some consider "soft" management. They treat their employees as adults. They genuinely trust and respect the workers as individuals. This respect for the individual creates a strong family feeling within the corporation. The authors found that the "Delta Family Feeling" was real—unlike the gimmicks they saw in so many less successful firms. But, on the other hand, the authors also noticed a *tough side* to this people orientation.

> The excellent companies are measurement happy and performance-oriented, but this toughness is borne of mutually high expectations and peer review rather than emanating from table-pounding managers and complicated control systems. *The tough side is, in fact, probably tougher* than that found in the less excellent and typically more formal system-driven companies, for nothing is more enticing than the feeling of being needed, which is the magic that produces high expectations.[19] (Emphasis added.)

Nothing illustrates this tough measurement-happy, performance-oriented side to people management as well as Dana Corporation. At Dana, very few written reports are required, but divisions report "their invoice total, and approximate profit earned, *at the end of each working day.*"[20] (Emphasis added.) Thus, successful firms in the private-sector have a balanced approach to people management; they treat their employees with trust and respect, but they also expect results.

For the conservative political executive, people-oriented management is also essential, but with important differences. Since it is often impossible to measure performance in the public sector (because inventory totals and approximate profit earned are not available), public managers tend to emphasize the "soft" side of people management. Public employees are trusted and respected, but honest measures of their output are lacking. Often the "results," the content of policy, are by definition non-quantifiable and difficult to evaluate.

The performance appraisal system can assist the political executive by holding staff accountable for results. But he should not use performance appraisal by searching for some quantifiable "bottom line" comparable to the private-sector. Nothing important is accurately quantifiable in government. In government, even such seemingly objective figures as number of cases processed can be "fuzzed up" when it is in the interest of the staff to do so. Therefore, the political executive must aggressively implement performance appraisal, not by using objective, quantifiable standards, but by stressing subjective policy-implementation standards.[21] Career employees, especially top-level career executives, must know that they are expected to assist the political executive with his task of conservative policy change. Once policy-change objectives are spelled out in performance appraisal documents, political executives must have the courage to evaluate and rate the performance of their subordinates. Those career employees who assist in the implementation of conservative policy should be rewarded. Those who do not, should not.

Habit-Breaking Reorganizations

As part of their study, Peters and Waterman studied the organizational structures of successful companies. They noticed that it is extremely difficult for firms to maintain rapid growth. Most experience a period of growth, but then they stop innovating and stagnate. Excellent corporations avoid this by breaking dysfunctional habits that cause stagnation. They do this primarily by regular reorganization and by reorganizing on a temporary basis to attack specific problems. For example, GM created a temporary organization called the Project Center to lead the effort to downsize its cars. The typical organization of a successful firm does not meet our image of a stable framework in which employees are assigned specific duties. The traditional notions of organizational structure, chain of command, rationally defined units with specific functions, are turned on their head. A new vocabulary arises to describe the structure: fluid organizations, experimentation, internal markets. These are the terms used to describe the organization, or lack of organization, in excellent companies. In short, to the outsider the organizational structures of these excellent firms looks like nothing more than "structured chaos."[22]

Political executives face agencies that are some of the most stagnant and calcified organizations in existence. Innovation and change rarely occur. In the absence of market forces that compel institutional change, government employees often stay in the same position for years doing the same job in the same way. Government agencies become very tradition-bound; change and innovation rarely enter the vocabulary of the average bureaucrat.

An additional, perhaps more important, organizational factor that the political executive must consider is that organization equals policy. Organizational structure, while seemingly unrelated to broad policy, is in reality very important for politics and policy. The organizational position of a program in an agency or a department determines its competitors for budget funds and closeness to the power of the agency head or department secretary. One of the clearest examples of this was the successful push by the National Education Association (NEA) to have education removed from the Department of Health, Education, and Welfare and given separate department status.[23] Liberal interest groups are well versed in the politics of organizational structure.

The NEA's political purpose was clearly expressed through the establishment of the separate organizational identity of the Department of Education. At lower levels, this is also true. Politically interested groups attempt to establish organizational units or move existing units to serve their political purposes. The conservative political executive must be aware of this and play the game. Organizational units can be moved to increase or decrease their visibility. New organizational units can be created. For example, in every department or agency, conservative political appointees should create units whose sole task is to suggest agency functions that might be privatized. Another example is to create units to engage in long-term planning and public information regarding the negative aspects of government and agency operations. As the case study on the Small Business Administration (Chapter 22) indicates, the Office of Management and Budget at times performs this function when there is a short-term budgetary goal of abolishing an agency, but organizational units devoted to long-term planning and public information are nonexistent. These units should exist in a conservative administration.

In addition to creating organizational units to further conservative policy, the political executive must engage in habit-breaking reorganizations, not to encourage growth or to prevent stagnation, but for policy reasons. First, political executives should review their organizational structure to identify programs supported by previous liberal administrations and to identify key career personnel who may help or hinder the implementation of policy. Second, habit-breaking reorganizations should take place that deemphasize or eliminate liberal programs and shift personnel around so that cooperative and productive career staff are given important policy positions. Third, reorganization should not be considered a one-shot affair. To be effective, the political executive should reorganize often, taking advantage of the learning which takes place during his tenure. Fourth, temporary task forces, as described above, should be used to elevate lower-level career staff members. Many "Young Turks" may exist in the career ranks. They have been stifled at lower levels of the stagnant bureaucracy and are eager to innovate. Because they have lower grades, they cannot be given senior positions in a formal organization, but they can be placed on very important and influential task forces where they can assist the conservative political executive.

Thus the traditional idea of formal, stable organizational structure which is supposed to produce efficiency actually hinders the political executive in achieving conservative policy change. Reorganizations, fluid organizations, temporary organizational units, create a much more hospitable environment for the conservative political executive.

Avoiding False Lessons

Let us return to the point we began with—namely, that many of the lessons drawn from Peters and Waterman for the political appointees in the public sector are *false lessons*. We have noted that our lessons are different from those conventionally drawn. They are in many respects paradoxical lessons. The heart of the paradox lies in the fact that Peters and Waterman describe organizations based on unified values and culture, while in the public sector there is often a dichotomy of values between the manager and the institution. Thus, the attempt of a conservative appointee to draw lessons from McDonald's and apply them at, for example, HUD will produce results which are at best silly.

The following is a brief summary of typical *false lessons* that can arise when advice written for the private-sector is applied directly to the public sector. It is accompanied by corrections based on an understanding of the differences between the two sectors. Areas where private-sector techniques can be most appropriately applied are indicated.

1. *Organizational Culture.* Many political appointees enter government and are quickly socialized into the agency culture. When this happens, all is lost. Executive branch leaders must recognize that they are not in the same position as leaders of private firms who have had decades to create a culture within their organization based on

their own values. Instead, conservative appointees are generally surrounded by an alien organizational culture. A related error is the belief among some appointees that they can easily instill new values in an institution, almost as if they were working in a vacuum. Appointees must recognize that they are implicitly confronted by the historic culture of the agency; cultural change will be slow and at times impossible.

2 . *Management of Values.* Many political appointees recognize that "management of values" is important, but they manage the agency's values, not the President's. When this happens, they become cheerleaders for the agency interests. Instead, they must bring political values with them, and work to replace the agency values with the President's political values.

3 . *Use of Hands-On Management.* This principle has many direct applications to the public sector, except that imparting values will be more difficult. Unfortunately, many political executives manage in a "hands-on" way, but become preoccupied with the operational efficiency of the organization. This serves the interests of the career staff. Instead, political appointees must learn the details of their agency operations and personnel in order to make decisions that change policy, not just operations.

4 . *Bias for Action.* Many political appointees have a "bias for action," but seem to be indifferent as to whose agenda they are acting on. Just as water always flows downhill, "action" in government will always have a bias toward public-sector expansion and statist solutions; it takes a very deliberate and consistent effort to move policy in any other direction. Public appointees need to be aware of this. Some seem to think that action means seizing the first item in their in-box and charging toward the goal line with it. In the very first months of the Reagan Administration, Secretary of Transportation Drew Lewis stumbled across an auto import quota plan that had been left over from the Carter Administration and began vigorously promoting it, even though it had nothing to do with the Reagan agenda and had been judged "too liberal" during much of the Carter Administration. Action in this case led to nothing but consternation among Lewis's fellow appointees.[24]

A similar misplaced bias for action among appointees is the desire for visible results, leading to a tendency to make undesirable compromises on policy substance in order to produce "a bill" or "a regulation" that can be entered on one's record of achievement.

5 . *People-Oriented Management.* Simplistic adoption of "people-oriented management" in government leads to a complete loss of control over institutions and policy. Direct borrowing of such ideas founders over the simple fact that in government there is not a single set of overarching values but rather competing sets of values.

6. *Habit-Breaking Reorganization.* This principle is directly applicable to the public sector with few negative side effects. As long as the appointee has a definite policy agenda and uses reorganization to facilitate that agenda, the technique will be effective.

Conclusion

We have noted that many of the lessons drawn from *In Search of Excellence* are paradoxical. Perhaps the most paradoxical lesson we may draw from this book on business management is that businessmen are not likely to be the most successful managers in government. Entrepreneurs such as Ray Kroc of McDonald's are successful because they have strong personal business values, relating to efficiency, detail, concern for customers, etc., which they instill into their organizations. Strong values are needed in government, but it is not business values that are needed—rather it is political values: a strongly articulated viewpoint on the fundamental issues of political economy and foreign policy. It is not likely that we will find such strong political values in the average successful businessman. Although some businessmen do make successful political executives, often we must look elsewhere for leadership in government.[25]

Four stars from the first Reagan term were academics. Don Devine, formerly the Director of the Office of Personnel Management, was a political science professor at the University of Maryland. Bill Bennett, who served as head of the National Endowment for the Humanities and is now Secretary of Education, was a professor of philosophy at the University of North Carolina. Jim Miller, former Federal Trade Commission Chairman and presently Director of the Office of Management and Budget, was a professor of economics at Texas A&M and a resident scholar at the American Enterprise Institute. And finally, Jeane Kirkpatrick, former U.S. Ambassador to the United Nations, was a political science professor at Georgetown University.

These academics recognized that success in public-sector management is not dependent on good business management of existing government operations, but rather on managing the President's political philosophy and values. They recognized that the existing organizational culture of their agencies would often be in violent conflict with the President's conservative policy agenda. They knew that implementation of their political change agenda would not be without controversy, but their job demanded that they manage the President's values within the context of their agency culture. These four stars met the challenge by establishing a firm set of political values, and generally managed those values with hands-on techniques that got them deeply involved in the details of their agency operations. In addition, they were all action-oriented managers. A political executive's tenure in office is much too short not to take an action orientation.

With regard to their career bureaucracies, they all communicated the President's values and stood firm behind the values of responsive competency. Career officials were expected to use their skills to advance the President's agenda, and bureaucratic resistance was not tolerated. Finally, calcified organizations were often reorganized. Bureaucratic structures that had been created to serve the political values of previous liberal administrations were changed in the shift from those liberal values to the conservative values of the President.

The successes of these four academics were based on a fundamental recognition that is missed by many political executives—a recognition that Peters and Waterman found in their study of successful private businesses. These academics recognized that the business of public-sector management is the management of political values and not the static management of government operations. Peters and Waterman discovered the importance of organizational values in the private sector. More political executives must recognize the importance of political values in the public sector.

Notes

1.   Thomas Peters and Robert Waterman, *In Search of Excellence: Lessons from America's Best-Run Companies* (New York: Warner Books, 1982).

2.   Susan Dentzer, "Al Casey's New P.O. Box," *Newsweek*, January 20, 1986, p. 34.

3.   Peters and Waterman, pp. 103, 134, 319.

4.   Ibid., p. 75.

5.   Ibid., p. 214.

6.   Ibid., p. 167, also see p. 160.

7.   It also conflicts with recent social science research which shows that government action to help the poor has actually made the plight of the poor worse. See Charles Murray, *Losing Ground: American Social Policy, 1950–1980* (New York: Basic Books, 1985).

8.   Peters and Waterman, p. 26.

9.   Ibid., p. 85.

10.   Ibid., p. 96.

11.   Ibid., p. 96.

12.   Ibid., p. 77.

13.   Ibid., p. 289.

14. Terry M. Moe, "The Politicized Presidency," in John Chubb and Paul Peterson (eds.), *The New Direction in American Politics* (Washington: The Brookings Institution, 1958), p. 239.

15. Peters and Waterman, p. 279.

16. Ibid., p. 287.

17. Ibid., p. 141.

18. Ibid., p. 142.

19. Ibid., p. 240.

20. Ibid., p. 153.

21. Peters and Waterman found that as far as mission and goals statements were concerned, companies with "broader, less precise, more qualitative statements of corporate purpose" did better financially than those with focused, quantified statements of mission (p. 281).

22. Peters and Waterman, p. 22.

23. A case history of this is contained in Constance Diamant Soll, "The Creation of the Department of Education in 1979." Also, the general conceptual basis for the importance of reorganization to policy is contained in Herbert Kaufman, "Reflections on Administrative Reorganization." Both articles are found in Richard J. Stillman II, *Public Administration: Concepts and Cases,* 3d ed. (Boston: Houghton Mifflin, 1984), pp. 353-79.

24. Paul Craig Roberts, *The Supply Side Revolution: An Insider's Account of Policymaking in Washington* (Cambridge, Mass.: Harvard University Press, 1984), pp. 122-24.

25. Examples of effective businessmen in the first Reagan Administration include Tom Pauken, Gerald Carmen, and Dan Sawyer.

18 ACTION: The Times They Are A-Changin'

TOM PAUKEN

Editors' Note: Tom Pauken served as head of ACTION from 1981 to 1984. His experience serves as a perfect case model in establishing control over government programs. It is also an excellent example of how an effective appointee can transform what others might regard as an administrative problem into a social and political opportunity.

The ACTION agency is a paradox: a federal agency designed to encourage private voluntarism. An independent umbrella agency, ACTION oversees such federally-assisted programs as VISTA, the Retired Senior Volunteer Program (RSVP), Foster Grandparents, Senior Companies, and other volunteer efforts. Paradoxes are not necessarily bad and ACTION, if governed with constraint and good purpose, can serve as a useful adjunct to the strong American tradition of charitable giving.

Such was not the case prior to the election of President Reagan. Under the Carter Administration, the ACTION agency had been headed by anti-Vietnam activist Sam Brown, one of the leaders of the student radical movement in the United States during the late 1960's and early 1970's. During Brown's tenure from 1977 to 1980, the agency used its VISTA program to fund what seemed to be virtually every remnant of the New Left hanging over from the turbulent 1960's, in a continuation of their radical political endeavors. This article relates my efforts to alter that situation, the pitfalls that this entailed, and the lessons that may be gained.

The Tax-Funded Left

From the mid-1970's to the early 80's, tax-funded left-wing politics flourished. It is a great irony that, at the same time that the liberal/left alliance sought to impose limits on how much private individuals might voluntarily contribute to election campaigns, they were taking funds from the American public involuntarily through taxation and injecting those funds quietly into the political arena to support left-wing causes. Tax revenue has been—and still is—used to support political advocacy, propaganda, lobbying, grassroots organizing, and the training of political activists. Tax funds have financed election campaigns of left-wing candidates and causes and union organizing. Often the ostensible purpose of federal funding has been for more legitimate activities, but since the mode of funding was generally to support staff salaries in radical organizations, it is very difficult to account for the actual use of tax funds; invariably they were used for whatever cause the funded group wished to promote.

The amount of money involved by the end of the 70's was staggering. The recent book *Destroying Democracy*, by James T. Bennett and Thomas DiLorenzo, while providing only a fragmentary record of federal grants, lists annual taxpayer funding to left-wing groups and activities that exceeded the sum of contributions expended in Presidential, Senate, and House election campaigns in 1980. It is clear that much of this activity is not only contemptuous of ordinary democratic processes, but if continued indefinitely will actually unbalance and jeopardize those processes.

At the center of these efforts was Sam Brown's ACTION. Among those funded by Brown and his cohorts were the Ralph Nader-related PIRGs (Public Interest Research Groups), organizations affiliated with radical activist Tom Hayden, Alinsky-style community activist groups operating under a variety of different names and ostensible causes in urban areas throughout the United States, and ACORN, a national leftist organization which utilizes the politics of confrontation to intimidate and hound local officials into acceding to their demands.

Typical of the organizations ACTION funded during the Carter era was the Mid West Academy, a training center for left-wing political activists. According to the Academy's brochures, the objective of the Academy is to create a "majority movement" to begin "the job of redistributing social wealth." The following description gives a flavor of the political training dispensed at the Academy:

> In the two-week course, students learn histories of grassroots organizations, techniques of meetings, press relations, leaflet making, and methods for holding effective demonstrations and doing research. . . . Steve Max, the main Academy teacher, who himself helped found the Students for a Democratic Society, adds a wealth of practical detail from years of experience in election campaigns, union battles, and community fights. . . . The students sing songs from the range of people's struggles in the century—"Solidarity Forever," "Union Maids," "We Shall Overcome," "Gonna Study War No More," "I Am Woman." They go out with groups like the Illinois Public Action Council on demonstrations or show up at press conferences of senior citizen groups. They plan skits for confronting city officials.[1]

Another recipient of ACTION funding was the Campaign for Economic

Democracy (CED) run by anti-Vietnam radical Tom Hayden with the support of his wife, the actress Jane Fonda. As late as the mid-70's Hayden was still clinging to extreme left ideology, stating that communism "can improve people's lives."[2] The goal of his political movement is quite simply socialism—to free America, in Hayden's words, from "the stink . . .called corporate capitalism."[3] However, not even Hayden is far enough removed from reality to fail to notice that socialism has an unhealthy reputation in the United States. Some repackaging is required. Consequently Hayden and his compatriots have adopted as their cardinal principle:

> Activists should avoid using the word socialism. We have found in the greatest tradition of American advertising that the word "economic democracy" sells. You can take it door to door like Fuller Brushes and the door will not be slammed in your face.[4]

Still it takes more than clever and deceptive advertising to promote social change. Among other things, it takes money—and if you have a hard time getting the average American family to fork over a few bucks to help promote socialism in America, you can always turn to Uncle Sam, who is generally known to have a spare million or two in his pockets to give to deserving causes.

The federal government provided funds for a wide range of CED political activity. ACTION supplied funding to train political organizations at the CED's Laurel Springs Institute; other government agencies provided funds to the CED's "Communitas" project. Ostensibly a crime prevention program, "Communitas" personnel focused much of their efforts on block organizing and precinct work for a rent control referendum and to propel a CED slate of candidates into control of the city government of Santa Monica, California. At least part of CED's government funding was diverted into these endeavors. The following is typical of the activities of the tax-funded CED and its affiliates:

> We sent out a postcard of an elderly family, somewhat haggard—they looked a bit like an Auschwitz picture. Stamped across their chest was the word EVICTED. We found a senior citizen who was dying of cancer who was being evicted. We reprinted an article [about him in the local paper]; the headline was "Before I Die I'm Going to Vote for Ruth Yannatta and Rent Control." We distributed that on the door of every tenant in the city two days before the election. . . . We considered techniques that played on people's feelings and emotions around a very simple idea: that housing is a basic human right, that it comes before the need to profit.[5]

Nearly a half million dollars in federal funds was channeled into the CED and related groups in Santa Monica. An extremely large sum in the world of local politics, this money was no doubt at least partially responsible for the success of CED candidates in taking over the municipal government. With the objective of using the "power of the city government to control the wealth of the city,"[6] Santa Monica's radical government was envisioned as a beachhead for similar movements throughout California and the nation.

Of course, the goals of the New Left do not stop at the borders of the United States; nor did the political vision of Sam Brown. Brown wished to use the Peace Corps, at that time a part of ACTION, to promote radical policies domestically and internationally. Carter's ACTION Director charged that, in the past, the Peace Corps had been guilty of "cultural imperialism"; under President Carter it would cease "elitist" practices such as teaching English to give natives access to scientific and technical information. Instead, Sam Brown would promote the notion that the United States had much to learn from Third World states, particularly radical and socialist states. He sought to establish a "reverse Peace Corps" in which volunteers from Third World countries would be brought to work in American cities. Similarly, American volunteers would be sent to radical Third World states to be trained in community organizing and other political techniques and then returned to American urban centers to spread their new-found values and skills. One such ideal tutor for American volunteers was the disastrous socialist government of Jamaican Prime Minister Michael Manley, which could provide instruction in "community mobilization." "We are going to Jamaica to learn from their experience; Jamaica can teach us much," said Brown.[7]

Other countries from which the United States could learn included Tanzania, Cuba, and Yugoslavia. The fact that what these regimes had most succeeded in accomplishing (besides establishing tyranny) was impoverishing their own people does not seem to have bothered Brown. In effect, he had similar goals in mind for the United States which was *too wealthy* for his tastes.

> We are so damned wealthy, as long as we try to hang on to that we haven't got a chance and morally ought not to have a chance [of surviving in the world community]. It is not right for us to have the kind of extravagant, consumptive society we have—it just isn't.[8]

The appropriate response to this dilemma was, presumably, to replace policies of economic expansion with a transfer of excess U.S. wealth to the rest of the world.

All this was too much for the Peace Corps Director, Dr. Carolyn R. Payton. A professor from Howard University and former Peace Corps administrator, Dr. Payton was the first black woman to head that agency. After repeated confrontations with Sam Brown over his policies, Dr. Payton resigned, charging that Brown was "operating outside the Peace Corps mandate" and was trying to impose American intellectual fads on host countries.

Dr. Payton sought to "sound the alarm" over the potential ruination of the Peace Corps. In particular, she condemned the New Left's efforts to use the Peace Corps "to export a particular ideology" and the notion that Peace Corps volunteers should engage in protests and political activities against American multinational corporations.[9] Brown's supporters countered with charges of Payton's "elitism." The confrontation between Payton and Brown demonstrates how far from the mainstream of American politics ACTION and the Carter Administration had drifted by the late 1970's.

A Personal Challenge

From the very beginning, the one job I wanted in the Reagan Administration was to be Director of the ACTION agency. There were a number of reasons for my interest in being appointed to a relatively obscure federal agency. I, like Sam Brown, was a product of the 60's' generation. There was only a small difference between us—I was on the other side of the Vietnam debate. While Brown was organizing protests against the war, I was serving as National Chairman of the College Republicans and defending our attempt to prevent a Communist takeover of Indochina. I had come out of the conservative movement in the 60's fueled by the writings of Bill Buckley and the presidential candidacy of Barry Goldwater. Later I would enlist in the Army and serve as an Army intelligence officer in Vietnam. I was one of the early opponents of the authoritarian New Left on college campuses. That opposition continued in the 70's after the fall of Indochina to the Communists and the Left's development of new political causes to rally round when the Vietnam issue went away.

I knew their goals, their tactics, and their key players. Thus, I figured that I would have an easier time changing the direction of the ACTION agency than would others who were less familiar with the way the New Left operates. Dramatic change was necessary, and I believed that I could bring about such change in a short time frame if all of the pieces fell into place.

I was selected by President Reagan to be Director of ACTION in February 1981. My nomination to this post drew immediate attention for a variety of reasons. From the Left's perspective, I was the worst possible choice to succeed Brown and disrupt their ongoing use of VISTA to fund their grassroots, left-wing organizations. A Democratic friend of mine was at a party with Sam Brown when Brown first learned that I had been named by President Reagan to head up ACTION. His reponse reportedly was, "Oh, no. Not that ————— fascist." So much for tolerance from the Left.

Essential Questions

ACTION is, of course, small as federal agencies go and far from the mainstream of public policy-making. Nevertheless, I think the record at ACTION during the first four years of the Reagan Administration raises a number of questions that have broader applications. The key questions as I see them are as follows:

1. How do conservatives get nominated for policy-making positions? Or, in the alternative, why have conservatives fared so poorly in the nomination process in the Reagan Administration?

2. How do conservatives in presidentially appointed positions which require Senate confirmation get approved by a majority of Senators in a Washington environment that is often hostile to conservatives?

3. Can a conservative govern effectively as an agency or department head and remain true to his or her principles?

Nomination

First, as to the matter of getting nominated to serve in top-level policy-making positions, conservatives did not fare particularly well in the selection process of the Reagan Administration, which seems somewhat unusual given the conservative philosophy of the President. There are a number of reasons for this, and conservatives need to be aware of how the system tends to operate—often to their disadvantage.

Washington insiders, who previously served in the Nixon and Ford administrations and who by and large worked against Ronald Reagan in the presidential primaries in 1976 and 1980, were shrewd enough to grab control of the key personnel-selection positions on the Reagan transition team. Pendleton James, who had been in White House Personnel in the Nixon-Ford Administration, was the nominal head of the personnel-selection process, while the operational director was his deputy, Jim Cavanaugh, who had been Nelson Rockefeller's Chief of Staff when Rockefeller was Vice President. Immediately after the November election, conservatives were pushed aside by the James-Cavanaugh crowd who grabbed control of the White House personnel-selection machinery. Those who were part of the old boy network that came out of the Nixon and Ford administrations fared very well in the placement process although few of them had done much, if anything, to aid in Ronald

Reagan's nomination and election to the Presidency. It was only when longtime Reagan aide Lyn Nofziger returned to Washington and joined the transition team that conservatives began to fare better. Nofziger almost singlehandedly prevented a bad situation from becoming a disaster for conservatives in the early going; the result was the placement of a few conservatives who were longtime supporters of Ronald Reagan, such as Don Devine and myself as the heads of departments and agencies.

The lesson to be learned from what happened after the election of Ronald Reagan in 1980 is to make sure the next time a conservative wins the presidency, the White House personnel office is staffed by knowledgeable and politically sophisticated conservatives who know how to find and bring in talented conservatives to fill the key positions in that administration.

Confirmation

But to be nominated is not enough; one must also be confirmed. When Sam Brown was selected to serve as head of ACTION, Senator Alan Cranston (D.-Calif.) had declared it was "another remarkable nomination of the President" and that Brown was an "outstanding young American." With regard to my nomination, Cranston took a slightly different attitude. Aided by his ideological staffer Jonathan Steinberg, a hard-left anti-Vietnam activist, Cranston led a vendetta to derail my nomination. That I was able to avoid the landmines set for me by Cranston and his staff was a combination of luck, skill, and a lot of help from friends—but not necessarily from the White House.

Many conservative nominees have not fared as well in the process. That is due partially to the fragile Republican majority in the Senate, combined with the unreliability of certain more liberal Republican Senators when it comes to voting for a conservative nominee. Moreover, if liberals in the Senate can knock off a conservative nominee for an important post, they generally have been able to get the Reagan Administration to nominate a "safe" choice the next time, i.e., a more moderate, pragmatic Republican who will not rock the boat so much. In my view, the Reagan Administration could have put a halt to this liberal sniping at conservative nominees by setting an example. Every time the Senate rejects a well-qualified conservative nominee for ideological reasons, the White House should submit an equally conservative nominee as his or her replacement the next time around. This would end the political profit of witch-hunting to liberals and bring it to a close. Finally, the White House could reinforce this process by dealing in a much more sophisticated fashion with those swing votes in the Senate— Democrats as well as Republicans—who can be won over with the right approach.

To return to my own experience, I was originally supposed to be confirmed by the Senate Labor and Human Resources Committee headed by Senator Orrin Hatch. I expected no problems in that Committee. But Senator Cranston began his campaign against me by arguing that since the Peace Corps was still under ACTION, I should be confirmed by the Senate Foreign Relations Committee.[10] Old reliable Republican Senator Chuck Percy, then Chairman of the Senate Foreign Relations Committee, helped Cranston in his endeavor by demanding that I go before his Committee as well. When I met personally with Percy trying to explain to him that this was simply a maneuver by Cranston to try to block my nomination, Percy assured me that I need not worry and that I had his "full support," even as he acceded to Cranston's request.

Cranston focused his attack on my one-year service in Vietnam as a lieutenant in military intelligence, claiming that this service would create the appearance that the Peace Corps was engaged in "espionage" activities, thereby jeopardizing the lives of Peace Corps volunteers. According to the opinions of the White House Counsel to the President, the fact that I had served briefly in Army intelligence in Vietnam did not violate the standing principle of separating the Peace Corps from U.S. intelligence activity. Nor did it violate established Peace Corps personnel policy regarding individuals with prior intelligence experience. In fact, the Deputy Director slot *inside* the Peace Corps had in the past been held by a former top-level military intelligence official! None of this deterred Senator Cranston and other liberals.

Although Cranston declared that his only concern was the safety of Peace Corps volunteers and that he would be willing to consider me for other positions in government, his actions declared otherwise. His staff undertook a lengthy and laborious search to dig up any imaginable sort of political or personal "dirt" that could be used to discredit me. Only part of these efforts ever came to public attention. This vehement opposition was rooted in my conservatism, or in Steinberg's case, seemed to grow out of unending malevolence toward anyone supportive of the American cause in Vietnam against which he had labored so intently in the past.[11]

At one point, Cranston and company embarked on a ludicrous effort to link me with the CIA. That effort failing, they devised a clever scheme to pull my military records without my knowledge or consent. The apparent objective was to question me publicly about my military service in Vietnam, hoping that I would omit some information because of its confidential nature, so that they could then claim I had "lied" about my military service and sink my nomination. All of this was, of course, extremely remote from any real issues related to my nomination as head of ACTION; however, I had become quite suspicious of my opponents, having reached the conclusion that they would do anything to block my nomination. Thus, I was very much on guard when I walked into the Senate Committee chamber for my confirmation hearing. My testimony—while adhering to the Army guidelines I had been given years earlier—was general enough and factually accurate so that the "deceit" bombshell fizzled. Still, the hostility in the hearing room was palpable. As Cranston repeatedly sought to uncover something sinister in my service in Vietnam, the entire proceeding took on, in the words of the *Washington Star,* the "taint of soldier baiting."

Despite the remarkable lack of substance in their bitter antics, liberal pressure began to pay off: White House backing for my nomination wavered. In contrast, a number of conservative Senators held firm; to this was added the support of many Vietnam veterans who started to raise a protest that whereas my draft-avoiding predecessor had sailed through his nomination without a sneeze, my Vietnam service was deliberately being used to force me out of government. I was finally reported out of Committee with a favorable recommendation (though seven Senators voted against me), and confirmed by the U.S. Senate by voice vote. (As a footnote to this story, Cranston and Percy, with the assistance of Peace Corps Director Lorette Ruppe, would later succeed in separating the Peace Corps from ACTION. That move ensured that business would continue as usual at the Peace Corps throughout the tenure of Lorette Ruppe at the helm.)

Of course, many Reagan appointees suffered far worse than I. There was, for example, Larry Uzzell who was forced out of a low-level (non-Senate-confirmed) political position under Education Secretary Bennett for the deeply heretical belief that the *federal* government had no proper role in education. (Liberals are, we all know, joyous in welcoming diversity of opinion, but even they must draw the line when faced with such extreme views.) Another notable victim was Eileen Gardner, a young black female policy researcher from the conservative Heritage Foundation. Miss Gardner, who holds a doctoral degree from Harvard University, was booted from a similar job in government in the wake of liberal tirades; her sin rested in her personal religious belief that no suffering in the universe is accidental and without divine purpose.[12] This was deliberately and fantastically distorted by liberal Senators and media to suggest that Dr. Gardner harbored a secret malevolence toward handicapped persons—despite the fact that she had served for nearly a half-decade as an exceptionally talented and effective teacher of handicapped children! (This last endeavor must rival any of the excesses attempted during an earlier "McCarthy" era.)

The fact that I faced hostile pressure during my confirmation and that appointees such as Larry Uzzell and Eileen Gardner were forced out of government, while only a few years earlier Sam Brown—who had publicly proclaimed in the late 60's that his political goal was communist victory in Vietnam—was confirmed by the Senate to a position in the second-highest level of responsibility in the executive branch without a single negative comment or question, says a great deal about the political environment in the United States today.[13] It says a great deal about the temperament, intentions, and mode of conduct of the conservatives and liberals.

Despite the obvious reality that there is in the United States today a strong political movement that openly harbors violent intentions toward economic liberty, that is contemptuous or indifferent to democratic principles, and that is openly sympathetic to almost every variety of Marxist cause or regime, "red-baiting" simply does not occur. On the other hand, right-baiting has become fashionable and prevalent in Washington. Liberals have never been tolerant of intellectual opposition; today, they have become fanatical and vindictive in their attacks on even the slightest deviation from the overripe liberal orthodoxy. All of this is, of course, the opposite of images conveyed by the liberal establishment. (When did we last hear of a "liberal ideologue"?) It may provide some comfort to conservatives to look forward to revisionist historians who a few decades from now will discover these obvious but currently "invisible" facts about American politics in the 70's and 80's.

At present, a conservative, waiting to be confirmed by the U.S. Senate after having been nominated by the President, must understand the rules of the game: The Left does not play fair in these hearings. Leftist Senate staffers are on "search and destroy" missions when it comes to conservative nominees. While their real objection is ideological, they often try to cloak it in other terms by finding some "dirt" that they can use against conservative nominees in Committee hearings. It is character assassination, pure and simple; and the liberal media—to their discredit—are a willing partner to this charade. Great caution is required.

Managing the Agency

Despite the efforts of Senator Cranston, I found myself at the helm of ACTION. In setting about to manage the agency, I adopted as my first rule: *PERSONNEL MAKE POLICY.* Changing the direction of an agency or department takes a team of committed people. I began to work immediately on recruiting a team of appointees to fill the key positions at the agency. Although we had some problems and made some mistakes, I was able to collect a band of tough-minded and able conservatives who were not afraid of making decisions and taking action to change the direction of the agency. I cannot overemphasize the importance of a team of people working together.

I was personally involved from the beginning in this selection process. One has only a limited number of noncareer/political appointments, and it was important to make wise choices in the early going—otherwise all we wanted to accomplish could have come undone. If I were the one ultimately held responsible for whether ACTION did well or badly, I wanted to involve myself heavily in the key political appointments that we would make. By and large we were successful in pulling together a talented group of people at ACTION committed to the Reagan Revolution. That made a big difference in making the changes that needed to be made.

In retrospect, we made mistakes in the personnel selection process when we recruited persons who (a) lacked a philosophy or value system that was fundamentally conservative or (b) were not men and women of good character. Good character is a key ingredient. Each of us has flaws, none of us is perfect; some are well qualified to be policy analysts but disasters as administrators; others cannot handle the pressure of making those kinds of decisions that essentially are "Hobson's choices" (choosing from between or among unpleasant alternatives); still others are more susceptible to the carefully developed charms of the sycophants who would tell us what we want to hear in order to win favor. But a character flaw—as opposed to the weaknesses in skills that all of us have—is another matter. One prevalent type of character flaw is found in those who are so enamored of power that they flaunt and abuse it when they take office; this can be highly disruptive within an agency. Another flaw may be found in individuals who have political convictions but who subordinate those convictions to personal ambition; thus policy substance will be compromised whenever career considerations become involved. Lack of character of this sort can undo the best of intentions when it comes to changing the direction of a federal agency. On the other hand, good character plus a philosophical commitment to conservative values makes for an unbeatable combination. One should look for both in the selection of personnel.

As a second principle, we set forth for the entire ACTION staff, political and career, a clearly defined strategy on the policy direction of the ACTION agency under the Reagan Administration so that there would be no misunderstanding between the political appointees and the career civil servants as to our goals and objectives. I never asked a career civil servant what his or her politics were. Nor did I put a career employee in a position where he had to adopt a particular political point of view. What we did was to outline the policy objectives that we, as Reagan appointees, planned to follow and asked that the career people do their job as professionals by helping to execute that policy. If a careerist did not agree with a particular policy we were considering, he or she had every right to voice objections. But once a policy had been decided upon, the career people were expected to do their part in executing the policy. What I would not abide were career bureaucrats who tried to hide the ball from us and either contravene the policy direction of the Reagan appointees at ACTION or set their own policy course independent of our decision-making process. We had some careerists who tried to play those games with us, and we made sure that they were not in positions of authority where they could do harm to our overall objectives.

A third rule that I learned in politics a long time ago and that I tried to pass on to our political appointees at ACTION is not to write any memoranda, make any public statements, or take any action as federal appointees that we would not mind seeing on the front page of *The Washington Post*. Political appointees have to assume that any memorandum they write as federal officials, no matter how restricted its access, will fall into unfriendly hands, and craft such a memo with that in mind. It is a good rule to follow, and one that might have saved the careers of more than a few Reagan Administration appointees if they had heeded it.

I had a political appointee in the early days of my tenure as ACTION Director who loved to write memos and send them to various offices throughout the agency. He would write up memos of meetings where no memoranda were requested or needed. He had fallen in love with the Washington memorandum fetish, and no amount of quiet counsel could convince him that there was no purpose served in expanding the paper flow at the ACTION agency unnecessarily and, in some specific cases, perhaps unwisely. He declined to heed the advice he was given; and shortly thereafter he left us.

The final related rule applies to personal conduct: Think how it will look in the press the next day. I remember, early in my tenure as ACTION Director, a staffer came into my office and said that I should redecorate my office and get new furniture. I laughed and declined the offer. One of the fastest ways to get press attention—and not of the favorable sort—is to become attached to the "perks" that go along with appointment to a high federal position. Not long afterward, in another agency, one of our Reagan Administration appointees got a lot of highly critical press for his excessive use of his perks; and one of the things included in the story was his complete refurbishing of his office at taxpayer expense. Shortly thereafter, he resigned his post.

Scandals relating to perks will occur in every administration. In some cases, infractions will take place because political appointees are ignorant of elaborate government regulations or simply unaware that very different standards apply in government than in business. An agency head can stave off this type of problem among political staff by making sure everyone understands all the rules, making sure they appreciate the potential serious consequences of even minor infractions, and closely monitoring things such as travel vouchers and use of government cars from the outset. This last step ensures that everyone comprehends the seriousness of the matter and nips potential misuse in the bud before a real problem gets started. In every case, conservative appointees intent on rocking the boat must remain "clean as a hound's tooth" or they will be publicly pilloried for offenses that would be simply overlooked in other appointees.

Establishing Control

A political appointee has to understand that the career people have seen a lot of administrations come and go, and the attitude of some of them is: We were here before you arrived, we will put up with you during your temporary stay here, but we will be here long after you are gone. Over the years, there naturally develop various networks of careerists who view the agency as their own. The career infrastructure tends to run the agency or the department day in, day out. Such was the case at ACTION when I arrived. While Sam Brown got his funding for a variety of his favorite leftist groups, a group of careerists ran ACTION on a day-to-day basis.

We set out to change all that. The first thing I did was to put political appointees in positions of line authority so that they were overseeing the various divisions of the ACTION agency. Thus, career personnel were reporting directly to Reagan appointees. We also placed a political appointee as executive officer overseeing personnel and administration. These are steps that are absolutely essential if the intent is to control the bureaucracy rather than be controlled by it. Unfortunately, in some other agencies and departments, the Reagan political appointees were put in staff positions while the line and administrative authority continued to reside in the hands of careerists. This, in my judgment, is no way to change an agency or department in any meaningful way.

Of course, as I have described, when I got there, ACTION was plagued with an extensive array of grants throughout the country under the VISTA program to virtually every kind of leftist political organization one can imagine. We wanted to stop that quickly. So I reversed the normal conservative approach of decentralization, and we centralized authority over all VISTA grants in our national office in Washington. Thus, to be approved, a VISTA grant had to pass muster not only with the state office and the regional office but also at the national office where our Reagan appointees personally would review each grant application to make sure that it fell within our guidelines. This approach may have slowed the bureaucratic process down to a virtual crawl for several months, but it saved a lot of taxpayer dollars from falling into the hands of left-wing activist groups.

Ironically, under Brown ACTION had been distributing books such as Saul Alinsky's *Rules for Radicals* and Harry Boyte's *The Background Revolution: Understanding the New Citizen Movement* to facilitate left-wing political organizing. The latter book contained a listing of virtually every leftist political group in operation nationwide—which proved very useful to us. However, it still required months and months of painstaking detailed research on the part of the political staff to find out about the hundreds of groups receiving or applying for grants: who they were and what they actually did. This investigation process was assisted by our maintaining noncareer staffing at the rather substantial levels established during Brown's tenure.

Another factor that assisted us in our tasks was that, as mentioned briefly, Sam Brown had not institutionalized his programs. For example, at ACTION we had no "grant review panels," a process wherein outside "experts" (who are really affiliates and friends of the normal grantees or even the grantees themselves) are used to evaluate and choose new grantees. To gain control in such a situation is a two-stage process: One must eliminate or totally transform the panels of experts before affecting the grants themselves. This will prove time-consuming and will inevitably bring the political appointee under fire for "politicizing" a process that was intensely and deliberately political to begin with. In this respect, we were fortunate that Brown was not as bureaucratically savvy as some of his counterparts in the Carter Administration.

Finally, our efforts to control ACTION grants had a positive as well as a negative side. Left-wing groups are protean; if defunded, they will quickly reappear in new organizational variants, with new acronyms, and with bleached resumes. Because these groups had long monopolized ACTION programs and were experts in the federal grant process, they often dominated the application lines despite the change of administrations. Our experiences in the details of the grant process quickly showed us the same old faces arriving at the door wearing "wigs" and a little "make-up," with hands out as usual. If we had limited ourselves to simply trying to say no to Brown-era recipients, we would invariably have ended up simply funding the same old liberal network under a variety of new guises. Instead, we made a positive effort to search out alternative groups beyond the usual application lines: groups which embodied other ideals of social service and were not necessarily in the habit of asking the federal government for assistance. This search was not simple; it took a lot of work, but eventually we found enough alternative nonideological groups and were able to shift all our funding. This was essential to our success.

By maintaining a substantial noncareer staff, placing political appointees in line positions, and centralizing the grant process, we, in effect, put appointees down on the playing field where they could block and carry the ball themselves instead of trying to direct the game from the press box (or even worse, waiting to read about the game on Monday morning, which seems to be the management style of some Reagan appointees). This was absolutely essential to our success. Because of it we were able, in a very short period, to stop funding left-wing groups— something that has not happened in many departments and agencies even now, nearly six years after Reagan was first elected!

An Alternative Vision

In our efforts to alter the ACTION grant system, however, we wanted to be intellectually consistent. I was opposed to the use of taxpayer monies to fund political groups of whatever persuasion, and so we refused to use ACTION funds to support conservative political organizations and activities. While leftists on Capitol Hill regularly attacked me for defunding left-wing, community activist groups and occasionally charged that I was funding conservative political organizations, they never once made that charge stick because we did not fund any such activist conservative organizations.

This does not mean that we were socially neutral or indifferent in designing our grant programs. As stated above, we actively sought out groups with an alternative social vision: groups that were not waiting for the millenium to be rung in through class conflict and social upheaval; groups that were interested in helping their fellow man but who understood social improvement as being centered on the improvement of the individual and the community and not as occurring as an incidental byproduct of an avalanche of billions of dollars out of the federal bureaucracy. But we did not fund any group engaged in political activity. For example, while we *would* fund groups seeking to materially assist poor, unwed women who wished to have a child rather than an abortion, we *would not* fund "Right-to-Life" groups engaged in political activity.

While I was at ACTION, we established a worthwhile alternative agenda with social programs addressing drug abuse, illiteracy, runaway children, and food banks for the poor. One common denominator in all these programs was limited financial support augmented by substantial volunteer effort. Another important factor was that all of them were efforts supported by the mainstream of the public. Even *The Washington Post* was forced to admit that we were more effective in carrying out our initiatives than had been our Carter predecessors.[14]

One particularly effective undertaking was to provide a small amount of money to sympathetic groups exploring the idea of providing owner-ship to tenants in existing public housing as a means of breaking de-pendency, encouraging responsibility, and improving the community. In early 1981 this concept was barely even discussed. Now, five years later, it is being implemented through legislation that is backed by both conservatives and liberals. I am certain that ACTION's early support of this idea contributed to its eventual success; it is an excellent example of how a small amount of "seed" money devoted to an incisive idea can reap extremely large rewards some years down the line.

However, the area in which we achieved the greatest results was our Vietnam Veterans Leadership Program. In the late 70's it was fashionable to treat Vietnam veterans as societal victims, as "sick puppies" deserving sympathy. Like so many liberal initiatives, this one had only negative consequences for the alleged "victims" it purported to serve. Clearly, Vietnam vets as a group were harmed by the extreme negative publicity depicting them by and large as sufferers of social and psychological problems. (Based on the prevalent media image in the late 70's, if I had been a prospective employer interviewing a job applicant who was a Vietnam veteran, I would have half expected him to pull out a gun and take me hostage.) Even those with real problems were obviously not helped by the obsessive focus on their handicaps and the efforts to pin them into a dead end, victim's role.

The overwhelming majority of Vietnam vets, myself included, resented the public image of veterans as guilt-ridden victims of an unjust war. Like veterans from previous wars we were proud of our service to our country and often strengthened by it for tasks in later life. The Vietnam Veterans Leadership Program grew out of these sentiments. It was an effort to help Vietnam veterans as a group by countering the derogatory publicity that hampered their prospects socially and economically; at the same time, it provided those who really needed help with positive direct service.

The program sought to change the public image of Vietnam veterans by stressing the real facts: that as in any war, the overwhelming majority of those who returned have not only adjusted but have gone on to succeed in life. We reinforced this by publicizing the examples of thousands of veterans who have produced great accomplishments in private life. The program then harnessed the volunteer services of those same successful veterans to provide counseling for other veterans who were having prob-lems, whether related to the war or not. We assumed, correctly, that pro-viding positive role models and counseling from those who had gone through the same experiences and problems would have a favorable impact. The approach was correct, possibly because for the first time it was sincere; certainly it was better than preoccupation with the past; certainly it was better than suggesting to those who were having serious and continuing problems adjusting that they were somehow victims of a malevolent conspiracy on the part of the government and society. (The cynical and exploitative nature of these last efforts should be apparent to all.)

In the last five years, the transformation in the public perception of Vietnam veterans has been tremendous. In the late 70's, nearly everything concerning Vietnam veterans was negative. Today this has been reversed; public opinion, treatment in the press and the popular media are overwhelmingly favorable. The Vietnam Veterans Leadership Program at work in communities across the nation contributed greatly to this transformation.

Like most Vietnam veterans, I do not believe that the war in Vietnam was meaningless. I, like President Reagan, regard it as a noble cause—a cause hundreds of thousands are proud to have served. That the war was "lost" was certainly no fault of those who fought bravely in it. (That responsibility should be more appropriately laid close to the doorstep of those who later conveniently discovered veterans as social victims.) I am as proud of my efforts at ACTION to serve my fellow Vietnam veterans as I was to serve with them in the struggle against communism in Vietnam fifteen years earlier.

Conclusion

The question still remains: Can a conservative govern effectively? In my judgment, the answer unreservedly is Yes. It can be difficult at times, and frustrating to no end. Yet a team of conservatives, working together with a clear agenda, can effect dramatic change in an agency or department. Within a four-year period at ACTION, the Reagan team managed to cut the staff from more than 1,000 to 500, cut our budget by 25 percent (from $160,000,000 to $120,000,000), and eliminate agency funding of leftist political organizations. Simultaneously, we developed an alternative policy course, consistent with the Reagan philosophy.

When someone says change is too difficult, the bureaucracy is too entrenched, or Congress will not cooperate, my response is: You are doing something wrong. If one has the substantive ability to handle the job, is sophisticated politically, and (most important of all) has the courage of one's convictions, one can govern effectively even in Washington. Perhaps, in the next conservative administration, conservatives will have more of an opportunity to prove that case.

Notes

1. Harry C. Boyte, *The Backyard Revolution: Understanding the New Citizen Movement* (Philadelphia: Temple University Press, 1980), p. 39, cited

in James T. Bennett and Thomas J. DiLorenzo, *Destroying Democracy,* (Washington, D.C.: Cato Institute, 1985), pp. 19–20.

2. William T. Poole, "Campaign for Economic Democracy, Part I: The New Left in Government," Heritage Foundation Institution Analysis, no. 13 (Washington, September 1980), p. 3, cited in *Destroying Democracy,* p. 65. Hayden stated that communism is one mode of human improvement.

3. Ibid., p. 47. See also *Destroying Democracy,* p. 63.

4. Bennett and DiLorenzo, p. 63.

5. John Boland, "Nader Crusade: The Anti-Business Lobby Is Alive and Kicking," *Barron's,* October 27, 1976, p. 7, cited in *Destroying Democracy,* p. 67.

6. Derek Shearer, as cited in *Destroying Democracy,* p. 62.

7. Warren Brown, "Efforts to Change Peace Corps Image Have Gone Nowhere," *The Washington Post,* December 25, 1978, p. A2.

8. Interview with Sam Brown, *Penthouse,* December 1977, p. 218.

9. Warren Brown, "Political Activism Peace Corps Goal Ex-Director Asserts," *The Washington Post,* December 8, 1978, p. A8.

10. The Peace Corps was made semiautonomous within ACTION after the Brown-Payton confrontation.

11. See James Fallows, "The Vietnam Generation," *Atlantic Monthly,* July 1981, pp. 18–22.

12. Eileen Gardner's personal religious convictions hold that adversity and suffering exist to help an individual grow toward internal spiritual perfection and that in some way such events are willed by both the human soul and by God. Her experience in teaching handicapped children also led to her conviction that an underlying philosophy that there is no universal order and that a handicap is simply a cruel, pointless trick of fate can often have a very negative influence on the development of handicapped persons. The most remarkable aspect of this affair was that in the hearings held by Senator Weicker, Weicker repeatedly attacked Dr. Gardner for statements directly tied to her religious beliefs but refused to allow her to fully explain those statements in their spiritual context—because religious views were a "matter of individual choice" and it was "not the business of government" to listen to or inquire into such individual beliefs. Sham of religious tolerance and kangaroo court tactics were the order of the day.

13. In 1969, TV commentator Martin Abend informed his viewers that Brown had admitted he favored communist victory in Vietnam. Brown, of course, was not alone. He had a great many ideological compatriots in the Carter Administration. For example, one of Carter's White House speech-writers favored "unilateral nuclear disarmament" and declared that the communists were "the good guys in Vietnam War" whose triumph was a "victory for something honorable in the human spirit" which would bring a "more benevolent totalitarianism." See William Poole, op. cit., pp. 10, 34, 35.

14. Cass Peterson, "Men of ACTION Have Many Differences—And a Lot in Common," *The Washington Post,* January 27, 1983, p. A21.

19 Conservative Policy and the Poor: Enterprise Zones

HERMAN A. MELLOR

Editors' Note: This case provides an excellent description of policy-making in Washington from the perspective of an energetic and able lower-level political appointee. Mr. Mellor, a pseudonym for a knowledgeable policy analyst, underscores the salience of ideas in the policy process, and the importance of philosophical commitment in the work of a political appointee; without the latter, an appointee is often simply adrift in the enormous apparatus of government. A number of techniques for advancing policy change are also presented: Hard work, attention to detail, and a willingness to bypass bureaucratic channels seem to be essential.

The central urban policy proposal of Ronald Reagan's 1980 presidential campaign was to establish an enterprise zone program. Under the proposal, certain distressed inner-city areas would be designated as enterprise zones, and within these zones taxes, regulations, and other government burdens on economic activity would be reduced as much as possible. The reduction of these burdens would then stimulate an economic renaissance within the zones, producing new enterprises, expansion, and jobs.

This enterprise zone concept was in direct contrast to the direct subsidies and central planning regulations of typical government economic development programs. The idea behind enterprise zones was to examine what the government was doing to prevent prosperity in depressed areas, and stop it, rather than to adopt new plans for government intervention in the private economy, through either subsidies or regulation.

Enterprise zones appealed to Ronald Reagan because the concept provided a special opportunity to reduce government sharply, even if limited to a few small areas, and offered the potential for building showcases of free-market capitalism. These showcases might then lead to wider adoption of free-market policies across the whole country. Enterprise zones also enabled Reagan to address an important public-policy problem in a politically appealing manner that was still consistent with his overall conservative philosophy.

Congressman Jack Kemp (R.-NY) and The Heritage Foundation had already taken the lead in popularizing the program. Kemp had first introduced an enterprise zone bill in 1979, and he introduced a new bill in 1981.

The Players

Samuel Pierce was appointed Secretary of Housing and Urban Development (HUD) at the start of the Reagan Administration. Pierce was a moderate black Republican from New York City. He was staunchly loyal to the President, and felt fundamental policy changes were necessary to save the nation from economic disaster. He did not, however, have a strong personal understanding of conservative ideology. He was vaguely familiar with enterprise zones as a program proposed by the President to help depressed inner-city areas, but did not have strong opinions or preferences regarding the details of the program.

The chief policy official at HUD was E. S. Savas, Assistant Secretary for Policy Development and Research. He also was from New York City, with government experience as a Deputy Mayor in the Lindsay Administration. Savas had most recently been a Professor of Government at Columbia University, where he had built a solid reputation as a careful academic analyst and researcher. Savas did have a strong commitment toward seeing that ideology translated into policy. He knew what enterprise zones were supposed to be, according to the philosophy and proposals of Reagan, Kemp, and Heritage, and wanted the program to be done right.

One of Savas's deputy assistant secretaries was Feather O'Connor, a career official who had worked at HUD for many years. She professed to be a Reagan supporter, but had been promoted to the top of the career bureaucracy by the Carter Administration. O'Connor, in truth, had very little sympathy for or understanding of most elements of conservative philosophy, and knew little about enterprise zones. But she was very experienced, savvy, and sophisticated regarding how to operate in Washington. Other political appointees under Savas at the deputy assistant secretary level were skeptical about enterprise zones in general, either through a lack of conservative commitment or because they believed that special rules for certain areas of the country would simply distort the economy.

One of Savas's special assistants was a 26-year-old attorney named Peter Ferrara. He was a recent graduate of Harvard College and Harvard Law School and was so excited by the election of Reagan that he left a job with one of New York City's most prestigious law firms to come to Washington. Ferrara was intelligent, hard working, and ferociously aggressive. He had a thorough intellectual grasp of conservative ideology and was passionately committed to its advance. He had published several articles on enterprise zones and understood the concept and its details well. He had close ties to Heritage and Kemp. But Ferrara also had no government experience and was totally unfamiliar with the ways of Washington.

Another Savas special assistant was Richard Francis, an ex-marine colonel in his mid-50's. Francis had recently served as head of a landlords' lobbying organization in Washington. He was sophisticated regarding Washington, and a competent advocate. He had a general feeling of support for conservative philosophy, but not a deep-rooted intellectual commitment. He knew little about enterprise zones in the beginning and was skeptical about the idea.

At the White House, Martin Anderson was the President's Chief Domestic Policy Advisor. He had run domestic policy for the Reagan campaign and was now the keeper of the ideological flame within the Administration. He knew exactly what the President wanted in regard to enterprise zones.

Robert Carleson worked for Anderson on the White House domestic policy staff. Carleson had been close to Reagan and Ed Meese for many years, having been the architect of Reagan's welfare policies in California. Carleson also was a strong conservative ideologue and understood what Reagan intended in regard to enterprise zones.

Shaping the Policy

Starting from the beginning of the first Reagan term, HUD had the lead for the Administration in the enterprise zone initiative, and the primary responsibility for developing the program within HUD naturally fell to Savas. The first decision Savas had to make was who would take lead responsibility on his staff for the project. Savas chose Ferrara.

This choice was in large measure due to Ferrara's aggressiveness and enthusiasm for the project. While everyone else around Savas shied away from the concept as vague and undefined, Ferrara stepped in with a well-defined concept of the program which he repeatedly articulated to Savas and others at every chance. Ferrara saw the enterprise zone opportunity coming and aggressively went after it.

Though the President had vigorously campaigned on the enterprise zone concept, and it was endorsed in the Republican platform, the proposal was under heavy fire in early 1981 throughout the Administration. Commerce Department bureaucrats were upset that the program had been given to HUD, and feared that it would become a HUD substitute for Commerce's own Economic Development Administration. Though Commerce Secretary Malcolm Baldrige supported the idea because he was close to the President, all those below him, from the undersecretary on down, lobbied against it.

The Treasury Department was also upset that HUD had been given the lead, because Treasury considered enterprise zone legislation to be a tax bill, which should naturally be Treasury's responsibility. Treasury also saw the idea as just creating new tax loopholes. Again, though Treasury Secretary Donald Regan supported the idea because he understood the President's support for it, Treasury representatives in Administration councils, usually career bureaucrats, opposed it vociferously.

The newly-appointed Undersecretary of Labor had been retained by a large manufacturing association to lobby against enterprise zones just prior to entering the Administration. The Council of Economic Advisors (CEA) opposed the idea because they thought enterprise zones would distort the market. Even Reaganites within the White House were concerned that the program would be inconsistent with the Administration's federalism policy favoring state and local control.

This heavy criticism was all focused on the numerous enterprise zone bills pending in Congress, which were the only concrete versions of the idea at the time. To cut through the criticism and get Administration approval for an enterprise zone plan, White House Domestic Policy Chief Martin Anderson asked Savas in May 1981 to develop a new enterprise zone plan from the ground up, consistent with the President's philosophy across the board. Anderson wanted Savas to develop the plan quietly and secretly within three weeks and to send it directly to him for his personal consideration and evaluation. Savas asked Ferrara to take on the project. (This quick study would largely preempt a major study of enterprise zones which Savas had started before Anderson made his request. Study groups of mostly career officials throughout HUD and other departments were involved in this larger effort, with Ferrara coordinating the project for Savas; but the process had obviously become too cumbersome and far flung to produce the quick, decisive action needed by Anderson.)

Ferrara burrowed into the effort to produce a new plan for Anderson. He consciously avoided any contact with the career bureaucracy regarding the project. This was partly due to the project's mandate of secrecy, which Ferrara seized on as the justification for career bureaucrat exclusion. But Ferrara also believed that the career bureaucracy at HUD did not understand enterprise zones and would at best dilute its ideological foundation, if not pervert it altogether. Ferrara instead sought input from the conservative community which had been working on enterprise zones, particularly The Heritage Foundation. He also scoured the many existing congressional proposals for good ideas, but mainly worked off Kemp's 1981 bill as the basis for the new plan.

After three weeks, Ferrara produced a voluminous set of notebooks describing a new enterprise zone plan. The plan was composed of four basic elements:

1. *Federal, state, and local tax relief within the zones.* Federal tax relief would focus on reduction of individual and corporate income taxes within the enterprise zones. Relief from tariffs and capital-gains taxes would also be included. State and local governments could choose among reductions in state and local income taxes, sales taxes, and property taxes, among others.

2. *Federal, state, and local regulatory relief within the zones.* Mayors and governors with enterprise zones in their jurisdictions could appeal to federal agencies to relax federal regulations within the zones, except for regulations involving health, safety, and civil rights. State and local governments could choose regulatory relief among such areas as zoning, occupational licensing laws, building codes, and others.

3. *Privatization of state and local services within the zones.* State and local governments were given incentives to allow as many of their services as possible to be provided by private entrepreneurs within the zones.

4. *Involvement of private, grassroots, neighborhood organizations.* State and local governments were given incentives to provide for strong participation by private, grassroots, neighborhood organizations in the enterprise zones program. These organizations could be supported in delivering some state and local services, helping local zone residents to participate in new economic development within the zones, and adopting programs to deal with social problems within the zones, such as alcohol and drug abuse, teenage pregnancy, crime, and others.

Discretion of state and local governments was maximized within the program's framework, satisfying federalism concerns.

Savas personally liked the plan and passed it on to Anderson, who was ecstatic over it. He felt it was exactly what the President had in mind. Anderson decided he would immediately take it to a Cabinet Council meeting to get final Administration approval for the plan.

Ferrara did not realize it at the time, but he later learned that he, Savas, and Anderson had violated a cardinal rule of bureaucracy through this process. The type of document Ferrara produced is usually not sent out of a department like HUD without being circulated throughout the department for comment and approval.

Based on the reaction of the HUD career bureaucracy to the plan, this inadvertent bypass of the entire Department was fortuitous. The HUD career bureaucrats objected to every element of Ferrara's plan. They said

tax relief was irrelevant to start-up businesses, deregulation was impractical, and privatization and neighborhood groups were unimportant.
    The career bureaucrats, however, did not oppose enterprise zones per se. They instead sought to change all the elements of the plan so that nothing was left of the original conservative idea except the name. The career bureaucrats argued that the key to new business formation was for the government to offer subsidized, guaranteed, front-end capital loans to new businesses. Another key, they argued, was grants to state and local governments for construction of infrastructure. If the HUD career bureaucracy had had its way, the enterprise zone plan presented to the White House would have had just these two types of subsidies targeted to distressed inner-city areas, rather than Ferrara's four elements. In short, the career bureaucrats would have turned Reagan's enterprise zones into just another big government spending program.
    The career bureaucrats ridiculed Ferrara as a neophyte political hack and sought to undermine Savas's confidence in him by telling Savas that if he took Ferrara's plan to the Cabinet Council, he would be laughed out of the White House. They made this argument even though Ferrara's approach was based on the clear statements of the President through the 1980 campaign, as well as the Kemp legislation which the President had endorsed, and Martin Anderson recognized that the plan followed the President's views. Because Savas was a strong ideologue and had a deep intellectual understanding of the conservative philosophy of the President, he was not persuaded by these arguments, though even he was a little shaken by them.
    It was obvious from this career bureaucrat reaction that if the usual procedure regarding comment and approval throughout the Department had been followed, no remotely conservative enterprise zone plan would ever have emerged. The liberal appointees and career bureaucrats would have deflected it into the big government program described above or would have buried it altogether within the Department in endless debate.
    Breaking the rules in this context was consequently essential to the success of the program. But this was possible only because of the leadership of Martin Anderson at the White House. Savas and Ferrara's plan would have been roasted back at HUD except for the fact that Savas could say he was only following White House orders and that the White House loved the plan. Without this White House cover and support, the HUD bypass play would have backfired, the plan would have been withdrawn by HUD, and Savas and Ferrara might have been ruined.
    As it stood, however, Martin Anderson was planning to take Ferrara's plan to the Cabinet Council as the HUD proposal. The key to final success of the bypass was that Savas was able to convince Pierce to accept the proposal as HUD's. This was easy to do because Pierce initially had no

strong feelings as to the content of the program and the ideology behind it, Pierce knew the White House liked the plan, and the known White House support discouraged any expression of opposition within HUD. Moreover, Pierce delved into Ferrara's notebooks over the ensuing weeks, was attracted to the ideological coherence of the plan, and came to embrace and support it enthusiastically.

Further Maneuvers

The enterprise zone program had already been assigned to the Cabinet Council on Commerce and Trade headed by Commerce Secretary Baldrige. The White House policy assistant coordinating this Cabinet Council was Dennis Kass, a young investment banker from New York who was quite skeptical regarding enterprise zones. Because of this skepticism, Anderson asked Robert Carleson of his staff to coordinate enterprise zones in the Cabinet Council with Kass. Carleson was responsible at the White House for coordinating the Cabinet Council on Human Resources, whose domain naturally overlapped with enterprise zones anyway.

The first Cabinet Council meeting to consider the new plan, in July 1981, had many of the Cabinet secretaries present, plus Anderson, and CEA Chairman Murray Weidenbaum. Most of the secretaries had little to say, probably due to the ambivalence or opposition of their underlings toward the plan and to an attitude of waiting to see which way the wind would blow. The exception was Treasury Secretary Regan, who, though still strongly supporting the overall enterprise zone concept, attacked the tax reduction elements as far too rich and administratively unworkable. The discussion at the meeting was thus dominated by a debate between Regan and his staff against Savas and Ferrara. The meeting concluded with an agreement that HUD would meet with Treasury to work out the tax provisions: These and the other details of the plan would then be presented at a later Cabinet Council meeting for final approval before being submitted to the President.

This approval plan was actually drawn out into an extended process involving several Cabinet Council meetings over many months. During this process, Savas continued to have the lead responsibility for HUD, with Ferrara having the chief responsibility for the project on Savas's staff. In practice, Savas was overwhelmed with the many other policy responsibilities he had. Ferrara reacted to this situation by aggressively seeking to seize responsibility as much as possible. As a result, Ferrara personally dealt as the representative of HUD on this issue with the officials of other departments and agencies.

Sensing that he had almost no allies in HUD, Ferrara sought to work alone as much as possible. He made a conscious decision to avoid interfering in any of O'Connor's projects, so that she would leave him alone on enterprise zones, even though he felt she was having a negative effect on other policy areas. Other political appointees under Savas seemed uninterested, and Ferrara did nothing to stimulate their interest. Occasionally other assistant secretaries sought to get involved, reflecting the career bureaucracy's general distaste for Ferrara's plan, but these individuals were again too busy with other matters to cause serious problems.

Ferrara's fears regarding the career bureaucracy were clearly justified by their continuing opposition to the enterprise zone plan. The career bureaucrats persisted in wanting to reopen the plan in order to substitute their liberal big government approach for the conservative approach. They convinced many nonconservative, nonideological political appointees within HUD to favor their view. But Savas and Ferrara repeatedly shrugged off their criticism on the grounds that the issue was closed within the Department. HUD had already made a proposal to the White House, Pierce and the White House supported it, and the task now was simply to win overall Administration approval. Ferrara's opponents within the Department viewed him as a crazy lone wolf who would never be able to get complete Administration approval for his plan alone. Their strategy seemed to be to allow him to fail first, and then they would remake the enterprise zone program, rather than take any positions overtly contrary to the White House, Pierce, and Savas.

The career bureaucrats naturally had a battery of studies from their usual run of urban institutes, central planners, and liberal professors to support their views. But the purpose of enterprise zones was precisely to try a radically different approach from this old establishment line, tried and failed so often in the past. Both Ferrara and Savas knew this, and consequently these studies did not intimidate them.

But they also knew that such studies could not be ignored. Consequently, Savas and Ferrara mustered counterrebuttals from all the outside conservative sources they could. They marshalled papers, books, and studies from The Heritage Foundation, American Legislative Exchange Council, Sabre Foundation, Arthur Laffer, and others, and suggested further studies they could conduct. They gathered supporting materials from Kemp's office and other congressional offices. At one point, Savas and Ferrara, aided by Francis, organized a private conference within HUD composed of outside business leaders and state and local representatives to give their opinions on various issues, and the results of the conference supported Ferrara's enterprise zone plan.

In the meantime, Ferrara let the original, extended enterprise zone study process, with study groups throughout the Administration, die quietly. He took the results that trickled in and used what was helpful.

But he didn't exactly crack the whip to meet deadlines and complete assignments. Nor did he seek to keep the process alive by circulating completed assignments to ask for comments and resolve disagreements. Ferrara felt that most of those involved in this process again were not conservative supporters of enterprise zones, and would undermine the effort. Moreover, Ferrara felt the longer any questioning and study process went on, the longer final approval of an Administration enterprise zone proposal would be delayed. While Ferrara stayed quiet, everyone else just forgot about this study process.

Ferrara also made a conscious decision to focus all his energies on the enterprise zone issue alone and not get involved in any other issues. He quickly learned that from a special assistant position he could not command the authority necessary to have meaningful and determinative input on issues on which he did not work full time. Instead of focusing just on enterprise zones, he could have had merely tangential influence on a wide range of issues. By focusing exclusively on enterprise zones, he came to be recognized as the expert and could dominate policy decisions.

In dealing with officials from other departments Ferrara noted that a pattern emerged similar to that within HUD; he repeatedly took advantage of the fact that they were all too busy on a wide range of other issues to counter him effectively as a full-time operator on the issue. This was particularly important since every single sub-Cabinet official Ferrara dealt with in the Cabinet Council approval process, except Carleson at the White House, opposed the enterprise zone plan. Only the Cabinet secretaries themselves supported it—since they were close to the President and understood his philosophy. The secretaries only spoke up, however, during the Cabinet Council meetings themselves, and were represented by contrary subordinates during the preparation meetings.

Because no one else was working on the issue full time, the opposition never got organized. In meeting after meeting to iron out the details of the proposal, Commerce would attack the plan as likely to be ineffective and consequently an embarrassment to the Administration. At the same time, Treasury would argue that the plan was likely to be overwhelmingly effective, and therefore the tax provisions could be cut back sharply. Savas and Ferrara responded to these attacks by contrasting them with each other, and consequently each attack canceled the other out.

Ferrara recognized that such meetings of Administration officials on enterprise zone issues were counterproductive, and sought to have as few as possible. Ferrara also insisted on writing any memorandum memorializing any decisions or positions taken at these meetings. This was essential for him to maintain control over the process, because he was able to define and memorialize what happened in the most favorable terms possible. Because the others were not involved in the issue full time, they were not paying enough attention to challenge effectively Ferrara's interpretations of what had taken place.

For the Cabinet Council meetings, a decision memorandum was necessary to state the issues for consideration and to list the different options for resolving each issue. Ferrara also insisted on writing every decision memorandum, which again was crucial for maintaining control. Ferrara was consequently able to frame the issues in the most favorable light and lead the decision-makers toward the favored conclusion. A common tactic in the bureaucracy regarding decision memoranda is always to list three options to resolve every issue, with the favored option in the middle and the other two on each end as extreme in opposing directions as is reasonable and effective. Ferrara employed this tactic as well.

Ferrara found in dealing with nonconservative political appointees, and even with career bureaucrats, that he was sharply challenged and sometimes ridiculed when he sought to invoke the President's philosophy as justification for a position. These opponents would not challenge the President or his conservative philosophy directly. Rather they would challenge Ferrara's interpretation of it. "You don't speak for the President," and "How do you know what the President believes?" they would tell him. This was so even though the President had clearly articulated his conservative conception of enterprise zones during the campaign, and Ferrara was stating what should have been obvious, conservative, vintage Reagan views, such as, for example, that the President favored including tax cuts and deregulation in the enterprise zone plan rather than government-subsidized loans and federal grants. Nevertheless, Ferrara found he could safely cite the President and his philosophy in support of a position only when he had a White House official to back him up, such as Carleson or Anderson.

Savas had instructed Ferrara to keep in touch with the conservative community regarding enterprise zones, and keep getting their input. Ferrara seized upon this mandate to gain the help of conservatives in influencing the Administration decision-making process. For example, a high-level official in another department might oppose Ferrara on a key issue and hold up the process. As a young special assistant to an assistant secretary, Ferrara often did not personally have the clout to counter this opposition. Generally in this situation, the assistant should turn to his boss, in this case Savas, to carry the fight. But sometimes Savas wanted to avoid controversies and antagonisms with other Administration officials, and so Ferrara would turn to the conservative community for help. In gaining input on this issue, Ferrara might indicate to Stuart Butler of The Heritage Foundation that a certain official might profit from a better understanding of the question. Butler could then himself go see the official in a friendly visit to explain the conservative cause, without giving any firm indication that he had spoken to Ferrara. If the official was not dissuaded, he would at least become concerned that outside conservatives would finger him as an obstructionist on this issue, and generally back off.

Similarly, in seeking input from Jack Kemp's staff, Ferrara was able to alert them as to how they could use their influence to ease the Administration decision-making process and counter troublesome officials in other departments. Kemp's staff was very aggressive, and if a little persuasion did not work, they turned to harsh criticism, sometimes public. This was highly effective and productive, but only because Ferrara was able to distance himself from any participation or encouragement regarding harsh criticism or public activities. Kemp and his staff had the clout and position to pull off these actions effectively whereas Ferrara did not.

As the process continued, the Cabinet Council meetings approved one by one every major feature of Ferrara's original plan, except the tax provisions, which were being saved for the end. Commerce Secretary Baldrige chaired these meetings, and served a key role in leading the group to agree to each of the provisions, recognizing that the provisions were in accordance with the President's preferences.

The battle between Ferrara and Treasury bureaucrats over the tax provisions, however, was a real donnybrook. Treasury assigned a number of career bureaucrats from the Office of Tax Analysis under the Assistant Secretary for Tax Policy to represent the Department on this issue. These career bureaucrats, some of them with decades of government service on tax policy issues, sought to intimidate Ferrara with their detailed knowledge of the tax code. They were intransigent, opposing any federal tax relief as part of the enterprise zone program. They argued that tax relief targeted to certain zone areas was administratively unworkable and would turn into a huge loophole. They argued that such tax relief was unjustified, virtual welfare. They argued that the President had never said he was in favor of federal tax relief for enterprise zones.

Fortunately, Kemp's office was able to get a Treasury ally, Deputy Assistant Secretary for Economic Policy Steve Entin, involved in the process. Entin had formerly worked for Kemp, and understood the enterprise zone concept well. Entin was able to distinguish between what was valid in the career bureaucrat criticisms and what was not, in a way that Ferrara could not have. The career bureaucrats were forced to defer to Entin, and he took control of the process within Treasury. Entin worked with Ferrara in developing a realistic package of federal tax relief for enterprise zones, though Ferrara was forced to compromise on many issues to gain Entin's agreement, as Entin in turn had to reflect to at least some extent the pressures and views of the Treasury Department generally.

The final enterprise zone tax package agreed to by Ferrara and Entin included a 50 percent increase in the investment tax credit for enterprise zone investment; elimination of capital-gains taxes on such investment; a 10 percent tax credit to employers for wages paid in the zone; a 5 percent tax credit to employees for wages received in the zone; a special 50 percent tax credit to employers for wages paid to disadvantaged workers; and relief from tariffs. Together, these elements would likely have eliminated almost all federal taxation on business activity in an enterprise zone.

This tax package was supposed to represent a final compromise between Treasury and HUD. But Treasury balked at the last moment and Entin was replaced on the issue by other political appointees, who did not understand enterprise zones or why the President supported the idea. They led the Treasury Department to propose an alternative enterprise zone tax package, including only two elements—Industrial Development Bonds (IDB's) and the Targeted Jobs Tax Credit (TJTC).

IDB's would provide a tax exemption for interest on bonds approved by state and local governments but used by private businesses. The TJTC would provide a modest tax credit for hiring disadvantaged workers. Ironically, IDB's and the TJTC were already in the tax code for the nation as a whole, but the Administration had already proposed abolishing them. Conservatives regarded TJTC as an ineffective waste. Industrial Development Bonds simply provided for greater government favoritism and intrusion into the credit market, as opposed to genuine tax relief which would allow a citizen to retain more of the money he justly earned in the marketplace. The Treasury proposal was that IDB's and TJTC be preserved only in enterprise zones. Not only would this proposal provide a mere portion of the tax relief of the Ferrara/Entin plan; but, more important, the proposal was clearly calculated to discredit enterprise zones themselves. By including only tax provisions the Administration had otherwise chosen to abolish as undesirable, the Treasury bureaucrats would have converted enterprise zones into a repository for discredited notions, a tactic which could easily have led to the demise of enterprise zones altogether.

Carleson weighed in at this point, advancing a third tax package that added many of the elements Ferrara had compromised with Entin. Carleson's strategy was again to leave the original Ferrara/Entin compromise as the middle alternative, with two more extreme alternatives on either side. The decision memorandum for a final Cabinet Council meeting with the President was written up with these three alternative sets of tax provisions.

Treasury sought to write this final decision memorandum, recognizing the value in authoring the document. But Ferrara resisted. Treasury responded to Ferrara's original version by rewriting it and sending it back to the White House. Ferrara took it and rewrote it again. Treasury held the draft until late Friday afternoon before the scheduled Monday morning meeting and then sent another Treasury rewrite back to the White House. Ferrara went to the White House over the weekend and was able to convince Dennis Kass to let him rewrite the final version for Monday morning.

The final Cabinet meeting with the President was held in late November 1981. Regan, who had continued to support enterprise zones personally, did not attend, leaving the opposing role at the meeting to his deputy Tim McNamar. The result was bitter for the Treasury bureaucrats. The President at the Cabinet Council meeting decided to adopt the Ferrara/Entin compromise proposal, plus the IDB's from the Treasury proposal. At this point, Administration approval for the enterprise zone plan had finally been won. The approval process had taken six months.

Promoting the Administration Policy

Enterprise zones now shifted into an entirely new phase, carrying out rather than developing policy. Savas and Ferrara recognized, however, that the policy decisions made could be gutted entirely in their implementation. Consequently, instead of switching to a new policy development issue, Ferrara continued to serve the same leading role on enterprise zones into the implementation phase.

This new phase had some key differences from the policy development phase. Since the President himself had approved the plan, all expressed opposition within the Administration ceased. The attitude within HUD changed dramatically. Everyone in the Department now saw the plan as HUD's own, for which they wanted to win congressional approval, creating new power, authority, and front-line Administration attention for the Department.

Moreover, there was no way Ferrara could work alone anymore. Winning congressional approval would entail an enormous public relations and lobbying effort, with hundreds of Administration employees involved. Savas responded to this new reality by asking Richard Assisi to team up with Ferrara in heading the effort.

Ferrara's first task was to explain the proposal to the others who would be working on it. He did this by preparing a set of materials describing the program. He emphasized up front in these materials the ideological and philosophical foundation for the program, so that people would understand the why as well as the what regarding enterprise zones. HUD officials took these documents seriously, studied them carefully, and began themselves repeating the Administration line as explained by Ferrara.

An immediate problem Savas and Ferrara both recognized was the tendency within HUD to be willing to compromise away key elements of the plan to win quick congressional approval. Savas and Ferrara responded by seeking and winning a ruling from the White House that no element in the plan could be changed without going back to the Cabinet Council for approval or at least getting White House assent.

In addition, the enterprise zone program was slated to be administered within HUD by the Office of Community Planning and Development (CPD), which was controlled by liberal political appointees. These appointees began consideration of how they would administer the program, and almost immediately began planning how they would change the heavy conservative emphasis in the program through HUD regulations and administrative actions. Instead of getting immediately involved in this battle, Ferrara determined that he would wait until congressional passage of the proposal was closer on the horizon, and then attempt to change responsibility for the program's administration.

Another major implementation task for Ferrara was taking the lead in overseeing the legislative drafting for the proposal. The White House decided that Treasury would draft the tax components and HUD would draft everything else. Ferrara sat down with the HUD drafters in the Department's General Counsel's office and sought to explain the proposal. Often, they could not imagine how a particular provision could be drafted, in which case Ferrara drafted it himself. Ferrara also freely rewrote what they did draft to suit the intentions and philosophical basis behind the approved plan.

Treasury's drafting of the tax provisions resulted in a whole new round of battles that Savas and Ferrara had to fight. Savas and Ferrara recognized that by drafting the details of the approved tax incentives narrowly Treasury could take away the substance of what had been approved. With the same deputy assistant secretaries from the Office of Tax Policy who opposed the plan during the development stage now overseeing the drafting for Treasury, this is precisely what the Treasury drafters tried to do. Savas and Ferrara fought them tooth and nail over every clause and appealed the issue to the White House. Ultimately, Ferrara had to write up a new decision memorandum covering each dispute separately, about three dozen individual items. Carleson then sat in judgment on each dispute and sided in most cases with Savas and Ferrara.

Another task was finalizing the Treasury revenue loss estimates for the enterprise zone bill. These estimates would define the cost of the bill and therefore would have a fundamental influence on the prospects for congressional approval. Career Treasury bureaucrats in the dreaded Office of Tax Policy were responsible for this task as well. The estimation process by these bureaucrats had actually begun when Ferrara was developing the enterprise zone tax package with Entin. Ferrara never trusted the estimators and insisted on attending the internal Treasury meetings where the estimation methodology was developed. He argued in these meetings for the proper methodology and assumptions, and did heavily influence what they finally decided to do.

Ferrara's skepticism regarding the estimators was well founded. There is no precise, correct methodology for estimating the revenue effects of tax changes, and Treasury is notorious for biasing its estimations depending on whether it opposes or favors a proposal. This institutional characteristic now worked in Ferrara's favor, however, since the higher-level political appointees were now committed to the program's passage, given the President's approval. As a result, Ferrara was able to eliminate many biases against the enterprise zone proposal in the revenue loss estimates.

However, Ferrara was still not able to get Treasury to consider adequately the positive economic impact of the program in reviving depressed areas and consequently producing new revenue to offset any initial revenue loss. The Treasury usually estimates revenue impact from a tax code change on the basis of "static" analysis—assuming taxpayer behavior does not change in any way in response to the tax code change. The supply-side view is that such static analysis is grossly in error. With respect to enterprise zones, supply-side analysis held that substantial new economic activity would result not only from the zone tax relief but from the other components of the program as well, leading to substantial new revenues which would largely offset any revenue loss.

In estimating the revenue impact of enterprise zones, the Treasury did not adopt a totally static analysis. But it assumed only a modest economic improvement in the zones, and in addition assumed that virtually all of the improvement came from relocation of economic activity from elsewhere in the country, resulting in virtually no new revenue to offset the program's static revenue loss. This was probably the most important revenue estimation bias against the program by far.

Still another task Ferrara took on was to prepare the public descriptions of the program. He prepared memoranda describing the program for the press, city officials, and affected constituent groups, and developed accompanying packets of information and materials. He also seized every opportunity to write the speeches for high-level Administration officials who would speak on the subject, and eventually was routinely asked to write such speeches. As a result, he was able to write speeches, not only for Pierce and Savas, but also for Commerce Secretary Baldrige, Treasury

Secretary Regan, and even the Vice President and President. Ferrara sent a speech to the White House speechwriters office for the President to announce the program, and they adopted the text for the President almost verbatim.

From the start, Ferrara adopted a special strategy for all of these public materials and speeches. He would include in the beginning a few paragraphs regarding the ideology and principles underlying the program. Moreover, he insisted on including the exact same paragraphs with the exact same words in every document and speech. Ferrara did this to further lock in the policy. Expressing the ideas of free-markets and removing big government would naturally make it difficult to dump the conservative components of the program and substitute traditional spending and regulation elements. Having the same words used over and over, and by leading Administration officials, hammered the point home and made changes even more difficult. Moreover, each leading official was more comfortable expressing these policy views, because he saw others and the President himself expressing them. They also came to a better understanding of the philosophy behind the program and were led to support it.

Of course, simply being able to write the President's speeches on the subject, and expressing carefully stated, ideological principles in those speeches, itself helped to lock in the policy, because the President himself was naturally in effect endorsing every word written in his name and then ultimately spoken by him. Any opportunity to write a presidential speech should consequently be seized. In writing the speech, careful thought should be given to what words should be included in the speech to express presidential endorsement of a policy, words which can then be quoted later to enforce that policy within the Administration.

It was during this implementation stage that Ferrara benefited most from focusing all his time exclusively on enterprise zones. He became the recognized Administration expert on the program and virtually everyone deferred to him. All questions were referred to him; everyone called him to be briefed on the issue, and, as noted, everyone sought to have him write the public speeches, even for officials in other departments, the Vice President and President. This expert reputation was generally enough to intimidate any potential opponents. If anyone still dared to challenge his policy directions, he could bury them with detailed knowledge, and with the mandate of the Cabinet Council decision-making process, which was commemorated in documents he had written.

Administration enterprise zone legislation was sent to Congress in March 1982, occasioned by a Rose Garden ceremony. The next month, Carleson hired Ferrara to work for him at the White House. With the continuing mandate that any policy changes in the program had to be approved by the White House or the Cabinet Council, it was clear that any alterations HUD wanted to make in the program would have to be referred to Ferrara. Before Ferrara's move to the White House, the liberal Office of Community Planning and Development (CPD) in HUD was planning a series of proposed changes for White House approval. After the move, CPD shut down all such activities.

Though Ferrara was consequently successful in winning Administration approval of a credible, conservative-oriented enterprise zone program, the question remains whether opponents were in fact able to stall the decision-making process long enough to upset the proposal's momentum and consequently scotch congressional passage, for enterprise zone legislation on a federal level has not been adopted to this day.

Editors' Postscript

This case is a remarkable story about pushing a new policy through the labyrinths of the executive branch. Unfortunately, enterprise zone legislation has not yet been passed. In retrospect, it seems that the fifteen months required to fight the policy through the executive branch effectively killed the prospects for real reform. By the time the proposed legislation reached Congress, President Reagan's "honeymoon" period had passed and support for tax-cutting was waning. (Some have also argued that enterprise zones were subsequently blocked in Congress because liberals did not wish to give the Reagan Administration credit for an effective anti-poverty program.)

It could be contended that a greater willingness to compromise on the part of enterprise zone proponents might have brought the bill out of the executive branch more quickly and facilitated its passage. This seems unlikely but, even if true, has a number of drawbacks worth noting. Overall, among political appointees there is a desire to demonstrate "accomplishments," which often leads to a bias toward "producing results" at the cost of compromising away the contents of legislation or policy. In policy-making the rule "Something is better than nothing" may often be misleading. Compromise which emasculates policy or repudiates the philosophical premises of the policy is never helpful. In this particular case the passage of a diluted form of enterprise zones legislation would have led to policy failure in the field which in turn would be used to discredit the central concepts of the program.

The protagonist in this piece seems to have taken another approach to his work. While never abandoning the practical, he seems to have operated with an implicit recognition of the principles advanced by Bruce

Fein in "Politics: The Art of Public Education" (see Chapter 2), i.e., that the intellectual foundations of policy are the point at which real, long-term change occurs. By forging a distinct conservative policy, the protagonist helped to articulate an alternative approach to the problem of poverty, permanently altering the context of the debate. As such, the effects of his efforts will endure and will transcend the fate of any particular piece of legislation.

20 Permanent Guerrilla Government: Legal Services Corporation

LEAANNE BERNSTEIN

*Editors' Note: This case history serves as an excellent intro-
duction to the concept of a "permanent nonelected government"
in Washington. The author is a member of the Board of Directors
of the Legal Services Corporation and thus is able to provide a
detailed view of the inner workings of that complex and
controversial organization. There is a wide discrepancy between
events as they are described in this narrative and the perception
of "government" held by the general public.*

On November 5, 1980, the American people elected Ronald Reagan
president, taking the first step in an historic break with the liberalism that
had dominated American politics for a half-century. Five days later, on
November 9, droves of "poverty lawyers" gathered at the Dupont Plaza
Hotel in San Juan, Puerto Rico, for the annual meeting of the National
Legal Aid and Defender Association (NLADA), an offshoot of the Legal
Services Corporation (LSC). Over 100 LSC employees—nearly one-third
of the work force in its Washington and regional offices—were scheduled
to participate in this conference. Airfare alone cost the taxpayers over
$100,000. The purpose of this meeting of affluent lawyers, held by the
beaches of San Juan, was to mobilize the LSC and its grantee network to
counteract the devastating election defeat of five days earlier. The conference saw the inception, under the close supervision of top LSC officials,
of a "survival plan": a strategy to block any significant change within LSC
on the part of the Reagan Administration and beyond that to thwart
Reagan policies on the full range of domestic and international issues.

The following case describes this political struggle by one component
of the federal government against an elected president—a struggle carried
out with considerable success; a struggle which continues today, funded
by the same taxpayers who elected Ronald Reagan to office in 1980 and
again in 1984.

It is, at the same time, the story of the efforts of Reagan appointees to
establish control over a government bureaucracy—efforts which were far
from successful. It was only in 1986, more than a year after the reelection
of Ronald Reagan, that the Administration began to establish some form
of supervision over the LSC.

The events at the Legal Services Corporation demonstrate that winning an election is not enough. After an election is won, a whole new battle must be waged to actually control the "permanent government" in Washington—a government which has become, in many cases, not only contemptuous of electoral processes, but of the law itself.

What Is the Legal Services Corporation?

The Legal Services Corporation was created in 1974. Its predecessor, the Office of Legal Services within the Office of Economic Opportunity (OEO), was an executive agency slated for abolition under President Nixon. Legal services activists mobilized the organized bar to support an "independent" legal services structure. Since it would not be a government agency, the Corporation would not be subject to "political pressure." This was in accord with the earlier recommendations of the presidential advisory council, the Ash Commission, which in 1971 urged President Nixon to remove legal services from the auspices of OEO and organize a quasi-governmental Corporation "as a first step toward reprivatization of what has traditionally been a function of the private sector."

Established as a nonprofit Corporation in the District of Columbia, LSC is a funding conduit. Congress appropriates funds; LSC then makes grants to and contracts with other entities theoretically for the provision of legal services to indigent persons. LSC absorbed the OEO grantees in 1974; additional grantees were established with greatly increased appropriations between 1974 and 1979 until geographic coverage of the country was accomplished.

Thus the de facto organizational structure of the LSC has three levels:

- The Board of Directors
- The LSC president and the formal headquarters staff
- The grantees

The LSC is "governed" by an eleven-member, bipartisan Board of Directors who are appointed by the president and confirmed by the Senate for fixed three-year terms. Once confirmed, the Board members cannot be dismissed by the president.

Board members serve on a part-time basis. The Board selects the full-time LSC president, who, in turn, has complete control over staff employment. At the beginning of the Reagan Administration, this headquarters staff consisted of about 90 employees in the central Washington office and 60 employees in regional offices.

The first two levels of the LSC organization serve to channel money to the third level: the grantees. Three major types of grantees are funded. The most numerous are the field legal services offices. Their function is to deliver direct legal representation to clients. They are organized as private nonprofit Corporations with separate Boards of Directors. By statute, these Boards must include one-third client eligible members ("poor persons") as well as attorneys.

The second type of grantee is the state support center. Of the 67 state support grantees, some are separate entities and some joint ventures with field programs. These centers may serve clients directly, but their function is generally that of organization, research, and backup for the local providers.

National support think tanks are another category of grantee. They are geographically and functionally removed from client service. Operating like public interest law firms, these centers formulate strategies for stimulating test-case litigation. They publish manuals and newsletters advocating positions on substantive legal and political issues.

Although there was little oversight over the activities of individual grantees, the law originally provided that grantees offering direct delivery of services could not be unfunded or have their funds radically reduced without a full and fair hearing before the Board establishing wrongful misconduct or mismanagement. Support centers were not covered by this "hearing" clause. Moreover, the Board did have full control over allocation of increases to the total LSC budget and could reduce the funding of any particular grantee by as much as 10 percent per annum without a hearing. Used cumulatively over a number of years, these provisions provided substantial long-term discretionary control over the allocation of the LSC funds.

As an "independent" Corporation, the LSC and its grantees are not subject to the regulation of the executive branch agencies such as the Office of Management and Budget (OMB), the Office of Personnel Management (OPM), or the General Services Administration (GSA). The LSC submits its budget requests directly to Congress rather than through the White House, although the president may comment on the requests.

From an OEO program controlled locally and initially funded at less than $20 million per year, the LSC grew rapidly during the 1970's. By 1981 the budget was $321 million. Over 1,450 local offices were staffed by 6,200 attorneys and 2,800 paralegals. Current direct federal funding is $305.5 million; additional funds provided by state and local government, federal agencies, and other sources, bring the total budget to $411 million.

As a putative effort to "depoliticize" the delivery of legal services to the poor, the LSC has been, as the following text will show, a remarkable failure. What the independent structure of the LSC has provided is access, for a certain part of the legal community, to nearly $3 billion in taxpayer's funds with virtually no oversight or accountability as to what the funds were used for.

The LSC Mission—Perception vs. Reality

The perception of federally-funded legal services is that of a safety net. Lawyers in legal aid offices meet immediate problems of individual clients. The poor client whose Social Security benefits have wrongfully been terminated will have an advocate; mothers will have access to an attorney to seek child support payments; indigent renters will have recourse against landlords who fail to provide heat or make repairs. These mundane but significant legal problems raise concerns for a system of justice that should provide equal access.

However, from the inception of the Legal Services Corporation, another function was envisioned: the use of litigation and related activities to change existing law and policy and to restructure American society through political class struggle. As part of the overall welfare state, the activist lawyers were to promote legislative and regulatory advocacy and develop organizations to assist poor peoples' "movements." Legal services programs were set up to be "general counsel to the poor." The notion of the individual eligible client was thus replaced with "poor people" or "the client community." The eligible client's "uninformed" demand was replaced with a social engineer's perception of "client community" need.

As LSC absorbed OEO's programs, local offices were given the statutory right to set service case priorities (the kind of problem most urgent). Many offices set priorities by consulting with local welfare rights organizations, labor unions, tenants' unions, and civil rights groups. The notion of a poor individual walking into an office, first come-first serve, to seek legal help is a popular perception of legal services, but in reality the federal system provides jobs and discretion to thousands of attorneys many of whom are bent on social reform and the redistribution of wealth. According to LSC training materials, the Legal Services Corporation funded attorney was to be

> an arm of community organizations, that is, the lawyer was to function
> as part of a political effort, at times as a lawyer, at times as an organizer,
> an educator, teacher, and PR man.[1]

The end pursued, according to the same batch of documents, is simply power—"power over the distribution of wealth, power over the means of production and distribution."[2]

Thus, as an activist agency in pursuit of its own vision of a just society, the LSC for over a decade has engaged in a wide range of blatantly political functions. These include:

- litigation to establish public policy at the local, state, and federal levels
- establishment of local grassroots political organizations and networks to promote a left-wing agenda
- broad-based lobbying for or against legislation
- direct partisan support for specific candidates for office
- general public relations activities on behalf of liberal "anti-poverty" programs

No one knows precisely what percentage of LSC activities is devoted to radical reform activities as opposed to routine client-oriented services. Indeed, the LSC grantees have fiercely resisted any effort to survey exactly what they do. However, it can be easily estimated that 50 percent of the work of LSC's staff attorneys over the years has consisted of social activism as opposed to traditional services. This translates into a 1985 expenditure of over $150 million in direct federal tax revenue devoted to activities to promote the legal service movement's notions of radical social change. Since 1971, the figure approaches $1.5 billion. Although this is not a great sum in terms of total federal spending, it is a very substantial sum in terms of its potential impact on the public policy arena. The annual amount represents, for example, 10 to 15 times the annual operating budgets of such influential think tanks as The Brookings Institution or The Heritage Foundation.

The list of political/advocacy activities that LSC's radical lawyers have inflicted on the American political system is lengthy. For example, LSC has engaged in numerous redistricting suits on behalf of the "poor." LSC lawyers sued to prevent the holding of the special election won by Phil Gramm in Texas. In Florida, LSC sued to prevent a bank merger. Legal services offices all over California were mobilized in 1980 to defeat Howard Jarvis's Proposition 9, a ballot initiative which, if passed, would have lowered individual income taxes. (The LSC Act expressly prohibits such political activity, yet Senate hearings and a General Accounting Office investigation revealed that hundreds of thousands of dollars were, in fact, devoted to the campaign that defeated Proposition 9.) Legal Services attorneys argued that lower taxes would result in lower state treasury funds, which would mean less money for public entitlement programs which would harm their clients. Of course, lower taxes could result in additional capital investment, more jobs, less unemployment, reaping productivity gains and economic and social independence for clients, thus obviating the need for public benefits or legal services lawyers.

One of the national LSC think tanks, the Center for Law and Education, sued to overturn Florida's high school functional literacy examination policy, asserting that the test is racially discriminatory because a higher percentage of black students fail. After years of litigation, Florida's requirement has been upheld. The legal services attorneys' position would have undercut the value of a high school diploma for all students, but hard-working poor students would have suffered the most. The LSC grantee has now sought $500,000 in attorneys' fees from Florida taxpayers for the same suit.[3]

An LSC program in Memphis, Tennessee, has filed numerous questionable lawsuits to obstruct child support enforcement activities of the Juvenile Court. Coincidentally, the program's Executive Director was himself cited by the court four times for failing to comply with a child support order. When Congressman Don Sundquist requested an audit of the program, anonymous calls were reported to have been made threatening the lives of the judge who issued the contempt citations and the congressman's son.[4]

The Network and the New Priesthood

In pursuit of its political goals, LSC has engaged in coalition building with other liberal groups. An LSC memo of 1980 relates a small sample of LSC efforts to build activist networks:

• Michigan—A broad-based coalition including labor unions and legal services local programs has helped to defeat a severe tax cutting initiative, the Tisch amendment, in 1978 and 1980. Terry Black with Michigan Legal Services . . . has also worked with the UAW and other progressive unions . . . for the past two years to pass legislation helping low-income and working class families deal with sky-rocketing energy bills.

• Florida—Last year legal services offices state-wide joined with public sector unions—AFSCME, AFT, NEA, and the Firefighters and the State AFL-CIO—to oppose a restrictive state spending limitation referendum. Their role was important in the defeat of that measure.

• Maine—Marshall Cohen of Pine Tree Legal Assistance, Inc. has worked hand-in-glove with the State AFL-CIO for as long as he has directed the legislative office . . . . [the LSC office drafts the bills for the AFL-CIO]—Chris Hastedt from his office . . . is a member of the state Executive Board of AFSCME, and she drafts most of the major labor bills for the State AFL-CIO.[5]

Although, as the above list indicates, LSC can be very active in the field of legislation, LSC doctrine is ultimately marked by a disdain for democratic processes and a belief that social policy should be developed in the judicial as opposed to the legislative branch. In accordance with this premise, LSC has, at the taxpayer's expense, initiated litigation to: require state disability payments for homosexuals; force state governments to use tax funds to pay for sex-change operations; establish the constitutional right to free public education for illegal aliens; require local school boards to introduce "black English" into the schools; block research on labor-saving agricultural machinery; and return two-thirds of the state of Maine to a tribe of Indians.

Clearly the LSC attorneys recognize no demarcation between legislation and litigation. According to LSC's own practice, there is virtually no question of public policy that should not ultimately be resolved by lawyers and judges as opposed to mere elected bodies. Doctrinally, the LSC seeks to erect a new category of constitutional, economic "rights and entitlements" for the poor—thus taking all questions of the welfare state and economic policy itself out of the hands of the elected government and into the hands of the courts. According to LSC materials,

> on an ideological level, we do now conceive of the citizen as rights-bearing and the citizen's relationship with the state and other large areas of life in terms of entitlements.[6]

Finally, in these endeavors of tax-funded social engineering, the LSC wishes to be accountable to no one. Its structure has dictated that there will be no direct supervision by any elected official. The policies it pursues are chosen by the officials of its 1,450 local offices, in accordance with their own social consciences, i.e., as high priests of the emerging social order. Much of LSC's political activity violates the intent of Congress and various prohibitions in the LSC statute. This, of course, does not deter the legal activists. Under the guise of providing routine legal services to the poor, operating in frank contempt of the law, the LSC continues its crusade for social revolution.

The Survival Campaign: 1981

The election of Ronald Reagan was a deep shock to the Legal Services Corporation. In the words of one LSC lawyer,

> . . . . [W]e woke up on November 5th and realized the extent of what we could see coming in these events, and realized the extent of it was much greater than we anticipated. It scared the shit out of us. And we realized after two days of terrible depression that we needed to do something. Allowing ourselves two weeks of grieving, we then decided we had to get on with doing what we had to do—either pack up our bags—or pick a place and stay and fight. And we have decided that we needed to fight. . . . The base bottom line is that we are in a political campaign. . . .[7]

The LSC began to fight back in its conference in Puerto Rico just five days after the election. At that conference, the LSC "survival plan" was born. Over the next few months, LSC President Dan Bradley gave responsibility for development of the survival plan to Alan Houseman, Director of the Corporation's in-house think tank, the Research Institute, and one of the drafters of the original LSC legislation.[8] Houseman wrote:

> What is at stake is not solely the survival of the Legal Services program. What is at stake is the survival of many social benefits—entitlement programs that we struggled, since 1965, to make real for poor people. We have struggled since 1965 to bring into the belt federal, state and local benefits. What is at stake is a number of other kinds of programs like affirmative action, civil rights programs. That, in the end, is what is at stake in this battle. Those, in the end, are far more important than legal services. Legal services is a tool to get them. Both of those kinds of things, both of those problems—legal services, social benefits, entitlement programs, civil rights. Those are what are at stake in this battle.[9]

With respect to the immediate situation at LSC, there was the threat that the agency would be eliminated and, even if this did not come about, a threat that the Reagan Administration would seek to seriously control LSC activities. Houseman stated, "We are in the end not subject to the control, to the immediate control, of the President."[10] He had no intention of allowing that situation to be altered, either administratively or legislatively. To preserve the LSC and ward off presidential supervision, Houseman thought that it was necessary to "manipulate the political situation to our advantage"[11] by building a local political base on behalf of the agency.

While the LSC staff was frantically working to "manipulate the political situation," the Reagan Administration did little at all.

The Grace Period

President Reagan had promised during his campaign that the elimination of LSC would be accomplished while he was in office. William J. Olson, a Washington, D.C., attorney, served as team captain of the Administration's transition team for the Legal Services Corporation. Olson assembled a group that formulated recommendations for the Corporation. However, the Administration strategy in reaction to the transition report was never clear.

In fact, the Reagan Administration was at that point tactically paralyzed. Strong conservatives, pushing for the abolition of LSC, felt it would be an admission of defeat to appoint a Reagan Board to the Corporation. The Administration tried and failed to cut off funding during 1981 but made no actual effort to control the organization. Reagan made no nominations to the Board until December 1981—14 months after the election. For all of 1981, LSC was governed by the Carter holdover Board; the Reagan Administration in effect gave the LSC a "grace period" in which to mobilize for its struggle. During that period, federal funding remained at the highest level in LSC history—$321 million.

During the winter of 1980 and spring of 1981, the elements of Houseman's "survival plan" quickly materialized and were put into action. The plan incorporated several different tactics: (1) affect the Reagan appointments to the LSC Board to ensure a moderate leadership; (2) mobilize grassroots lobbying to influence Congress against any restrictions on grantee organizations; (3) mobilize grassroots organizations to fight Reagan policies in general; (4) create a shadow structure outside of the Corporation so that when a Reagan Board was appointed, the Congressionally-protected grantee organizations would have leadership; and (5) protect resources for the long-term political struggle by granting increased funding and independence to those organizations designated as crucial to radical activism. (This last element was dubbed "saving the rubies" by LSC leaders in reference to Tsar Nicholas's actions to save the Russian crown jewels in 1917 by sending them to Switzerland when the Bolsheviks were coming over the palace walls.) In addition, LSC staff conducted training sessions for field programs on how to create "mirror corporations" for the hoarding and hiding of federal funds.

Throughout the 1981 grace period, many regional meetings were held for grantees to explain and coordinate the survival effort. Corporate headquarters staff provided supervision for the networking and organizing activities carried out by the grantees. President Carter's Board of Directors supported the survival activities by allocating increased funds to the "rubies" and by its acquiescence to the activities of LSC staff.

Legal services staffers were urged to contact hundreds of potentially sympathetic organizations in their localities, such as the League of Women Voters, the NAACP, and the elderly groups, to gain their support; staffers were instructed to *write LSC endorsement letters for these organizations* which could then be mailed to local congressmen. The survival plan also called for influencing Congress through the media; LSC lawyers unleashed a blitz of op-ed pieces, talk show appearances, and strategic press releases. In addition, the regional support centers were expected to maintain a presence in Washington to lobby directly for their case.

A memo from Clint Lyons, Director of the LSC Office of Field Services, suggested that local offices "send notices to all poor people groups, agency officials that deliver services to poor, handicapped and elderly people" notifying them of the threat to LSC and of the LSC survival meetings.[12] Thus, instead of providing services to the poor, LSC sought to reverse the situation, to mobilize its clients to work for the organization.

A particularly effective ploy for mobilizing the "public" was the "services cut because of impending budget cuts" panic. In many local offices, new clients were refused service because of the "Reagan budget cuts"; clients were then given a pen and paper and asked to write a letter to their congressman protesting the "Reagan cutbacks." If the client did not wish to write a letter, LSC staffers were instructed to write it for him. In fact, the cutbacks were "proposed," not actual, and were for fiscal year 1982, not 1981. In reality, LSC offices in 1981, as noted, were receiving their highest funding ever, and were busily diverting the funds to political activity or stockpiling money for future years. (Total fund balance carry-over for LSC during 1979-82 has been estimated to have been about $140 million. Some individual programs had fund balances exceeding $2 million. As a political war chest available for the congressional elections of 1982, neither the Republican nor the Democratic Party could match its size nationally.)

As LSC became increasingly confident of its ability to survive, it began to shift the survival campaign to broader political targets. It mobilized tens of thousands of LSC workers and client volunteers to lobby against the full range of Reagan policies. LSC funding served as a focal point in building broad-based coalitions to attack the Reagan budget, economic policies, etc. For example, the Migrant Legal Action Program was given $40,000 to hold conferences in cities across the country for the purpose of "networking and coalition building in support of farmworkers."[13] These conferences brought together activists from the AFL-CIO, United Farm Workers, NAACP, PUSH, SCLC, the League of Women voters, ACLU, NOW, the National Council of Churches, environmental groups, and many others.

In Missouri, LSC funded the Coalition for Sensible and Humane Solutions. In its grant application the groups proposed to "fight Reagan budget cuts." In its midterm report, it listed its accomplishments:

> 500 Coalition members attended Congressman Richard Gephardt's St. Louis Budget hearings—150 low-income people attended a People's Forum providing testimony to representatives of Senators John Danforth and Thomas Eagleton—The Coalition has sponsored massive letter-writing campaigns to Congressmen and Senators—The Coalition distributed solid up-to-date information about proposed cuts and opposition strategies.[14]

Meanwhile, the LSC prepared for the inevitable arrival of a Reagan Board of Directors. Funds for the most salient political activities and for the management of the survival campaign were transferred to external organizations. Contracts were written in such a way as to bar even minimal oversight of the use of these funds; "survival" leaders such as Director of the Office of Field Services Clint Lyons subsequently assumed the management of this "government in exile."

Senator Jeremiah Denton summed up the "grace period" and survival plan at LSC during 1981 in the following way:

> The initial reluctance to appoint a Board in January of 1981 was compounded by a similar reluctance after passage of HR 3480 [a measure which would have, if adopted by the Senate, significantly restricted LSC activities and would have eliminated presumptive refunding of LSC grantees]. The proponents of defunding LSC were undercut by the additional six months of independence given to LSC holdovers as a result of the failure to appoint a new Board.
>
> To my mind, the failure to move in the summer of 1981 to replace the Carter Board majority was a compound error of the gravest consequences. That failure allowed the final steps of the survival strategy to occur—the creation of an "LSC in exile," the transfer of funds to LSC surrogate entities, and program beyond any real control.
>
> This new [survival] strategy was twofold: a hedge against the future for LSC itself and a hedge for its grant recipients. In both elements, the strategy was designed simply to wait out the Reagan years.
>
> In essence, the leadership of LSC planned to place the most powerful elements of the LSC apparatus as far away from direct control of a new board as was possible—and they intended to provide similar insulation for field programs.[15]

The First Reagan Appointments

Finally, after the year of grace, President Reagan announced seven recess appointments to the LSC Board of Directors. William Olson of the transition team was among those appointed.

Although the seven appointments provided a majority on the eleven-member Board, the decision not to replace the entire Board reflected the Administration's lack of attention to this program.

Nevertheless, Olson attempted to assert control over the Corporation. After his appointment as acting Chairman of the LSC Board, he held a meeting of the Board on New Year's Eve, 1981. The urgency of that meeting reflected Olson's hope that grant checks for fiscal year 1982 would not yet have been sent. The Board voted to suspend issuing any new grants until further notice, thereby restricting LSC expenditures to 1981 amounts. The Board's resolution had little effect; its main purpose had been frustrated by LSC President Dan Bradley's early issuance of checks to grantees in December. Bradley spent $260 million in two weeks, before the new Board could take power and stop him. He reportedly "stayed up late many nights signing checks and cover letters, personally dropping packets into the mail for programs all over the country. When he mailed the last checks on December 15, there was not a dime left in the next year's budget."[16]

In mid-January 1982, the Administration named an additional three members to the Board. This left only one representative from the Carter Board. With nearly a full Reagan Board appointed, Olson arranged with LSC President Bradley that two assistants be hired to help the new Board during the confirmation process. However, it was early February before any Reagan personnel were actually allowed to work within the Corporation headquarters.

When the new Board was constituted, Bradley told them that he intended to resign as of March 31, 1982. Although it was certain that they would have replaced him, his imminent departure imposed the first major organizational responsibility on this group of virtual strangers. The selection of a permanent president would be a lengthy process; the Board needed a temporary full-time executive to serve until a permanent replacement could be found. Based in part upon a recommendation from the White House, Gerald Caplan, a law professor at George Washington University, was approved by the Board in March. The selection of Caplan as the interim executive was a major mistake, as Caplan would seek to thwart every effort of the Board to actually control the Corporation.

Indecision at the White House also crippled the Board at the outset. The White House delayed sending Board member nominations to the Senate (more media questions; another example of bad public relations strategy). At some point, the White House indicated that William Harvey, former Indiana University Law School Dean, not Olson, should be the permanent chairman of the Board. This abrupt and unexplained switch, after Olson's aborted attempt to exert control over the grant process, seemed disloyal, and it promoted rivalry and suspicion on the Board itself.

During the spring the Board met on a monthly basis. Olson's Transition Team work had introduced him to Corporate operations, but the balance of the Board began the process of learning. It soon became apparent that there were significant differences in political outlooks and philosophies toward the federal funding of legal services. Early voting isolated and identified factions among the Board. Reagan had appointed ten members to an eleven-member Board and only five were consistently willing to take an objective or critical view of the Corporation; the others were either opposed to changing the structure of LSC or were willing to accept the recommendations of staff "on faith." The Administration evidently had failed to understand the appointees' positions.

In the legal services community, this divisiveness among Board members was gleefully received. Outwardly there was a semblance of deference to the Board. In reality, the LSC staff had begun a campaign of disinformation, while seeking to gain the confidence of the Board so that business could go on as usual.

Caplan's perfidy in the Corporation did not improve matters. The confirmation process was being delayed, and media coverage of the nominees and Reagan's pledge to abolish LSC increased. The LSC public affairs office continued to disseminate photocopies of anti-Reagan, pro-LSC press clippings to the legal services "community" and Congress. During most of 1982, the LSC press kit itself included propaganda about the Corporation (how it was necessary and wonderful), President Reagan's attempt to abolish it, and the political manipulations President Reagan had engaged in by naming recess appointees.

Though the Board held monthly meetings to get information, material was uniformly prepared and screened by "survivalist" Clint Lyons, Director of the Office of Field Services. The Board's unconfirmed status was continually used as justification for "waiting" to take action. At the same time, the temporary President Caplan would refer to the Board at staff meetings as "inexperienced" and unfocused. Caplan set up a procedure whereby any Board requests for information would be routed through him, thus preventing Board members from asking natural "follow-up" questions of the responsible staff person. This also resulted in "survival" manager Lyons being informed of every substantive Board interest.

Caplan brought on only a few new people to help him. Instead, he worked to promote the credibility of career staff in the eyes of the Board. A charade was devised in which Lyons, a key leader in the survival plan, was portrayed as a hard-liner, insisting that grantee fund balances be recovered from field programs. (Memoranda and Lyons's prior actions demonstrate that Lyons was hardly in favor of recovering fund balances.)[17] It is not clear from Corporate records whether Caplan understood all of the survival program, but his reliance on liberal staff such as Lyons prevented effective control by the Board. Records do indicate that instead of encouraging the anti-Reagan forces to resign, Caplan and Lyons worked out "salary adjustments" to reward them for staying.[18]

In order to cloak LSC and grantee activities, much had already been done toward purging and hiding files, and omitting descriptive information from required reporting documents. A memo from the government relations Director to her secretary outlined that some Corporate files were to be moved to NLADA and others to her home, "in the event that we have to get out fast."[19] By July, the survival leadership had reconstructed the Corporation's organizational chart so that Lyons would have effective control. In meetings of senior staff, the phrase "the Board doesn't need to know about this" was common. (Only later, in July 1983, when new headquarters personnel seized files at all regional offices, was the full extent of this subversion understood.)

The Struggle to Select a President

One of the most volatile issues that the Board faced was naming a permanent president for the Corporation. The selection of the president, as it would directly affect control of the Corporation, was marked by no small degree of byzantine intrigue. In addition to Board Chairman William Harvey, three other individuals played key roles in the complex manuvering: Gerald Caplan, the temporary LSC president, appointed by the Reagan Board; Clint Lyons, career official in the Carter LSC and in-house "survival" planner; and Howard Dana, Reagan-appointed Board member.

Although a Reagan appointee who had headed the 1980 Reagan-Bush campaign in Maine, Howard Dana was actually among the more liberal Board members. Characterized as a "silk stocking Republican," Dana was also a practioner of hardball politics; for example, at one point he sought to intimidate a younger Board member by stating that if that individual sided with the conservative Board members it would damage any future career in politics in Washington or with the Bar.[20]

Since the Carter Board in 1979 had included advisory persons in its selection process, pressure to "involve" client groups, the trade associations, unions, and the organized bar began immediately with the formation of the presidential search committee. Board Chairman Harvey resisted such intrusions, stressing the private nature of the process and the integrity of the Board itself. But, Howard Dana, named Chairman of the presidential search committee, permitted himself to be lobbied constantly, especially by the American Bar Association, the National Clients Council, and the National Organization of Legal Services Workers (a labor union of staff attorneys affiliated with the United Auto Workers). As a compromise, the Board agreed to have an advisory panel review résumés and separately interview the final candidates.

The extreme publicity and controversy surrounding this process produced delay. In addition, the unconfirmed Board was told to hold off on such an important decision because it might affect the confirmation vote. The selection process was not yet complete when the temporary President Caplan was to return to George Washington University in September 1982. Accordingly, the Board needed yet another acting president. But when the search committee met in Chicago on September 14 the question of naming another acting President was not on the agenda. Such a decision could not legally be made without prior notice, and the decision needed to be made by the entire Board rather than by the search committee alone. At the meeting, both Board Member Dana and temporary President Caplan supported "survivalist" Clint Lyons as acting president. Caplan had already elevated Lyons from Director of the Office of Field Services to acting Vice President in order that Lyons would be "in line" should no person be named.

Lyons's role in the still largely hidden survival campaign was at the time unknown, but he had clearly demonstrated intense hostility to certain conservative Board members at public meetings.[21] Fortunately, there was no majority on the search committee to support Lyons as acting president. Unable to actually appoint another acting president until the Board met, the committee specified that there would be *no acting president.* Consequently, Lyons as acting vice president would be the top Corporation officer, but the powers of the acting president (to make grants, hire or fire) would be specifically withheld. Caplan and Lyons chose to ignore the Board's clear intention. When the committee decided not to appoint Lyons as acting president, Caplan attempted to delegate his powers to Lyons through internal corporate documents.[22] These delegated powers included "the making of grants and the entering into of contracts." At a staff meeting, Caplan made clear that he considered Lyons to be the immediate successor to all of his authority. He did not mention that the Board had retained control of certain functions until a permanent president was named.

When Board Chairman Harvey learned of Caplan's "delegation," he informed both Caplan and Lyons that no delegation could grant Lyons powers the Board had not extended.[23] Board Member Dana attempted to muddy the issue by writing Harvey to express *his* understanding that Lyons would remain acting vice president but be "delegated the duties and responsibilities (but not the title) of Chief Executive Officer" when Caplan left.[24]

The reason for the Board's apprehension was clear: Former President Bradley had specifically committed all of the available funds for the FY 1982, knowing that a new Board was being appointed. They did not wish a repetition. Chairman Harvey took no chances. He notified all grantees that Lyons did not have the authority to issue grants or enter into contracts, and he sent a telegram on October 1 to the Treasury that the office of the President of the Corporation was vacant and that any decisions to draw down funds must be made by the Board as communicated through him as Chairman.[25]

Lyons's intention of exercising the statutory powers of the president (including making grants) was later revealed. He consulted an attorney for an opinion on the "Authority of Executive Officer and Board." The attorney wrote encouraging him on October 5, 1982, stating that Lyons "does not lack authority to do any of those activities which are normally within the scope of the Corporation's Chief Executive Officer."[26] While he sought counsel for an opinion that he had all the powers of the presidency, Lyons wrote cloying memos to the Board disavowing any intention to use these powers.[27] The first year of Reagan "control" at the Legal Services Corporation was marked by such treachery. Caplan, Dana, and other Republicans on the Board itself openly opposed initiatives by members promoting close scrutiny of LSC.

Muckraking

Meanwhile, aggressive action by the legal services network placed the Board in a defensive posture. This strategy had been mapped out in manuals produced with federal funds during 1980 and 1981, such as *Strategic and Tactical Research*. In that particular volume a tactic called "muckraking" was described.[28] Muckraking, or mud-slinging, as it is ofttimes termed, is designed to put pressure on the opposition. The legal services community began assembling background information, "muck," on the Board members. Harvey, Olson, and others were targeted.

These efforts quickly paid off in the case of Board Member Marc Sandstrom. Assertions were made that Sandstrom had a conflict of interest because the financial institution of which he was an officer had foreclosed on mortgages of clients represented by legal services programs. This conflict did not, in fact, legally exist. However, the media distortions were of such severity that Sandstrom resigned to protect his employer from further harassment. In his May 7, 1982 resignation statement, he concluded with the sad commentary that "While I can deal with attacks on my personal actions, I cannot in good conscience continue a course of conduct which would unfairly involve others."[29] The Executive Director of the Senior Citizens Law Center, an LSC grantee, Bert Fretz, openly told Congress that it had been his assigned job (again diverting resources from client services) to do such strategic research on the Reagan nominees.[30] Sandstrom's resignation tilted the balance on the Board; only four of ten were then committed to reform.

Former members of the Carter Board played a role as well. In February 1982, the Carter Board filed suit to prevent the Reagan Board from holding a meeting, alleging that the recess appointments were unlawful. *The Washington Post* coverage of the lawsuit failed to mention that several members of the Carter Board had themselves been recess appointments in 1979. That litigation finally became moot when a Reagan-appointed Board was confirmed in 1985; but, as a diversion from the real issues, it was a successful ploy. It forced the appointees into a defensive posture; it facilitated propaganda about Reagan's attitudes being "above the law," and it confused potential supporters in Congress. The Administration's reaction to the suit was unsupportive and confused. The Board members had to hire a private attorney to represent them until the Justice Department finally acquiesced. It was, after all, the President's power that was being questioned.

The Administration made recess appointments of two additional members prior to the vote on the Corporation president. The last Carter member was finally replaced, and Marc Sandstrom's slot was filled. There was a slim 6–5 critical majority on the Board out of eleven Reagan appointments.

The advisory panel to the Presidential search committee leaked information regarding the final LSC presidential candidates prior to the Board's vote. The clear conservatives, Alfred Regnery and Robert D'Agostino, were again targeted for "muckraking." For days, *The Washington Post* carried stories on those "being considered by the unconfirmed Board."

Meanwhile, the confirmation process suffered from lack of commitment. Although the White House professed support for the conservatives on the Board, the individuals in charge of relations with the Hill were passive in their approach. Deals to drop Olson or Harvey or both in exchange for the confirmation of the rest were countenanced by White House legislative staff. In view of the wealth of publicity adverse to the Reaganites, liberals held up confirmation through the 1982 elections. Had the White House made it clear that a *more conservative* Board would be appointed if this one were not confirmed, there might have been action.

The Washington Post Attacks

LSC published a manual in 1981 on manipulating the media. During aı. of the Harvey-Olson Board tenure, misinformation was disseminated by legal services operatives; it was printed in newspapers all over the country. Most of it was designed to denigrate President Reagan and the Board. But nothing topped the bias and malevolence of *The Washington Post* in particular.

The *Post* tried hard to bully the Board out of making a decision on a permanent president. When the Board did choose, the *Post* began its attack on the man selected. The *Post* attacked his employment contract even though it duplicated provisions contained in every previous LSC contract and despite the fact that the compensation is set by statute.

To this attack was soon added the "consulting fee scandal." On

December 14, 1982, just as the Board was about to make decisions about grants for FY 1983, a House Judiciary subcommittee hearing "revealed" that Board members had been paid thousands in compensation and expenses. Congressmen angrily denounced the Board's extravagance. One charged, "It sounds a lot like the first thing they did was put all four feet and a snout into the trough."[31] Representative Robert Kastenmeier and Senators Edward Kennedy and Lowell Weicker immediately demanded a GAO investigation.

Newspapers carried stories about the Board members robbing the poor. Leading the charge was *The Washington Post* with a December 15 headline: "Legal Services Appointees Get Fat Fees." Over the next two weeks the *Post* unleashed 14 articles and editorials about the LSC "scandal." Egged on by the media blitz, liberal Rep. Harold S. Sawyer (R.– Michigan) notified President Reagan that a congressional delegation would like to meet with him "regarding the removal of the Board, the repayment of the consulting fees, the removal of the corporate president...and the selection and confirmation of qualified [Board] members."[32] Even the White House fell under the sway of media hysteria; President Reagan declared the fees paid to be "highly unfortunate."[33]

This media avalanche worked as a smokescreen behind which the real issue was silently fought out: control over LSC. Fed by the *Post's* front page stories, Senator Weicker presented an amendment to the LSC appropriations bill barring the board and the new corporate president from making any policy decisions concerning funding and grant-making during 1983. Funds to grantees were to be locked in according to prior allocation patterns, essentially depriving the Board of the power to change the program.[34] Congress, deeply distressed by the scandals over the Board presented daily in the papers and too busy just prior to adjournment to examine the details, approved the Weicker amendment.

In early January 1983, after weeks of media blitz which made it seem certain that the Board had engorged itself with unprecedented debauchery at taxpayers' expense, OMB issued a report stating, strangely, that it could find no improprieties in Board compensation or expenses. This information was presented on the back pages of the *Post* and largely discounted.

Finally, six months later, GAO issued a complete report.[35] It found that all payments had been lawful and consistent with previous LSC practices. The Board had received higher compensation than previous boards because it had devoted far more actual time to its oversight duties. (Ironically, the "scandalous" compensation can now be seen to have been yet another consequence of the survival plan; covert efforts to neutralize and circumvent the Board's authority required an increased reciprocal effort from a Board intent on fulfilling its responsibilities.) Board Member

Dana, favorite of the liberals, was found to have received more compensation and expenses than conservative members who had been singled out for attack. Harvey, who had come under particularly heavy abuse, was found to have actually contributed over 450 hours of voluntary uncompensated time to LSC duties. The *Post* again relegated the GAO findings to the back pages.

Board Chairman Harvey charged that the ethics "scandal" had been intended to discredit the Board and divert attention from information about the survival plan which was beginning to emerge. The new corporate President Donald Bogard advised that the *Post* "should reorient itself to its function of reporting the news, not creating the news."[36] But it was too late; the damage was done; the Board's power had been largely emasculated; effective control over the LSC had been blocked for a third year.

Not all of the Reagan Board members, however, were displeased with the smear campaign. In a speech to legal services attorneys, Dana described the smear campaign as a story with a "happy ending." With an obvious degree of satisfaction he described the process:

> When some people in high places began to show an inordinate interest in the internal workings of the Legal Services Corporation, it became evident to the generals in the legal services community that their adversaries were not going to be playing by the conventional rules. The generals needed a counter-strategy. . . .
>
> The constituency in Congress prepared to fight the White House over the fate of the Legal Services Corporation needed to be galvanized. They needed a banner to act behind. . . . The consulting fee issue had headline potential. It could compete with "the Jobs Bill" and "the MX" for front page coverage. More importantly it could provide the necessary smoke to cover what was happening in Congress: the locking in place of the protective clauses in the Continuing Resolution[CR]. . . . The issue put the Board and the Administration on the defensive while the friends of Legal Services were quietly inserting provisions in the CR unmolested by their distracted foes.[37]

Dana continued to describe himself as a "Ronald Reagan Republican" even as he demanded that Ed Meese be thrown out of the White House for "mismanagement," and encouraged the audience of LSC attorneys to "keep up the fight" against the Administration and accountability in LSC.[38]

Caretakers and, Finally, A Confirmed Board

When the Congress adjourned in 1982, the terms of the Harvey-Olson Board expired. For several weeks, LSC had a president but no Board.

Singed by the smear tactics of the press and the hostility of Congress, the White House failed to take decisive action. It missed the chance to register its support for a policy of accountability.

Instead, the White House itself psychologically and politically stripped the next group of recess Board members of their statutory right to make changes in the Corporation. The individuals who agreed to serve President Reagan as "caretaker" Board members during 1983 and 1984 were to be water-treaders at LSC. It is to their credit that they ignored controversy and made some of the needed regulatory changes.

The "caretaker board" passed stricter lobbying and eligibility regulations, increased the percentage of funds dedicated to private attorney involvement, and authorized corporate-sponsored privatization experiments. But, at the adjournment of Congress in 1984 the "caretaker" members vacated their seats.

In November 1984, the White House once again made recess Board appointments. But this time, nominations had preceded the appointments[39] and the confirmation process was under control. By May 1985, a confirmed Reagan LSC Board was assured. By July 1985, a new LSC president chosen by the confirmed Board was at work.

Postscript

By the fifth year of the Reagan Administration, LSC's grantees' total funding had increased by at least $60 million per annum. A few programs were defunded. The National Clients Council (NCC), one of the most blatant activist organizations, was one. The cost of the defunding proceeding exceeded $500,000, and the NCC received over $800,000 in interim funding while the eighteen-month process was going on.

LSC central staff, now under control of the Reagan Board, is attempting to exercise its duty to monitor use of grant funds. However, several grantees have locked corporate officials out, refusing access to books. Congress still mandates that appropriations be passed on to the same grantees. The grantees, figures show, have passed increases in appropriations onto themselves in the form of raises; benefits alone have risen 44%.

The story of the LSC over a five-year period demonstrates that the skills needed to win an election and the skills needed to control government bureaucracies—which have been in liberal hands for decades—are separate and dissimilar. All too often the clear will of the people expressed in the elections has been thwarted by a Washington-based "permanent government," pampered and supported by sympathetic liberal media. Let us hope that the misfortunes of the Reagan Administration with regard to the LSC will provide lessons for conservative appointees in the future.

Notes

1. Rael Jean Isaac, "Bringing Down the System," *The Robber Barons of the Poor?* (Washington: Washington Legal Foundation, 1985), p. 103, quoting *Working with Community Organizations: Conference Materials* (Marcy, New York: California Legal Services, June 16–18, 1981), p. 80.

2. Isaac, p. 108, quoting Si Kahn, "How People Get Power," *Working with Community Organizations*, op. cit, p. 28.

3. Judith A. Brechner, General Counsel, Florida State Board of Education, testified before the Senate Committee on Labor and Human Resources on July 12, 1983 that there were at least three federally funded legal services organizations involved. The attorneys at each program were compensated through the taxpayer-funded grants, but a motion for attorneys' fees was filed in the trial court for $580,316.89, reflecting hourly rates of $70 to $100 per hour plus a 10 percent enhancement factor. Transcript of "Oversight of Certain Activities of the Legal Services Corporation," focusing on policies of the Corporation and political activities, Senate Committee on Labor and Human Resources, July 12 and 15, 1983, pp. 449 and 458.

4. Judge Kenneth Turner to Tom Apsut, Office of Compliance and Review, Legal Services Corporation, January 21, 1985.

5. "Russ" to "Alan" [Houseman] memorandum entitled, "Examples of Coalition Efforts at the State and Local Level Around Issues Affecting Lower Income and Working Class Groups."

6. 9 *Clearinghouse Review*, No. 4, p. 371.

7. Don Wharton, Oregon Legal Services, in a speech given at the Denver Regional Project Directors Meeting in Boulder, Colorado, January 12-15, 1981. Quoted by Senator Jeremiah Denton in "The LSC Survival Campaign: Manipulating Against the Mandate," *The Robber Barons of the Poor?*, p. 21.

8. Senator Denton, p. 37.

9. Senator Denton, p. 38. The videotape was submitted and shown to the Committee on Labor and Human Resources of the United States Senate as part of the LSC oversight hearings. Senator Edward Kennedy walked out, refusing to watch the evidence.

10. Senator Denton, p. 38.

11. Senator Denton, p. 39.

12. Senator Denton, p. 49.

13. Senator Denton, p. 68.

14. Senator Denton, p. 61.

15. Senator Denton, p. 64.

16. Taylor Branch, "Closets of Power," *Harper's*, October 1982, p. 50.

17. In fact, a large fund balance was predicted by a House of Representatives Investigative Report in 1979, and the 1980 (existing) fund balance "policy" at LSC was tougher than the weakened version Lyons and Caplan put over on the Reagan Board. According to Bucky Askew's handwritten notes, the goal of the fund balance charade was to "make ourselves look credible."

18. Clint Lyons to Gerald M. Caplan memorandum, July 20, 1982.

19. Mary Bourdette, Director of the Office of Government Relations, to her secretary in an undated memorandum.

20. Interview with former Board member Dan Rathburn who stated that the incident occurred in a private conversation between Dana and himself. Rathburn was a "client eligible" Board member at the time and a college senior. Howard Dana states that he has no specific recollection of the conversation.

21. Lyons, at a public Board meeting, accused Olson of running a mini-corporation out of his office. Transcript, LSC Board Meeting, October 29, 1982, p. 99.

22. "Gerald M. Caplan, Acting President," to "Clint Lyons, Acting Vice President," memorandum entitled, "Delegation of Authority," September 15, 1982.

23. William F. Harvey, Chairman of the Board, Legal Services Corporation, to Acting President Gerald M. Caplan, September 17, 1982.

24. Howard H. Dana, Jr. to Professor William F. Harvey, September 17, 1982.

25. William F. Harvey, Chairman of the Board, Legal Services Corporation, to Honorable Donald T. Regan, Department of Treasury, mailgram of October 1, 1982.

26. Rita L. Bender, attorney (Seattle, Washington), to Clint Lyons and Bucky Askew, memorandum of October 5, 1982.

27. "Clint Lyons, Acting Vice President," to Board of Directors, memorandum of September 28, 1982.

28. Barry Greever, *Strategic and Tactical Research: Power Structure Analysis*, Advocacy Training and Development Unit, Legal Services Corporation, September 1981, p. 16.

29. Marc Sandstrom, statement relating to nomination to Legal Services Corporation Board, May 7, 1982.

30. Francis X. Clines, "Inquiry Begins Into Fees Paid Legal Services Board," *The New York Times*, December 16, 1982.

31. *The Washington Post*, December 15, 1982, p. A1.

32. *The Washington Post*, December 18, 1982, p. A1.

33. *The Washington Post*, December 16, 1982, p. A1.

34. The Weicker amendment did the following: removed the Board's discretionary control over allocation of total funding increases; removed the Board's authority to adjust funding to particular grantees by 10 percent per annum without a "full and fair hearing"; and removed discretionary authority over funding to support centers. The amendment essentially froze the existing program in place.

35. "The Legal Services Corporation Board of Directors' Compensation and Expenses and the New President's Employment Contract," General Accounting Office report to Honorable Robert W. Kastenmeier, Honorable Edward M. Kennedy, and Honorable Lowell P. Weicker, Jr., GAO/HRD-83-69, B-210338, August 31, 1983.

36. *The Washington Post*, September 24, 1983, p. A13.

36. Dana, speech before the Greater Boston Legal Services Annual Meeting, January 20, 1983.

37. Dana, Greater Boston speech.

38. Dana, Greater Boston speech.

39. The majority were first nominated in 1983; their nominations "pended" in a "Republican" Senate for nearly two years.

21 Commerce and the Public Interest: James C. Miller at the Federal Trade Commission

EMILY ROCK

Editors' Note: Emily Rock served as Secretary to the Federal Trade Commission under James C. Miller III and worked on the Reagan domestic policy Transition Team. This chapter describes forceful non-confrontational leadership based on a strong personal sense of agenda and an understanding of the public education aspects of a political appointee's work.

At the tip of the Federal Triangle, in front of the Federal Trade Commission, stand statues of two powerful horses. Next to each horse is a man, straining to hold the horse back. The statues are said to represent "man restraining commerce." Any equestrian will tell you that is no way to control a horse. Pulling back on a horse's mouth only provokes a horse to run away from the pain. The way to control a horse is to sit firmly in the saddle, signal with light pressure on the reins, and guide the horse in the direction that the rider wants to go. This is true not only of horses, but also of institutions.

During the 1970's, the FTC had strayed far from its original mandate, and was viewed by many as out of control. Then Jim Miller was appointed Chairman. By exerting firm leadership and providing clear direction through a positive agenda, Chairman Miller guided the FTC to enforcement activities that make sense, are effective, and are consistent with the overall deregulatory policy of the Reagan Administration.

Overview

The Federal Trade Commission was founded in 1914. Section 5 of the FTC Act gives the Commission broad authority to regulate "unfair methods of competition in or affecting commerce, and unfair or deceptive acts or practices." As stated in the U.S. Government Manual, "In brief, the Commission is charged with keeping competition both free and fair." There are three major bureaus at the FTC: the Bureau of Consumer Protection, which regulates unfair or deceptive practices that affect consumers: the Bureau of Competition, the Commission's antitrust arm which shares jurisdiction with the Department of Justice; and the Bureau of Economics, which collects data for preparation of antitrust matters and provides analysis to the Bureau of Consumer Protection to test competition on economic efficiency grounds. The work of the Bureau staffs is reviewed and decided upon by five independent Commissioners, one of whom serves as Chairman.

The FTC has substantial enforcement authority, including the power to institute formal litigation proceedings that can result in monetary fines and/or cease-and-desist orders. In 1975 the Magnuson-Moss Act empowered the FTC to conduct industry-wide rulemakings, which can have a significant impact upon domestic business enterprises.

During the Carter Administration, the FTC achieved new levels of activism, becoming notorious as the "National Nanny" for its campaign against "unfair" advertising on children's TV programs. This expansive exercise of the FTC's authority caused Congress to reserve for itself a legislative veto on all new FTC regulations (a veto that was declared unconstitutional in 1983). In 1980, Congress actually shut down the agency for a day, and it took President Jimmy Carter's personal intervention to get it going again. At the same time, the Commission was faring poorly in the courts, losing more than 60 percent of its antitrust decisions on appeal.

In 1986, the FTC is bringing cases that are not overturned by the courts; it has improved the level of industry compliance; it has increased reliance on economic analysis in antitrust enforcement; it has developed a protocol that describes its approach to the analysis of deceptive practices; and it has stepped up efforts to inform businesses and consumers about its enforcement policies. All this was accomplished while reducing personnel by 30 percent over a three-year period.

The FTC changed direction because James Miller is a strong leader with a positive agenda to translate his philosophy into action. Others have tried pulling back on the reins in order to stop an institution and have found, to their surprise and dismay, that the institution responds by running away in unpredictable directions. Miller's successful approach to managing the FTC was to change the basic direction of the agency rather than merely attempting to trim its activities. He moved forcefully to transform the FTC into an institution that promotes the free market by taking on government-inspired barriers to competition such as municipal taxi licensing systems. He has turned the FTC into an advocate of deregulation and free trade within the government and a model of policymaking based on sober economic analysis. This article discusses and analyzes Miller's tactics; hopefully it will provide insights on successful management of a government agency.

FTC Under Carter

In March 1977, President Carter appointed Mike Pertschuk as Chairman of the FTC. The appointment followed Carter's pattern of selecting "public interest advocates" for prominent sub-Cabinet posts, as with the selection of Joan Claybrook, from Ralph Nader's Congress Watch, to head the National Highway Traffic Safety Commission. Pertschuk was not at all satisfied with the FTC's traditional role of policing the marketplace to maintain competition and to prevent fraud and deception. Instead, he intended to bring a new "consumerism" to the FTC: to save the American public from the machinations of corporate America and to restructure the American economy.

Pertschuk consistently sought to expand the regulatory ambit of FTC. In the words of one report, "Pertschuk encouraged all his managers to give free rein to their creative spirits and to let every flower bloom. He placed a premium on innovative ideas that would probe the outer limits of FTC's mandate."[1] This was later dubbed by Reagan appointees as "Star Trek" law enforcement: "to boldly go where no man has gone before." The result of this regulatory renaissance was an expanding network of minute regulation over the marketplace.

How consumers benefited from all this or whether they benefited at all was far from clear. Perhaps consumer benefit was never the central issue. As Robert Reich, a political subordinate to Pertschuck, put it:

Pertschuk is a great, clever politician, in the sense that he understands the symbolic role of politics. He understands that you need symbolic issues that have certain ingredients—public drama—that can easily be communicated to the public, that draw almost a gut reaction from the people, and perhaps most importantly, that open up other issues, which are kind of key foot-in-the-door issues. Nader's Corvair was a perfect kind of issue, because *Unsafe At Any Speed* had all of those aspects to it.[2]

In other words, Pertschuk was a master of a theatrical scene-setting for dramas in which business wears the black hat, government wears the white hat, and the public plays the role of the helpless maiden. Most of the notable FTC initiatives of the Carter era had this theatrical quality: FTC versus nefarious funeral directors bilking bereaved widows; FTC versus used car salesmen foisting defective autos on an unsuspecting public; FTC versus Madison Avenue exploitation of four-year-olds. (To the extent that the FTC's automatic rule-making process on these

Pertschukian issues persisted through the early 1980's, they continued to generate anti-business sentiment well into the Reagan era.)

The major concern, again, would seem to be not over whether the public will gain from a particular rule but to demonstrate to the public who wears the black and white hats, with the understanding that this will affect broader social perceptions. It is not a coincidence that Robert B. Reich, who spoke so glowingly of Pertschuk's political savvy, has since become famous as America's leading proponent of national industrial planning: government control of all the major functions of the economy.

The centerpiece of Pertschuk's plans was the children's video (Kidvid) crusade. This regulatory initiative had nothing to do with the FTC's lawful power to prevent deception and fraud in the marketplace and everything to do with broader social goals not germane to the FTC, such as reducing sugar in children's diets or eliminating violence on television. A number of Kidvid regulations were considered, from a flat ban on advertising for children to limits on the number of ads for sugared products directed at children. To many, the Kidvid campaign was seen as direct and obvious usurpation of a legislative function. The advertising, television, and toy industries, faced with losses of billions in income, were infuriated by an FTC that seemed too arrogant even to discuss its policies.

By the late seventies, however, the country was becoming exhausted by intrusive regulation generated by nonelected bureaucracies. Even *The Washington Post* chided the FTC over "Kidvid," stating that the government would seem to have better things to do with the taxpayer's money and that there were perhaps some aspects of life that should not be subject to federal regulation. The Kidvid issue collapsed.

But the reaction to Kidvid was not isolated. Increasing regulation threatened the livelihood of thousands of businesses; FTC's conduct both in rule-making and enforcement had become "highly adversarial."[3] By the third year of the Carter Administration, the country and the Congress were swept up in a backlash to the regulatory abuses of agencies such as the FTC, OSHA, and EPA. Liberal Senator Carl Levin (D.-Mich.) referred to regulators as "arrogant," "unaccountable," "inflexible," and "stupid." "You are dealing with people who are so wound up in their own bureaucracy that they begin to take power unto themselves that Congress never intended. . . .[It is] a system that has run wild," he said.[4] In a hostile congressional hearing Pertschuk was forced to admit that some of his staff had not been impartial but had engaged in a "vendetta" against business.[5]

By 1981, President Reagan's new Director of OMB, David Stockman, was talking of eliminating FTC's antitrust responsibility entirely. There were rumors that the entire agency would be abolished.

Enter Jim Miller

Jim Miller was born and raised in Conyers, Georgia, where his family still resides. He is an economist of the "Chicago School," and is known for his deregulatory philosophy. He taught economics at Georgia State University in Atlanta (1969) and Texas A&M University in College Station (1972–74). Aside from his academic experience, his professional background is primarily in government. He worked at the Department of Transportation, the Council of Economic Advisors, and the Council on Wage & Price Stability during the Nixon Administration. He spent four years at the American Enterprise Institute before joining the Reagan Administration in 1981 as head of OMB's regulatory division. He assumed the Chairmanship of the FTC on October 5, 1981.

Transition Team

As head of the 1980 transition team unit responsible for reporting to the President-Elect on the policy agenda for the FTC, Jim Miller gathered an experienced and loyal team to develop specific recommendations and goals for the FTC. Transition from one administration to another takes place over a period of seven short weeks from the day of the national election until January 20 at 12:00 noon, when the new president is sworn in on Capitol Hill. Miller and his team threw themselves into the effort of learning about and critiquing the Commission. They were a visible presence at the Commission, conducting numerous interviews with the existing staff.

Although generally familiar with regulatory issues, Miller knew little about the FTC when he began his transition efforts. Indeed, that was part of the challenge. By the time the report was completed, however, he had developed an in-depth understanding of the FTC. Miller's ability to become an expert in an impressively short time was a hallmark of his transition efforts and characterized Miller's enthusiastic approach to his job as head of OMB's regulatory division and later as Chairman of the FTC.

During Miller's confirmation hearings, Senator Howard Metzenbaum (D.-Ohio) inserted in the *Congressional Record* a document he claimed was a copy of the transition report. Whether or not this was the case, Miller immediately stated that the hard-hitting recommendations contained in the document made eminent good sense and that as Chairman he would attempt to carry them out. The twenty-nine recommendations, termed the "Metzenbaum Document" by Miller, were as general as

"Terminate all cases based on social theories" and as specific as "Evaluate the Line of Business and Quarterly Financial Report programs."

The themes of the report were clear. The Reagan FTC should seek to:

- analyze the imperfections of regulation as well as the imperfections of the market
- avoid moralistic posturing and focus on sober calculation
- ensure that antitrust and other regulatory activity benefited rather than harmed the consumer
- make economic analysis central to policy formation and evaluation
- examine the anti-competitive effects of government activity, especially of government regulation.

Building a Political Senior Staff

All the members of Miller's senior staff at the FTC had three things in common: They shared a common political philosophy; they had some kind of relevant experience; and they were personally loyal to Jim Miller.

Collectively, the original Miller team at the FTC had extensive Hill experience either from having worked on the Capitol Hill staff or from having worked on Hill issues from the public and private sectors. One member of the team, Tim Muris, was a strong free-market economist who had written a book critical of the FTC. Muris had previously served at the FTC in other capacities and brought an in-depth understanding of the internal workings and office politics of the Commission. Individuals with experience in working with the press on a day-to-day basis and in developing effective long-term public affairs strategies were included in the original group. The academic world was well represented and helped to keep an eye on the big picture as day-to-day decisions were made.

Miller was also careful to include people who had proved to be effective managers in order not to neglect administrative areas that could have an impact on the policy areas. (It is too often the case that heads of agencies assume that if they have appointed people to the policy areas of an organization that implementing policy can be left to others. This analysis excludes the real power that individuals wield when they manage areas such as budget, personnel, and paper flow.)

When members of the original team left the FTC, they generally went to the White House or other places in government and continued to keep in touch with Miller on issues of shared concern. Replacements usually brought political and/or management experience with them. Because the political team was both experienced and loyal, Miller was able to delegate a great deal of responsibility to his senior staff, which allowed him to be an effective outside spokesman while the team managed the day-to-day business of the agency according to plan.

Miller's management style encouraged close coordination and communication among the senior political staff. For example, if he received a policy recommendation or proposal from one member of the senior staff, he routinely would ask, in writing, if the report, suggestion, or analysis had been cleared with other members of the political staff. Not only did he encourage political staff to clear policy recommendations with other political staff members, he did not tolerate political staffers undermining each other. Indeed, he would become visibly irritated if he detected any infighting. Miller was accessible to individual members of the team and was in the habit of swooping into an individual's office unannounced to discuss points of interest. We never knew what he might ask next, so it was best to keep track of everything that was going on that was of major interest to the Chairman.

As a general rule, before Miller hired new members of the team, he had them read the 29 goals from the "Metzenbaum Document," familiarize themselves with his major policy speeches, and meet individually with each member of the senior political staff. This gave the political staff an opportunity to advise the Chairman before he brought a new member on board and sent the clear message that the senior political staff worked as a group.

While Miller cultivated agreement among the staff, at least in his presence, and encouraged people to share their views with him on a wide range of issues, it was always clear that he was the one who made the final decisions. Not that the senior political staff were without resources. They learned to coordinate if they could not individually convince Miller to take a recommended course of action. Political staff members would hunt around for the person who had the most capital at any given moment to take to the Chairman a matter that he had rejected from someone else. Sometimes this approach would work and other times it failed miserably.

The working relationships among the senior political staff of the Miller team were extraordinary because while one might disagree on tactics there was very little disagreement about goals. One member of the original team says, "We got along better together than any similar group I could imagine. This is to Jim's great credit." Because all the individuals shared a common philosophy and because the overall goals were clear, little time was lost on discussions or intrastaff fights on basic issues. Opportunities for communication were provided and encouraged while a great deal of autonomy was granted to individuals in running their own shops.

Managing a Responsive Bureaucracy

Managing the bureaucracy, or career staff—those individuals who are virtually a permanent part of the government—required entirely different methods from those used with the political staff. There are over 1,300 career positions at FTC. Because FTC personnel consist mostly of lawyers and, in lesser numbers, economists, both of whom are in a special federal schedule (Schedule A) that does not grant full civil service protection, Miller technically had more leeway in hiring and firing than did some other heads of departments and agencies. There is, however, a danger in cutting too wide a path among Schedule A's, even if one has the power, because the effects on overall morale can be devastating. Disruption of staff and the attendant negative impact on morale were kept to a minimum by Miller because he had included in his senior staff someone who had worked at the FTC in the past and knew which career individuals were likely to support the changing agenda and which individuals were unlikely to do so. Reorganizing at the Bureau level allowed those who were actively supportive of the Miller agenda to participate at fairly high levels in implementing the agenda.

Some heads of government institutions assume that the career staff are by definition the enemy, that they are impossible to guide and manage, and thus must be stopped by virtually any means possible. Miller likes to say that when he became Chairman he assumed that 20 percent of the career staff were sympathetic and 80 percent were actively opposed to the Administration's goals. This assumption led to his decision to introduce himself and his political staff to the career employees in a manner designed to "get their attention." He gathered his senior political staff in his office, which is adjacent to the main Commission meeting room where the career staff had gathered for their first introduction to the new Chairman. He put a trumpet fanfare on the record player, donned a pair of devil horns, and he marched himself and his senior staff out to meet the FTC. The silence, as they say, was deafening.

Miller proceeded to introduce his senior political staff and to tell a little about each individual. He described one attorney as his "personnel specialist from the Office of Personnel Management," thereby seeming to confirm the rumor that his goal was to fire the staff and shut FTC down. After this event, a photocopy appeared throughout the Commission. The image was that of the creature from the black lagoon carrying a fainting woman in his arms. Miller's face was superimposed on the creature and the limp woman was labeled the FTC. The senior political staff's affectionate name for Miller thereupon became "The Creature."

Miller's views about the career staff have since altered dramatically. Miller now contends that he had it exactly backward; 80 percent of the career staff are loyal employees and only about 20 percent actively opposed the goals of the Administration. He believes that he would have entered the FTC on a different note had he had his numbers straight at the beginning. In retrospect, it is fairly clear that the FTC career staff were looking forward to a new Chairman. They had been chafing, due to the previous Chairman's penchant for taking the agency into uncharted and unpopular enforcement activities which ultimately jeopardized the agency. Miller could have won over the career staff earlier if he had realized that the agency's low morale under his predecessor had predisposed the staff to be receptive to a positive agenda and good management. Moreover, since previous excesses had weakened the forces of regulatory expansion both inside the FTC bureaucracy and on the Hill, Miller did not have to face resistance to change from a triangular alliance of bureaucrats, lobbyists, and Hill staffers to nearly the same degree as some other Reagan appointees.

Miller maintained a high profile and personal presence at the FTC. He made special efforts to visit career staff in their organizations and practiced MBWA—management by walking around. He made it a practice to circulate copies of his speeches to career staff so that they could be well aware of his philosophy and agenda. He was quick to recognize and participate in the annual events of the FTC, presiding over the Annual Awards ceremony with great gusto and obvious pleasure. The FTC Christmas party will never be the same without his trumpet and enthusiastic rendition of "When the Saints Go Marching In." He was quick to publicly recognize the contributions of career staff in furthering the agenda that he continued to articulate. Individuals who were obviously committed to his goals were identified and included in the decision-making process. One was not excluded just by virtue of being a member of the career staff. (This was possible to a large degree because Miller had an exceptionally strong background in deregulatory theory and a very clear sense of his own agenda; for political appointees who have hazier policy goals and shallower philosophical roots such practices may backfire.)

Finally, Miller is easy to like. He has a generous and open personality. He is willing to ask questions and to listen to what people have to say. One may not agree with Miller, but it is hard not to like him. He made it part of his business to get to know and be known by as many people at the FTC as was possible, given the real constraints on his time. Miller was well aware that attention and positive feedback from the Chairman go a long way toward building morale. Basically he treated career staff as professionals. It is not surprising that most of them eventually responded to him in a positive way.

Capitol Hill

In his tenure at FTC, Jim Miller fought many long battles. For example, he was able to ward off attacks on FTC's antitrust enforcement authority over professional groups. Despite a bleak political landscape dominated by a powerful lobbying effort against the FTC led by the American Medical Association, Miller succeeded in upholding the principles of competition, because he took the time to carefully, clearly, and consistently articulate his views to other commissioners and to the Congress, on one occasion even remaining near the Senate floor during a crucial all-night session so he could be available for discussions with senators.

Miller did not win in some of his efforts to assure that the redirection of the FTC was codified. But overall, he did develop a working relationship with the oversight committees that allowed him some leeway to run the agency without constant review and hearings. His general rule of thumb in dealing with members of Congress was to be pleasant, be responsive, stick to his guns, tell the truth, and take the time to explain in detail what it is that he wanted to do and why. During hearings on another issue in March 1984, the chairman of the Subcommittee on Oversight and Investigations, Representative Dingell (D.-Mich.), concluded by saying to Miller, "We have kept you a long time. In spite of our differences on the policy questions, you still retain my affection for you. . . . I must confess I do like you, and I thank you for being present."

This may seem unimportant in the larger scheme of things, but it is critical to the success of any government official that members of Congress respect and trust those who testify before their committees. Washington abounds with stories of individuals who lost their ability to accomplish important goals because they lost their credibility on the Hill. Miller let it be known publicly what his intentions were as FTC Chairman, and thus as he proceeded to accomplish the individual goals, no one could accuse him of having hidden the agenda. Indeed, he earned their respect by his tenacity and consistency.

The Press and the Public

Miller made a very great effort to present his agenda and the reasons for it to the public. He took every opportunity he could to offer his message by speaking to groups with an interest in FTC activities: state attorneys, trade groups, economists, lawyers, etc. A second method of communicating with the public and industries that are regulated by the FTC was via the press. Many government press offices quickly fall into the mode of reacting to reporters' questions. They tend to see their jobs as fighting fires that are created by the reporters who cover that particular beat. Miller realized early on that press relations could be utilized to clarify and publicize the FTC's new agenda. Despite this realization, Miller too often found himself in the position of responding to press stories based on internal disagreements that were made public by other commissioners.

It made good copy, over and over again, to have public statements by Commissioner Pertschuk compared to public statements by Chairman Miller when they disagreed about something.[6] The impression from the press stories was that the Commission was in disarray and that tempers were running high. It was difficult not to respond to accusations that Miller and his staff were more concerned about whether or not their desks were polished than they were about substantive issues at the FTC, but countercharges and defensiveness lent little to reasoned public debate. Miller eventually kept his responses to a minimum and concentrated on getting positive stories out to the public via the press.

In order to spread the word about specific programs and in order to keep the agenda in public view, Miller held informal discussions with the press, usually in the form of a breakfast, about once a month. He tended to be candid and accessible to the press at the press breakfasts and on a day-to-day basis. He also made substantial use of his Public Affairs Office to prepare background materials explaining the impact and reasons for Commission actions, sometimes even involving a pre-decisional briefing about the facts, so that the press could more effectively follow the proceedings at the Commission table.

Keeping the press informed does not always assure that the facts will be reported fairly and accurately, but it mitigates press stories that misinform because education of the reporters has been neglected. Supplying the press with information is a much more effective way of assuring that one's views will be fairly represented than is merely responding to questions.

The Agenda: Antitrust and the Marketplace

Antitrust policy was an area of major innovation under Jim Miller. Under Carter, the FTC had operated according to the belief espoused by Pertschuk in congressional testimony that "bigness is necessarily bad."[7] Therefore, bigness needed to be punished; the motivation for antitrust activity became more social than economic. The goal was not the most efficient competitive marketplace but, in Pertschuk's words, to alter "the structure and behavior of major industries and, indeed, of the economy itself [to bring it] in line with the nation's democratic, political and social ideals."[8]

Ambitious antitrust theories were developed. The FTC became preoccupied with industry concentration (the share of a market held by the few largest firms), despite the evidence that concentration was at best a crude preliminary indicator of the extent of competition in an industry. Analysts experimented with the idea of "no-fault monopoly," a notion that structural concentration should be broken up independent of noticeable effects on competition. This in turn led to hostile attention to firms that increased their market share despite the obvious fact that these firms were expanding precisely because they were providing the greatest benefit to consumers through reduced costs or product innovation.

In keeping with the "transition team report," Miller brought sound economic analysis back into antitrust policy, eschewing the blind assumption that big business must covertly be out to "get" the American public. The goal of antitrust policy must be, Miller stressed, to achieve economic efficiency and productivity: The hard facts showed that most corporate mergers had beneficial consequences, producing efficiency and even enhancing competitition by strengthening weaker firms. Mergers would restrain competitive forces only in very specific economic conditions—e.g., where barriers to entry of new firms existed—antitrust policy should concentrate on those situations where harmful anti-competitive effects would occur.

Rejecting hysterical charges by liberal opponents that "mergers were at an all-time high,"[9] Miller demonstrated that merger activity was at a normal level and that there was no increasing trend of industry concentration in the United States as some alleged. Because FTC rulings were once again based on real economic evidence, the courts began upholding the FTC's antitrust actions, in marked contrast to the Carter era.

A related antitrust issue was prosecution for "predatory pricing": the idea that by pricing below cost a large firm can drive out its competitors and then reap monopoly profits when it is left alone in the market. Empirical studies had shown predatory pricing to be a problem largely residing in the minds of idle regulators; such a practice could again be profitable only if there were substantial barriers to firms' entering or reentering the field and if there was no substitute for the product; investigation showed predatory pricing to be rare if not nonexistent.

Nonetheless, in the 1970's the FTC had brought suits against companies such as Borden for selling its product "ReaLemon" at an "unreasonably low price," even though Borden was following normal business practices and was not setting prices below the cost of production. The theory seemed to be that an "unreasonably low price" was a price that less efficient firms could not match! Rather than enhancing competition, FTC litigation blocked it, raising prices artificially for the consumer. Under Miller, these practices were reversed and the FTC became the supporter of market competition, not its opponent.

Regulatory Style

A key difference between the policy agendas of Pertschuk and Miller was that Pertschuk believed that the FTC should keep its distance from the business community. At his confirmation hearings, Pertschuk testified,

"I believe that it is essential for government servants to scrupulously avoid even the appearance of collusive relationships."[10] Chairman Pertschuk significantly reduced the traditional role of the FTC Chairman by not serving as a member of the governing council of the American Bar Association, by speaking less frequently to industry groups, and by limiting his speeches to congressional testimony. Limited contact with the business community that is regulated by the FTC helped to create an adversarial relationship between the FTC and trade associations. Miller, on the other hand, strongly believed that those who are regulated by government agencies have a right to know the rules of the game. Chairman Miller made every reasonable effort to inform the consumer and industry about FTC regulations. He spent a considerable amount of time speaking to trade associations, advertising groups, and chambers of commerce.

Miller sought to replace the "sue first, talk later" strategy with more constructive alternatives. For example, the FTC's Bureau of Consumer Protection has the responsibility of monitoring advertising. The Bureau assists commissioners in enforcing statutes that are designed to assure that consumers can rely on the truthfulness of messages disseminated to them by advertising. In the past, if a firm was not in compliance with FTC rules, the FTC sued. It is Miller's view that confrontation does not always get the best results. In the fall of 1983, the FTC observed that falling interest rates were leading builders and developers to advertise homes aggressively by claiming they could be purchased through very attractive financing terms. Surveys of major newspapers in 16 major cities revealed massive noncompliance with the credit advertising provisions of the Truth in Lending Act. From 1975 to 1983, the FTC had sued 19 firms for noncompliance and the compliance rate still remained at less than 20 percent. Miller decided to try a less litigious approach. He alerted the home building industry that there was widespread noncompliance and offered to work with it and its advertising agents to curb the deceptive ads. The Bureau of Consumer Protection and the Public Affairs Office worked together to develop and distribute materials to explain to industry how to comply with the act. The Public Affairs Office made sure that local newspapers and trade journals had access to this information. The FTC contacted over 1,300 companies individually. As a result of this cooperative effort, compliance in the market rose from less than 20 percent to 80 percent in nine months.

The Government and the Consumer

Under Carter, the FTC sought out new and innovative ways of protecting the consumer. One Carter official had suggested that the Geritol ad—"My wife, I think I'll keep her"—might be deceptive and subject to a ban because the company could not substantiate that its product would generate a state of marital happiness.[11] Jim Miller arrived at the FTC with a better appreciation of the needs of the American public and a more serious agenda. In doing so, he confounded the traditional scenario of the white and black hats. Miller demonstrated that regulation not only imposes direct costs on the taxpayer and raises prices through the expense of industry compliance—it often creates substantial indirect costs as well. Regulators erecting multiple hoops for industry to jump through in an effort to eliminate "deceptive" or "misleading" advertising often deprive the public of valuable information. Thus, the FTC had blocked advertisements concerning tar and nicotine content in cigarettes in the 1950's and auto mileage claims in the 1970's on the grounds that such information was "misleading" or could be misinterpreted. This counter-productive situation was not accidental but was an inherent byproduct of any regulatory system; the urge to regulate, Miller emphasized, should be limited to circumstances where the benefits were indisputable and should always be tempered by an understanding that the full costs of regulation may not be immediately apparent. Moreover, reasonable regulation should proceed from an understanding that the marketplace is ultimately the most effective regulator; firms producing shoddy and deceptive goods cannot long remain in the economic mainstream.

A well-publicized case of this sort was the proposed national regulation of the used car industry. (Rule-making on this issue was initiated under Pertschuk but came before the full Commmission only after Miller became Chairman.) Miller's staff demonstrated that this apparent "apple pie" issue was far from clear cut. In fact, the state of Wisconsin had already established a regulatory system similar to the one the Pertschuk FTC had proposed for the entire country. To the distress of "consumer groups," Miller presented an independent study from Wisconsin which showed that the regulatory system produced no benefits at all; purchasers of used cars in Wisconsin were actually slightly worse off than those in the rest of the nation. The only clear consequence of extensive regulation was to penalize honest car dealers. (There is not necessarily a government solution to all imaginable social problems.)[12]

Positive Agenda: Government and the Public Interest

Miller did not limit his efforts to staving off past regulatory excesses. In keeping with FTC's lawful responsibility to protect the consumer by promoting competition, Miller established an aggressive antitrust agenda— to attack government restraints on competition. Under Miller, the FTC pushed for deregulation of taxicabs by bringing antitrust suits against the cities of Minneapolis and New Orleans. The suits sought to force the city governments to stop setting rates and limiting the entry of new cabs. Evidence showed that cities with unregulated taxi industries had fares 15 percent lower than cities with regulation, as well as more service; the city of Minneapolis had only 248 cabs, compared to the taxi market of Washington, D.C. with unrestricted entry and over 9,000 cabs. Deregulation would bring better service, lower prices, and create more jobs.

Under Miller, the FTC also began a critical examination of the Marketing Order system under which the U.S. Department of Agriculture establishes industry cartels to restrict supply and raise the prices of oranges, milk, and other products. Similarly, Miller fought hard to maintain the FTC's antitrust authority over professional associations like the American Bar Association and the American Medical Association. In the past, the ABA had used the cartel authority granted by state governments to stifle competition by banning informational advertising concerning fees. The AMA had used its guildlike powers in a similar manner. Miller stoutly and successfully defended the FTC's authority to enforce the right of advertising and other competitive practices within the professions, against massive lobbying efforts in Congress.

In the case of taxi deregulation and agriculture marketing orders, on the other hand, Miller it would seem was ahead of his time; Congress stepped in to block FTC activity. But by focusing attention on these issues, Miller conducted a valuable exercise in public education that will eventually contribute to the demise of such indefensible systems; more important, the FTC demonstrated that the free market supports the public interest while the government often willfully abuses it.

Conclusion

The single most important ingredient of Miller's success at the FTC is that he brought with him a well-reasoned, publicly articulated, nonconfrontational agenda. It is easy, in the day-to-day business of running an agency, to get caught up in minutiae and responses to other people's agendas. Miller was singularly effective because in making the day-to-day decisions concerning political staff, career staff, the Congress, the public, and the press, he acted within the context of his own agenda. The effect of the agenda was greatly enhanced by the fact that Miller gathered a loyal, knowledgeable, and effective political staff who were committed to achieving the goals that Miller had articulated.

Horseback riding lessons help the beginning rider a lot. The rider learns about what motivates the horse and what signals are most effective in directing the horse. A new rider can spend hours practicing correct leg position and refining hand signals. But there is a moment when the lessons and the practice and the experience come together and the horse and rider are one. No one can teach how to create the union between the animal and the man that looks effortless but is the result of constant practice and experience; an observer can see when it happens and describe some of the elements that make it happen, but there are intangibles that do not lend themselves to words. Ultimately, this inability to fully capture the essence of excellent riding also applies to descriptions of effective leadership. One has to experience the process and the results in order to fully understand how and why individual approaches work with what seems to be breathtaking ease and grace.

Notes

1. Arthur Applbaum, under the supervision of Stephanie Gould, ed., case study entitled "Mike Pertschuk and the Federal Trade Commission," for use in the Senior Managers in Government Program at the John F. Kennedy School of Government, Harvard University (copyright Cambridge: the President and Fellows of Harvard College, 1981), p. 8.

3. Applbaum, p. 14.

3. Applbaum, p. 9.

4. *Forbes*, November 12, 1979, p. 38.

5. *Forbes*, p. 39.

6. President Carter appointed Michael Pertschuk as an FTC Commissioner in 1980 after Pertschuk ended his tenure as Chairman.

7. Applbaum, p. 33.

8. Applbaum, p. 12.

9. U.S. Congress, House of Representatives, *Report of the Federal Trade Commission to the Subcommittee on Oversight and Investigations, House Committee on Energy and Commerce*, 98th Congress, 2nd Session, September 1984.

10. Applbaum, p. 9.

11. U.S. Congress, House of Representatives, *Review of the FTC Report to the Subcommittee on Oversight and Investigations, House Committee on Energy and Commerce*, 98th Congress, 2nd Session, September 21, 1984.

12. Editors' Note: This is a classic example of the "government failure" or two-singers problem discussed by Fred Smith in Chapter 4. It is also a striking instance of the value of social research appropriately directed. If the Wisconsin study had not already existed, it would have been far more difficult to argue the case against regulation. The value of public policy research is neglected by conservatives; much more research into "government failure" questions should be undertaken.

22 Agenda Deflection: James Sanders and the Small Business Administration

ROBERT RECTOR

Editors' Note: This case study underscores many of the points made in preceding chapters, particularly in Chapters 6 and 14. As the narrative illustrates, defining policy goals is the most important and the most difficult task of a political executive; all else is secondary. The incidents described here are not at all uncommon; political appointees "go native" with alarming frequency. The results are a loss of electoral accountability, fragmentation of presidential authority, and political inertia. The following history is set apart from dozens of others largely by the public manner in which the controversy was enacted.

During World War II when large defense contractors began shutting down assembly lines for lack of screws and bolts, Congress responded by creating the Small Defense Plant Administration (SDPA) to encourage entrepreneurs to set up small businesses to feed vital components into the nation's war machine. After the war, the SDPA was phased out only to be resurrected during the Korean War; in 1953 it was continued as a peacetime agency, the Small Business Administration (SBA). Politically, the SBA was intended to serve as the vanguard of a Democratic effort to woo small businessmen away from the Republican Party, making them part of the expanding system of federal largess.

At present, the SBA carries out six basic functions in aid of small business:

- providing direct loans and equity capital to small businesses
- providing guarantees to loans made by banks to small businesses
- serving as a small business advocate within the federal government
- supplying "management assistance" to small firms
- operating procurement programs that reserve certain federal contracts for small businesses
- providing various forms of assistance to minority small businesses.

Of these functions the first two are by far the most important, absorbing more SBA resources than all the other functions combined. This is in keeping with the original conception of SBA as a federally owned and operated bank for small business.

The SBA is authorized to make direct loans of up to $350,000 to small firms. Currently, interest rates are set by statute at levels equal to the cost of borrowing money to the federal government; however, due to a deliberate policy of interest rate subsidies in the past, the bulk of outstanding SBA loans bear interest charges of less than 5 percent.

During the Nixon Administration, the SBA was permitted to guarantee ordinary bank loans as well as to provide its own direct loans. This enabled the SBA to greatly expand both its activities and the number of small businesses affected. The SBA guarantees 90 percent of the value of the loan made by the bank, up to a total of $500,000 per loan. Loan duration can be up to ten years; interest rates are determined by the bank, but cannot be more than 2.75 percentage points above the prime rate. All loan guarantees must be specifically approved by the SBA. When a borrower defaults on an SBA guaranteed loan, the SBA buys the guaranteed portion of the loan from the bank at face value and places the loan under SBA "management" in an effort to recover some part of the loss from the continued operation of the borrowing firm.

The SBA is intended to be a lender of "last resort." Thus a small business is eligible for SBA direct and guaranteed loans only if its loan requests have been previously rejected by two commercial banks. Because it was less costly to administer and entailed lower initial costs, the loan guarantee program came to overshadow earlier direct loan programs; in 1980, for example, the SBA provided $3.17 billion in guarantees and only $0.393 billion in direct loans to general business. However, in the area of physical disaster lending (to rebuild businesses and homes following a flood, fire, etc.) direct lending remained strong— $1.118 billion in 1980.

In addition to providing loan guarantees and direct loans, the SBA regulates privately-owned small business investment companies (SBICs). SBICs provide financing to small business in two ways—by straight loans and by venture capital or equity-type investment. In the latter case, the SBIC will receive stock in the company in return for funding. SBICs obtain their funding through the sale of SBA-guaranteed debentures. In 1980, SBICs provided $181 million to small businesses.

The Office of Advocacy was established by law within the SBA in 1976. It is intended to represent the views and interests of small businesses before other federal agencies whose policies and activities may affect small business; accordingly, it develops proposals for changes in the policies of the federal government. The office also serves as a focal point for receipt of criticism from small businesses concerning the conduct of federal agencies, and counsels small businesses on the resolution of problems arising between the business and the federal government. The Office of Advocacy, which in 1980 employed 80 of SBA's 5,800-member staff, is generally regarded favorably both within and without the government.

SBA's management assistance program provides individual counseling, conferences, and management publications to help small businesses overcome management problems. SBA management assistance officers identify management problems and offer advice to specific small business firms; in addition, SBA maintains SCORE—an organization of 8,100 volunteer, retired business executives who provide free counsulting services to small business owners. SBA also sponsors conferences and management training activities by universities, professional associations, and chambers of commerce. The efficacy of these programs is often questioned; in particular, the university programs that entail business students offering advice to business owners have been criticized as mere subsidies to business schools.

SBA's procurement assistance program exists to make certain that small businesses obtain a fair proportion of federal purchases and contracts. Through a network of procurement representatives placed throughout the government, the SBA assures that certain federal purchasing is set aside for small business bidders alone. The SBA also monitors procurement processes for policies and practices that may discourage small business involvement and seeks to correct such problems.

SBA's minority small business programs offer three types of assistance. The "8(a)" program provides for a percentage of government contracts to be set aside for minority small businesses; SBA, in effect, contracts with other government agencies for specific procurement services and then subcontracts with selected minority firms. Minority firms also receive preference in funding for SBA direct loans, and the SBA maintains minority enterprise small business investment companies (MESBICs) which are SBICs that work exclusively with minority-owned firms.

An Agency Without a Purpose

Despite its other functions, the main task of the SBA has always been to channel credit to small businesses. In this respect, SBA has remained somewhat schizophrenic, unable to determine whether it wished to be a prudent socialist banker or a specialized welfare agency injecting ever-greater streams of "Keynesian stimulus" into the economy. For years the bureaucratic operations of the agency revealed the second emphasis. SBA managers were given loan quotas to be fulfilled; the faster the quotas were filled, the more evidence would exist for Congress to raise future funding.

Moreover, since SBA's pool of potential customers (small businesses whose loan applications have been rejected by bankers) has always greatly exceeded its resources, and its procedures for choosing among clients have been somewhat arbitrary, SBA has been a fertile ground for favoritism and bribery. SBA's thirty-year output of unremitting scandal is truly prodigious and its blotchy reputation is perhaps rivaled only by the venerable GSA.

Although SBA's mechanisms for making and guaranteeing loans are relatively straightforward, its pattern of selective targets in lending is nearly unfathomable. SBA lending is subdivided into a myriad of programs dictated by passing congressional whims and fancies. Thus SBA has a special program devoted to landscaping, others to "strategic arms control injury loans" and military base closing assistance. The most intriguing program of the lot is "nonphysical disaster loans." Under this program, ski lodge owners and snowplow operators, for example, may receive special assistance when their area suffers a substandard snow fall. Recently SBA used this program in 18 agricultural states where fertilizer and other agricultural suppliers had their sales reduced by the Payment-In-Kind (PIK) program—thus providing relief against one of America's greatest "nonphysical disasters," the federal government.

Even in its "general business" lending efforts, SBA selection of clientele is peculiar. Over two-thirds of SBA-guaranteed loans are directed toward the retail, wholesale, and service sectors of the economy. This needy clientele includes lawyers, doctors, liquor stores, restaurants, golf courses, photographic studios, funeral homes, grocery stores, motels, dance studios, and gift shops. In 1984 SBA aided 12,541 wholesale/retail/service firms. The beneficiaries included:

835 doctors
130 car washes
 76 bowling alleys and pool halls
252 coin-operated launderies
126 barber and beauty shops
458 furniture stores
 15 detective agencies
242 motels
112 bars
164 radio, TV and music stores
593 repair and body shops and
 27 boat dealers.

However, even in those sectors where its efforts are concentrated, SBA assists only a tiny fraction of small businesses. For example, in 1984 SBA provided guaranteed loans to 0.3 percent of American used car dealers. Among the 14 million small business firms in the U.S. economy, less than 1 percent have ever received SBA lending assistance. In any given year, less than 0.2 percent will receive aid. Rather than providing a general program of assistance to small business, the SBA provides "special advantages for a relative handful of government-wise loan seekers."[1] Ninety-nine percent of American small businesses operate without any government aid, in competition with those few who get special treatment.

SBA lending activities are unrelated to public rationalizations for SBA's existence. SBA apologists refer to the need to assist "sunrise" industries, but less than 4 percent of SBA aid reaches these sectors, and less than 1 percent of all high-growth sunrise firms have ever received SBA funding.[2] A second proposed rationalization for SBA is that it serves as a catalyst generating new business starts and injecting "fresh entrepreneurial blood" into the economy; however, SBA's role in creating new competition is minimal; again less than 1 percent of small business starts are affected by the SBA. Finally, SBA propaganda applauds the agency's creation of over 350,000 jobs, an argument which ignores the fact that SBA, for the most part, merely diverts existing credit resources from one firm to another; indeed, since SBA requires a firm to be a poor credit risk to receive backing, it is quite likely that SBA routinely diverts investment funds from more efficient to less efficient firms. It is not for nothing that the business community refers to SBA clientele as the "cream of the crap."

The SBA's lack of impact is reflected in the relative indifference of the small business community to the agency. A survey of small business owners found that 80 percent said the agency had a neutral or negative effect on them. Seventy percent stated that they had never written or phoned the SBA.

Yet although small businesses may be indifferent to the SBA, Congress is not. On Capitol Hill, the SBA serves as a "petty cash drawer" enabling congressmen to fulfill important symbolic functions within their states and districts. For example, in 1980 when the influx of Cuban refugees was allegedly hurting tourism in south Florida, Rep. Dante B. Fascell (D.-Fla.) persuaded the SBA to channel low-interest loans to local gift shops, charter boat companies, and a hot tub emporium. In 1983, when weather fluctuations reduced the salmon catch on the Northwest coast, Sen. Slade Gorton (R.-Wash.) and Rep. Douglas H. Bosco (D.-Calif.) passed a bill declaring their states to be "nonphysical" disaster areas. The SBA plays a role in presidential politics, too; while Nixon campaigned in 1972, SBA loans were increased a modest 44.5 percent.

The Cost of SBA to the Taxpayer

The cost of providing "disaster relief" to snowplow operators and other assorted functions is not insubstantial. In pure administrative costs, SBA's 5,000 employees required over $230 million in payroll in 1985.

However, administrative costs are only a small part of the picture; as a banking enterprise, SBA was always intended to run at a loss, and in this respect it has proved eminently successful. Since the inception of the program in 1971, for example, SBA has disbursed nearly $24 billion in guaranteed loans. Of this amount, over 20 percent have gone or will go into default, requiring the SBA to repurchase the loans from the bank. Once a defaulted loan is repurchased, the SBA attempts to "work out" the loan in an effort to recover part or all of the loan amount from the debtor; this process involves considerable forbearance on the part of SBA, including extending the terms of the loan and reducing or suspending interest payments. Currently there are over $1 billion in repurchased loans in suspended payment status. Despite this forbearance, over half of the value of SBA's repurchased loans is never repaid at all and is simply charged off as a dead loss. Thus, with each annual installment of new SBA loan guarantees (over $3 billion in 1985), the taxpayer can expect a complete loss of 11–12 percent. This figure does not include the implicit cost of interest subsidies.

However, guaranteed loans have an excellent track record in comparison to the direct loan programs. An astonishing 42 percent of all SBA direct loans go into default and 33 percent of the funds lent are never repaid at all. Some critics charge that this is an inherent consequence of the government trying to second-guess the banking community; others argue that the direct loan program in fact works the way it is implicitly intended to, since as a government "make-work" program the question of repayment was never important. The program generates the headlines essential to the New Deal/Great Society style of symbolic government: "SBA and Congressman Jones create 1,500 jobs in Newark!" The headlines are shifted to new government-funded miracles while the subsidized company quietly goes bankrupt.

Inc. magazine has referred to the SBA as a "thinly disguised welfare agency for small business."[3] Unfortunately, like welfare programs for the rest of society, the negative effects of SBA generally outweigh the positive. Overall SBA lending programs between 1978 and 1985 resulted in a net loss to the taxpayer of $10.5 billion; scarce funds were diverted from worthwhile companies; labor and managerial resources were wasted on infeasible projects; and substantial personal savings were lost as "make-work" companies have gone belly up.

James Sanders and the SBA

In March 1982, James C. Sanders was appointed head of the SBA by President Reagan. He replaced Michael Cardenas, who had served ten months at the SBA before succumbing to allegations of mismanagement and financial favoritism, thereby adding another notch to the SBA's unrelieved tradition of scandal. Sanders had served on the California State Republican Central Committee and the State United Republican Finance Committee. He brought to the SBA strong experience as a successful small businessman, having built an independent insurance brokerage firm from scratch into one of the largest firms in Southern California; Sanders sold his interest in the firm before coming to Washington in 1981 to serve as head of SBA's Management Assistance Office under Cardenas.

In becoming SBA Administrator, Sanders assumed control of an agency that was frequently identified as a candidate for eradication. (The last serious effort to abolish SBA had been led by Senator Proxmire in 1979; although the Reagan administration had not sought to immediately eliminate the agency, the Administration's out-year budget projections had shown a virtual elimination of the agency's lending function by the late 1980's.) Sanders, however, would have none of that. In his nomination hearing, he testified:

> Rumors abound concerning the future of the SBA. I want to state unequivocally from the outset that I would not accept this job if I were merely to preside over the agency's demise. I am convinced of the Administration's commitment to a strong and independent SBA. . . . Some say that my task will be to prove to you that there is a continuing reason for SBA to exist and function. This, it seems to me, is the negative and far less productive approach to the same central issue. . . . The task, upon which I will need [the Senate's] counsel and active help is to give it new vitality.[4]

Sanders also repeatedly emphasized the current desperate situation facing American small business, and the need for the federal government to take a strong role in providing assistance. He stated that SBA's efforts on behalf of small business had often been inadequate and needed improvement; he saw that improvement coming in two ways: first, through an increase in the efficiency of existing programs; second, through the creation of new programs that would aid small business.

> I intend to concentrate on the improvement of quality and efficiency in the delivery of Agency programs. . . . [However], we live in times of change. We cannot simply proceed by going through the motions with programs designed, and perhaps well designed, for the 1950's or 1960's. I have said that I must look to [the Senate] for guidance and assistance. It is here in the realm of new approaches, new ideas, new ways to make existing programs better, that this cooperative endeavor is most essential.[5]

In office Sanders attempted to live up to his goal of instilling management efficiency. Noting that the SBA maintained only 65 percent of its personnel in the field, the new Administrator worked to cut top-heavy bureaucracy, eliminating unnecessary administrative layers and shifting personnel into service delivery. Whereas officers in direct loan programs under the Carter Administration had been given bonuses based on the numbers of loans issued, Sanders reversed this practice, stating that bonuses instead should be linked to repayment rates; this led Democrats within Congress to charge that Sanders did not understand the difference between banking where the goal was to "make money" and the government where the goal was to "make jobs."

Sanders also established the "preferred lender" program in which selected banks were authorized to issue loans with a 75 percent guarantee without consulting SBA officials. This resulted in a streamlining of the loan application process and was seen as a significant step toward removing SBA bureaucracy from the banking business. Sanders also reformed the "8(a)" program which set aside a percentage of government procurement for minority firms. Of the 2,000 "disadvantaged" firms that had participated in this program over the preceding decade, only 170 had matured to face competition in the open market. Noting that the government's "helping hand" was being transformed into a hereditary fiefdom, the SBA sought to place limits on the program. Against congressional opposition, Sanders maintained that participation would be restricted to five years, at the end of which the minority firm would lose its preferential status and enter the competitive market.

Sanders's most significant reform was his attempt to eliminate the scandal-ridden direct loan program. For three years (FY83, FY84, FY85), SBA proposed to Congress that the program be abandoned. Sanders argued that the program was not only inefficient but that it often placed too great a repayment burden on new firms, lending them more than they could realistically repay and thereby ruining them. He stated that a preferable alternative which Congress should consider for future funding was some form of direct equity participation by the government in new businesses. Such a scheme would provide needed funds while reducing the initial repayment problem. However, for three years in succession, Congress rejected Sanders's efforts and saved the direct loan program.

Overall, the SBA changed little during the first four years of the Reagan Administration. Staffing levels were reduced slightly; salaries and expenses actually increased from $216 million to $230 million. Total business lending also increased slightly from $3.56 billion in FY80 to $3.7 billion in FY85; however, direct loans which Sanders had sought to eliminate were cut by 35 percent in the same period. By and large, the Reagan revolution had passed the SBA by.

Sanders and Stockman

After the election of 1984, things changed drastically. In December 1984, Sanders went to the White House for a briefing on the FY86 budget.

According to his accounts, he had prepared himself for cuts in the SBA budget of up to 25 percent. However, the Office of Management and Budget (OMB) had other plans, proposing to save $1.46 billion in the next year by abolishing the agency. Loans and guarantees would be terminated. Certain minor functions (procurement assistance, advocacy, and minority set-asides) would be transferred to other agencies. Sanders was shocked, stating that he had "no idea this was coming." (Since OMB had internally supported the abolition of the SBA for the first four years of the Reagan Administration, and since Administration off-year budget projections had consistently indicated a reduction of overall SBA lending of 80 percent by the late 1980's, Sanders's professed surprise was certainly more feigned than real.)

In an interview with *Washington Post* reporters a few days later, Sanders commented on the SBA's future. Stating that "I want to to be careful not to say anything to you that would indicate that I am planning to take on the Administration," Sanders did express reservations to the OMB proposal:

> Some Draconian measures are necessary to reduce that deficit, and we all want to do our part to contribute to that. But I am not sure that the benefits should be eliminated with the wasteful parts of the agency.[6]

Sanders then recommended an alternative trimming plan that conformed to his proposals in previous years: eliminating direct loans while preserving the "good" programs such as management assistance and loan guarantees. Sanders also complained that he did not have enough political clout to obtain an objective hearing from the White House.

A week later, Sanders did obtain a meeting with White House Chief of Staff James A. Baker III. Sanders lobbied vigorously to preserve his agency, presenting his alternative plan of budget reductions and arguing that preserving the good SBA programs would in some circuitous manner save the government more in the long run than the OMB/ Stockman plan.

Sanders was not content, however, to leave the fate of his agency in the hands of White House officials. According to reports in several newspapers, the "mild-mannered Republican administrator" began to work quietly with sympathetic interest groups and with Senator Lowell P. Weicker, Jr., Chairman of the Senate Small Business Committee, to ward off the Administration's attack on the SBA.[7] A key Sanders aide offered this rationale to *Washington Post* reporters:

> There have been enormous changes at the SBA since Jim came, positive changes that the White House has acknowledged. Now there are a solid core of programs here *which are vital to expanding the economy* and some which should be eliminated.[8] (Emphasis added.)

Lobbying groups took up the rallying cry that the reformed SBA should be trimmed but preserved; deficit reduction should not come at the expense of the "pro-growth" SBA. In the House of Representatives, subcommittee Chairman Parren J. Mitchell announced that "this assault on small business would inflict the final blow on this important sector of the economy."[9]

Within a few weeks, however, it became apparent to Sanders that his appeal to the White House had not borne fruit; the White House rejected Sanders's proposals and reaffirmed the Administration's intention to abolish the SBA. This rejection did not end Sanders's activities on behalf of his agency. *The New York Times* reported that Sanders was conducting "a discreet campaign" to mobilize support for SBA within the key components of its iron triangle, e.g., the congressional committees and small business lobbying groups.[10]

Sanders's unique interpretation of the "Reagan Revolution," as it pertained to the SBA, brought dismay to White House officials who had hoped that some sense of political loyalty would keep the Administrator in line. Rumors circulated that Sanders would be removed from office, thus creating "a crucial void in the defenders' ranks."[11] However, within SBA, Sanders's continuing defense of the agency began to have a reviving effect on morale. While acknowledging that the Stockman proposal was the most serious threat to SBA in its 30-year history, agency defenders began to express increasing confidence in the agency's survival, declaring abolition to be "an almost unthinkably bad idea."[12]

Through January and early February 1985, Sanders maintained a mode of détente with the Administration by suspending his public criticism while continuing his covert lobbying activities.[13] However, in mid-February when Stockman referred to SBA as "a billion-dollar waste, a rathole," Sanders could no longer restrain himself. Lashing out in defense of his employees, the SBA head accused Stockman of "slandering" an important federal agency.

> It's unthinkable that anyone in a responsible position would use that kind of excessive and abrasive language. You can't call an agency a rathole. That slanders the achievements of everyone in the agency.[14]

On February 21, Stockman appeared before the Senate Committee on Small Business to outline and justify the Administration's plans for the SBA. In accordance with the December plan, Stockman stated that small business advocacy, procurement programs, and minority "8(a)" set-aside programs would not be eliminated but would continue to operate as part of the Commerce Department. Other SBA functions including management assistance, direct loans, and loan guarantees would be abolished and the agency would be eliminated as a separate entity. In addition, the SBA's existing portfolio of outstanding direct loans and repurchased guaranteed loans (loans taken over from the bank when the debtor defaulted) would be sold.

To accomplish this, Stockman proposed to terminate all new lending and to phase down and disband SBA credit service operations. Reduction of SBA administrative costs plus the sale of part of the SBA portfolio would produce savings of at least $1.46 billion in FY86. Savings over three years would be at least $5.3 billion, and would continue indefinitely in the future, particularly through ending the cost of future defaults by ending additional guarantees.

In presenting his case for abolishing the SBA, Stockman stressed the basic theme that the SBA did not create additional investment resources for small businesses.

> As a matter of *pure economics*, SBA does not *enlarge* the national pool of business credit resources—it just *reallocates* funds away from more credit worthy firms. By definition, therefore, it *reduces* marketplace efficiency and national investment, job creation and economic growth by substituting political and bureaucratic judgments of profitability and risk for market judgments.[15] (Emphasis in original.)

SBA lending guarantees might be justified if it was found that the nation's banks were clogged with idle funds which could only be shaken loose with government guarantees. But this was certainly not the case. As it was, the SBA, like most government agencies, merely reshuffled a small part of existing resources in a capricious manner.

Stockman stated that while at times it was necessary for government to override rational market allocations for specific public policy objectives, in the case of SBA no such public policy objectives existed. There was no rational motive behind SBA's traditional activities:

> No case has ever been made that the federal government can improve national economic prosperity by fostering more or bigger car washes, bars, accounting firms, real estate agencies or hardware stores. . . . SBA conducts a $3–4 billion annual lending program which indiscrim- inately sprays a faint mist of subsidized credit into the weakest and most prosaic nooks and crannies of the nation's $4 trillion economy.[16]

SBA's existence would be justified if there were some vast market im- perfection in U.S credit networks which prevented funds from reaching competitive small firms and channeled them instead to less successful giants. However, no evidence of the existence of such imperfections had ever been presented. Moreover, the myth that SBA helped small firms operate against large firms and thereby stimulated needed competition was, itself, totally unfounded. The overwhelming bulk of SBA lending occurred in sectors of the economy where competition between large and small firms was irrelevant (as in the case of subsidized beauty parlors). Stockman stated:

> No case has ever been made that [the business sectors where SBA lending was concentrated] are characterized by significant market imperfections, such as too few firms; too little innovation; entry barriers to new firm start-up; or inadequate responsiveness to consumer demand and welfare.[17]

Each of the markets where SBA lending was concentrated was abundantly populated by thousands of efficient, profitable firms. Moreover, well over 99 percent of the small firms in each of these market sectors would operate either by using market-rate bank loans or, more commonly, personal savings for capital. Rather than helping small firms compete against large, the SBA "helps a tiny fraction of weak small businesses compete with unsubsidized firms in naturally competitive, healthy markets." At best, an SBA guarantee would shift a bank loan from an efficient pizza parlor to a less efficient/less creditworthy pizza parlor on the next block; at worst, it would provide a taxpayer subsidy for one firm to compete against another which was relying on family savings.

> SBA lending does not improve the structure of markets—it just *unbalances the competitive playing field* on which thousands of tax-paying small businesses have staked their entire economic wealth.[18] (Emphasis in original.)

Thus, rather than interfering in the market to serve a public good, SBA guarantees actually have counterproductive public policy effects by decreasing economic efficiency, by creating unfair competition, and by arbitrarily benefiting a few thousand citizens at the expense of millions of others who are striving to make a living in competitive markets without taxpayer handouts. As a type of government expenditure that actually produces public harm rather than good, the SBA was a prime candidate in any deficit reduction plan.

Stockman was criticized for his plan to sell off SBA's $9.8-billion portfolio of direct loans and repurchased guaranteed loans at well below face value. In the case of direct loans, OMB had projected an average selling price of 30 to 40 percent of the original face value of the loan. Critics maintained that these loan "assets" would bring more revenue to the government if they remained under SBA ownership and management. Stockman responded that the 30–40 percent figure was simply a preliminary OMB estimate; the actual sales price would be determined by auctioning the loans in an open market; the loans would sell below face value because of the high risk of default and the low interest rates they bore, resulting in an actual income-producing potential well below the face value. If the SBA portfolio would really bring the higher revenue levels to the owner (federal or private) alleged by SBA proponents, then the sales prices as determined by the market would reflect this. This would in fact argue in favor of selling the loans since the higher price would make an even greater contribution to deficit reduction. Whatever the actual market value of the loans, it made no sense for the U.S. government to hold on to low-interest yielding "assets" at the same time that it was borrowing funds at higher interest rates to finance the deficit.

Under questioning, Stockman acknowledged that the Administration's plans had been vigorously appealed by officials at SBA. His proposals for the SBA met firm resistance from both Republicans and Democrats on the Senate Small Business Committee.

In late April, Sanders unleashed yet another attack on Stockman and OMB in the pages of *The Washington Post*. Stockman, he declared, had become "an embarrassment" to the Reagan Administration who was damaging the President through his inability to work with senior Administration officials. Sanders mentioned Environmental Protection Agency head William Ruckelshaus and Veterans Administration head Harry Walters as other Administration officials who had had emotional confrontations with the Director of OMB.

Sanders complained that Stockman was "surrounded by fanatics [who] have no real life experience" and was taking the advice of senior staffers who were "acting like zombies on some issues—mechanical prostitutes." Sanders stated that he had been deeply angered and shocked by the December decision to abolish his agency. The decision made no apparent sense, and the move to tear the agency literally right from under his feet after his ongoing successes in improving efficiency and correcting past abuses led him to wonder "what I'm doing here." Stockman and the OMB "zombies" were wrong to "treat agency heads as the enemy," he said. OMB needed to see things in a broader perspective; agency heads were "on the same side as the President. That's why we were appointed. That's why we're here."[19]

Sanders further charged that Stockman's reliance on OMB fanatics and his failure to consult with agency heads had impeded the functioning of the annual budget process. Greater consultation, he held, would at least make Stockman's public remarks on budget cutting "more coherent." Sanders concluded his attack on Stockman and the OMB "mechanical prostitutes" by stating:

Stockman and I both believe in a free-market economy. We both disagree with subsidies, with interference [sic]. But I believe there are programs in which the federal government can come in and help small businesses succeed. And we have some—no many—good people to run them. . . . [OMB] cannot expect to understand the inner working of all the federal agencies. They cannot continue to deal in micro-management. They have to arrive at the overall tough decisions in the budget process. But it's one thing to study, teach and listen, and evaluate. It's another to impose [their will]. The issue [of Stockman's role] is going to surface eventually and steps will have to be taken to curb Stockman's uncontrolled nature. Continuing to increase OMB's power is sheer idiocy.[20]

Conclusion

Although *The Wall Street Journal* supported abolition of the SBA and even *The Washington Post* ran an article highly critical of the agency, in the end the Senate was unmoved. Senators Weicker and Bumpers introduced legislation providing new authorization for the SBA in FY86, FY87, and FY88. Overall ceilings on SBA business lending were actually increased over the three-year period, from $3.4 billion in FY85 to $3.7 billion in FY88. However, direct loans were cut sharply. The nonphysical disaster program was eliminated. The Weicker/Bumpers bill passed as part of the Senate budget authorization with few modifications. The SBA would survive to serve the nation's economy.[21]

Notes

1. Tom Richman, "Will the Real SBA Please Stand up?" *Inc.*, February 1984, p. 86.
2. Sunrise industries are new industries with high potential growth rates. In the 1940's television was a sunrise industry, as robotics is today.
3. Richman, p. 86.
4. Testimony of James C. Sanders before the Committee on Small Business, March 9, 1982. p. 12.
5. Ibid. p. 11.
6. Myron Struck, "Chief Wages Quiet Battle for SBA Survival," *The Washington Post*, December 18, 1984, p. A17.
7. Struck, December 18, 1984, and Robert D. Hershey, Jr. "Plans to Keep Agency from the Ax," *The New York Times*, January 31, 1985, p. A20.
8. Struck, December 18, 1984.
9. Hershey, January 31, 1985.
10. Ibid.
11. Ibid.

12. Ibid.

13. Ibid.

14. Howard Kurtz, "SBA Chief Says Stockman's Comments 'Slander' Agency," *The Washington Post,* February 16, 1985.

15. David A. Stockman, Director OMB, Testimony before Senate Committee on Small Business, February 21, 1985, p. 1.

16. Ibid., pp. 4 and 27.

17. Ibid., p. 3.

18. Ibid.

19. Myron Struck, "Stockman's Style Ripped," *The Washington Post,* April 28, 1985, p. A6.

20. Ibid.

21. In 1986, one year after the events described in this chapter, the scenario repeated itself. The White House again proposed the abolition of SBA; Sanders, however, finally submitted his resignation. With his departure set, Sanders's control over the Agency was loosened; a handful of subordinate political appointees began, for the first time, to work quietly in support of the President's initiative. This unprecedented activity threw Parren J. Mitchell, (D.-Md.), Chairman of the House Committee on Small Business, into a rage. Mitchell sent a mass mailing to career employees at SBA, stating:

> Last year while the Congress and the President carried out the negotiations over the future of the agency, I believe that most SBA employees, commencing with Jim Sanders at the top on down to the GS-2 clerks, carried out their duties and continued the programs. Apparently, however, such is not going to be the case this year. With the Administrator leaving at the end of the month, there are numerous indications that individuals within the agency are going to go out and actively campaign for the abolishment of SBA. Even worse they have started spreading false information and previously discredited statistics. For that reason I believe that this year I must communicate with the field officers on a regular basis in order to correct the record and let you and your subordinates know what is going on in Washington. . . . Carried to the degree some of these Judases would do it, we might save the agency but find nothing but a hollow shell remains.

The notion that the president as head of the executive branch should have authority over political and career staff is scoffed at. A proper presidential appointee, according to Congressman Mitchell's presumptions, should have his first loyalty to the agency and then to the relevant congressional committee; the elected president and his policies are mere flukes to be discounted. Unfortunately, a great number of presidential appointees, like James Sanders, live up to Congressman Mitchell's expectations. On the other hand, President Reagan is lucky to have a number of "Judases" in the ranks as well. (Source: Parren J. Mitchell, letter to SBA career employees dated March 13, 1986.)

23 UMTA and the Golden Fleece

RALPH STANLEY

Editors' Note: The job of a political executive has many dimensions, public education being one that is generally neglected or ignored. In this case, the Administrator of the Urban Mass Transportation Administration demonstrates one example of a skillful public education effort. All conservative appointees can draw a lesson from the initiative and common sense displayed in the following story.

A ring of the telephone infused what had become a rather drab early December day with a ray of opportunity. The call was from a reporter I'd gotten to know during one of my recent battles with Congress over excessive government spending. "Ralph, I've got great news," he said. "You're about to be the lucky winner of Proxmire's Golden Fleece." I *was* lucky. Many "winners" don't know about the honor until they read about it in the papers. I had a whole day to absorb the news.

Every month since January 1975, Wisconsin's senior Senator, William Proxmire, has selected some government agency upon which to bestow his Golden Fleece Award. This dubious honor goes to projects deemed "a wasteful, ridiculous, or ironic use of the taxpayer's money." The Urban Mass Transportation Administration (UMTA) was about to share the limelight with such past notables as:

- a $40,000 study entitled "Food Preferences and Society Identity"
- $1.2 million spent to preserve a sewer as an historical monument
- a $97,000 grant to study behavior and social relationships in a Peruvian brothel
- a $3.4 million ad campaign to make Americans write more letters to one another

The news didn't actually surprise me. After all, for months I had been calling attention to some of the more disastrous UMTA-funded projects: the empty, half-finished Downtown People Mover in Detroit; the billion-dollar Miami system that the press had nicknamed "Metrofail"; and the 63rd Street tunnel, New York's $800-million white elephant on the bottom of the East River. This last project, if it is ever finished, will connect New

York's Upper East Side to a wasteland of warehouses and railyards in Queens. Experts project that this mausoleum will carry only around 200 passengers a day. For the cost of the project the government could have bought each of these potential riders 45 to 50 Rolls Royces.

All these projects seemed more than qualified as Fleece candidates. Then I saw Proxmire's prospective press release, stating that UMTA would receive this month's award:

> for playing Santa Claus to the nation's mass transit systems at a 20-year cost of over $30 billion and to what end: transit revenues per vehicle mile have dropped 26 percent, costs have increased 78 percent, and the taxpayers' subsidy per passenger has jumped by a whopping 1,250 percent. As for the broad social improvements expected—decreased congestion, air pollution, and energy use—not one has come up to snuff—federal support of mass transit has been a spectacular flop, the Edsel of federal programs.

UMTA was not being cited for one bad project. Proxmire's attack was more fundamental. The entire UMTA program—in fact, the very concept of federal involvement in urban transportation—was being challenged!

I called various staff members to my office and asked for their reaction to Proxmire's announcement. Some suggested that I apprise Mr. Proxmire of UMTA's many accomplishments. I should point out, they said, that UMTA was vital to public transportation. Or, they argued, I could take a more subtle approach: I could admit some of UMTA's past failings while stressing our current efforts to clean up the program and eliminate waste. In short, the agency's reaction was to defend its program. But, having a first-hand knowledge of UMTA, I was dubious.

In fact, I had to admit that Senator Proxmire was right. He was only confirming what I had been saying for the past two years: that the billions of federal tax dollars invested in transit have not bought what they were intended to buy. Moreover, in many ways, the program has usurped a legitimate state and local responsibility.

From its outset, UMTA was based on shaky premises. Public transit was touted as a service for the poor, the handicapped, and the elderly; whereas these groups were in fact no more likely to use public transit than any other segment of the population. UMTA legislation had granted extensive bargaining leverage to public transit workers; work-force reductions were prohibited, and unions were, in essence, empowered to write their own contracts. The upshot was a rapid increase in transit workers' salaries at the same time public use of transit systems was shrinking rapidly.

Seeking to modernize the urban landscape, UMTA discouraged modest improvements to existing transit systems and promoted vast new undertakings. Faced with rising costs and a steady decline in demand for urban mass transit, UMTA had pushed new urban rail systems—by far the most expensive mode of urban transportation. These new rail lines would actually require a dramatic increase in numbers of users in order to break even.

The new rail lines, however, had worked at cross purposes to real transportation needs. Following the historic hub-and-spoke pattern, they sought to shuttle commuters directly from the suburbs to the "urban core." But the suburbs had been spreading away from the radial "spokes," and suburb-to-center trips were increasingly being displaced by "lateral commutes" between suburban centers. While urban residents needed greater flexibility in transportation, UMTA "modernized" our cities with rigid, gargantuan systems based on ideas dating back to the previous century.

UMTA's programs seemed to be deliberately designed to encourage the unnecessary and the exorbitant. Since the federal government would pay for 80 percent of construction costs and the state government paid for most of the rest, cities hurried to sign up for new "free" transit systems. For the first time in 50 years, new urban rail systems sprang up in cities across the country. Many were white elephants. Few if any would have been built if residents had been asked to foot the bill; local taxpayers possess a remarkable degree of foresight and common sense, qualities lacking in Washington-based experts.

Moreover, cities blessed with "free" rail systems soon began to regret their good fortune. Overly elaborate and costly, the new rail lines bore only a fraction of the riders originally projected, creating huge annual operating deficits and straining city budgets. To cope, many cities were forced to cut back on other less expensive transit services. Thus overall public transportation service was reduced; despite the enormous investment, the public-transit dependent population actually became worse off.

Senator Proxmire was correct in criticizing UMTA. Ironically, the figures in Senator Proxmire's charges came from a 1985 report by the General Accounting Office (GAO), an arm of Congress. That meant that for perhaps the first time since I'd become UMTA's Administrator, Congress and I agreed about something!

I thought back on the frustration I had experienced before that distinguished assembly. I'd spent hundreds of hours testifying—fruitlessly—to convince Congress to address the problem of wasteful and excessive federal spending. They responded by making the situation worse.

In 1982, Congress had raised federal taxes on gasoline. From a nickel increase in the gasoline tax, one cent entered a special fund to upgrade and reinforce our nation's urban transit infrastructure. The idea was that urban transit would have a reliable, stable funding source—a "trust fund." My chief concern was that such a fund, if needed, be spent wisely and not merely squandered as so often in the past.

When Congress directed that a portion of the trust fund monies go for new construction, I established a set of criteria to guide UMTA's investment in this area. Past experience indicated that new construction or "new starts" are the least efficient use of federal transit dollars. "New starts" tend to mushroom into enormously expensive undertakings. If poorly planned, they can bleed a community dry economically. Therefore, strict, objective criteria for choosing new construction projects are essential.

This was the only prudent and fair solution: fair to taxpayers, fair to communities that do spend wisely, and fair to people who depend on transit. With all I'd been hearing on the floor of Congress about fiscal restraint, I had dared hope that our nation's elected representatives would embrace my idea of basing any future new start funding on objective, merit-based guidelines.

Not so. The House and Senate Appropriations Committees flatly rejected the investment guidelines and instead earmarked the entire amount available in FY 1985 for new construction projects in a few politically powerful districts. Many of these projects were economically unsound. Beyond that, the sheer number of "new starts" promised staggering future costs. In effect, the congressional earmarks would make a mockery of the trust fund by exceeding its limits and establishing a rationale for enormous new expenditures.

The interested members of Congress knew that once UMTA began funding specific projects, the agency would be obliged to see them to completion, rather than "waste" the initial investment. The history of UMTA showed this pattern repeated over and over. A bad project would be initiated; periodically it would be reviewed, always with a negative conclusion—but always the result would be the same: more spending. Once a program is in place, it takes on a life of its own, building up momentum until it is impossible to stop.

Each program develops its own constituency, rather like the "military-industrial complex" President Eisenhower spoke of. In the transit program, it's the "special-interest consultant constituent complex" that has remained steadfast and uncompromising. And in their view, it has paid off. They know that administrations come and go, but all are vulnerable to the same political pressures.

Facing an extravagant array of congressionally proposed "new starts" promising inevitably to soak the taxpayer for tens of billions, I felt like the Dutch man with his finger in the hole in the dike. To avert the flood, I attempted to reprogram, then to defer a portion of the earmarked funds.

The congressional answer was a firm "No!" accompanied by wails of protest even from those legislators professing a "deep concern" about government waste. It was a prime example of institutional irresponsibility at its worst. Through micromanagement and pork barreling, Congress had squandered and would continue to squander billions, inflating transit costs beyond reasonable proportions and causing real harm to the transit user.

All these problems remained. But at the moment, I had a more immediate issue to address: How to deal with Senator Proxmire? To his credit, the Senator had had the courage to vote against the noxious earmarks. At the same time, he continued to sit on the Senate Appropriations Committee, a body that could do something about excessive government spending but fails to defy the system perpetuating it. The Fleece, in my view, would be an outstanding opportunity to illustrate the real reason such an award exists.

Despite those who counseled me to take the usual course, to "keep a low profile" or defend UMTA, I decided that if I were going to criticize Congress's "institutional irresponsibility," I should avoid reacting in a typically institutional way myself. So I elected to accept the Fleece in person, just as enthusiastically as if it were an Academy Award. In my acceptance speech, I would modestly share the honor with the "ones who make it all possible: my friends in the United States Congress."

Ironically, retrieving the prize was almost as frustrating as qualifying for it. When I could not reach Senator Proxmire by phone, I spoke to a baffled staff member who refused to believe I was serious about accepting the award publicly. Apparently, there was no place at the award ceremony for the awardee. It had never been done.

Had I waited for an invitation, UMTA's "Fleece" may well have been nothing more than a tiny headline buried on the newspaper's back page. Not willing to let this opportunity escape, I drove over to the Capitol on the morning the award was given. Outside the committee room, I cornered Senator Proxmire. Once I convinced him I was serious, Proxmire graciously agreed to my plan. I would deliver a statement at his press conference.

Reporters in the committee room were somewhat bored; waste of taxpayers' money had become routine news. But this time something was different; as Proxmire recited the facts behind the selection of the award, reporters began to murmur, "Who's that fellow up there on the platform with the Senator?" "Well," said Proxmire's staffers, "that's the recipient of the award, the Administrator of UMTA. He's come to receive his Golden Fleece personally."

The following morning, *The Washington Post* carried the story and a photo. The headline read: "Winner Says Golden Fleece Wasn't Wasted."

Not only had I been the first to accept the award in person, I was the first to share it with Congress! Afterward, Senator Proxmire told me he would work with me to ensure that the waste in UMTA is not repeated.

Will this small government official's adventure mean anything in the long run? After all, UMTA is but one program among many; it's no secret that the congressional budget process encourages the "cookie jar" approach to spending, regardless of an administration's budget requests. Even so, Gramm-Rudman has riveted public attention on the issue of waste. I can only hope that what I've done will convince other agency heads to become bolder in criticizing their programs. There is no shame in publicizing the truth—in fact, the taxpayers deserve nothing less.

24 Conspiracy Against the Taxpayers: Contracting Out at NOAA

JOHN HIRAM CALDWELL

Editors' Note: Much of the real work of political appointees is carried out far from the headlines. Silent struggles amid a myriad of bureaucratic details play an immense role in setting the course of government policy. In this case history, John Caldwell, a pseudonym for an official close to the struggle, describes the events eloquently—no further introduction is needed.

We must never again abuse the trust of working men and women, by sending their earnings on a futile chase after the spiraling demands of a bloated federal establishment. The time has come for a new American Emancipation—a great national drive to . . . liberate the spirit of enterprise. . . . If we meet this challenge, these will be years . . . when our economy was finally freed from government's grip, and the American eagle soared to new heights.

> *President Ronald Reagan*
> *Second Inaugural Address*
> *January 22, 1985*

This statement by the President is merely a recent synopsis of his long-held beliefs in limited government and the free enterprise system. The need to make such a statement in his Second Inaugural Address resulted from the failure of the first Reagan Administration to free our economy "from government's grip." This failure was caused, in large measure, by a "conspiracy against the taxpayers." Some members of the conspiracy are precisely those one would expect—the career bureaucracy, program beneficiaries, and certain members of Congress. But these conspirators have been quietly joined by others less expected—political appointees of the President. This case study examines the efforts of a few political appointees in the National Oceanic and Atmospheric Administration (NOAA) in the Department of Commerce to implement the President's agenda and details their conflicts with the "conspiracy against the taxpayers."

The Agency: NOAA

NOAA was formed in 1970 by President Nixon through the merger of a number of government activities into a single agency. Its mission is to

establish policy for the nation's oceanic, coastal, and atmospheric resources and to provide services and products related to the oceanic and
atmospheric environment. NOAA's most common services are storm
warnings, weather forecasts, ocean wave and current predictions, navi-
gational charts, and satellite imagery.

NOAA employs about 13,000 people and has an annual budget of
approximately $1.3 billion, which represents more than one-half of the
total Department of Commerce budget and about 40 percent of the Department's employees. NOAA is headed by three presidential appointees
requiring Senate confirmation—the administrator, deputy administrator,
and associate administrator. It has five line offices, the largest being the
National Weather Service.

The record of Reagan appointments in NOAA is merely one example of
the failure of the White House to be consistently guided by the Reagan
philosophy when making presidential appointments. The first appointment, of John V. Byrne as Administrator set the stage for failure to implement the Reagan agenda in NOAA. Byrne, although a pleasant person,
was anything but a Reaganite. A professor from Oregon State University,
he was a self-described "liberal Republican in the stamp of Lowell
Weicker." Byrne had never been active in the Republican Party or in
Reagan campaigns. He was a registered Democrat when Reagan was
elected in 1980 and switched parties two weeks later. (In fact, Byrne had
a long record as an apparent party switcher, having changed party
registrations six times in twenty years.) An oceanographer, he was a member of the oceanographic constituent community of university research-
ers which relied on grants and contracts from NOAA for their livelihood.
Given such a background, it is difficult to see why anyone would expect
Byrne to be committed to drastic change within NOAA.[1]

The second Reagan appointment was of Anthony J. Calio as Deputy
Administrator. Calio, a twenty-year career bureaucrat from NASA, was
recommended as a strong administrator. Like Byrne, he had no Reagan
credentials. In fact, Calio had closer ties to the Carter White House than
to Reagan since his wife had been a speechwriter for President Carter.

The third Reagan appointee, James W. Winchester, was the only one
of the three with true Reagan credentials. A meteorologist and oceanographer, Winchester had worked in NOAA for five years, and had over
40 years experience in both industry and government. Winchester had
an established record for trimming government spending and waste, and
was well known for his opposition to limitless research and the continuing expansion of "free" NOAA services and products, which in most cases
competed with private industry. Winchester had been actively and continuously identified as a Reaganite since Reagan's election as Governor
of California.

After Reagan was elected in 1980, Winchester wanted to come and help the President rein in the bureaucracy in the agency he knew best, NOAA. He had very strong support from Senator Thad Cochran and House Republican Whip Trent Lott. But he had strong opposition from Byrne, Calio, NOAA bureaucrats, and the university research community. Winchester's nomination was under consideration for eight months; finally, the deadlock was broken and Winchester's nomination was made. He was confirmed as Associate Administrator by the Senate on March 15, 1982.

Upon Winchester's arrival at NOAA, every effort was made to control and contain him. The first step was a nimble reshuffling of responsibilities. During the first eleven years of NOAA's existence, the day-to-day general manager of the agency had been the Associate Administrator—the position to be held by Winchester. However, upon Winchester's confirmation, almost all power and responsibility were stripped from that position by Byrne and transferred to Calio.

Next, Winchester was informed that hiring a political staff would needlessly "alienate" NOAA career professionals. It was recommended that he have no political subordinates, a very unusual situation for someone at that level of responsibility. But this effort to neutralize Winchester by placing him in a padded cell lined with career staffers loyal to agency interests failed. Winchester named Jack Coleman, a 28-year-old attorney, as his special assistant. Coleman was a native Mississippian with a long record of conservative activism. All subsequent members of Winchester's political staff followed this ideological mold.

Other incidents quickly followed that would prove symptomatic of the political struggle that would develop within NOAA over the next four years. Winchester's office soon found itself left out of the information loop, bypassed on correspondence, and excluded from the clearance system for any decision documents. Winchester spoke with Byrne about the problem; Byrne asserted he was imagining things and denied that anyone was trying to keep him uninformed. However, the situation continued unchanged and Winchester's frustration level increased. Finally, Coleman spoke with the special assistant to Commerce Secretary Malcolm Baldrige about the correspondence problem. The special assistant was quite concerned and spoke with the Secretary who went directly to Byrne and told him to correct the problem. The result was a memo from Byrne to Calio and the executive secretariat stating that Winchester would receive copies of all incoming and outgoing correspondence and could be on clearance for any correspondence he desired.

Finally, some weeks after Winchester's arrival at NOAA, Byrne issued a memo stating that the Associate Administrator's only role would be to conduct special studies assigned by the Administrator. Winchester objected to this, but to no avail. At this time Winchester still had a vague sense that all Reagan appointees were playing on the same team and that he could still be helpful, even if in a limited role. Since Winchester and Coleman had effectively been cut out of any role in the management of the agency, they vowed to become the watchdogs for the Administration.

Winchester's Agenda

Based on his experience in government and industry, Winchester understood the fundamental differences between the public and private sectors. He understood the futility of public-sector "efficiency campaigns," which invariably fail because of a lack of an inherent disciplinary mechanism such as the marketplace which punishes inefficiency. His agenda from the beginning was to terminate programs, reduce expenditures, and move as many support services to the private sector as possible.

Since his role had been reduced to conducting special studies, in April 1982 Winchester requested authority from Byrne to conduct a large-scale study to determine areas where NOAA should rely more heavily on support services from private industry. Winchester's idea was to travel around to major NOAA installations, conduct detailed inspections, and write a report to Byrne containing recommendations after each inspection. Byrne readily agreed to this request from Winchester. (It would be time consuming and keep Winchester on the road and away from day-to-day operations.)

Winchester made several of these trips and after each wrote a lengthy report to Byrne; all of them just sat on Byrne's desk for several months. Somehow, Byrne could never find the time to discuss them. Winchester came to realize that Byrne never intended to read them. His frustration level was at an all-time high. His efforts to contribute to a conservative revolution in government were being thwarted by another appointee who was not even a consistent member of the President's party. Winchester had given up his company, taken a cut in pay, incurred large expenses to move to Washington, given up his residence on the Gulf Coast with his sailboat docked at his back door—all against his wife's wishes and all apparently for nothing.

Then Coleman suggested to Winchester that maybe they could yet be effective. He told Winchester about the little-known Office of Management and Budget (OMB) Circular "A-76," which provides that functions conducted by government employees that could be provided by the private sector could be placed in direct cost competition with private-sector firms, with the low-cost method being selected. Coleman had been involved with the A-76 program as an Army procurement attorney. Although the Department of Defense (DOD) was implementing the A-76

Circular fairly extensively, most civilian agencies had merely ignored it since its origination under President Eisenhower in 1955.

Coleman said that if they could quietly get an A-76 program going, real cost reductions could be forced on NOAA because of the automatic competitive bidding mechanisms contained in the program. Winchester immediately saw the potential. He directed Coleman to draft a memo for Byrne's signature elevating responsibility for the A-76 program to the Associate Administrator, Winchester. Winchester took the memo to Byrne for him to sign, stating that A-76 was merely a variant on the special projects he was already doing. Byrne, not understanding the potential of A-76 and the controversy surrounding it, signed the memo, giving Winchester full authority over A-76 in NOAA.

Background of OMB Circular A-76

The A-76 program, or "contracting out," is a type of privatization: the return of "public" functions to the private sector. In contrast with pure privatization, under "contracting out" the government remains the overall authority and funding source for a given activity. For example, under the "contracting out" principle, a local government would retain responsibility for fire protection services but might contract with a private-sector firm to run the operation, provide the equipment, staff, etc. Or the government might simply contract with private firms to perform certain subfunctions within the fire department such as vehicle maintenance or health services. In the United States, various levels of government currently contract out a wide range of activities including fire protection, park maintenance, jails, street repair, data processing, garbage collection, and legal services.

The federal A-76 contract program was begun under Eisenhower in 1955. The original requirements stated that:

> The federal government will not start or carry on any commercial activity to provide a service or product for its own use if such a product or service can be procured from private enterprise.

The rules recognized the inherent inefficiency of government bureaucracy; simple cost effectiveness required that government organizations would not undertake commercial activities that could be routinely performed by private-sector firms. Instead, private firms would bid for a contract to perform the activity for the government. Contracting firms would be forced to maintain their efficiency through a periodic renewal of bids in competition against other private firms.

However, one general principle about government operations is that while the federal government expects firms in the private sector to obey the voluminous rules and regulations that the government establishes, rules designed to control the operation of the government itself are another matter. These "self-governing" rules will frequently be violated when it is in the interest of the bureaucracy to do so. Such is the case with A-76. Since the mid-fifties, the federal government has not only continued to perform "commercial" activities but has started new commercial activities involving hundreds of thousands of career employees. By the early 1980's, there were over a million employees in the federal government performing commercial activities at a cost of $40 billion per annum. In most cases the idea of contracting out was simply ignored.

Even when contracting out has been pursued, it has often been blocked by Congress. This occurred despite the long record of the A-76 program of achieving cost savings of 20 to 40 percent when utilized. Congressional barriers are the result of a second general principle of government: When a focused and organized interest group confronts a broad-based unorganized interest, it is the organized group that will win. In the case of A-76, Congress had quickly heeded the protests of federal unions and employees hostile to A-76, and ignored the interest of the taxpayer. The history of the A-76 program has thus been marked by a long series of moratoriums and exemptions on contracting out imposed by Congress in various agencies and departments.

In an effort to make the program more palatable to its opponents, the A-76 Circular was revised in 1979. The simple rule that commercial activities should be performed by the private sector was modified. Instead, each government unit was to be given a chance to "compete" with private-sector companies; agencies were required to conduct "cost comparisons" between internal suppliers and contract bidders from the private sector before awarding a contract. The low-cost alternative would then be chosen. However, private-sector firms were not permitted to bid against the actual cost of the activities as performed by the government organization. Instead, the government bureaucracy would be given a chance to "reform" itself—by determining how much the activity would cost if the government unit operated in its most efficient manner. The private sector would then bid against this in-house estimate. An award is given to the least-cost organization.

The A-76 cost comparison process as inherited by Winchester and Coleman thus had five basic steps.

1. A determination is made as to which activities are commercial in nature.

2. Certain commercial activities are selected for A-76 review.

3 . The government, either through internal management reviews
   or through outside consultants, determines where waste exists
   in its current operations. It then determines the cost of conducting a waste-free government operation, the so-called "most efficient organization" (MEO). This becomes the government bid.

4 . A contract—including performance requirements—is developed
   for private-sector firms. A solicitation of external bids is made;
   private-sector firms bid against the government's cost estimate
   (MEO).

5 . An award is given to the least-cost bidder. But to "win," a private-
   sector bid must be at least 10 percent less than the government's.

However, as befits a government-designed efficiency program, the
actual A-76 process is far more byzantine and laborious than this five-
step outline suggests. The average time required to award an A-76 contract to a private-sector firm is two and one-half years compared to six
months for other government contract programs. In addition, since the
federal bureaucracy operates the program and evaluates the cost comparison, it in effect plays the roles of both defendant and jury. This has
led to a system that is heavily biased against private-sector bidders.
Nevertheless, Coleman knew from his experience at DOD that the
program, if properly managed, could be made to work. He also knew that
the road to success would be a difficult one.

Winchester Moves Out

In the fall of 1982, with A-76 authority from Byrne in hand, Winchester
set about exercising it. As noted, the first step in the A-76 process is to
determine which activities are "commercial," i.e., those that could be
performed by contracts with the private sector. When Winchester took
control of the NOAA A-76 program, only about 300 civil service positions
out of a total of 13,000 were on the "commercial activities" inventory. So
as not to give away their plans, Coleman personally reviewed every
activity in NOAA over a three-month period and made recommendations
to Winchester as to their applicability to OMB Circular A-76.

His method was nothing ingenious, but required rolling up his sleeves
and getting his hands dirty—something many political appointees do not
want to do, but something they must do to be truly successful. First, he
asked for a list of all civil service job series of NOAA employees. With this
list, Coleman made some judgments, following guidance in the Circular,
as to which jobs were most likely to be "commercial," e.g., computer
operators, electronic technicians, cartographers, supply clerks, and
warehousemen. With the list of commercial job series in hand, he had

the computer designate by organizational unit the location of the employees in each series. Where he saw aggregations of commercial series, or large numbers in even one series, the activity was automatically targeted for further analysis. He then read the organization mission statement for each of these targeted units. If Colemen felt they were commercial in the nature of their operations, he included them on a list to be given to Winchester. After three months of review, the list was totaled and came to 5,700 positions, nearly 44 percent of the entire NOAA bureaucracy.

Both Winchester and Coleman knew that, given the fact that almost no other agency outside of Defense was active in A-76, Byrne would not allow them to run such an aggressive program. So they decided to start with a mere 750 positions and gradually to increase it. In December 1982, Winchester sent this abbreviated list out for comment by the top career staff. As you might expect, some line officers were very upset, but others knew they were getting off lightly. Still, there was criticism from both political and career officials. They complained that the Reagan Administration had no particular interest in "contracting out" and that Winchester and Coleman were simply mavericks off on their own private crusade.

Fortunately, in January of 1983 Winchester got some surprise assistance. The Office of Management and Budget (OMB) published a revised A-76 Circular in the *Federal Register*. The revised Circular emphasized the Administration's support for the program, and called on the agencies to complete all existing A-76 studies as expeditiously as possible. The revised Circular gave Winchester the apparent impetus he needed. Relying on the call for expeditious treatment of existing A-76 studies, Winchester gambled; he abandoned his go-slow approach and took the chance of pushing his entire program forward all at one time.

Winchester sent out the entire list of 5,700 positions for comment. The bureaucracy was apoplectic. Both Byrne and Calio immediately called for a cutback in the proposal. Winchester responded that he would give the career staff a chance to demonstrate to him which of the listed activities were actually "noncommercial" and thus inappropriate for outside contracting. Following discussion with the career offices, Winchester pruned the list back to 3,000 positions. This did not mean that both sides had agreed on the commercial nature of these 3,000 positions, but it did mean that formal management studies (step #3 of the A-76 process) would be begun on nearly one-fourth of NOAA activities. Since A-76 management studies alone historically resulted in cost savings of 20 percent, this was an enormous step forward. It also meant that NOAA went from having one of the smallest A-76 programs in the government to having one of the largest, as a percentage of agency employment. Moreover, while other agencies had traditionally restricted A-76 reviews to blue-collar activities, the NOAA program for the first time included a wide range of professional, white-collar functions.

Winchester's gamble paid off. Byrne was afraid to tangle with him openly because his dramatic proposal had caught the favorable attention of OMB. Still, there was a confident feeling within NOAA that, given time, the A-76 program would collapse under its own weight—with a little help from the career bureaucracy, special interest groups, and the Hill.

First Steps

With such a large program to push through in such a short time, Winchester and Coleman realized they could not do it alone. They also knew they could not trust the career bureaucracy to be honest in the management studies or fair in writing the work statements for contractors to bid on. So they proceeded to contract with respected management consulting firms to conduct the management studies with assistance from career technical personnel. They also sent 125 employees through intensive five-day courses on how to conduct A-76 reviews. Two of these employees were detailed to each study and were made personally responsible for achieving the aggressive milestones set by Winchester. As one might expect, studies soon bogged down. The contracting office was unable to get the consulting contracts awarded in a timely manner because of insufficient contracting staff and foot dragging.

In an effort to improve progress, in late summer 1983 Winchester hired an expert A-76 management analyst from DOD. Slowly but surely, things began moving faster. One initiative was to develop the most detailed "how-to" A-76 study guide in the federal government. In order to award the consultant contracts faster, a Special Projects Branch was carved out of the Procurement Office to work only on A-76 matters.

However, as the program progressed, it drew increasing attention from a hostile Congress. Since its beginning, NOAA has had a powerful group of lawmakers and staff on Capitol Hill who have felt it was "their" agency. Only they knew what was best for it. This same group has thwarted just about every NOAA budget reduction proposed by President Reagan over the last five years. Not content to block budget reductions, these lawmakers have even added new pet projects to NOAA's budget. As a consequence, NOAA's budget authority increased from $851M in fiscal year (FY) 1981 to $1,327M in FY 85, which is quite remarkable for a civilian agency during that period. As one might expect, the members of this group were outraged over Winchester's A-76 program. Many saw the program as the Administration's attempt to take revenge on NOAA through the back door after having been thwarted in its efforts to reduce the agency through the budget process. These congressmen envisioned OMB at work behind the scenes, and refused to believe that this program had merely been a pleasant surprise to Stockman's budget examiners.

During the spring of 1983, in an effort to contain the congressional fury, either Winchester or Coleman visited the office of each Senator and Representative who was to have an A-76 study in his state or district. They explained the process, step by step, and provided reference materials indicating all of the protections afforded to the incumbent government personnel, such as the right of first refusal for jobs with the contractor. Similar briefings were conducted for all staff on the authorizing and appropriating subcommittees.

Meanwhile, Winchester and Coleman attempted to cultivate outside support to help their efforts. Luckily, a coalition called the Business Alliance on Government Competition, composed of approximately 50 trade associations and private-sector labor unions, was formed in the spring of 1983 to counteract the legislative pressure against contracting out from public-sector unions like the American Federation of Government Employees (AFGE) and the National Federation of Federal Employees (NFFE). The Business Alliance, with a highly capable Staff Director, Frank Sellers, worked closely with Winchester and Coleman to coordinate the support efforts of associations like the Electronic Industries Association (EIA), the National Council of Technical Service Industries (NCTSI), the American Consulting Engineers Council (ACEC), and private-sector unions like the Marine Engineer's Beneficial Association (MEBA). Winchester also developed friends at White House Personnel, OMB, The Heritage Foundation, the Grace Commission, and elsewhere.

Rough Sledding

As part of his overall plan, Winchester had scheduled the high payoff A-76 studies first. This may have been a tactical error—because these studies also tended to be the most controversial. They included operations such as the Marine Chart and the Aeronautical Chart offices. Confrontation over these activities began with the management studies prepared by an external consulting firm, Arthur Young, Inc. Although intended to be cooperative endeavors to make these organizations more efficient so they could compete with the private sector and possibly win—in fact, these efforts quickly deteriorated into acrimonious debate. For every position recommended for elimination by Arthur Young, the bureaucrats would present multiple reasons why the position was absolutely essential to the "safety of navigation." The truth was that the bureaucrats did not intend to become more efficient and, apparently, did not believe they would ever have to compete with the private sector. As an example of the pervasiveness of this attitude, managers of one organization argued that they actually needed more government employees to be able to accomplish the work they were already performing with existing staff.

Nevertheless, the management studies were completed and it soon became apparent that the activities were good candidates for outside contracting. The NOAA bureaucracy and its allied special interest groups fought back. The House Merchant Marine and Fisheries Committee and the Senate Commerce Committee were inundated by a national letter-writing campaign from NOAA employees and outside interest groups. These outside groups included the Aircraft Owners and Pilots Association; Boat U.S.; Potomac River, Delaware Bay, and other Pilots Associations; the Coast Guard Auxiliary and the U.S. Power Squadrons. The allegations, from whatever source, were similar: NOAA would cause loss of life, ship groundings, and airplane crashes if it contracted out the production, warehousing, and distribution of NOAA marine and aeronautical charts. Winchester was accused of everything from incompetence to having personal economic and business interests in the potential contracts. Both committees convened hearings on the NOAA A-76 program. In the hearings, Winchester was harassed by members of both parties. Each hearing was attended by more than 100 NOAA career employees who would boo and hiss when Winchester spoke. They attended on government time, at taxpayer expense, to—in effect—lobby against the taxpayers.

The motive of the special interest groups was easy to ascertain. The price of nautical and aeronautical charts was about 25 percent of the actual production cost. Since these groups represented hundreds of thousands of organizations and individuals that purchased charts from NOAA, they did not want to risk any program changes that might eventually result in an increase in the price of charts to anything resembling a market level.

Not only were the outside special interest groups active against the NOAA program, but so were representatives of the Federal Aviation Administration (FAA), the Defense Mapping Agency (DMA), and the Coast Guard. Clearly, success of the NOAA program could serve as a model for contracting out activities in other agencies. Indeed, OMB had long targeted the traffic control operations in the FAA and the entire range of mapping and charting activities in DMA as candidates for contracting out under A-76. These agencies had a strong interest in supporting the idea that A-76 did not apply to their operations or anything similar to them in another federal agency. All of these agencies, along with the special interest groups, testified at the oversight hearing. All opposed NOAA's A-76 program.

Winchester and Coleman fought back with the facts. It was pointed out that not a single commercial airline in the United States used NOAA charts. Instead, they used charts produced by a private-sector company that did not have its products reviewed by government "quality assurance inspectors." This had been the case for more than 30 years and had not caused a safety problem. The airlines told Winchester that they used the private-sector charts because they were more "user friendly" and more informative.

Much to the chagrin of the special interests, NOAA did award the chart distribution contract to a private firm. Since this was the first new NOAA contract under A-76, it took on special significance to the bureaucracy. If this contract could be discredited, the entire program would collapse. The result was an organized sabotage effort by a group of career employees. The wrong packing material was "accidentally" ordered for the contractor, so that the charts would be damaged in shipment. A similar "accident" provided the contractor with incorrect addresses and shipment schedules for delivery of the charts. The objective was simple: Make it look like the contractor could not perform, cancel the contract, and bring the work back in-house. It was only through Winchester's persistent personal supervision in this transition period that these "mistakes" were discovered and the effort to discredit and terminate the contractor was stopped. The private contractor performed his agreed functions; costs were reduced from $2.8 million per year to $1.1 million. Savings of $1.7 million per year, or 60 percent, were achieved for U.S. taxpayers.

Bureaucratic resistance continued in other A-76 studies, although in a more subtle manner. A simple ploy was for career employees to include in the contract proposals—on which private-sector firms were to bid—performance requirements that had never been fulfilled by the current government operations. Thus the bids of outside firms would be artificially inflated. Similarly, the private-sector firms could be forced to submit fixed price bids on contracts that had highly variable and fluctuating work requirements. Perhaps the most effective means of resistance was the tactic of repeatedly modifying the proposed contract (solicitation of bids) sent out to private-sector firms. Under the guise of "fine tuning," the NOAA bureaucracy could repeatedly modify the requirements of the contract, forcing the private-sector firms to reevaluate and submit new bids. Since the process of tracking revised solicitations and preparing multiple bids is very expensive—in some cases running into hundreds of thousands of dollars—repeated modifications force many firms to drop out of the process. From the perspective of the NOAA bureaucracy, the game of endless modifications to proposed contracts was thus doubly rewarding; it delayed the ultimate cost comparison and it narrowed the field against which the federal bureaucracy must compete. The champion in this process was an ingenious NOAA library director who managed to amend one solicitation for bid fifteen times, thereby squeezing out nearly all private-sector interest. In the face of these obstacles, constant detailed oversight was required by Winchester's political staff to ensure that the bureaucracy did not derail the program.

Quiet Struggles Behind the Scenes

However, Winchester's struggles to keep the A-76 program on track received no support from NOAA's other presidential appointees—quite the contrary. During his tenure at NOAA, Administrator Byrne seldom, if ever, expressed support for A-76, publicly or privately. This silence at the top sent strong signals to the career ranks within NOAA and no doubt encouraged resistance to implementing the program. Although Winchester had full formal authority for the A-76 program, he was not permitted to answer general public inquiries about the program. Such inquiries were handled by other political appointees in an effort to keep a low profile on the program. When Coleman had an opportunity to speak about NOAA's A-76 on national television, Byrne refused to let him appear on the grounds that it would needlessly "alarm" NOAA employees.

In an effort to demonstrate that the Commerce Department and the Administration did, in fact, support the program, Coleman briefed the Electronics Industries Association (EIA) in the fall of 1983 on the NOAA A-76 program, mentioning some of the problems. This resulted in a letter that EIA wrote to the Deputy Secretary of Commerce expressing its support for NOAA's program. The Deputy Secretary responded by committing his support to the NOAA program, stating, "I expect all elements of the Department to strive to meet the high standards that NOAA has set." To bolster his position, Winchester made sure that this letter received wide distribution inside NOAA.

But the lack of support by Byrne went beyond verbal fencing. Much of the work in the A-76 process was under the control of the top career managers in NOAA's line offices; their professional staffs possessed most of the information necessary to prepare the management studies and the solicitations for contract bids. As noted, Winchester had been relieved of his managerial authority over these career officials, during his first weeks at NOAA. This lack of management activity now posed a serious obstacle to carrying out his A-76 plans. As a minimal step, Winchester requested that A-76 be included as a work objective within the formal performance appraisals of NOAA's top career managers. (Top-level career civil servants have performance appraisal systems that spell out the work they are to fulfill in a given year. These appraisals serve as a contract between career managers and their political supervisors; the pay of the career civil servants is, in part, determined by their successful completion of the specified work objectives.) Byrne and Calio refused to include A-76 in the performance appraisal system. Similarly, when Winchester and Coleman requested managerial control over personnel in the NOAA Procurement Office working solely on A-76, they were again refused.

Under the circumstances, it was remarkable that the A-76 program survived. But it not only survived, it advanced. One by one the management studies were completed, solicitations for bids were made, and bids were received. This progress was facilitated by the use of outside consultants for many of the management studies and by the fact that key phases of the program such as bidding were driven by external forces. Nevertheless, long hours of bureaucratic trench warfare were required by Winchester and his political staff.

By the fall of 1983, Byrne was becoming seriously concerned about the changes A-76 was wreaking in his previously tranquil agency. He attempted to move directly against the program, repeatedly seeking to overturn Winchester's decisions concerning the scope and timing of the reviews, the details of the cost comparisons, and the actual award of the contracts. Winchester responded to these overtures by declaring that OMB regulations clearly stated that one political appointee in each agency was to have charge of the A-76 program and that Byrne had given that authority to him. If Byrne wished to second-guess his decisions, Winchester stated that he would simply return entire authority for the program to Byrne. This represented an implicit threat of resignation and was sufficient to balk Byrne. He was apparently reluctant to tackle Winchester's political supporters and unwilling to directly challenge a program that had drawn OMB support.

Thus Winchester was able to protect the essential elements of the A-76 program from direct intervention by the program's internal political opponents, but he found it harder to rectify the problems stemming from his lack of direct managerial control. The A-76 program stayed on track but its implementation was seriously delayed. Winchester and Coleman estimate that by denying them even minimal managerial oversight of the program, Byrne succeeded in doubling the time required for each stage of implementation.

Congressional Opposition and Presidential Support

Slowed but not stopped, the A-76 program continued to nibble away at the layers of fat in the NOAA bureaucracy—to the horror of NOAA employees. A favored agency, traditionally pampered by Congress, NOAA was for the first time facing the specter of serious belt-tightening and, even worse, of permanent competition with lean, aggressive private-sector organizations. Cries of alarm and lamentation poured out to the agency's benefactors on the Hill. Ever alert, Congress responded.

It was alleged that the NOAA A-76 program must be illegal. More than 40 Congressmen and Senators, both Republicans and Democrats, requested the General Accounting Office (GAO) to investigate the NOAA program for compliance with law and the Circular. The GAO initiated its review in December 1983, and the review lasted for more than a year. The investigating team spoke with scores of NOAA officials and employees and representatives of constituent groups. The very existence of this review was a blow to Winchester's efforts. But when GAO finally issued its report in June 1985, the investigation was revealed to be a complete waste of time and taxpayers' money. The report stated, "NOAA has been complying with the policy and procedures of the Circular." While damage had been done to the program by encouraging even more dissension and foot dragging, at least the report vindicated Winchester and Coleman.

In January 1984, the House passed H.R. 2900, the NOAA Authorization Bill, which contained a provision for a 90-day legislative review period between an A-76 contract decision and the actual award of the contract. This would have, in effect, crippled the program by the threat of continual congressional override. Once again, the private-sector coalition, the Business Alliance on Government Competition, was active in fighting this legislation in the Senate. Although somewhat diluted, the measure, now S. 1097, was passed and sent to the President for his signature. Industry groups urged the President to veto the bill. What these groups had to say to the President about the NOAA program is significant. The Committee on Contracting Out, an umbrella group of 26 associations, stated:

> The National Oceanic and Atmospheric Administration, under the leadership of Associate Administrator Jim Winchester, is the only civilian agency that has made a sincere effort to implement OMB Circular A-76 in response to White House direction. It was that effective program which stimulated congressional opposition. Your action provides encouragement for those few dedicated officials who have taken this program seriously and should set an example for other agencies.

The Electronic Industries Association wrote:

> With commitment and enthusiasm perhaps unique among government agencies, the NOAA commercial activities program under Associate Administrator Jim Winchester continues to generate the potential for millions of dollars of savings to the taxpayer without diminution of essential programs and services. If every manager charged with implementation of Circular A-76 would approach this

responsibility with the fairness and commitment of the NOAA program, the resultant savings would begin to have a marked positive effect on the federal deficit.

Industry's efforts succeeded; President Reagan vetoed the bill. NOAA's A-76 program was saved.

The President's veto provided Winchester with new impetus. Although the rate of progress remained exasperatingly slow, one by one, reviews were completed and contracts awarded. With each review completed, cost savings of 20 to 30 percent were achieved; staff in the relevant activities, whether inside the government or in the contractors' organization, were cut by 33 percent. The savings began to mount; relative to the size of the agency, the NOAA A-76 program moved from an initial level of insignificance to being the largest and most successful in the government. Based on the program's consistent rate of success, Winchester was able to demonstrate that when his full A-76 program was completed, savings of $40 million would be achieved. These savings represent 10 percent of total NOAA personnel costs. Similarly, the program would enable NOAA and its outside contractors to reduce staff by 1,200 positions without a reduction in services delivered. Winchester's only regret was that these savings could not have been achieved earlier due to the indifference and hostility of other NOAA officials.

By the end of President Reagan's first term in office, the NOAA A-76 program had achieved renown. Jack Coleman found he was spending half of his time explaining the success of the NOAA program to political appointees from other agencies. NOAA materials on how to implement A-76 were circulated throughout the government. Despite his nearly impossible position, Jim Winchester had cleared a path for other political appointees to follow.

Conclusion

There are a number of lessons that can be drawn from Jim Winchester's experiences in NOAA. The first is the importance of the selection of political personnel. To select personnel is truly to select policy. The battle over policy itself begins with a struggle over the selection of the individuals who will develop and implement that policy. Like any other political process, personnel selection is fraught with compromise. The result has been a conservative Administration that holds within its ranks appointees who are indifferent or even hostile to conservative policy goals. The fact that these appointees hold key positions within the Administration at points where policy is originated gives them ample opportunity to quietly frustrate conservative policy initiatives.

Thus the political personnel selection process lies at the core of the policy process within the executive branch. Largely unheralded, it is a political arena as important as the more conspicuous arena of legislative debate with its celebrated votes over Contra aid, MX funding, etc. Outcomes in the personnel selection process within the executive branch will often spell the difference between success and failure for a conservative agenda.

Second, the actions of Jim Winchester in NOAA offer insights concerning the ubiquitous question of "efficiency" in government. Productivity enhancement and "efficiency" in government are will-o'-the-wisps ceaselessly pursued—with little success. The history of modern government is studded with the attempts by "whiz kid" executives to bring the latest in management and productivity techniques from the private sector into lethargic public bureaucracies. More often than not, little change is accomplished; in those cases where exceptional executives have boosted government performance, their achievements generally evaporate after a few years. Failures in the quest for "efficient government" stem from a lack of recognition of the true cause of government inefficiency.

Private-sector firms are more efficient than government organizations not because government managers are inept or government workers are lazy. Private-sector firms are efficient because the marketplace leaves them no choice; inefficient firms will simply perish. Competition is the prime mover from which all private-sector performance ensues; government bureaucracies will always remain relatively less efficient because they do not confront the impetus of external competition. As a result of his long experience in both the public and private sectors, Winchester was aware of the inherent nature of inefficiency in government. He moved directly to the source of the problem—seeking to eliminate nonessential government functions, and to introduce competitive forces wherever appropriate in remaining government operations. This, he correctly assessed, was the only way to achieve permanent reductions in cost.

In their efforts, Winchester and Coleman always sought not only to achieve cost savings within NOAA but also to create a model for cost reduction across government. Currently there are $40 billion of "commercial" activities performed within the federal government. If a policy of "contracting out," based on the principles of the NOAA program, were implemented government-wide, cost savings of $10 billion to $15 billion per annum could result. The opportunity exists, but the success of such a program will clearly depend on the selection of political personnel with the vision and commitment of James Winchester and his political staff.

Note

1. When Byrne left NOAA in 1985, Senator Lowell Weicker, who had fought the Reagan Administration vigorously over all NOAA issues as well as most other government policy, appropriately complimented Byrne as a Reagan appointee. Weicker praised Byrne's leadership and lamented that his departure from NOAA would be a "great loss."

25 Turning the Iron Triangle
Upside Down: Alfred Regnery and
Juvenile Justice

LEO HUNTER

*Editors' Note: In this case study, Leo Hunter, a pseudonym for
someone knowledgeable about Washington affairs, describes
one of the few grant programs successfully transformed by the
Reagan Administration. Degree of commitment to change was
perhaps the determining factor. The passions of an intense
political battle, recently fought, are still very much present in the
following narrative.*

Theories about social policy are theories dearly held. When social policy
and federal money are combined, emotions run even higher. But when
social policy affects children, and an annual federal subsidy of $70 million
to a narrow ideological group of activists is at stake, emotions reach the
boiling point. Confrontation between those who wish to change policy
and a constituency dedicated to maintaining the agency's "integrity" (as
defined by the beneficiaries) is inevitable.

All these factors are reflected in the Office of Juvenile Justice and
Delinquency Prevention (OJJDP) at the Department of Justice. Established by Senators Birch Bayh and John Culver, the office was intended to
spread the "juvenile justice gospel" according to Bayh and Culver across
the nation. Efforts in this behalf included:

- over $1 million to Jazz Mobile Inc., a mobile jazz show, located in
  Harlem, intended to divert youngsters from delinquent activity
- $678,000 to the YMCA to purchase minibikes for juvenile delin-
  quents to "establish rapport between the alienated youth and the
  YMCA outreach worker"
- nearly $1.7 million to the National Juvenile Law Center of St.
  Louis, Missouri, to sue state and local governments on behalf of
  delinquent youth

Although $70 million per annum may be small potatoes in terms of
federal spending, it is enough to provide ample stocks of white wine, Brie,
and Volvos to "juvenile justice" professionals in OJJDP's grantee network.

The Bayh and Culver gospel as articulated by OJJDP rested on a long
tradition of liberal social policy. At its philosophic base, it held that

children are incapable of determining between right and wrong. Therefore, children are not responsible for their misdeeds, no matter how serious, and should not be punished. When juveniles do something wrong, they need to be "rehabilitated" but should never be held accountable for what they have done. Concomitantly, crime is viewed as the product of social factors beyond the individual child's control. Those strongly advocating this philosophy believe that the worst thing that can be done to juvenile offenders is to lock them up; accordingly, juvenile correctional institutions should be closed. They also believe that children have—or should have—virtually the same legal rights as adults, and that their rights exceed the need for the safety of other children or society.

Since 1974, OJJDP has directed its funding at three main goals. First, it sought to separate and ultimately remove all juveniles from adult jails. Second, it sought to remove from juvenile correction facilities all "status offenders"—those individuals whose offenses would not be deemed offenses if committed by adults, e.g., incorrigibility, running away from home, alcohol violations, and truancy. (States could not receive OJJDP funds unless they agreed to these policies.) Third, and most important, it sought through a variety of research grants and special projects to spread its liberal philosophy, promote children's legal "rights," and generally protect juvenile offenders from the "evils" of the criminal justice system. By the early 1980's the first, generally laudable, goal was largely accomplished, and the focus remained on the last, far broader endeavor.

Through a series of strong and forceful moves on the part of the Reagan Administration, the Office of Juvenile Justice and Delinquency Prevention has been turned around as have few other offices in the government. It currently reflects a strong law enforcement view and is recognized across the juvenile justice community for its effectiveness, concern for juvenile victims, and commitment to holding juveniles accountable for their crimes. The following pages describe how this change was accomplished: how the expenditure of juvenile justice funds has been completely altered; how the OJJDP staff has been brought under control; and how the "iron triangle" of bureaucrat, congressional staffer, and grantee has been emasculated.

The First Eighteen Months of the Reagan Administration

When Ed Meese came to Washington as Counselor to the President after the 1980 election, his contact with the federal government had been limited to serving as a member of the National Advisory Committee to the Office of Juvenile Justice and Delinquency Prevention. From that experience he has said he realized one thing: He did not like OJJDP. He did not like the way the Office spent money, and he did not like the philosophy it espoused. He knew that one of the objectives he wanted to accomplish while in Washington was to shut down the Office.

To the shock of those who had shared in OJJDP's generous funding over the years, President Reagan's first budget requested no money for OJJDP. The Justice Department, headed by Attorney General William French Smith, argued that OJJDP's mission of removing children from adult jails had been accomplished and further funding was not needed. Congress was not impressed with the Administration's arguments. In fact, spurred by clamoring from the juvenile justice lobby, it provided more funds for the Office! The Administration has sought to abolish the agency each year since, but Congress has responded by doling out even higher funding.

However, since the Administration was initially determined to close down OJJDP, the decision was made not to appoint an Administrator of the Office. Accordingly, the Attorney General appointed an acting Administrator, a career Justice Department lawyer who was well versed on the workings of the Office, named Charles Lauer. Lauer, an able bureaucrat who recognized the potential hot spot he was in, worked to keep both sides relatively happy; he provided enough money to the juvenile justice lobby and the Office's constituents so they would not protest too loudly, while maintaining a low profile himself within the Justice Department.

Lauer stayed on as the acting Administrator until November 1982. During that time not much changed at OJJDP: the money appropriated by Congress (against the Administration's wishes) continued to be spent along traditional liberal lines. By 1982, however, it had become clear to the Department of Justice, as well as to Ed Meese, then Counselor to the President, that Congress was not going to acquiesce and eliminate the Office. Therefore a permanent Administrator was clearly needed.

Appointment of a New Administrator

In November 1982, Attorney General Smith appointed Alfred S. Regnery as the acting Administrator of OJJDP. Regnery, a Deputy Assistant Attorney General in the Land and Natural Resources Division at the Justice Department and former counsel to Senator Paul Laxalt, was an articulate and outspoken attorney who had received his early political training in the conservative movement.

Regnery had spent three or four weeks prior to his appointment researching the OJJDP and educating himself on juvenile justice policy and philosophy. While in private law practice, Regnery had had no experience in working with juvenile justice issues; Smith appointed him largely because of his administrative abilities and because Smith needed someone in the Office who was a reliable Administration spokesman and who would stand up to predictable attacks from the Office's liberal constituency.

"I knew the perils of taking on an office such as OJJDP on an acting basis," Regnery said. "I had a choice of either doing nothing and remaining anonymous while I was being confirmed or confronting the issues head on, risking the possibility that I would become vulnerable during the confirmation process. Because I had been a former staff member on the Senate committee which would confirm me, because of my close ties with Senator Laxalt, and because of support that I would get from the Administration, I thought that I could take a tough stand right from the start and still survive confirmation."

Regnery decided to approach his new job as if he had already been confirmed. On the day following his appointment, at his first meeting with OJJDP staff, he stated that he was a strong conservative who was going to say what he believed. He said that he expected the staff to be professional and serve the new Administration. He then took immediate action to change the existing grant system.

But Regnery's forebodings about the perils of serving in an acting capacity prior to confirmation proved to be correct—if underestimated. He was subject to a barrage of criticism. Congress, the liberal justice establishment, and the media were outraged that someone who actually believed in punishing juvenile criminals should administer the government office charged with "saving children." In an editorial entitled "A Fox for the Juvenile Justice Coop," *The New York Times* said President Reagan's "choice of Mr. Regnery seems designed to destroy the agency." *The New York Times, The Washington Post*, and other papers demanded that he not be confirmed. Regnery was called back to the Senate Judiciary Committee twice after his initial confirmation hearing, once in closed session, but he was finally confirmed by the full Senate by a vote of 69 to 22.

During the confirmation process, the Justice Department received a telegram from a pediatrician in Madison, Wisconsin, where Regnery had previously lived, indicating that the pediatrician had some confidential information about Regnery. The doctor charged that Regnery was psychologically unfit for the job and, if confirmed, would be a menace to the health of American children. The FBI was dispatched to Madison to investigate, and after an exhaustive search, was able to turn up nothing to substantiate the pediatrician's claim. It later turned out that the pediatrician's daughter was a large grantee of OJJDP, and thus was possibly concerned that if Regnery were confirmed her grant might be terminated.

"There was never any substance to what this doctor was saying,"

Regnery said. "I knew there wasn't. The point was that it gave the people who were otherwise opposing my nomination some ammunition with which to criticize me. *The Washington Post,* for example, would refer to the allegations every time it mentioned my name, which it did at least ten times before I was confirmed, even though there was no substance to the story. When the truth finally was learned, the *Post* hardly mentioned it."

Still, Regnery retained confidence through the confirmation process. Although he had a tough fight, he credited his knowledge of Washington and his experience working on the Senate staff with helping him to persevere. "If I had come to Washington from elsewhere, and gone through what I went through in confirmation, I probably would have withdrawn," Regnery said. "But having worked on the Hill and having a fairly good idea of what went on in this town, I knew what I was up against, I knew where my support and my opposition lay, and I knew how to handle it."

Regnery says he recalls sitting by himself in a private office behind the Judiciary Committee while the Committee was deliberating his confirmation. "Senator Laxalt walked in. He was, of course, my former employer and a good friend; he told me that if I wanted to withdraw, he would support that decision, but if that I wanted to stick with it and go through confirmation, he would support me in that regard as well. Having that kind of support, I decided to stick with it."

One lesson reinforced by the confirmation process was that normal standards of decency do not apply in Washington politics; even Regnery's family was not immune from assault. "It gave me a taste of things to come. I realized that liberals view their government money very dearly, and don't like other people fooling around with what they think is theirs by right," Regnery said. He also didn't waver from his original position. He was quoted, in fact, in *The Washington Post* in April 1983, just before his confirmation hearing, as follows:

> There is an interesting phenomenon in juvenile justice, a network of people involved in the system . . . . they talk to each other every day. Rumors are rampant. That network has a fear that the conventional wisdom, the traditional orthodoxy, will be challenged. . . . [T]hey are right. I think there needs to be a breath of fresh air.[1]

Controlling the Bureaucracy

When he arrived, Regnery found OJJDP to be a paradigm of the interworkings of the iron triangle. Most individuals within the small community of "experts" were well known to each other; career paths led from the bureaucracy to Capitol Hill staffs, into the grantee organizations and back again. So tightly interlocked was this network that Regnery had employees of grantees and Capitol Hill staffers working on temporary assignments in his own office. Open channels of communication between the various parts of the network worked to bolster the status quo and ward off challenges to the system that was providing an ample livelihood to all. There was even a newsletter, published in Washington, and subscribed to by those in the network, ever ready to start rumors and personally attack anyone who proved a threat.

"They had an amazing communications network," Regnery said. "I would make a decision and within half an hour be called by one of Senator Specter's staffers, wondering, in amazement, if I had really done what she had heard. Then I would be called by a grantee in California to tell me what a bad decision I had made. And all the while anxious bureaucrats would be waiting at my door to learn whether they had heard of the decision correctly. From time to time, I would even plant some disinformation to see how fast it came back. True to form, the fictionalized event would be back on my desk on the same day."

In dismantling the iron triangle establishment, Regnery directed his first efforts at the OJJDP bureaucracy over which he had direct control. "An iron triangle is like a three-legged stool," he said. "If you pull out one leg the stool will fall over. By tightly controlling and restructuring your own bureaucracy, you sever long-standing connections and rip out that leg."

As a first step in controlling his career staff, Regnery moved to install as many political appointees as possible. Tom Dailey, his special assistant, was hired on the first day. James M. Wootton, a University of Virginia Law School graduate, was brought on speedily as a consultant, and later became Deputy Administrator. Regnery never fails to emphasize the importance of hiring compatible and trustworthy political appointees. "You simply cannot do it without them. Some people have tried to run their agencies with only the bureaucrats, and they have failed miserably. The bureaucrats capture you right away. They have their own agenda, which is largely to protect themselves and the interests which they represent. Those interests are very different from ours," Regnery stressed.

It didn't really matter that his political staff was not well versed in juvenile justice policy. "None of us were," said Regnery. "I didn't know much about it when I was appointed; Jim Wootton had been working on Social Security issues. So none of us were experts. But that didn't really matter. The important thing was that we were loyal to the Administration and to each other—we knew where we were going and had the ability to learn the issues quickly." Throughout his tenure Regnery has maintained a ratio of one political staffer for each 12 careerists.

Regnery and Wootton made a careful analysis of the structure of the Office, who was placed where, and what sorts of shifts could be made. They found only a small cadre of people who were adamantly opposed to what they were doing. But those people were outspoken and provided crucial links to the staffs of the Senate and House committees and to many of the grantees. Particularly troublesome was a group of four or five old-time employees dedicated to making life as miserable as possible for anybody from the Reagan Administration. "I had even been told about them before I took over, and was again told when I got here," Regnery said. He knew that he couldn't fire them, but that he had to split them up in one way or another. And he did.

One case involved a senior-level employee who had been acting Administrator during the Carter Administration. When Regnery arrived, this individual had a budget of some $40 million, 20 employees working for him, and the ability to stay in close contact with the liberal juvenile justice lobby. He was openly scornful of the Reagan Administration's policies. In one of his bolder personnel moves, Regnery removed this individual from his job on the very day that he was confirmed in office. He gave the employee the title of Technical Advisor to the Administrator, put him in an office with no windows, and stripped him of his duties. Shortly thereafter, the man was detailed to another department, where he was to continue to do research on juvenile crime in the nation's subway systems. Two and one-half years later, he is still there. All of this was accomplished without violating any right guaranteed the employee by the civil service laws.

The rest of the troublesome employees were scattered around in different divisions under new supervisors, given new duties, and closely watched to see that they performed according to their job descriptions. The Administrator also shuffled around all the Division Directors—there were four of them—into new positions, effectively breaking up cliques that had developed in the Office and grabbing the staff's attention. Regnery also rescinded all delegations of authority, assuring that only he could sign anything official, including grant adjustment notices and personnel actions. "I got immediate control; *everything* had to go through me. It told the staff, clearly and unequivocally, that I was the boss," he said.

But there was also a positive side to relations with the career staff. "We went out of our way to find the career people who were trustworthy and who did a good job, and to reward them," Regnery said. "We used every personnel tactic we could find—cash awards, promotions, commendations, as well as the rating system—to reward those people who deserved it." In all their personnel matters, Regnery and his political staff went out of their way to be fair, relying on the counsel of their personnel office. As a result, only one personnel grievance was filed against them during their entire tenure, and that was dismissed as meritless. The effect was very positive; Regnery soon found that he had a loyal group of staff people who were interested in what he was doing and who worked to help him accomplish his goals.

The Other Leg of the Triangle: Grants and Grantees

OJJDP's primary function is to distribute money for the purpose of "improving" the juvenile justice system. Its $70-million budget is divided into two main areas. Sixty percent goes directly to the states. The remainder is devoted to discretionary grants for training, research, and special projects. Since 1974, OJJDP had spent nearly half a billion dollars to implement Birch Bayh's statute. For example, between 1980 and the end of 1982, the Office had spent over $16 million on a project promoting "children's rights" through litigation, lobbying in the state legislatures, and a variety of other methods. Tens of millions of dollars had been spent on "delinquency prevention," even after an evaluation of the programs found that virtually no delinquency had been prevented. The Office had spent $8 million on "Alternative Education," a project through which special schools were established for delinquent children. Some $6 million was spent on a project disingenuously called Capacity Building, a project by which funds were channeled to political friends of the Carter Administration.

Regnery and his politically appointed staff immediately started reviewing all of the grants. They discovered that grants could not be terminated except for cause, meaning the grantee had to have done something fairly drastic in order to justify cancellation. On the other hand, if a grantee came to the end of his grant period designated in the original document, and still had money left, he had to get permission from the Administrator to use the rest of the money, a process known as a "no-cost extension."

"We revamped the whole policy," Regnery said. "We implemented a new policy on no-cost extensions, making the grantee justify receiving one. We adopted a policy that we would not approve continuations unless we felt the project was consistent with the goals of the Administration." By the end of his first year, Regnery did a calculation of projects that had not been extended or that had been cancelled. He found that a total of 123 grants, valued at over $67 million, had been terminated.

Many were controversial. For example, in his first week as acting Administrator, Regnery received a no-cost extension request for a group in Milwaukee called Jewish Vocational Services. They hadn't used up all of their grant money and wanted more time in which to spend it. Regnery asked about what the grantee was doing, and was told that they were helping delinquent youth get jobs. Regnery then asked his staff to find out for how many youths the agency had actually gotten jobs. Professional staffers seemed surprised by the question, but after a few days they reported that the government was spending far too much money for each job found and that kids coming out of the Milwaukee courts who did not go to the grantee had a better record than those who did! Regnery refused to sign the grant extension notice.

"Within a day or so, I knew what I was in for," Regnery said. "I got frantic calls from the head of the organization in Milwaukee, telling me I had no right not to extend them, and that they would sue me. I had calls from Senators and Congressmen, and the press. I was accused of being anti-Semitic, capricious, and unfair. I was advised by the General Counsel that they had no grounds on which to sue. I stood my ground and never heard from anybody again after a week or so."

Regnery and his staff also visited many of the old grantees to find out first hand what they were doing. They would often arrive unannounced asking to see the books and records, to meet the staff, and to observe their projects. One such visit to a group on the West Coast was particularly illuminating. This "youth advocacy" grantee had received $634,000 from OJJDP between 1978 and 1982. Regnery's staffer was astonished at what he saw. There were left-wing political posters in the lobby. "Gay rights" was obviously a big issue with them. People were sitting around planning rallies and projects. It looked like something out of the sixties. The final straw was when the staffer noticed a large picture of President and Mrs. Reagan on the wall; it was being used as a dart board. Funding for this project was not continued.

Another case that materialized prior to Regnery's confirmation involved an organization in St. Louis, Missouri, called the National Juvenile Law Center. It had received over $2 million from the Office to sue state and local officials on behalf of delinquent children. Harry Swanger, the head of the organization, was a long-time legal services lawyer who depended totally on OJJDP for his funds. Swanger was a regular in Regnery's office, trying to convince him that the project had to be continued. When the expiration date came, Regnery declined to give Swanger a new grant, even though Swanger had told him he would sue if cut off.

Swanger sued Regnery on the remarkable grounds that once the federal government starts to fund public interest litigation, it has a duty to continue funding indefinitely until that litigation is completed. The case, which had serious implications for the Legal Services Corporation, was filed in the District of Columbia District Court. At the trial level,

Swanger was successful. The case was immediately appealed to the D.C. Circuit Court of Appeals where it was summarily reversed, Regnery winning on all counts.

There were many more cases. "I was accused of everything you could imagine," Regnery said. "When I terminated a contract to a minority-owned firm, I was accused of being a racist. When I declined to re-fund an organization headed by a wealthy woman lawyer in Washington, D.C., I was accused publicly of being a sexist. People simply couldn't believe that I was carrying out what I said I was going to do: to fund projects that were compatible with the Administration's conservative philosophy, projects that could make a positive difference in the juvenile justice system, and to terminate everything else that I could."

But Regnery realized that simply cutting off the old grantees was only half the battle: He had $70 million of new money appropriated by the Congress. Congress said he had to spend it all. "We immediately tried to establish what our priorities would be by talking to as many people as possible, to get as much information as we could about juvenile delinquency," Regnery said. Particular efforts were made to maintain close contact with conservative sources outside the usual OJJDP networks. It became apparent that the most pressing issue was serious juvenile crime, i.e., the large number of major crimes such as rape, robbery, and murder committed by minors. This was an issue OJJDP had always ignored. Other new issues included the victimization of children through child abuse and through crime, and crime in the schools.

In tackling the grant process, Regnery and his aides learned their statute almost by memory. "It was very important to know just what we had to do, and what was merely traditional practice but not really required," he said. The vague nature of the statute provided many avenues for changing the program. "Congress had to make many compromises to get this law passed, and where they did, the law was very broadly worded. I would determine what I wanted to do first, and then figure whether I could do it under the statute. In almost every case, I could find a way to do what I wanted."

The new team at OJJDP was entrepreneurial in funding new conservative programs. Whenever it made such a grant, the "iron triangle" would clang with alarm; charges would be leveled saying the intent of the statute was being violated. "I would quickly respond that if that's what they intended, they should have said so in the statute," Regnery said. "Legally, of course, it was the words of the statute, not the assumed intentions that counted."

Because the Office had been intended to be staffed by liberals and run for liberal purposes, the statute had provided OJJDP with ample discretion which its originators now began to rue. In particular, the statute allowed Regnery to provide some grants on a noncompetitive sole-source basis. "It was clear that the competitive process did not guarantee that the best applicant would get the grant. The application usually had nothing to do with the way the project would actually be run," Regnery said. "Instead, the best grantsman, or people with the closest ties to the agency bureaucracy would win. Merit had little to do with it."

Liberals, of course, objected to the new use of the noncompetitive provision they had placed in the statute. Accordingly, in 1984 they eliminated it. This did not mean, however, that Regnery lost control over the grant process. The competitive review process continued to operate through small panels of outside experts (who evaluate and rank the grant applications). Following initial confrontation between the political appointees and the career staff over who would select the members of these peer review panels, Regnery was able to ensure that the panels were balanced and honestly run. Through persistent efforts Regnery was able to substantially alter both the population of grantees and the content of direction of the grants. "I knew that I was outraging the liberals, but in some ways, that made my job easier," Regnery says. "It laid out the proper course more clearly. I would go up to the Senate to testify in an oversight hearing, and listen to Senators Metzenbaum and Specter rant and rave about all the awful things we were doing. That just confirmed to me that we were doing the right thing."

Seizing the Agenda Initiative: Serious Crime and Chronic Offenders

The one issue that seemed most potent, and where Regnery thought the Administration could have the most effect, was the chronic juvenile offender problem. Most serious juvenile crime—about 75 percent—is committed by 5 to 10 percent of the juvenile offender population. These offenders often commit literally hundreds of felony offenses during their juvenile years. The juvenile courts have virtually no control over them; they often go on to become career criminals. In the past, OJJDP had not concerned itself with this group of offenders. In fact, the liberal juvenile justice community would hardly admit that they existed; they were difficult people for the liberals to deal with philosophically, since these young chronic offenders demonstrated the inability of the juvenile court system to function effectively.

The chronic juvenile offender became the core around which much of the new policy would be based. In every speech Regnery and Deputy Administrator Wootton gave, they hammered away at the necessity of doing something about these young criminals. Similarly, in press interviews, panel discussions and anywhere people would listen, the policy was expounded: Identify, arrest, prosecute, and lock up young chronic offenders. The National Advisory Committee to OJJDP also issued and distributed a report entitled *Serious Juvenile Crime—a Redirected Federal Effort* strongly supporting the new policy and condemning past neglect of the problem.

In addition, the Office set up new programs to deal with the phenomenon of the *habitual offender*. It established programs in 13 major urban prosecutors' offices, providing funds to hire special prosecutors and investigators to prosecute habitual offenders. This program became one of the most popular the Office funded. In Cook County, Illinois, for example, over 500 young offenders were prosecuted in the new program in the first year, each of whom had been arrested more than five times. Considering that each of the offenders probably had committed ten serious offenses for each arrest, the young offenders who were locked up had committed in the aggregate up to 25,000 offenses. The prosecutorial success rate was also exceptionally high; nearly 90 percent of the cases brought to court were successfully prosecuted.

A similar program was funded within police departments to target the chronic offender. An independent evaluation showed that by using techniques developed for adult offenders, police could identify and arrest chronic juvenile offenders, collecting good evidence that resulted in convictions and a reduction in the crime rate. Early opposition, loudly expressed by the OJJDP liberal constituency, subsided as time went on. The liberals realized that the Reagan Administration's concept of juvenile justice was so strong that it was basically beyond criticism. At the end of 1985, Regnery was asked to appear on the PBS television show "Crossfire" to debate the issue. The show was canceled when PBS could find no one to debate for the liberal side.

Networking for Change

Regnery set about finding allies who would support him. These included professionals in the juvenile justice field who agreed with the Administration's position on juvenile crime, politically active conservatives, and scholars concerned about social policy but who had not necessarily been involved in juvenile justice issues before. The National Council of Juvenile and Family Court Judges situated in Reno, Nevada, was both supportive and helpful. It had received millions of dollars from OJJDP in the past, but basically agreed with Regnery's policies. Similarly, the National District Attorney Association, law enforcement groups, and academics who had studied the issue agreed both that serious juvenile crime needed to be addressed and that OJJDP, as it had been run during the Carter Administration, had contributed nothing to protecting society.

Another helpful group was OJJDP's National Advisory Committee, a group of 15 outside advisors appointed by the President. Although Committee members were supposed to serve for staggered terms, Reagan had appointed all 15 early in his first term. The Committee was strongly supportive, both managerially and programmatically—so much so, in fact, that Congress abolished it in 1984.

One more early ally was Bob Woodson, a black conservative and head of the National Center for Neighborhood Enterprise, and a long-time critic of OJJDP. Woodson had testified in Congress during the Carter Administration that OJJDP's policies neglected minority youth and often had an adverse effect on them. Woodson stated that all of the Office's money was spent on doing things that helped middle-class white delinquents, and virtually none benefited poor blacks. Senator Bayh was so upset by the allegation that his statute might actually be promoting white liberal elitism that he appointed two outsiders to look into the allegations that Woodson had made. The reviewers concluded that Woodson was right; their report was, accordingly, buried. In any case, Woodson supported Regnery strongly in what he was trying to do. Woodson says:

> Since its inception in 1975, the Office of Juvenile Justice and Delinquency Prevention's policies and programs have been injurious to low-income and minority youngsters. While the agency was created to control and prevent delinquent behavior—a major concern of the minority community—once funds were appropriated, OJJDP emphasized the deinstitutionalization of status offenders most of whom were white and middle-class. Under the leadership of Al Regnery, however, this concern has dramatically improved with the emphasis shifting toward the repression of violent youth crime and assistance to low-income neighborhood groups capable of exercising social control over their young people. Al Regnery supported the Office's first conference that brought together hundreds of minority youth workers from around the country so they could share their experiences of dealing effectively with youth crime. Al Regnery is an outstanding individual who is committed to the original goal of OJJDP to control and prevent youth crime.[2]

"I found myself in the ironic position of being a conservative Reagan appointee whose policies were admired by minorities, while running an Office which had been accused during the Carter Administration of being racist," Regnery said. "That kind of support helped my state of mind considerably."

Although Regnery's approach had outraged the liberal community, he found support among the "front line" workers in the juvenile justice system. Meetings were held with district attorneys, police chiefs, judges, foundation executives, academics, and other professionals. Regnery and his staff went to juvenile institutions, sat in juvenile courts, visited shelters, police lockups, and wilderness camps. He found considerable dissatisfaction with what OJJDP had done in the past, and recognized immediately that most critical juvenile justice issues had been ignored. "Since the office was founded," Regnery said, "it was obvious that most of the money had been spent trying to undermine the criminal justice system rather than trying to make it better. Many of the people working within the system, on the front lines, had been largely neglected. It was those people we wanted to assist. Contacts at these levels built support for our policies."

Liberals Attack the Process, Not the Substance: Crime in Schools

Increasingly unable to confront Regnery on the substance of policy, the liberal establishment turned to other avenues of attack. All of OJJDP's grants and actions were reviewed in minute detail. For example, during the fall of 1983, Regnery participated in a White House working group on the issue of crime in schools. Chaired by Gary Bauer, a Deputy Under Secretary at the Department of Education (ED), with the close cooperation of Mike Horowitz, Counsel to the Director, at the Office of Management and Budget (OMB), the group prepared a report entitled "Disorder in Our Schools," which was delivered to the President in January 1984.

The Justice Department had been involved in school crime during the Carter Administration, but the emphasis had been completely different. The old philosophy centered on the belief that crime in schools was the fault of the schools, not of the students; everything should be done to protect "student rights" rather than to hold the students accountable. "Disorder in Our Schools" took a different approach, calling for a return to "old-fashioned discipline." Liberals hit the roof. Congressman Pat Williams held hearings on school crime, in which he claimed that tougher discipline was racially discriminatory and stated that discipline "is indeed not a problem which should attract the undivided attention of the most powerful public official in the world. So it is puzzling why the President would focus the Nation's attention on discipline."[3]

One of the recommendations in the report was that the federal government establish a center to provide assistance and training to school districts concerned with crime in schools, and to make school crime an ongoing issue. Because of its large discretionary budget, OJJDP was given responsibility to fund the center. Regnery began a search for the proper candidate to head the center, ultimately selecting George Nicholson, a top aide to Governor George Deukmejian of California. While in the California Attorney General's office as Deukmejian's assistant, Nicholson had set up a California School Safety Center and had devised many innovative and worthwhile projects throughout the state to suppress school crime. Following discussions with Regnery and Wootton, Nicholson approached Pepperdine University in Southern California, which agreed to sponsor the program. After extensive negotiations with OJJDP, a grant for over $3 million was given to Pepperdine, to establish the National School Safety Center.

Liberals immediately attacked the grant. The charge was led by Senator Howard Metzenbaum; in hearings and in the press, Metzenbaum and others blasted the grant to the National School Safety Center, alleging that Ed Meese had intervened to see that the grant went to his "buddies." (Meese's name appeared on a list of contributors to Pepperdine and he had once known Nicholson professionally in California.) The issue came up in Meese's confirmation hearings to be Attorney General and was examined by Special Prosecutor Jacob Stein, who concluded that Meese had done nothing wrong, and had not even known about the grant. That did not, of course, deter Metzenbaum, who went right on with his accusations.

Senator Specter felt compelled to take up the battle as well, ordering the General Accounting Office (GAO), an arm of Congress, to do a full investigation of the way the Center had been funded, whether it was performing the duties that it had agreed to perform, and whether employees were being treated unfairly. The GAO, after a month or so, concluded that everything was being done according to the book, and gave the National School Safety Center a clean bill of health.

Going by the Book

As the case of the National School Safety Center demonstrated, it had become apparent from the beginning of Regnery's tenure that everything he did would be under scrutiny. Those opposed to him would try to "get him" on anything they could find. Accordingly, he and the rest of his political staff realized that they would have to give their opponents as little ammunition as possible. The Regnery Rule became "*Do everything by the book.*"

Regnery stated, "As with the National School Safety Center, most of this was a smoke screen for the real issues. But liberal efforts to confront us directly on the issues lacked public credibility. They started looking around for other ways to discredit us. They became frantic to find some apparent impropriety." Accordingly, everything Regnery did was checked by Charles Lauer, a career lawyer serving as the General Counsel of the Office of Justice Programs who had been Regnery's predecessor as

Acting Administrator of OJJDP, before action was taken, to be certain it was permitted within the OJJDP statute. Regnery and Wootten were also particularly careful about financial matters, clearing every questionable item with the Comptroller's office, the Budget office, or the General Counsel.

Predictably, Congress ordered the General Accounting Office to do a far-ranging audit and review of Regnery's operation only six months after Regnery had become acting Administrator. GAO was asked to look at whether Regnery was complying with the law in a number of areas, whether he made grants to unqualified grantees, whether he had a "hit list" of dissident employees whose careers he was jeopardizing, whether his travel costs were excessive, and several other far-ranging issues. After an exhaustive investigation which took nearly a year, GAO concluded that everything was in order and, much to the liberals' disappointment, the investigation closed. Subsequently, congressmen asked for more investigations, and each time GAO came up with nothing whatsoever.

The "do everything by the book" principle was essential to the massive changes Regnery brought about in OJJDP. Any fault in management practice that did occur served as a beachhead for general attacks. A case in point was an $800,000 grant to American University to study the treatment of children in pornographic magazines. A survey of thousands of cartoons, pictures, and articles in *Penthouse, Playboy,* and *Hustler* magazines revealed that children were routinely depicted as possible participants in sexual acts with adults. Much of the material was presumably intended to be "merely facetious." But the fact that children were habitually depicted in this degrading and frightening manner, and that the idea of sexual relations between adults and children was routinely presented as a suitable topic for "humor," could only have the effect of lowering public moral standards and debasing attitudes in this critical area.

The grant had been awarded on a sole-source basis after a career staff member had written a memo stating the project could be completed at a lower cost. "Obviously the liberals were appalled at the subject matter of the research," Regnery said, "but by spending far too much money on it and awarding it on a noncompetitive basis, we gave them issues that they could use against us much more effectively than trying to criticize the substance of the grant." Regnery added:

> There is no question that the American University grant became an albatross. Once we got into it we couldn't get out, and it provided an easy target for those opposing everything we were doing to criticize us, which they did very successfully. Although the subject matter of the grant was something that needed to be done and something that fit in with the

rest of our program, we neglected to take proper steps at an early stage
to make it a credible project.

Choosing the Battles

Regnery found that there were new challenges, and new decisions to be
made, on a daily basis. "One of the first things that anybody in a position
like mine has to realize is that you cannot take on all of the fights that
come along and expect to win them. You have to learn to pick the ones
that you think you can win, and to try to avoid those that you will lose,"
Regnery said. "One of the things that I learned when I worked for Senator
Paul Laxalt was that you should never get out front on an issue unless you
have commitments from people who support what you are doing to
actively back you up."

As battles loomed, Regnery, with help from Wootton and others on his
staff, tried to predict what kind of reaction they would get, who would be
there to help them out when the going got tough, and make their decisions accordingly. One particular example stands out. OJJDP's formula
grant program, by which money is provided to the states, includes a long
set of regulations that had been promulgated before Regnery took over.
The regulations were bureaucratic, oppressive, and typified the way federal agencies fill interstices in vague statutes. In reviewing them, Regnery
concluded that they would be an ideal candidate for "deregulation."

Regnery talked to Mike Horowitz, the Counsel to the Director at OMB,
who introduced Regnery to OMB lawyers who helped to draft new
regulations. The old regulations filled about 15 pages of small type; the
new ones were less than one page long. The new regulations essentially
got the Office out of the business of regulating what the states did. They
were, of course, still in accord with the statute, and much closer to the
Reagan Administration's policy on relations with state governments. But
Regnery knew that promulgating such regulations would cause a storm
in the juvenile justice community. The House and Senate committees
would react negatively. Even those within the Administration who tried
to avoid controversy would be critical.

Regnery's staff checked around to find who would back them up on the
regulation fight, calling the National Council of Juvenile and Family
Court Judges, the National District Attorneys Association, and various
law enforcement organizations. Their calls were met with a yawn. "In
fact," Regnery said, "the only people we could find who really liked the
idea were the lawyers at OMB, and we knew that they would be no help
at all." Even the people in the states who administered the programs,
most of whom were bureaucrats themselves, liked the regulations that

existed and the way they worked. The result was that the regulation fight was abandoned, and the old bureaucratic regulations were kept in place.

Virtues of a Positive Agenda: Missing and Victimized Children

According to the traditional juvenile justice philosophy, so well reflected by OJJDP policy prior to 1982, the only "victims" in the juvenile justice system were the offenders themselves. The reason they were offenders, of course, was because they had been victimized by society, and they needed the full force of the juvenile justice system, and OJJDP, to protect them. The fact that nearly one-third of all crime victims in the country were forced to rely on the juvenile courts for protection against criminals, and that millions of children were victimized by crime themselves, was an embarrassment to the old Office, since these victims were living proof that some "children" were brutal victimizers of the rest of society.

Regnery, who had been involved in the victims' movement for several years, was aware of the impetus for change the movement could provide within the criminal and juvenile justice systems. Victims and those who are afraid they might be victims are potentially a strong political constituency for law enforcement. Sympathy for victims could be capitalized on to bring about changes that would otherwise be blocked. But although the victims' movement had made some progress in the adult criminal justice system, it remained, in 1982, in its infancy as far as juveniles were concerned. Thus it afforded a good opportunity to solicit the help of large segments of the population—those concerned with child victimization, as well as those concerned that they might be victims of juvenile offenders—as supporters for OJJDP's new efforts to bring change.

Shortly after he arrived on the scene, Wootton came up with the idea of establishing a national center to deal with the problem of missing and exploited children. NBC's showing of the film "Adam," about a missing child case, provided considerable impetus. A center was subsequently established with OJJDP funding. Its purpose was to coordinate missing children's activities on a national basis. Operating a toll-free telephone number which people with information about missing children would call, the center would be tied into the FBI's national crime information center computer, and would provide information to people across the country on missing and exploited children. Congress then followed suit, passing legislation that Regnery and Wootton helped to write, mandating that the center continue in largely the same form that had been created by OJJDP.

The missing children's effort is one of the most successful public relations campaigns of the Reagan Administration. In less than two years, the issue went from one that virtually no one knew about, to one that was on everybody's mind. Although there have been a few negative press stories, public reaction to the campaign has been overwhelmingly positive. As Regnery stated:

> Virtually nobody disagreed with us on the missing children's issue. They couldn't. It was a case of being at the right place at the right time and capitalizing on an issue that people are concerned about. Our campaign with missing children diffused a lot of other negative attitudes that might have been generated among certain constituencies and made us innumerable friends. Because of it, we were able to move forward with other things that we never would have been able to do otherwise.

Another consequence of the missing children's issue was the fact that it gave Regnery and Wootton an avenue by which to attack liberals' pernicious efforts to "emancipate" children from their parents. Most missing children have actually run away from home, ending up in the streets of major cities, often supporting themselves by drugs, theft, prostitution, and pornography. However, because of the movement of the 1960's and 1970's, to give children "rights" and emancipate them—a movement in which OJJDP had participated to a considerable extent—the law enforcement system had no control whatever over such children. Liberals found that allowing such children to live in the streets was one of the prices that had to be paid for its broader philosophy. By demonstrating that missing children were often the products of a social policy gone awry, OJJDP was able to garner considerable support for the notion that children weren't simply "little adults," free to go their own way regardless of the desires of their parents. Because of the concern for missing children that had been generated, the argument gained considerable credibility that it would have otherwise lacked.

Getting the Message Out: Many Public Relations Vehicles

OJJDP's function, as it was established by Senator Bayh, was to change national policy. He, his colleagues in the Congress, and their staffs, together with the rest of the "iron triangle," wrote the Juvenile Justice and Delinquency Prevention Act in such a way as to have maximum impact on public opinion and public policy affecting juvenile delinquency. Because much of that impact was anathema to the Reagan Administration, the new Administration had not only to undo what was being promoted by the Office, but also to make its own views known. Although a great deal could be accomplished through the grant-making process, a considerable amount had to come directly from the OJJDP as well.

For one thing, OJJDP had published, over the years, many booklets and monographs on various aspects of juvenile policy: on the courts, on the role of the police, on deinstitutionalization, and on many other topics. All were ultimately reviewed by the OJJDP political staff, with an eye toward whether they projected the policies of the new Administration. Those that did not were no longer distributed to the general public as policy statements of the Office, although they were kept available for reference purposes.

On the positive side, Regnery adopted a policy of making his position clearly known to the public through interviews with the press, through speeches, and through writings. "Over three years I must have made at least 100 speeches. I went to conferences, to meetings, to conventions. I spoke to groups of police officers, to prosecutors, to judges, to academics, literally anywhere where I could get a crowd of people who had something to do with the issue. I found that I could use such forums as a place to make policy statements, and then take the policy statements that I had given and have them published or otherwise written about," Regnery said.

These speeches became the policy statements for the Office and were widely distributed. Many were reprinted in publications going to the juvenile justice field. Others OJJDP published itself and mailed to people who might be interested. Regnery also adopted a program of publishing bulletins on particular topics, expounding the Office's policies on issues that it felt necessary to get to the public. Copies were sent to the media, to policy-makers, to juvenile justice officials, and to others who might be interested. This again resulted in interviews with newspapers, magazines, television and radio stations, providing added opportunities to present the conservative viewpoint.

Finally, Regnery adopted a policy of writing as much as he could for publication. He found a ready market for articles and op-ed pieces about juvenile justice and related issues. "I tried to aim my comments to nonprofessionals and to those other than the usual recipients, in order to broaden the scope of our market," Regnery said. In one particularly good example, he wrote an article entitled "Getting Away With Murder— Why the Juvenile Justice System Needs an Overhaul" for *Policy Review* magazine, and thereafter mailed 10,000 copies of reprints to policy-makers, public officials, and others across the country. "The response from the *Policy Review* piece was astounding," Regnery said. "I was interviewed on the *Today* show, and there was a piece that went out on the AP wire that was published in hundreds of papers. I appeared on PBS *Crossfire* and on the MacNeil-Lehrer Show. I was interviewed by many small papers and radio stations and the entire article was re-printed as the lead editorial in the *Hartford Courant*'s Sunday editorial supplement."

In all of his speeches and writings, Regnery always reiterated the same themes: Concentrate on serious crime; be concerned with victimization of children; and abandon the unsuccessful policies of the past. People listened, and what he said slowly became accepted policy.

Beyond making speeches and writing articles for immediate impact, Regnery also recognized the role of academic research in the long-term debate over policy. Early in his tenure, he contacted Harvard Professor James Q. Wilson, whose books Regnery had read and respected. Wilson was one of the leading academic spokesmen advocating a sane policy on crime. After making several trips to Harvard to visit with Wilson, Regnery agreed to provide Harvard with a grant to study the entire juvenile justice system. Wilson, his associates, and Regnery then picked a group of about 25 practitioners, academics, and others, representing different points of view—all of whom were highly credible—but who in the aggregate would take a fairly hard-headed approach toward the issues. The group met for 12 days at the Kennedy School for discussions, the results of which were to be combined in a book outlining the weaknesses of the existing juvenile justice system and providing a series of recommendations for change.

A subsequent undertaking, chaired by Wilson and Harvard Professor Glenn Loury, set out to review government involvement in family issues: how families affect juvenile crime, and how effective programs might be developed to strengthen the family structure. Loury and Wilson are currently working on a book stemming from that project, including papers and critiques from a number of noted experts.

Conclusion

The philosophical thrust of OJJDP has been completely reversed. Few if any of the original liberal grantee organizations still receive support. This is a degree of change unusual within the federal government over the last five years. Regnery and his political staff at the Office of Juvenile Justice were successful largely because they staked out a position in which they believed, stuck to that position even in the face of controversy, and developed programs that adhered to the position they had developed. They took the high ground in terms of the debate and did not let themselves get dragged into the personal attacks and muckraking that their opponents seemed to relish.

Additionally, Regnery believes that he came to office at an opportune time, a time when there was considerable discontent with a system that was not doing what it was supposed to do. There were allies available to back him up in what he wanted to get done. "There is no question that we turned OJJDP around," Regnery said. "Starting with what we said— and we said it very clearly—and ending with the grants that we made, the Office took on a completely different hue. In addition to that, I think that the programs that we started, and the debate that we encouraged, will eventually contribute to a change in the system. I can't say that we are completely responsible for that change, but I do think we took advantage of a situation that we saw, with the result that the change may come more quickly."

Woodrow Wilson once said that if you want to make enemies, just change something. Regnery, Wootton, and his other political appointees at OJJDP did make lots of enemies, but they also made lots of friends. Those who believe in a lawful society and the rights of innocent crime victims owe them a vote of thanks.

Notes

1. *The Washington Post*, April 3, 1983.

2. Interview with Robert Woodson, President, National Center for Neighborhood Enterprise, Washington, D.C., April 17, 1986.

3. Representative Pat Williams, Hearings before the Subcommittee on Elementary, Secondary and Vocational Education, 98th Cong. 2nd sess., January 23, 24, 1984, p. 63.

26 The Firing of Ed Curran

DOUGLAS ALEXANDER

Editors' Note: This chapter provides a microcosm of essential problems in the Reagan Administration. It demonstrates the initial passion and idealism that Reagan loyalists brought to Washington, a passion which has in many cases been replaced by a tired cynicism. An excellent case study, the following story raises fundamental questions about the Reagan presidency which will perhaps never be adequately answered.

Is federal research in education, especially as embodied in the National Institute of Education (NIE), essential to American education? Or is it a trivial, even dangerous, waste of taxpayer funds? The answer to that question depends on the answers to other very broad questions: What is proper education? What are the purposes of the federal government? What, if any, is the federal government's appropriate role in education?

For a hundred years, there has grown up in America an education establishment that sought, with great success, to assume new and different answers to such questions. Generations of theorists and teacher-activists turned American education into a "system," erected mostly after the turn of the century, with remarkable homogeneity from coast to coast. This homogeneity of thought and practice was achieved through an alliance among several universities, particularly Columbia, of professors of education with practitioners of a new experimental psychology.

The "system" was propagated through networks of like-minded activists at the state level, but it always implied a federal headquarters as guardian for the system once fully erected. President Lyndon Johnson, a former teacher-unionist, provided the beginnings of such a federal role, with Jimmy Carter elevating federal involvement to Cabinet status as the Department of Education (ED).

But just as this culmination was reached, grave deficiencies in the American public school system began to bring into question the long-unexamined assumptions on which the whole structure was based. With both conservatives and liberals beginning to divide among themselves on important questions of education policy, Ronald Reagan arrived in Washington, D.C. with a new Republican administration pledged to roll back some advances of the century-long education crusade.

Central to the question of the federal role in education is the role of sociological research, since, as stated, the original success of the systematizing movement in education had come about as an alliance of educationists and experimental psychologists. As the research arm of the Department of Education, the National Institute of Education was the natural place to expect fireworks to break out in an administration seeking to change the educational status quo. The breakout came rather earlier then anyone might have expected, with the appointment of Ed Curran as Director of NIE.

For fifteen years Edward Curran was the popular headmaster of Washington, D.C.'s National Cathedral School, a prestigious girls' preparatory school (paired with the boys' school, St. Albans) in association with the National Episcopal Cathedral. In 1979, he resigned his position and joined the Reagan campaign as a full-time volunteer. An educator, like Terrel Bell, the new Secretary of Education, but from a very different tradition, Curran had long been concerned that federal education efforts were having an adverse overall impact on American education. With the candidacy of Ronald Reagan, he saw a chance for a correction of that course.

First Experience: The Transition Team

When a new administration arrives in Washington, its first challenge is the necessity of making three thousand executive and bureaucratic appointments. No White House function is under more pressure and scrutiny than the Office of Presidential Personnel. After the election of Ronald Reagan, Ed Curran was asked to work there, dealing with the urgent need to find suitable people for the swarm of impending government appointments.

Since "people are policy," the appointing of a government is also the beginning of the long-term hopes of any administration for its impact on the nation. Ed Curran's introduction to Washington politics came with the responsibility to see that the Reagan agenda was truly embodied in the new federal executives. He had to produce people ready to effectively enter into a bureaucracy that had flourished for fifty years on the assumption of a growing federal role in American life and that now found itself under a President pledged to restraint and contraction.

In the course of that work, the Office of Presidential Personnel arrived at the task of finding a Director for the National Institute of Education. After considering a number of candidates, Curran's boss one day returned from a meeting on the question to ask Curran to take the job himself.

Director of NIE at that time was one of six hundred or so appointments requiring Senate confirmation. But before approaching this hurdle,

Curran was directed to privately seek the approval of the Administration's new Secretary of Education. Terrel Bell had been in office only a few months. After an amicable discussion in the Secretary's office, during the course of which Bell told Curran that NIE was very important to him, Curran was cleared for the confirmation hearing, and was officially appointed Director of the National Institute of Education in September 1981.

His was to be a brief time in office: only eight months. Starting without experience or borrowed opinions concerning education research at the federal level, Curran set out to understand how NIE should be fitted into the Reagan mandate. In time, he came to believe that abolishing NIE would be a service both to American education and to American tax-payers. Acting on that judgment, he lost his job and inadvertently brought to public view the divided counsel of the new Administration on education policy.

Terrel Bell

Reagan's Secretary of Education, Terrel Bell, had set out to explore the bureaucratic terrain with a very different mission: to save as much as possible of the federal role in education from an Administration likely to succeed at the very minimum in demoting the Department of Education (ED) from Cabinet-level status.

When President Carter and a Democratic Congress elevated the old Office of Education to Cabinet status as the Department of Education, it was widely understood to be a gesture of gratitude to the National Education Association (NEA), the nation's largest teacher union, for its ardent political support. When Ronald Reagan triumphed over Carter in the 1980 election, it was against the best efforts of the NEA and the education establishment. The new Administration was left with no reason to doubt their serious opposition to the Reagan agenda, which had included in particular the new President's promise to demote the Department of Education from Cabinet status.

It was doubly odd, then, for the Administration to choose as its nom-inee for Secretary of Education Terrel Bell, a man fully identified with the education establishment Reagan's people had set out to abolish. Bell had undergraduate, master's, and doctoral degrees in education studies, and his universe was molded by the thought and traditions of the education establishment. It is not too much to say that Bell has been and remains (he is a professor of education administration at the University of Utah in Salt Lake City) an articulate and accomplished opponent of Ronald Reagan's aims in education.

A year after leaving the Reagan Cabinet, in a famous article for the prestigious education journal, the *Phi Delta Kappan*, Bell wrote, "To this day I'm not certain why I was selected by the President, especially in view of the fact that I had once testified favorably on the bill that created the Department of Education."[1]

Before leading the Reagan Administration's efforts in education, Bell had served as Commissioner of Higher Education in the state of Utah, and as head of the Office of Education in HEW under Nixon and Ford. He had also served as one of the first members of the policy-making council of NIE, a role of which he remained very proud.

Working Cautiously

Bell came to the post of Secretary of Education as an experienced Washington bureaucrat, prepared to concede the demotion of ED from Cabinet status, but determined to prevent it from being submerged and parceled out among several federal agencies, as it had been before Jimmy Carter. Bell's aim was to bring about a single foundation to house federal education activities, a foundation on the model of the National Institutes of Health (NIH).

Like the NIH, which is devoted first of all to cancer research, Bell's new foundation was also to have a research function at its heart: the National Institute of Education.

> When President Reagan asked me to serve as Secretary of Education, I accepted with the understanding that I would take the lead in designing the alternative agency that would replace the Department of Education. . . . My purpose was to preserve the traditional federal role in education. To do so, I had to work cautiously.[2]

Bell worked both cautiously and successfully for four years, from January 1981 to January 1985, preserving even the forlorn seat at the Cabinet table for education. "In my view," he concluded his triumphant *Kappan* article, "the continued existence of that seat is now assured."[3]

Bell's success, from within the Administration and against even his own expectations, was largely possible because of the triumph of one of his earliest initiatives as Secretary, the appointment of the National Commission on Excellence in Education, staffed by members of NIE and housed at NIE headquarters in Washington, D.C. The commission at length produced a report on the failings of American education called *A Nation At Risk*, which generated great publicity and sympathy for public education.[4] For a season, it compelled American politicians to speak publicly and often about schools. Bell's *Nation At Risk* report gave education enduring national attention such as it had never had before.

The climate of opinion that resulted made demotion of the Department of Education from Cabinet status much more controversial. But before the release and success of the *Nation At Risk* report, Bell had to deal with a direct challenge to the existence of the NIE itself, a challenge from an unexpected quarter: the Director of NIE.

The National Institute of Education

In June 1972, hidden in the bowels of an omnibus education act, without comment or notice, Congress passed the statute authorizing the National Institute of Education.

> The Congress hereby declares it to be the policy of the United States to provide every person an equal opportunity to receive an education of high quality. . . . Although the American educational system has pursued this objective, it has not yet attained that objective. . . . To achieve quality will require far more dependable knowledge about the process of learning and education than now exists or can be expected from present research and experimentation. . . . The Institute shall, in accordance with the provisions of this section, seek to improve education in the United States through . . . improved dissemination of the results of, and knowledge gained from, educational research and development, including assistance to educational agencies and institutions in the application of such results and knowledge.

The words of this statute, largely written by Chester E. Finn, at that time a member of the staff of Senator Daniel Patrick Moynihan (D.-N.Y.), commit the federal government to social science research and applied technology as a means of improving the American people. Going beyond the provision of opportunity to all Americans, the aim of NIE is to create a federal ability to affect "outcomes." While NIE is intended only to discover and disseminate the methods which give that ability, nevertheless it remains true that knowledge is also power, and ability is easily confused with authority. And authority is perhaps the key question in all education.

"The central problems of high school humanities teaching today," Chester Finn has written elsewhere, "arise from uncertain convictions, confused ideas, and irresolute standards, not from insufficient knowledge, weak techniques, or inadequate resources."[5] The remedy, Finn goes on to say, is the restoration of clear standards through restoration of the authority of the teacher. "As Carlyle said," Finn writes, " 'Surely, of all "rights of man," this right of the ignorant man to be guided by the wiser, to be, gently or forcibly, held in the true course by him is the indisputablest.' "[6]

Whether or not it was the original intention, NIE, as the ultimate educational research organ of both the federal government and the community of American education sociologists, necessarily exercises immense inherent authority over education. It seems ready, whether it ever actually does so or not, to authorize its devotees to define who is ignorant, and then to "guide them," "gently or forcibly," in the path desired for them. The offhand establishment of NIE by Congress, and its undeniable potential as a tool of political tyranny, have made the agency controversial from the beginning.

For many reasons, NIE never met the expectations of even its founders. Half its budget (up to $100 million) went to 17 regional labs and centers of independently contracted education research, with the rest going to support hundreds of staff members in Washington, D.C. But as a decade passed and Johnny read less and less well, as parents began to doubt that public schools were even physically safe for children, and the crisis of the black family intensified in urban communities and began to overwhelm children's performance in school, NIE became an obvious failure. The applied research called for by Congress, carried out by NIE, made no perceptible contribution to solving the nation's education problems, though NIE had cost the taxpayers over $700 million.

In the last budget of the Carter Administration, Congress nearly deleted spending authority for NIE, and finally cut it sharply. By 1980, as the Reagan Administration arrived promising to cut the federal budget and demote the Department of Education from Cabinet status, NIE was a demoralized bureaucracy, expecting the worst.

Curran at NIE

Arriving at NIE to do a job similar to those to which he had helped send many others, Ed Curran entered a community of sociologists and educators basically unfriendly to that mission. Without the aid of other Reagan appointees at first, Curran set out to master the administration of the Institute, to learn the needs and expectations of the career bureaucrats, the federal educators and their staffs, and to determine what was the best course for NIE under the Reagan mandate. "I did not go to NIE with the intention to abolish it," Curran says. "Later, when I hired Larry Uzzell to be my executive assistant, and I knew he was committed to abolishing NIE, I had to wrestle with my conscience in bringing him in. We had several long talks and he promised he was willing to work within the President's intentions."

With Larry Uzzell, a former staffer on the most important congressional education committee, on board, Curran proceeded to add others to his team. Among the new appointments were Robert Sweet, a textbook expert from New Hampshire, who became acting Director after Curran left. (Sweet made his own brief six-month period as Director an effective continuation of Curran's before Terrel Bell passed him over in favor of a standard education liberal.) Don Senese had been appointed earlier to a related position—nominally above Curran's—as Assistant Secretary of the Office of Education Research and Improvement (OERI). Senese's appointment was resisted by the Secretary, and came about only after a great effort on the part of Curran and his supporters.

As his team assembled, Curran began a vigorous investigation of the possibilities at NIE. The political staff reviewed the research goals of the Institute, causing their first public controversy in February 1982, with the release of new guidelines for research. To be studied, for a change, were the effects of parental choice plans in school finance, such as tuition tax credits; merit pay for teachers; the worth of required curricula versus electives; and the impact of mothers' entry into the work force on the educational achievement of children.

The most controversial decision was to reconsider the status of the most scandalous part of NIE: its independently contracted research agencies scattered across the country, called labs and centers. Centers were usually located at a university and did research on a national level. Labs were small independent institutions with a local and regional orientation.

In the past, about half of the Institute budget had gone to a dozen or more of these labs and centers, scattered around the country: nests of education scholars with ongoing NIE-funded contracts to carry out unimportant research at great expense. Meanwhile, back in the Washington HQ, NIE's National Diffusion Network staff labored to find some way by which working teachers and principals could be gotten to show some interest in the resulting droves of papers, charts, and reports.

Chester Finn, one of the originators of NIE, who by then had become a professor of education at Vanderbilt University, writing in the *Phi Delta Kappan* deplored the situation in these terms:

> The resources of NIE have been captured by a group of educational R & D organizations, commonly known as the 'labs and centers,' that have gained a stranglehold on the annual appropriation through adroit manipulation of key members of Congress.[7]

Writing several months after Curran's departure, Finn noted that "several NIE Directors have sought to break this hold—usually without vigor, and always without success."[8]

Ending the labs and centers—a small delicacy on the menu of pork-barrel politics—was, Congressionally speaking, nearly impossible. They are a principal reason NIE itself has weathered so many storms.

But Curran set out merely to end their status as guaranteed grant recipients, not to abolish them, and to see that there would be competition for grants in the future. After obtaining a ruling from the Department legal counsel that it was within the Department's contract rights, Curran proposed to end all the contracts a year early and to introduce competitive review panels for new grants.

In the past, grant-review panels had been composed of the same kinds of educators and scholars who were requesting the grants, people who expected that on a future occasion their grant might well be under similar review. This situation did not make for the most effective oversight, and one of Ed Curran's first intentions was to arrange for a more neutral and effective way of appointing panel members. It was a job too large to accomplish during Curran's brief tenure, but the first steps were taken and lists of objective panelists were commissioned.

Meanwhile, the intense scuffle over eliminating the ongoing contracts with the labs and centers occupied much of the attention of Curran's small staff, but in the end, the change was made.

Another basic issue tackled was the large number of scholars who had been hired for three-year terms at the Washington HQ as "excepted service" (non-civil service) appointees. These educators were meant to carry fresh, federally oxygenated research blood back out to the peripheries of the nation's public education system after a brief time in Washington. By 1981, however, many had arrived and few had left, forming a stagnating pool of senior associates with over six years in "temporary" residence at NIE.

These were the same sorts of folks who, back home, were soaking up federal research largesse in the labs and centers, and Curran began the painful process of making honest visiting scholars of many by sending them home. Amid a variety of bureaucratic tactics to counter his efforts, Curran found himself facing the threat of a sexual discrimination suit by dismissed officials who seemingly were more inventive in their quest to hang onto "temporary" positions than they had been in their efforts to improve American education. In one particularly difficult case, a long-time standout had become especially hard to fire. Curran finally managed to do so, with reluctant approval from Terrel Bell, but after Curran's own departure, he was hired back at the Department of Education.

Another issue was the National Council of Education Research (NCER), originally the policy-making body for NIE. A council of presidentially appointed citizens (usually not educators), it was intended to give NIE political accountability to the current Administration. NCER had never functioned effectively, however, and on Curran's arrival, he still had to deal with Jimmy Carter's Council. He didn't manage to get a new Reagan-appointed Council for NIE until May 1982, just before he resigned.

These major difficulties, and many lesser ones, took up the whirlwind months of Ed Curran's tenure at NIE, surely one of the most active of any Reagan appointee. As he proceeded to deal almost simultaneously with the previous decade of disorders at NIE, Ed Curran found himself asking what real value the American taxpayers were receiving for their $53 million a year. As the weeks wore on, increasingly the answer he gave himself was "not enough."

The Attempt

Late in 1981, as the White House Office of Management and Budget was preparing the 1983 budget to be submitted to Congress in 1982, Curran heard a rumor that OMB head David Stockman had decided to delete funds for NIE from the new budget—in effect, to the kill the whole agency. Curran cautiously called OMB, asking if the deletion of NIE funds from the budget plan could be confirmed. Yes, he was told, and Curran briefly let OMB know that he, the Director of the agency, felt that that was a good idea, and that he could support it.

Soon after, Curran met with Bell in the Secretary's office and Bell mentioned the "problem" with NIE, telling Curran that it would be necessary to go over to the White House to make the case for keeping the research institute. Curran, put on the spot, shared his thoughts frankly with Bell, saying that he had his doubts about fighting for NIE. "Keep in mind," Curran says now, "I was new in the Administration. This was what the President wanted. And I was naive. I should have gone along with the Secretary to the first meetings."

But as a result of Curran's disclosure, Bell turned instead to the new Assistant Secretary of OERI, Don Senese, a Curran ally, to accompany him in his visits to the White House to defend NIE's appropriation. If Curran had been present at these first formal discussions, he would have had more legitimate and more effective influence on the challenged policy question. As it was, Curran was immediately set to one side, and Don Senese was brought front and center in the controversy. Curran and his team were left entirely unconsulted. The fate of NIE might still have been sealed if Senese had fully shared the convictions developed by his friends and fellow Curran appointees about the Institute. Senese could then have brought them directly into the discussions at the White House. But that was far from the case.

In fact, before one meeting that was expected to be especially crucial, Robert Sweet, Larry Uzzell, and Ed Curran pleaded with Senese to take their case to the White House. Senese flatly refused. In conversations with White House Counselor Ed Meese, Bell soon reached agreement to overrule OMB and save the NIE.

The final decision was taken between Meese and Bell in December 1981. But a little later, during Christmas time, President Reagan made a very moving, effective television speech about cutting the size of the federal government. One among the vast television audience that day was Ed Curran, who remembered that he was director of a federal agency that seemed to fit the President's bill perfectly. "You as an ordinary citizen," the President said, "can help." What Curran heard that day prompted him to quietly approach his assistant Larry Uzzell to try to reverse the deal Terrel Bell had struck with Ed Meese. Of that effort, Curran now says, "Larry Uzzell and I were neophytes, we didn't understand the significance of that deal—we never planned a long-range strategy."

Terrel Bell, an experienced Washington tactician, had made an arrangement with the strongest elements of the White House staff. Curran, with Larry Uzzell, set out to find a way to go around Bell and Meese to ask the President directly. The problem, as they well knew, was that open channels of communication with the President go through a vigilant and inquisitive staff. And the staff was part of the problem.

Discreet inquiries led Curran to Lyn Nofziger, a long-time political friend of the President's from California who had recently left the White House to do private consulting. In a personal meeting, Curran asked Nofziger if he thought the President would be open to his suggestion to abolish NIE. Nofziger said yes, but "If you're willing to do this, you realize, you may be out of a job." He supplied Curran with information on how to send a letter to the White House coded to go directly to the President, without being opened by anyone else. He also asked Curran to keep secret the method he had provided, as well as the source that had provided it. Curran did keep the secret. But Nofziger was later named in the press anyway on someone else's information, along with the method used.

As it happened, perhaps by chance, the plan did not succeed. The President was in California when Curran's letter arrived, and it was opened by Richard Darman of the President's staff. Darman immediately sent the letter to Terrel Bell.

Curran had planned to get a copy to Bell a day or two later. In the event, that was unnecessary.

Bell reacted with great anger and agitation. He asked for and received immediate assurances from the White House about NIE. The White House advised Curran that NIE would continue in the budget at Secretary Bell's request. As to whether or not Curran would resign, that was up to the Secretary. Curran was urged to meet with Bell to see what could be worked out.

Of the meeting, Bell says, "I asked him how he could continue as head of an agency he was committed to abolish." Curran responded with the same question to Bell. Bell offered to let Curran stay on if he would publicly repudiate the position taken in his letter to the President. Curran felt he must refuse. "I have a lot of respect for Ed Curran," Terrel Bell says now, "he could have kept his job—his was the opposite of the choice David Stockman made in a similar circumstance." (In an *Atlantic Monthly* interview by William Greider, Stockman was quoted as calling Ronald Reagan's budget plans "trickle down economics," the old liberal term of derision for the free market, but when called on the carpet, Stockman backtracked on his own remarks in order to remain with the Adminstration.[9])

The meeting lasted an hour. The next day, Bell called Curran and asked him to clean out his office by that evening.

Could It Have Worked?

Even if the President had seen Curran's letter, presidents do not commonly intervene against their top staff. Not commonly, but sometimes, and why not?

Curran's was an act of naive seriousness. It was also a likely enough prospect that one of the nation's most able political advisors, Lyn Nofziger, thought it worth a try. It was also a likely enough threat to surprise Secretary Bell (and make him personally very angry).

Education policy questions were never openly raised and discussed by the Reagan Administration. They were settled, at least as far as the NIE is concerned, in Reagan's presidency, when behind-the-scenes policy moves by Bell and Curran erupted in public, with Bell firing Curran while the White House stood conspicuously above the battle—on the procedural grounds that, as Secretary, Terrel Bell had the prerogative to decide.

It was not until about six months later that President Reagan saw a copy of Curran's letter. He sent it down to Jim Baker with a note in one corner: "So this is the reason Ed Curran was fired. I hope we haven't made a mistake."

Notes

1. Terrel H. Bell, "Education Policy Development in the Reagan Administration," *Phi Delta Kappan*, March 1986, p. 487.

2. *Ibid.*, p. 489.

3. *Ibid.*, p. 493.

4. The National Commission on Excellence in Education, *A Nation at Risk: The Imperative for Education Reform.* April 1983.

5. Chester E. Finn, Jr. and Diane Ravitch, *Against Mediocrity, The Humanities in America's High Schools* (New York and London: Holmes and Meyer, 1984), pp. 245 and 249.

6. *Ibid.*, p. 249.

7.   *Phi Delta Kappan*, Vol. 64 no. 6, Bloomington, Indiana, February 1983, p. 408.

8.   *Ibid.*, p. 408.

9.   William Grider, "The Education of David Stockman," *The Atlantic*, December 1981, pp. 27-54.

27 The Reagan Presidency and Policy Change

ROBERT RECTOR and MICHAEL SANERA

How successful has the Reagan Administration been? As might be expected with a President who has sought dramatic change, opinions on this question are sharply divided. Some commentators declare:

> The American political system, during the presidency of Ronald Reagan, has been transformed to an extent unknown since the days of Franklin Delano Roosevelt. The terms of political debate, the course of domestic and foreign policy, and the dominant line of partisan cleavage have all been fundamentally changed. Only rarely in American history has the political system broken as sharply with governing customs to address festering national problems or confront social and economic issues head-on.[1]

Congressional opponents charge that Reagan has cut domestic spending to the bone and engaged in unprecedented militarization of the economy. Tip O'Neill bemoans Reagan's alleged efforts to drag the government back to the days of Herbert Hoover. On the other hand, many of the authors of this volume tell a different tale: of useless spending which persists unchecked, of necrotic policies which remain unchallenged, of renitent bureaucracies which ignore or actively oppose a conservative presidency.

A second question is less common, but no less important: How has the struggle over policy change altered during the Reagan presidency? Over time governmental institutions and processes change; each president arrives in office with a different agenda and operates within a different political context. Each faces a unique set of challenges and opportunities. The process of policy change consists not only in emergence of new issues (which are widely reported), but also of continued changes in the arenas and tactics under which policy contests are fought.

The system of government in the United States was not designed for rapid and radical political change. Indeed, the structure of separation of powers, and checks and balances at the federal level was intended specifically to impede the accumulation of power and precipitous change.

Only occasionally in our history does a window of opportunity for dramatic change open: when the intellectual and political climate is ripe for assault on the old order and a strong change-oriented president is supported by like-minded majorities in Congress. Such a window of opportunity opened in the 1930's when economic trauma propelled Franklin Delano Roosevelt and solid Democratic majorities into power to lay the foundations of the modern welfare state. It opened again in the mid-sixties when, following the assassination of a young president, landslides in presidential and congressional elections set the stage for the welfare state's efflorescence.

In 1980 Ronald Reagan won a decisive victory against an incumbent President; in 1984 he was re-elected with one of the largest margins in U.S. history. The Republicans won and retained a majority in the Senate. The number of voters considering themselves Republicans grew considerably while the number regarding themselves as Democrats fell. The intellectual credibility of much liberal policy was shaken if not buried. Public attitudes were shifting in a conservative direction; and the strong ideological aura of President Reagan, coupled with the decisive repudiation of Walter Mondale's old-style liberalism in the 1984 election, reinforced the sense of intellectual realignment.

American politics is clearly in a period of transition, but unlike the presidents in the periods of change previously alluded to, Reagan has not been supported by stable majorities in both houses of Congress. A window of opportunity for conservative redirection opened, but it was a narrow one. This mixed state of affairs may well have been a result of the increase in the power of incumbency in the House, a development which may have made dramatic partisan realignments a thing of the past.[2] For whatever the reason, the problem of dramatic intellectual transformation within a divided power setting has provided the context for political change in the Reagan Administration.

Presidential administrations work for political change on four fronts. The first is the institutional arrangements which the presidency establishes to govern itself and to mobilize for change. The other three fronts are the avenues through which policy change occurs. These are respectively: regulation, public education, and legislation. The following sections discuss each of the four fronts of the change process in turn.

Institutional Change and the Presidency

For the last half-century, presidents have complained of the inadequacy of the institutions of the executive branch. Centrifugal and inertial forces within the departments and agencies have threatened the president's ability to create and control policy. Presidents have responded to these threats through increasing *centralization* in decision-making and by an expansion of *political control* across the executive branch. These patterns of institutional change have been continued by the Reagan Administration.

Over fifty years ago, Franklin Roosevelt arrived in Washington with a vision of profound social change, but found himself confronted by a federal bureaucracy inhospitable to innovation, and frankly incapable of meeting the President's demands for redirection. FDR's response was *centralization*: removing policy-making authority from the departments and agencies and relocating it within the White House. Subsequent presidents, particularly Kennedy, Johnson, and Nixon, responded to the same problems of inertia with further steps toward centralization of responsibility in the hands of the President's immediate White House staff, who alone seemed to provide loyalty to the President's direction.

Another technique utilized by presidents such as Roosevelt and Johnson was bypass: the creation of new agencies staffed with individuals capable of carrying out the presidential agenda with flexibility and initiative. Though this option has, for obvious reasons, been neglected by conservative presidents, presidents since Eisenhower have continued to seek greater *political control* as a means of instilling greater responsiveness in the bureaucracy. Political control has been pursued by a gradual increase in the number of political appointees and a growing tendency to regard the political appointment process less as patronage and more as an instrument of presidential policy coordination. Under President Carter's Civil Service Reform Act, the trend toward political control was strengthened by giving presidential appointees greater ability to reassign top-level career staff and to reward bureaucratic responsiveness financially.

The Reagan Administration has continued these historic trends. From the outset there was a perceived need to prevent the administrative chaos and lack of direction that had occurred in the Carter Administration by an improved process of policy direction based inside the White House. The newly formed Office of Domestic Policy, in conjunction with the cabinet councils, provided President Reagan with a decision-making mechanism that was more centralized than those of Presidents Ford and Carter (though less so than that which existed under Nixon). However, centralization increased to new heights through the changing role of OMB. Under Reagan, OMB became a focal point of policy-making, and for the first time acquired crucial responsibilities for policy advocacy. But most significant was the establishment of a centralized regulatory review system within OMB to rationalize a process which seemed to be proceeding almost without political supervision in many agencies.

The record of the Reagan Administration on *political control* is more ambiguous. Early on, the Administration expressed its understanding of the policy implications of the political personnel process; institutional arrangements reflected this perceived importance, and the review process described in Chapter 15 provided, in theory, unprecedented centralized control to the White House. On paper all the elements were in place for a fusion of policy and personnel and a dramatic initiative against the problems of centrifugalism and inertia which had plagued presidents since the New Deal.

Yet the results from the implementation of this strategy of political control have been far less than revolutionary. The Reagan Administration has attempted to govern with roughly the same number of political appointees as the Carter Administration, a policy which hardly seems practical in a presidency that sought to reverse the course of government of the preceding half-century, and whose policies invariably clashed with the institutional interests of most of the federal bureaucracy outside the Pentagon. The number of political appointees still remains at slightly more than one per thousand career civil servants, a number which seems inadequate even to monitor the activities of the bureaucracy, let alone to control it, or to mobilize resources for change. Although conventional wisdom holds that in the appointment process the Reagan presidency has stressed "ideology above all else," the facts speak otherwise.[3] As Becky Norton Dunlop noted, the first round of cabinet-level appointments differed only slightly from the past, and in most appearances, seemed as if they could have been made as easily by Presidents Ford and Nixon as by Reagan. Many seemed to be more suited to serve as managers of the status quo than as agents of change.

Although the personnel selection process as an instrument of policy control may have fared better at the lower political echelons, still a remarkable heterogeneity among appointees has existed throughout the Reagan presidency. Indeed, although the case studies in Part IV were not selected with this point in mind, it is worth noting that each story of marked policy failure (the Small Business Administration, the Department of Education, and the Legal Services Corporation) involved appointees with what might be best described as a tenuous relationship to a conservative presidential agenda. Other case studies at NOAA and HUD record controversies between appointees over conservative initiatives. These cases are not at all atypical of institutional realities during the Reagan era.

In part, these problems may be attributed to the inherent uncertainty of personnel selection, but they have been reinforced by the absence of centralized oversight and disciplinary mechanisms for appointees once they were in office. In addition, the prospects for political control over the bureaucracy have been dimmed by the failure of Reagan appointees to utilize the managerial tools created by the Carter Administration. The provisions of Carter's Civil Service Reform Act were designed to promote bureaucratic responsiveness by providing high or low salary differentials to top-level career civil servants based on effective performance or the lack thereof. Unfortunately, the Reagan Administration has for the most part acquiesced to the standard bureaucratic practice of rating nearly all top-level bureaucrats uniformly "excellent," thereby nullifying any potential incentive effects.[4]

Although centralization and political control are generally regarded as complementary trends in the institutional development of the presidency, they are in fact contradictory. The necessity of centralization reflects the failure of political control. The emergence of Stockman as the master budget cutter stemmed from the failure of department and agency heads to step vigorously into this role. Although a few appointees such as Donald Devine, former Director of the Office of Personnel Management, took the lead from OMB in cutting their own agencies' budgets, they were the exception not the rule. Far more common were efforts to blunt OMB's shears. Similarly, the establishment of a centralized regulatory review process in OMB derives from the failure of political appointees to control and rationalize the process at the agency level.

Nonetheless, the institutional reforms of the Reagan Administration, as far as they have gone, are salutary. They are in keeping with the changes in the political process that will be discussed in the following sections, and provide a structure for presidential effectiveness. It is likely that they will be retained and built upon by future presidents of either party.

The Battle for Administrative and Regulatory Control

As ably described by Joseph Morris in Chapter 7, many current legislative enactments seem to be more an effort to avoid difficult decisions and responsibility than to establish public policy. Since the early sixties, vague, ambiguous and self-contradictory legislation has increasingly become the norm—a trend which has been enhanced by the expansion in the sheer scope of government activity.[5] This has meant that actual determination of policy is left to the executive power vested in the President by Article II of the Constitution. The real content and impact of legislation is determined by the regulations formulated to implement the law and by the bureaucratic interpretation of these regulations. Academically, this ability to shape the content of broad legislation through regulation and administrative action has been termed *bureaucratic discretion*.

The importance of bureaucratic discretion has been increased by another trend in our political system: the semipermanent split between a Republican presidency and a Congress with one or both houses under Democratic control, which has evolved since the late 1960's. After the 1972 election, President Nixon—voted into office with an overwhelming majority, but finding himself blocked on the legislative front—decided that he could most effectively exercise his authority as president by focusing on the enormous policy discretion which existed in the operations of the executive branch under his charge. Richard Nathan has termed this strategy the "administrative presidency"—a concept which has grown, and continues to grow, in importance.[6] It is clearly a strategy that calls for an enhanced role for political appointees as operatives of the president within the executive branch.

However, this strategy—which has been adopted, perhaps, to a greater degree by Reagan than by any other president—cannot be implemented simply through presidential intent. Bureaucratic discretion implies a policy vacuum, which many forces will rush to fill, not the least of which is the career bureaucracy. The political power and resistance of the permanent bureaucracy will be least when the political component of the executive branch is united over policy and greatest when there are divisions among political appointees or between the presidency and Congress. In these circumstances, the bureaucracy will act not as a neutral pawn caught in a contest between legitimate political actors, but as an independent political actor in its own right, with its own interests and ideological perspective.

Into such a policy contest, the bureaucracy will throw the considerable power that derives from its technical knowledge and its control over government operations. Some commentators have even gone so far as to characterize the bureaucracy as an independent power broker mediating the conflicting interests of the President, Congress, and special interest groups.[7] As an independent political actor, the bureaucracy usurps power and function in violation of the framework of the Constitution and the principles of democratic accountability.

Competition and conflict with the permanent bureaucracy over policy development and implementation occurs in any presidency, but it is most severe in a conservative administration. This is not surprising given the political interests and attitudes of top-level career officials. It is especially true in "Great Society" era departments and agencies whose policies and *raison d'être* are called into question by conservative philosophy.

A recent study by Stanley Rothman and S. Robert Lichter confirms the prevalent perception of a liberal slant at the top levels of the federal bureaucracy.[8] Rothman and Lichter studied career executives from the top rungs of the bureaucratic hierarchy (the Senior Executive Service) in thirteen different domestic departments and agencies, dividing their sample into "traditional" agencies (the Departments of Agriculture, Commerce, and Treasury; and the Bureau of Prisons in the Department of Justice); and "activist" agencies, generally of more recent origin (the Environmental Protection Agency, the Federal Trade Commission, the Consumer Product Safety Commission, the Equal Employment Opportunity Commission, ACTION, the Food and Drug Administration, the Civil Rights Division within the Justice Department, and the Departments of Housing and Urban Development and Health and Human Services). In the traditional agencies, 48 percent of the career executives identified themselves as "liberals"; this was nearly two and one-half times greater than the rate for the American public at large. Within the activist agencies, 63 percent identified themselves as "liberal," while only 23 percent saw themselves as "conservative." Voting patterns of these same bureaucrats shown in Table 1 reaffirm the liberal patterns; while Washington bureaucracy is not uniform in its political beliefs, it is not surprising that, *en masse*, it is well to the left of the American public. Attitudes on specific issues reflect the moderate-liberal slant: 80 percent of Washington career executives support abortion; half feel the government should substantially redistribute income; and a third would like the government to guarantee jobs.

The confluence of these factors has meant that one of the most significant areas of political conflict in the last six years has been the efforts of the Reagan Administration to establish active control over the executive branch. This struggle has taken place with varying degrees of success and failure throughout the bureaucracy; as bureaucratic discretion becomes more important within our governmental framework, competition in this area will undoubtedly intensify. The overlap between this problem and the institutional questions raised in the preceding subsection is worth re-emphasis: Strong-minded appointees with an enthusiasm for the details of operations have tended to be effective in controlling the bureaucracy; but where uncertainty or division have existed in the political ranks, the interests of the bureaucracy and the status quo have generally prevailed.

The Battle for Public Opinion

A presidency must seek not only to change policy but to mobilize public support for that change. In this area conservative administrations face a particular constraint based on the structural biases of news media institutions.

The news system in the United States has two distinct levels. At the national level there are twelve principal print and broadcast organiza-

Table 1 Presidential Voting Record of Top-Level Bureaucrats, 1968–1980[9]
(Percent Voting For)

	Traditional Agencies	Activist Agencies	Combined
1968			
Nixon	33	23	28
Humphrey	67	76	72
1972			
Nixon	51	35	42
McGovern	47	65	57
1976			
Ford	35	24	28
Carter	65	76	71
1980			
Reagan	48	27	36
Carter	34	55	45
Anderson	19	18	18

tions. These are ABC, CBS, NBC, PBS, *The Washington Post, The New York Times, The Wall Street Journal,* AP, UPI, *Time, Newsweek,* and *U.S. News and World Report.* The second level of the news system comprises thousands of local newspapers, radio stations, and television stations. There is a dependency between the two levels; reporters at the local level receive virtually all of their information about national and international events by way of the twelve primary national organizations. For example, local reporters cite *The New York Times* as their foremost source of information.[10]

The broadcasting, reporting, and editorial personnel of the national news organizations are predominantly liberal.[11] A survey of these national media elites found that as a group they had voted for the Democratic candidate 86 percent of the time in presidential elections between 1960 and 1976. An astonishing 81 percent voted for George McGovern in 1972—more than twice the level of his support in the general public.[12] News personnel at the local level are not as liberal as those at the national level, but the ratio of self-professed liberals to conservatives among local journalists is still four times greater than among the general public.[13] Attitudes of news personnel at the local and national levels reveal that the news media are well to the left of the American public on nearly all issues. President Reagan's approval rating among the press is virtually a photographic negative of that of the public.

In 1985, 30 percent of the journalists "favored" the President and 60 percent "opposed" him. The figures for the general public were 56 percent and 17 percent respectively.[14]

The narrow ideological spectrum of the news media, particularly at the national level where most stories are generated, means that it is difficult to articulate the conservative side of many policy issues. This would be true even if the media were making the best possible effort to be balanced and objective (which is certainly not the case at all times). Journalists often lack the assumptions and perspectives that make conservative policies intelligible. This is true just as it would be if a group of reporters—80 percent of whom were supporters of Barry Goldwater—were asked to present in a convincing manner the liberal case on arms control, detente, wage and price controls, pornography, etc.

The biases of media institutions affect news coverage in three ways. The first is in the attitudes that are projected toward specific issues. For example, a study of the treatment of the U.S. military by CBS News over a two-year period in the mid-seventies found that there were five negative stories for every positive one. At the same time, CBS ran 20 favorable stories about detente and arms control for every negative story.[15] The second impact of institutional bias is in "agenda setting," focusing public attention on specific issues and problems. For example, a survey of the news coverage of the Democratic and Republican conventions in 1984 found that the major television networks were seven times more likely to mention a pro-Democratic issue as they were to mention a pro-Republican issue; most conservative issues were not addressed at all.[16]

Finally, media institutions automatically inject a "philosophical" bias into all public policy debate. By their very nature, news media institutions cover the activities of government. News coverage *per se* relates to public or collective problem solving, therefore issues covered by the media tend to be converted into public, i.e., governmental issues almost by instinct. Whatever enlarges the role and importance of government or the scope of government activities also enlarges the importance of the media that report on the government. Media coverage, by its very nature, distorts perceptions of the importance of government relative to the private sector or to other institutions such as the family, church, and voluntary associations. The very format of media reporting on most issues (particularly television reporting) leaves the implicit question: What is the government going to do about this problem? The presupposition that government can do little about many problems, or is actively harmful, is antithetical to the nature of the news industry.

The institutional bias of the media has its greatest impact on complex or novel conservative ideas. Very often arguments or policies are not even put on the table because they are certain to receive scant or negative press treatment. In a more practical vein, each political appointee at the middle and senior levels throughout the government begins the working day with a file of news-clippings pertaining to his or her self, programs, and policies, generally garnered from the national media. The appointee is aware that everyone else in Washington, particularly on the Hill, is reading these same articles, and a great deal of time and emotional effort is spent evaluating and responding to them. Best intentions to the contrary, such press attention does play a heavy role in future decision-making.

In sum, when a conservative presidency seeks to muster public support for its policies, it faces an uphill fight. Insufficient attention has been paid to the role of institutional bias in the media on the overall questions of political realignment. Nonetheless, it is a topic that is growing in both importance and interest.

The Legislative Front

The Reagan Administration began with a string of remarkable legislative victories. Teamwork with conservatives on the Hill, a working bipartisan majority in the House, a clear policy vision, and a confident legislative strategy, all contributed to early successes. However, as Clifford Barnhart indicates in Chapter 8, the aggressive legislative strategy of the early Reagan White House was soon replaced by a strategy of risk aversion aimed at preserving presidential prestige. This shift coupled with election losses in Congress led to a period of legislative stagnation.

Clifford Barnhart and Morton Blackwell (in Chapter 3) both stress that the deliberate neglect of the concerns of key components of President Reagan's electoral coalition has weakened the President. Sympathetic activist groups who were essential to the initial legislative successes diminished their support, and the absence of a strategy to use targeted legislation to mobilize electoral support and to weaken the political opposition, in all probability, eroded the conservative base in Congress in the 1982, 1984, and 1986 elections.

Lack of legislative aggressiveness is evident in other areas as well. For a man who possessed a dramatic agenda, and who is considered to be the most "clearly ideological" president in recent history, Reagan has made little use of the veto. In his first term, President Reagan vetoed less than half the bills struck down by Presidents Eisenhower or Ford and a sixth of those vetoed by Truman (prorated in each case by time in office). This had led some critics to charge that Reagan should be less concerned with legitimate institutional reforms such as the line item veto and more concerned with using those powers he already has.

Assessing Reagan's Legislative Impact: The Budget

The federal budget is a principal legislative vehicle by which presidents seek to translate their philosophical tenets into programmatic form. Because it is quantifiable, budgetary change also permits direct comparison between presidencies. A president's impact on public policy can in part be determined through his ability to alter: (1) the total level of spending, and (2) spending priorities. Examination of budgetary changes since 1980 shows that there has indeed been a "Reagan Revolution" of sorts—but that the nature and implications of this change are often misunderstood.

First of all, and obviously, Ronald Reagan has not cut government spending. Measured either in constant (inflation-adjusted) dollars or as a percentage of the GNP, federal spending has risen under Ronald Reagan. This should not be surprising; it is in keeping with the long-term trend of this century. Federal spending has risen from 2.8 percent of GNP in 1900 to 24 percent today. The last President to actually cut government spending was Calvin Coolidge; each President since has presided over increases both in real expenditures and in government's share of the total economy. (This analysis excludes temporary spending downturns at the end of World War II and the Korean War.) It should come as no surprise that the Reagan Administration has not succeeded in breaking this pattern. As a percentage of GNP, total outlays have risen from 22.2 percent to 24.0 percent during the Reagan era. Measured on a per annum basis, this is slightly less than the average rate of increase since the 1930s.

The change in *priorities* or the direction of spending, however, has been significant. Excluding the temporary costs of waging the war in Vietnam in the late 1960s, defense spending as a percentage of GNP had fallen since the mid-fifties. Even in absolute terms, defense spending was nearly 17 percent less in 1980 than in 1956. Under Ronald Reagan this trend has been reversed. Peacetime defense spending has risen both in constant dollars and as a percentage of GNP for the first time in a quarter-century.

Still the magnitude of the change, contrary to popular claims, has been small: Defense spending rose from 5.0 percent of GNP to 6.5 percent over six years. Far from being the "largest military spending increase in U.S. history" the Reagan military buildup—measured in constant dollars—is about half the size of Eisenhower's peacetime military increases. More remarkably, the "massive" expansion in Reagan's first term was less, in

Table 2 Federal Spending in Constant Dollars (in billions of 1982 dollars)

Fiscal Year	Total Outlays	Defense		Nondefense	Interest
1940	83.2	15.1		61.2	6.9
1944	638.0	522.1	(499.4)	101.5	14.4
1948	158.2	55.8		83.7	18.7
1952	349.3	258.9	(175.0)	72.0	18.4
1956	306.2	198.5		89.5	18.2
1960	340.4	192.1		126.0	22.3
1964	403.2	198.8		179.6	24.8
1968	525.8	254.8	(82.3)	241.2	29.8
1972	527.6	190.9	(17.8)	303.1	33.6
1976	609.8	153.6		413.2	43.0
1980	699.1	164.0		473.1	62.0
1984	788.8	210.4		475.9	102.5
1986 (est.)	850.0	232.0		495.0	123.0

Note: Figures in parentheses are war costs accrued in the given fiscal year.
Source: Office of Management and Budget *Historical Tables: Budget of the United States Government* (Washington, D.C.: U.S. Government Printing Office, 1986).

constant dollars, than the increase in domestic program spending that had occurred in each preceding four-year presidential term from 1960 to 1980. For example, under President Carter, constant dollar domestic spending increased more than did defense spending in Reagan's first term in office. But while there has been continuous heated debate over Reagan's "massive" increase in defense, the domestic spending increase under Carter was barely recognized or commented on. (For an understanding of the strength of the trend favoring increases in domestic spending as opposed to defense spending, it is interesting to note that even during the Vietnam War domestic spending rose more rapidly than defense spending!)

President Reagan's efforts to apply a policy of restraint on domestic spending have likewise met with mixed results. As Table 3 indicates, the growth in domestic spending slowed under President Carter, remaining virtually unchanged as a percentage of GNP. Under President Reagan domestic spending has continued to grow but the constant dollar increase has been less than at any time since the Eisenhower presidency. Constant dollar spending on nondefense programs increased by less than defense spending and has actually fallen as a percentage of GNP from 15.2 percent to 13.9 percent. If Social Security and Medicare (which Reagan declared out of bounds for vigorous budget cutting) are excluded

Table 3   Federal Spending as a Percentage of GNP

Year	1 Total Outlays	2 Defense	3 Interest	4 Non- defense	4a Non- defense: Social Security & Medicare	4b Non- defense: Other
1920	6.9	2.6	1.1	3.3	0	3.3
1924	3.4	0.8	1.1	1.5	0	1.5
1928	3.1	0.8	0.8	1.5	0	1.5
1932	8.0	1.4	1.0	5.6	0	5.6
1936	10.2	1.4	0.9	7.9	0	7.9
1940	9.9	1.7	0.9	7.2	0	7.2
1944	45.2	39.2 (37.5)	1.1	4.9	0.1	4.8
1948	12.0	3.7	1.7	6.6	0.2	6.3
1952	19.8	13.4 (9.1)	1.4	4.9	0.6	4.3
1956	16.9	10.2	1.2	5.5	1.3	4.2
1960	18.2	9.5	1.4	7.3	2.3	5.0
1964	18.8	8.7	1.3	8.8	2.6	6.2
1968	20.9	9.6 (3.1)	1.3	10.0	3.3	6.7
1972	20.0	6.9 (0.8)	1.3	11.8	4.1	7.7
1976	21.8	5.2	1.6	15.0	5.3	9.7
1980	22.2	5.0	2.0	15.2	5.6	9.5
1984	23.1	6.2	3.0	13.9	6.4	7.5
1985	24.0	6.4	3.3	14.3	6.5	7.9
1986	24.0	6.5	3.3	14.1	6.5	7.6

Note: Outlays equal defense plus nondefense plus interest (column 1 = 2 + 3 + 4). Nondefense equals Social Security and Medicare plus "other" (column 4 = 4a + 4b). Defense figures are for total defense spending; figures in parentheses are immediate war-related costs as distinct from readiness or peacetime force structure expenditures. [17]

from consideration, Reagan's policy of restraint appears even more effective. Domestic spending in this category has fallen from 9.5 percent to 7.6 percent of GNP; in constant dollars this category of spending programs has remained frozen since 1980. While this may seem like a small success for conservatives who have sat through a lifetime of government expansion waiting for their turn at bat, it is unprecedented in the last half-century.

Although Reagan has made a dramatic shift in spending priorities, the magnitude of actual change has not been "revolutionary." The rate of increase in prioritized programs and the rate of "decrease" in nonprioritized spending are well within the norms of most of the 20th Century. While real peacetime defense spending was actively cut in the 60's and

70's, domestic spending has not suffered the same fate under Reagan. It is not, perhaps, surprising that a conservative president has been more successful in increasing favored spending programs than in decreasing others—modern political calculus (at least in the pre-Gramm-Rudman era) has always found a greater affection for "more" than for "less."

The gradual nature of change under President Reagan should not have been unanticipated. Although we have had periods of abrupt shifts in peacetime federal spending (e.g., surges in domestic spending under Hoover and Nixon, in military spending under Eisenhower, and cutbacks under Harding), these were the exceptions not the rule. On average in this century, total federal spending in any broad category has increased or decreased by between 0.25 and 0.50 percentage points of GNP per annum. It is these incremental changes accumulating year after year that eventually yield massive transformations in the social and political landscape. "Revolutionary" policy realignment occurs when there is a sharp and permanent shift in *the direction of incremental change*. Thus, FDR and Lyndon Johnson achieved their greatest success not in their immediate impact of the federal spending, but in setting the stage for an expansion of government which came in subsequent years. President Reagan will be judged "revolutionary," not by his immediate successes, but only if he has initiated a lasting redirection of government, if he has inaugurated a shift in priorities and a process of incremental change which will endure through the rest of this century.

Public Education and Long-Run Policy Change

The long-run incremental nature of change has a direct bearing on the art of governing. Successful presidencies are those which set the stage for long-term change by altering public perceptions. As Bruce Fein outlined in Chapter 2, successful politics is the art of public education: The effectiveness of a presidency must be evaluated not simply by its short-term impact on public policy but by its long-term impact on public attitudes.

By public education in the long-term sense we mean not education about specific policies, but education that addresses public assumptions on which policies are built. The recent progress of liberalism is a record of fundamental change in public attitudes on integration, women's rights, poverty, and the environment. The process of change on these issues was complex, but in each case the government took a leading, and in certain respects, tutorial role. If conservatism is to prevail in the future, it must place its assumptions before the public on free trade, individual economic liberty, smaller government, the indispensable role of the family and religion as engines of social progress, and many other issues. If the nation is to evolve in a conservative direction, these ideas must be transformed from slogans into vital components of public understanding.

If the objective is long-term change, public education must become a primary policy goal, not a secondary or tertiary concern. In this respect, the Reagan Administration has often failed—an irony, given the President's undoubted abilities as the great communicator. Too often the function of public education has been subordinated to exigencies. For example, public understanding of the necessity of free trade has not advanced at all in the Reagan era. By focusing on "fair trade" instead of "free trade" from the outset, the Reagan Administration conceded the rhetorical initiative and began playing in its opponent's court. Indeed, the very notion "fair trade" rests on neo-mercantilist premises. By dwelling on what might be called the "balance of protectionism"—by portraying the United States with dubious accuracy as the aggrieved victim of more protectionist trading partners, instead of focusing on an indispensable role of trade expansion to United States prosperity past and present—the government invited charges it was "too soft" on trade. Occasional lip service on behalf of free trade could not offset the central message. Although the Administration might have been forced on the defensive on this issue anyway, conceding the intellectual and rhetorical battle early on only made matters worse.

In arguing for military defense in a hostile world, the Administration has done a better job. But the government has not consistently presented the case that the U.S. is weaker than the Soviet Union, has military forces less than half the size of its opponent, and is outspent militarily by 40 to 50 percent each year.[18] Reagan's critics often seem to understand the importance of public education far better than does the Administration. When Reagan made a rare remark regarding the "evil empire," the term was, no doubt, empirically correct (just as it is correct to say that we must live on the same planet with this empire indefinitely). But the result was consternation; the President was sternly warned that he must temper his words or risk offending Kremlin sensibilities. Such warnings ignore the reality that the U.S. government is supposed to and does put up with far worse from the Soviet government all the time—and, more important, that President Reagan has an audience other than the Soviet leadership. While the President's rhetorical tone, per se, has very little direct significance to the Kremlin, the way the President describes the USSR does have a substantial long-run influence on the perceptions of the American public. And the attitudes of the American public, unlike those in the Soviet Union, do have a direct impact on foreign policy. Therein lies the source of concern for Reagan's critics in the Kremlin and elsewhere. To allow Kremlin "sensitivity" to control how and what an American president says to the American public about the Soviet Union and the world does not bode well for the nation's future.[19]

But the failure of the Reagan Administration in public education lies not so much in themes which are misarticulated as in those that are not addressed at all. The most effective public education addresses "invisible" attitudes which have only an indirect bearing on immediate policy. For example, economic growth is, for conservatives, a cynosure of much government policy. Clearly, growth is of extreme importance. But why? For most Americans, economic growth is something vaguely nice, like the senior prom or the Kentucky Derby. It is remote; few can comprehend its overwhelming impact on every aspect of their lives. The public cannot relate to growth in personal terms as they can to unemployment or inflation. How many Americans understand that a real per capita income growth rate of 5 percent per annum means that an average family's income will double in fourteen years, while with a rate of 1 percent growth it would take 68 years for the same increase? How many understand that the free enterprise system has increased the real incomes of the average American almost ninefold since the Civil War, or understand how small a positive role the federal government has had in that process?[20]

Conservatives implicitly understand these facts and understand the relation of growth to many other social problems. But economic growth has never been an important topical concern to the public in the sense that "drugs" or "abortion" are concerns. How difficult would it be to create an explicit public understanding of the value of growth? Very difficult—but, on the other hand, it would seem impossible for an enduring consensus on conservative policies to emerge without such an understanding, especially when these policies call for perceived short-term sacrifice.

A related area is supply-side economics. Initially, the Administration's public education on supply-side economics was good; a tax-cutting policy was presented along with its rationale. But it soon became clear that supply-side philosophy was merely an adjunct to a specific piece of legislation, not an enduring public education effort in its own right. Once the specific legislation was no longer on the table, the underlying economic theory all but disappeared.

In a nutshell, supply-side theory argues that the expansion of government is a negative sum game, while reducing government (relative to GNP) is a positive sum game. Reducing the government's relative share of the economy increases economic growth and produces a more prosperous America for all. There seems to be indisputable evidence that nations with smaller government sectors have economies that grow faster. Witness Japan, South Korea, and Taiwan.

A recent cross-national study by the World Bank on the relationship of government expenditures to economic growth suggests that each additional $1.00 in government spending today may cut the standard of living of Americans by nearly $5.00 (measured in constant dollars) only ten years in the future.[21] If that is so, then the growth of government domestic spending in the Great Society and its aftermath—from 1960 to 1975—will, if uncorrected, have the effect of cutting the potential GNP of the United States in half by the year 2000.[22] This is indeed a very high price to pay for many of the "free" government benefits to which Americans have become accustomed.

Reducing government will make Americans more prosperous—but for the last few years the Reagan Administration has all but dropped this theme. Instead, the rationale for cutting government spending has been limited simply to avoiding a tax increase. More and more, cutting government has actually been presented as an "unpleasant necessity." The line "this is an excellent program and we hate to cut it, but regrettably we must because of the serious problem with the deficit" has come readily from the lips of a great many Administration officials. The theme that cutting government spending *per se* is a positive investment in America's future has not been presented.

Reducing government's share of the GNP should be a conservative goal. But, as outlined in the preceding section, reduction must be a long-term incremental process. Decades of restraint will be required to return government spending to the relative levels of 1960. Clearly, long-term restraint on spending will be more easily achieved if the public perceives governmental restraint as a policy producing a "positive future" instead of as a policy of "unpleasant necessity." But the economic ideas to be presented are complex; it will take a concerted effort to demonstrate to the American public the importance of economic growth, the relationship between the size of government and growth, and the implications of these facts for ordinary government programs. What is required is a consistent public education campaign over many years, not rhetoric which is turned on or off based on legislative and political vicissitudes. The task will not be simple, but unless the public comes to perceive the problem in terms similar to those outlined above, the prospects for weaning the public from big government seem bleak.

Many conservatives simply shrug their shoulders at the scope of such an undertaking. But fundamental policy change invariably entails vast changes in public opinion. Such changes have occurred in the recent past. For example, in 1950 the United States had no "poverty." Rather, it had a perceived problem of abundance. There was even discussion of what philanthropists would do with their money now that so many basic human needs had been met.[23] It took decades of endeavor to "discover" poverty in the "other America," but by 1970 most Americans had been convinced that the nation, far richer than it had been twenty years before, was caught in a "crisis of poverty," crying for some form of governmental solution. The government itself played no small part in this transformation of perceptions.

The blossoming of big government in this country did not occur accidentally. Rather, the government itself has always been involved in marketing the idea of government expansion to the public. Politicians first raise expectations concerning the benefits the government can provide to constituent groups, creating a demand where none existed. Bureaucracies develop and justify new programs which are gradually incorporated into the public's way of life, until life without big government becomes difficult to envision. To reverse this process conservatives cannot rely on the public's feeling vaguely disgruntled about paying taxes. Instead, they must aggressively market their own ideas to create a public demand for less government.

A new pattern of hopes and expectations must be instilled in the voters and, paradoxically, the government must play a major role in this process. Chapter 14 on "Statistics and Public Education" discusses some of the public education resources available within the executive branch. Other mechanisms include the assiduous use of White House commissions and public policy research conducted or funded by the government; traditionally such research has played an important part in enlarging the government by uncovering a widening array of problems and needs requiring state intervention. Under a conservative administration, this research should be aggressively redirected toward topics of government failure, social problems generated by big government itself, and related themes—but up to now this has not been the case. An additional method for promoting smaller government is *institution building* within the government and in quasi-governmental institutions.[24] Presently OMB is one of the few institutions within the executive branch oriented toward reducing government, but OMB operates on a short-term perspective and has no real public education capability; the creation of related institutions is a necessary step in providing the capacity and continuity needed for long-term change.

But conservatives within the Reagan Administration are unaccustomed to the idea of a long-term marketing strategy for conservative principles. Liberals, on the other hand, are much more comfortable with this approach, in part because for most of this century long-term incremental change has moved in a leftward direction, extending the liberal horizon of expectations. Conservatives have spent the same period fighting a series of rear guard actions, and have become habituated to thinking in the short-term, yielding what one political appointee has shrewdly termed a "strike at dawn" mentality about politics. Despite the potential for change brought by President Reagan, conservatives are still far from thinking and planning for the future with the confidence that characterized liberals in their heyday.

Ironically, the nature of our current news institutions means that the presentation of conservative ideas will depend heavily on a conservative government, much more so than has been the case with past liberal initiatives. But the public education efforts of a conservative administration will themselves continue to face the constraints of the liberal media; success will require both persistence and innovative strategies. There is no choice in these matters. Politics, like nature, abhors a vacuum. Political discourse will be filled with one set of ideas or another. If a conservative government does not market the long-term benefits of small government, it will find itself endlessly on the defensive before ad hoc proposals for expanded state action, for new programmatic band-aids to meet the most current social complaint. In public education there is no middle ground between offense and defense.

The preceding discussion has been limited largely to economic issues, but the same principles apply to the full range of the conservative agenda. For a fundamental change in public policy to occur in any area, the ground must be prepared through a change in the ideas and attitudes that provide the foundation of policy. It is precisely in the realm of ideas that a presidency is most free from practical and immediate political constraints; but ironically, the Reagan Administration has often failed to fully grasp and exploit that freedom.

Conclusion

Change in the American political system is incremental; significant change will be cumulative in origin. Fundamental political transformation, on the other hand, consists in a substantial shift in the direction of incremental and cumulative change, which persists for two decades or longer. For policy redirection to endure, it must be reinforced by change in the realm of ideas. Thus the importance of the Reagan Administration will be determined as much by its impact on the attitudes that the American public carry into the 21st century as by its impact on budget, legislation, regulation, and administration in the 1980s. History will judge Ronald Reagan most successful if the changes he has inaugurated are continued and developed by subsequent leaders.

The present era remains exciting because of its uncertainty. While public belief in the liberal orthodoxy, which has reigned since the Depression, is faltering if not shattered, and public attitudes are shifting in a conservative direction, no new conservative orthodoxy has yet emerged to replace the decaying liberal creed. Politics in the mid and late 1980s will pertain largely to the crystallization or frustration of such a new orthodoxy. To forge a new consensus, conservatives must employ all the tutelary techniques of government that liberals have used with such panache in the past. Success or failure in this endeavor will determine whether the changes, which the Reagan Administration seems to foreshadow, will come to fruition in future years: whether or not there has been a real "Reagan Revolution."

Notes

1. John E. Chubb and Paul E. Peterson, eds., *The New Direction in American Politics* (Washington, D.C.: The Brookings Institution, 1985), p. 1.

2. *Ibid.*, pp. 17-20.

3. *Ibid.*, p. 258.

4. The government evaluates managerial performance by five grades running from the first category, "outstanding," downward. Standard bureaucratic practice ranks nearly everyone into the top two performance categories. In some offices 90 percent of the staff will be judged "outstanding." In 1984, for example, over half of the entire Senior Executive Service was ranked "outstanding," while 0.3 percent were placed in the lowest two categories. Since the financial incentive system operates by dividing a fixed "bonus" pool among high performers, overranking of most of the managerial population means that the bonus per individual is quite low. Failure to differentiate between managers and to significantly reward high performers, effectively neutralizes the existing system as a motivating and control mechanism.

5. Theodore J. Lowi, *The End of Liberalism* (New York: Norton, 1979), pp. 212–216.

6. Richard P. Nathan, *The Administrative Presidency* (New York: Wiley, 1983).

7. Edie Goldenberg, "The Permanent Government in an Era of Retrenchment and Redirection," in Lester M. Salamen and Michael A. Lund, eds., *The Reagan Presidency and the Governing of America* (Washington, D.C.: The Urban Institute Press, 1985), pp. 386–387.

8. Stanley Rothman and S. Robert Lichter, "How Liberal Are Bureaucrats?" *Regulation*, November/December 1983, pp. 16-22. Additional data supplied by Rothman and Lichter.

9. Lichter and Rothman, *op. cit.*, p. 17. Reprinted by permission of *Regulation* magazine.

10. John W. C. Johnstone, Edward Slawski, Willliam Bowman, *The News People* (Urbana, Illinois: University of Illinois, 1976), p. 224.

11. For an account of the eastern media establishment and the socialization process in which media parvenus abandon philistine belief systems in order to assimilate into the cosmopolitan/liberal media culture, see Dinesh D'Souza, "TV News: The Politics of Social Climbing," *Policy Review*, Summer 1986, pp. 24-31.

12. S. Robert Lichter and Stanley Rothman, "Media and Business Elites," *Public Opinion*, October/November 1981, p. 43. Lichter and Rothman's sample did not include the two wire services, but a study by Barry Sussman of *The Washington Post* of Washington-based reporters, which would include the wire services, found voting patterns almost identical with the Rothman/Lichter survey. See Barry Sussman, "Elites in America" (reprinted from *The Washington Post*, September 26–30, 1976).

13. William Schneider and I. A. Lewis, "Views on the News," *Public Opinion*, September 1985, p. 7.

14. *Ibid.*, p. 7.

15. Ernest W. LeFever, *T.V. and the National Defense* (USA: Institute for American Strategy Press, 1974).

16. William L. Adams, "Convention Coverage," *Public Opinion*, December/January 1985, p. 48.

17. Source of budget data, 1940–1985: Office of Management and Budget, *Historical Tables: Budget of the United States Government* (Washington, D.C.: U.S. Government Printing Office, 1986). Estimates for FY 1986 suppplied by OMB. Estimates of war costs are for expenses that accrued in the immediate year. War costs for World War II and the Korean War were estimated by subtracting defense outlays in the last pre-war year from defense costs in FY 1944 and FY 1952. Annual costs of the Vietnam War are from *Congressional Quarterly Weekly Report*, April 26, 1975, p. 847. Pre-1940 data are from *Historical Statistics of the United States: Colonial Times to 1970, Vol. 1 (Washington, D.C.: U.S. Department of Commerce, Bureau of the Census, 1972), Series F1, Y457-461.*

18. Organization of the Joint Chiefs of Staff, *United States Military Posture: FY 1986*, p. 18. Moreover, there is compelling evidence that conventional government statistics underestimate Soviet military spending. See Steven Rosefielde, *False Science: Underestimating the Soviet Arms Buildup* (New Brunswick and London: Transaction Books, 1983). See also W. T. Lee, "Soviet Military Spending Still Growing," *National Security Record*, No. 91, May 1986.

19. A recent article by White House staffer Mona Charon records the ongoing efforts of the White House to emasculate the speeches of the President. Charon cites a scathing memo by White House speechwriter Peggy Noonan to the National Security Council staff, assuring them that the "c word" (communism) and the "f word" (free enterprise) had been struck from a presidential address as they requested. The efforts to reduce the President's utterances to the level of a fourth-grade basal reader also include a general policy of excising references to God. Charon describes a White House where many are indifferent to real questions of policy and most seem oblivious to the public education aspects of politics. See Mona Charon, "What the White House Women Think of the White House Men," *The Washingtonian*, September 1986.

20. See *Historical Statistics of the United States: Colonial Times to 1970, Vol. 1* (Washington, D.C.: U.S. Department of Commerce, Bureau of the Census, 1972), series F1-5; and *Statistical Abstract of the United States: 1986* (106th edition), table 723.

21. Keith Marsden, "Links Between Taxes and Economic Growth," World Bank Staff Working Papers No. 605 (Washington, D.C.: The World Bank, 1983). The Marsden study indicates that an increase of one percentage point in the tax/GNP ratio decreases the rate of economic growth by 0.36 percentage points. Assuming a one-point increase in the tax/GNP ratio and an initial growth rate of 3.5 percent, each dollar in increased taxes will reduce GNP by $4.84 in real terms ten years later. The Marsden study shows the long-term correlation between small government and growth but draws no conclusions on the specific, immediate consequences of short-term policies to cut taxes and spending.

22. Federal, state, and local nondefense spending rose from around 21 percent of GNP in 1960 to 30.6 percent in 1975.

23. Charles Murray, *Losing Ground: America's Social Policy, 1950–1980* (New York: Basic Books, 1984), pp. 3–5.

24. The effective use of quasi-governmental institutions for policy purposes is exemplified by the Institute for Research on Poverty Studies which has been built largely on continuing government grants. See Mark Huber, "Impoverished Scholarship at the Institute for Research on Poverty," Heritage Foundation *Institution Analysis* No. 37, December 23, 1985.

About the Authors

Douglas L. Alexander is the editor of the American Education Report, a newsletter covering American public and private education.

A Thomas Aquinas graduate, he received a masters degree in political philosophy from Claremont College. He is a former senior associate at the National Institute of Education.

Clifford Barnhart is a pseudonym.

LeaAnne C. Bernstein is an attorney in the Office of General Counsel of the Fidelity & Deposit Insurance Corporation and is a Board Member of the Legal Services Corporation.

She holds degrees from Butler University and the Indiana University Law School. She has practiced as an attorney in both Indiana and in Washington, D.C., and has been a staff attorney with the Marion County Department of Public Welfare in Indiana. She has taught at the University of Maryland, Baltimore County and Catonsville Community College. She is President of the Board of Directors of the Montessori Society of Central Maryland.

Morton C. Blackwell is an active member of the conservative movement, serving as the head of three organizations: the Leadership Institute, the International Policy Forum, and the Conservative Leadership Political Action Committee.

He served as Special Assistant to the President for Public Liaison for the first three years of the Reagan Administration. His experience includes positions as Policy Director for U.S. Senator Gordon Humphrey and Deputy Director of Congressional Clearance in the Office of the President-Elect. Mr. Blackwell has served as editor of *The New Right Report* and contributing editor of *Conservative Digest*.

John Hiram Caldwell is a pseudonym.

Donald J. Devine is President of Donald Devine Company, the Consulting Director of Campaign America, and the former Director of the U.S. Office of Personnel Management.

A key figure in the Republican Party, he is a veteran of dozens of campaigns and Republican National Conventions. He was an associate professor of government and politics at the University of Maryland, and then moved from theory to practice. In 1980, Dr. Devine was Deputy Director for Political Planning and Analysis and Regional Planning Director for the Reagan-Bush Committee and held similar responsibilities during the 1976 Reagan campaign. President Reagan's former personnel chief has written a number of books and articles on politics, including *The Political Culture of the United States*, *The Attentive Public*, *Does Freedom Work?*, and *Reagan Electionomics*.

Becky Norton Dunlop is Senior Special Assistant to the Attorney General for Cabinet Affairs at the Department of Justice and former Deputy Assistant to the President and Deputy Director, Office of Presidential Personnel in the White House.

A graduate of Miami University in Ohio, she previously served as Special Assistant to the President and Director of the Office of Cabinet Affairs. Mrs. Dunlop was associated with the American Conservative Union from 1973 to 1980, completing her service as assistant executive director and consultant to the board. During that period, she founded and was president of Century Communications, Inc.

M. Stanton Evans has made numerous contributions to the field of journalism on political issues. He is the Director of the National Journalism Center and the publisher of *Consumers' Research* magazine and a visiting professor of Journalism at Troy State University. Evans is an editor for the American News Service as well as a contributing editor and columnist for *Human Events*, having had experience as a syndicated columnist and as editor of the *Indianapolis News*. A former commentator for National Public Radio, CBS Radio, and CBS Television, he currently serves WGMS, Radio America, and Voice of America in this capacity.

Evans holds a B.A. in English from Yale University and has done graduate work in economics at New York University. He was awarded an honorary Doctorate of Law from Syracuse University. Evans is the author of numerous publications including *Revolt on the Campus*, *The Liberal Establishment*, *The Politics of Surrender*, *The Future of Conservatism*, *The Lawbreakers*, and *Clear and Present Dangers*.

Bruce E. Fein is President of Bruce Fein and Associates, a law and consulting firm, and is the Supreme Court editor of *Benchmark Magazine*. He is Adjunct Constitutional Scholar at the American Enterprise Institute and is a Heritage Foundation Adjunct Scholar.

He received degrees from the University of California at Berkeley and the Harvard Law School. Mr. Fein held several positions at the U.S. Department of Justice including Associate Deputy Attorney General, before serving as the General Counsel of the Federal Communications Commission from 1983 to 1984.

Leo Hunter is a pseudonym.

Jeane J. Kirkpatrick is Leavey University Professor at Georgetown University and a resident scholar at the American Enterprise Institute, both in Washington, D.C.

She is a graduate of Barnard College and received her M.A. and Ph.D. in Political Science from Columbia University. She has held academic positions at Trinity College, the University of Aix-Marseilles, France, and the Georgetown Center for Strategic and International Studies. She is a trustee of the Robert Taft Institute of Government and the Smith-Richardson Foundation, and served with the Twentieth Century Fund's Task Force on the Presidential Election Process. During the 1980 presidential campaign, she was a member of President Reagan's foreign policy advisory group. In 1981, President Reagan appointed Dr. Kirkpatrick U.S. Permanent Representative to the United Nations; she was also a member of the Cabinet and the National Security Council until her resignation in 1985. She has lectured throughout the world, often under the auspices of the U.S. Information Agency and the Department of State, and also has written extensively on political and international issues for such national publications as *Commentary, The Journal of Politics, The American Political Science Review,* and *The New Republic*.

Dr. Kirkpatrick is the author of *The Reagan Phenomenon, Dictatorships and Double Standards, The New Presidential Elite, Political Woman,* and *Leader and Vanguard in Mass Society*.

Patrick S. Korten is Deputy Director of Public Affairs for the U.S. Department of Justice, since 1985.

After studying political science at the University of Wisconsin–Madison, he worked on the staffs of several members of the House of Representatives and for the American Conservative Union. Mr. Korten was an anchor/reporter at the all-news radio station WTOP in Washington, D.C. He has had previous experience in the executive branch, serving the U.S. Office of Personnel Management as Executive Assistant Director for Policy and Communications, and prior to that position, as Assistant Director for Public Affairs.

Herman A. Mellor is a pseudonym.

Joseph A. Morris is Chief of Staff and Counsel to the Director of the U.S. Information Agency.

After receiving his college and law degrees from the University of Chicago, Mr. Morris was engaged in the private practice of law in the Chicago firm of Rothschild, Barry and Myers. Mr. Morris's previous government experience includes service during the Reagan Administration as General Counsel of the U.S. Office of Personnel Management, Special Counsel to the Chairman of the Equal Employment Opportunity Commission, and U.S. Delegate to the United Nations Committee on Human Rights in Geneva. He has chaired the Young Republican Organization of Cook County, Illinois, and Students for Capitalism and Freedom. Mr. Morris has litigated in numerous trial and appellate courts, is a member of several bars, and has written and lectured widely on legal and political topics.

William A. Niskanen, Jr. is Chairman of the Cato Institute, a public policy research institute in Washington, D.C., and a former member of the President's Council of Economic Advisers (1981–1985).

A graduate of Harvard College, he received his master's and doctorate degrees in economics from the University of Chicago. Dr. Niskanen is an active participant in politics, business, and academia. He was a professor at the Graduate School of Management at the University of California, Los Angeles. From 1975 to 1980, he was director of Economics at the Ford Motor Company. Dr. Niskanen was a founder of the National Tax Limitation Committee and has contributed to the drafting of several tax limitation amendments. He served on the President's economic task force during the 1976 campaign. He is the author of *Bureaucracy and Representative Government* and numerous articles on issues of bureaucracy, budgeting, environment, local government, and public policy.

Thomas W. Pauken is Vice President and Corporate Counsel to Garvon Inc. and President of KRZF Radio. He served on President Reagan's transition team and from 1981 to 1985 was Director of ACTION in the Reagan Administration.

In 1969 Mr. Pauken served as 1st lieutenant in the Army and as province intelligence officer in Vietnam. After receiving his law degree from Southern Methodist University, he became Associate Director of the White House Fellowship program and a White House staff assistant under President Nixon. He has been a practicing attorney in Dallas, Texas, and has run twice as a Republican candidate in closely contested elections for the U.S. House of Representatives.

Robert Rector is the Director of The Heritage Foundation's Executive Development Program which conducts political management seminars for senior Reagan Administration officials.

He holds a bachelor's degree in political science from William and Mary College and a master's degree in international relations from Johns Hopkins University. While at Heritage he has written on international trade, military policy, and the political process within the executive branch. Prior to his work at Heritage, he served as a staff member in the Virginia House of Delegates.

Emily Hackett Rock is the Secretary to the Federal Trade Commission. She is a graduate of Sonoma State University in California. Her experience in government began as a member of the Reagan-Bush Campaign/ Transition Team in 1980. In 1981–1982 she served as Special Assistant to the Deputy Director at the Office of Management and Budget. From there, she went to the White House to work for the Assistant to the President for Policy Development until her appointment to the FTC in 1983.

Michael Sanera is an Assistant Professor of Political Science at Northern Arizona University. A Ph.D. in political science from the University of Colorado, he has government experience as Assistant Director for Planning and Evaluation at the U.S. Office of Personnel Management in the Reagan Administration. Dr. Sanera has also worked as a consultant at the U.S. Department of Education and as a Visiting Scholar at The Heritage Foundation. He is the author of "Implementing the Mandate" in *Mandate for Leadership II.*

Fred L. Smith, Jr. is President of the Competitive Enterprise Institute, a pro-market public interest group organized to advance the cause of limited government. He is a Phi Beta Kappa graduate of Tulane University and pursued graduate studies in economics and operations research at the University of Pennsylvania. He has worked as a military and policy analyst at the Cornell Aeronautical Laboratory, for the U.S. Environmental Protection Agency, and as a senior research economist with the American Association of Railroads. Mr. Smith has written on economic issues for *The Wall Street Journal, The New York Times, Regulation,*

Reason, and the *Cato Journal.* He is the author of a chapter on the Department of Transportation in *Agenda 1983* published by the Heritage Foundation.

Ralph L. Stanley is the Administrator of the Urban Mass Transportation Administration. He has received degrees from Princeton University and the Georgetown University Law Center. Mr. Stanley previously served as Chief of Staff to Transportation Secretary Elizabeth Dole and as Special Assistant for Policy to her predecessor, Drew Lewis. In the private sector, he worked in the Washington office of a Houston law firm, and as a financial analyst for the Bank of New York.

Ronald D. Utt is the Deputy Chief Economist for Economic Policy at the U.S. Chamber of Commerce. He holds a B.S. from Pennsylvania State University and a Ph.D. from Indiana University. Dr. Utt served as the Director of Research for the National Association of Real Estate Investment Trusts and as a senior economist with both the Office of Management and Budget and the Department of Housing and Urban Development before his appointment to the U.S. Chamber of Commerce.

Jade West is the Executive Director of the Senate Steering Committee. Mrs. West attended Duke University and was a delegate to the GOP National Conventions in 1976 and 1980. Prior to her present position, Ms. West served as Research Director of the National Right to Work Legal Defense Fund.

Aaron Wildavsky, professor of political science and public policy at the University of California, Berkeley, and founding Dean of its Graduate School of Public Policy (1969–77), is one of the best-known political scientists in the country. His scholarly reputation is based on the authorship of eighteen books, including *The Politics of the Budgetary Process,* presently in its fourth edition, and more than one hundred articles published in the leading political science, public administration, and public policy journals. In addition, he has served on the editorial boards of many academic journals, including *Policy Sciences, Policy Studies Journal,* and the *Annals of Public Administration.* A recipient of numerous awards and honors, Dr. Wildavsky served as President of the American Political Science Association (1985–86). His work in the area of public administration led the American Society of Public Administration to honor him with two of its highest awards, the Dwight Waldo and William E. Mosher Awards.